Private Security Companies during the Iraq War

This book explores the use of deadly force by private security companies during the Iraq War.

The work focuses on and compares the activities of the US companies Blackwater and DynCorp. Despite sharing several important characteristics, such as working for the same client (the US State Department) during the same time period, the employees of Blackwater fired their weapons far more often, and killed and seriously injured far more people in Iraq than their counterparts in DynCorp. In order to explain this disparity, the book undertakes the most comprehensive analysis ever attempted on the use of violence by the employees of these firms. Based on extensive empirical research, it offers a credible explanation for this difference: Blackwater maintained a relatively bellicose military culture that placed strong emphasis on norms encouraging its personnel to exercise personal initiative, proactive use of force and an exclusive approach to security, which, together, motivated its personnel to use violence quite freely against anyone they suspected of posing a threat. Specifically, Blackwater's military culture motivated its personnel to fire upon suspected threats more quickly, at greater distances, and with a greater number of bullets, and to more readily abandon the people they shot at when compared to DynCorp's personnel, who maintained a military culture that encouraged far less violent behaviour. Utilizing the Private Security Company Violent Incident Dataset (PSCVID), created by the author in 2012, the book draws upon data on hundreds of violent incidents involving private security personnel in Iraq to identify trends in the behaviour exhibited by the employees of different firms. Based on this rich and original empirical data, the book provides the definitive study of contemporary private security personnel in the Iraq War.

This book will be of much interest to students of the Iraq War, Private Security Companies, Military Studies, War and Conflict Studies and IR in general.

Scott Fitzsimmons is Lecturer in International Relations at the University of Limerick, Ireland, and author of *Mercenaries in Asymmetric Conflicts* (2012).

Cass Military Studies

Intelligence Activities in Ancient Rome
Trust in the gods, but verify
Rose Mary Sheldon

Clausewitz and African War
Politics and strategy in Liberia and Somalia
Isabelle Duyvesteyn

Strategy and Politics in the Middle East, 1954–60
Defending the northern tier
Michael Cohen

The Cuban Intervention in Angola, 1965–1991
From Che Guevara to Cuito Cuanavale
Edward George

Military Leadership in the British Civil Wars, 1642–1651
'The genius of this age'
Stanley Carpenter

Israel's Reprisal Policy, 1953–1956
The dynamics of military retaliation
Ze'ev Drory

Bosnia and Herzegovina in the Second World War
Enver Redzic

Leaders in War
West Point remembers the 1991 Gulf War
Edited by Frederick Kagan and Christian Kubik

Khedive Ismail's Army
John Dunn

Yugoslav Military Industry 1918–1991
Amadeo Watkins

Corporal Hitler and the Great War 1914–1918
The list regiment
John Williams

Rostóv in the Russian Civil War, 1917–1920
The key to victory
Brian Murphy

The Tet Effect, Intelligence and the Public Perception of War
Jake Blood

The US Military Profession into the 21st Century
War, peace and politics
Edited by Sam C. Sarkesian and Robert E. Connor, Jr.

Civil–Military Relations in Europe
Learning from crisis and institutional change
Edited by Hans Born, Marina Caparini, Karl Haltiner and Jürgen Kuhlmann

Strategic Culture and Ways of War
Lawrence Sondhaus

Military Unionism in the Post-Cold War Era
A future reality?
Edited by Richard Bartle and Lindy Heinecken

Warriors and Politicians
U.S. civil–military relations under stress
Charles A. Stevenson

Military Honour and the Conduct of War
From Ancient Greece to Iraq
Paul Robinson

Military Industry and Regional Defense Policy
India, Iraq and Israel
Timothy D. Hoyt

Managing Defence in a Democracy
Edited by Laura R. Cleary and Teri McConville

Gender and the Military
Women in the armed forces of Western democracies
Helena Carreiras

Social Sciences and the Military
An interdisciplinary overview
Edited by Giuseppe Caforio

Cultural Diversity in the Armed Forces
An international comparison
Edited by Joseph Soeters and Jan van der Meulen

Railways and the Russo-Japanese War
Transporting war
Felix Patrikeeff and Harold Shukman

War and Media Operations
The US military and the press from Vietnam to Iraq
Thomas Rid

Ancient China on Postmodern War
Enduring ideas from the Chinese strategic tradition
Thomas Kane

Special Forces, Terrorism and Strategy
Warfare by other means
Alasdair Finlan

Imperial Defence, 1856–1956
The old world order
Greg Kennedy

Civil–Military Cooperation in Post-Conflict Operations
Emerging theory and practice
Christopher Ankersen

Military Advising and Assistance
From mercenaries to privatization, 1815–2007
Donald Stoker

Private Military and Security Companies
Ethics, policies and civil–military relations
Edited by Andrew Alexandra, Deane-Peter Baker and Marina Caparini

Military Cooperation in Multinational Peace Operations
Managing cultural diversity and crisis response
Edited by Joseph Soeters and Philippe Manigart

The Military and Domestic Politics
A concordance theory of civil–military relations
Rebecca L. Schiff

Conscription in the Napoleonic Era
A revolution in military affairs?
Edited by Donald Stoker, Frederick C. Schneid and Harold D. Blanton

Modernity, the Media and the Military
The creation of national mythologies on the Western Front 1914–1918
John F. Williams

American Soldiers in Iraq
McSoldiers or innovative professionals?
Morten Ender

Complex Peace Operations and Civil–Military Relations
Winning the peace
Robert Egnell

Strategy and the American War of Independence
A global approach
Edited by Donald Stoker, Kenneth J. Hagan and Michael T. McMaster

Managing Military Organisations
Theory and practice
Edited by Joseph Soeters, Paul C. van Fenema and Robert Beeres

Modern War and the Utility of Force
Challenges, methods and strategy
Edited by Jan Angstrom and Isabelle Duyvesteyn

Democratic Citizenship and War
Edited by Yoav Peled, Noah Lewin-Epstein and Guy Mundlak

Military Integration after Civil Wars
Multiethnic armies, identity and post-conflict reconstruction
Florence Gaub

Military Ethics and Virtues
An interdisciplinary approach for the 21st century
Peter Olsthoorn

The Counter-Insurgency Myth
The British experience of irregular warfare
Andrew Mumford

Europe, Strategy and Armed Forces
Towards military convergence
Sven Biscop and Jo Coelmont

Managing Diversity in the Military
The value of inclusion in a culture of uniformity
Edited by Daniel P. McDonald and Kizzy M. Parks

The US Military
A basic introduction
Judith Hicks Stiehm

Democratic Civil–Military Relations
Soldiering in 21st-century Europe
Edited by Sabine Mannitz

Contemporary Military Innovation
Between anticipation and adaptation
Edited by Dmitry (Dima) Adamsky and Kjell Inge Bjerga

Militarism and International Relations
Political economy, security and theory
Edited by Anna Stavrianakis and Jan Selby

Qualitative Methods in Military Studies
Research experiences and challenges
Edited by Helena Carreiras and Celso Castro

Educating America's Military
Joan Johnson-Freese

Military Health Care
From pre-deployment to post-separation
Jomana Amara and Ann M. Hendricks

Contemporary Military Culture and Strategic Studies
US and UK armed forces in the 21st century
Alastair Finlan

Understanding Military Doctrine
A multidisciplinary approach
Harald Hoiback

Military Strategy as Public Discourse
America's war in Afghanistan
Tadd Sholtis

Military Intervention, Stabilisation and Peace
The search for stability
Christian Dennys

International Military Operations in the 21st Century
Global trends and the future of intervention
Edited by Per M. Norheim-Martinsen and Tore Nyhamar

Security, Strategy and Military Change in the 21st Century
Cross-regional perspectives
Edited by Jo Inge Bekkevold, Ian Bowers and Michael Raska

Military Families and War in the 21st Century
Comparative perspectives
Edited by René Moelker, Manon Andres, Gary Bowen and Philippe Manigart

Private Security Companies during the Iraq War
Military performance and the use of deadly force
Scott Fitzsimmons

Private Security Companies during the Iraq War
Military performance and the use of deadly force

Scott Fitzsimmons

LONDON AND NEW YORK

First published 2016
by Routledge
2 Park Square, Milton Park, Abingdon, Oxon OX14 4RN

and by Routledge
711 Third Avenue, New York 10017

Routledge is an imprint of the Taylor & Francis Group, an informa business

© 2016 Scott Fitzsimmons

The right of Scott Fitzsimmons to be identified as author of this work has been asserted by him in accordance with sections 77 and 78 of the Copyright, Designs and Patents Act 1988.

All rights reserved. No part of this book may be reprinted or reproduced or utilized in any form or by any electronic, mechanical, or other means, now known or hereafter invented, including photocopying and recording, or in any information storage or retrieval system, without permission in writing from the publishers.

Trademark notice: Product or corporate names may be trademarks or registered trademarks, and are used only for identification and explanation without intent to infringe.

British Library Cataloguing-in-Publication Data
A catalogue record for this book is available from the British Library

Library of Congress Cataloging-in-Publication Data
A catalog record for this book has been requested

ISBN: 978-1-138-84426-1 (hbk)
ISBN: 978-1-315-72803-2 (ebk)

Typeset in Baskerville
by Wearset Ltd, Boldon, Tyne and Wear

Contents

List of tables   x
Acknowledgements   xi
List of abbreviations   xii

Introduction   1

1 The nature of Blackwater and DynCorp's security operations during the Iraq War   19

2 The ideational theory of tactical violence   65

3 The military cultures of Blackwater and DynCorp   82

4 The relationship between military culture, tactical behaviour and casualties inflicted on suspected threats   97

5 The relationship between military culture, tactical behaviour and friendly casualties   137

6 The implications of Blackwater and DynCorp's tactical behaviour in Iraq   176

7 Conclusion   213

Index   232

Tables

I.1	Casualties inflicted by Blackwater and DynCorp, 2003–2009	2
I.2	Casualties suffered by Blackwater and DynCorp, 2003–2009	3
2.1	Summary of predictions of the ideational theory of tactical violence	73
4.1	First behavioural responses to suspected threats	99
4.2	Second behavioural responses to suspected threats	99
4.3	Mean engagement distances during first four stages of incidents	106
4.4	Number of bullets fired	109
4.5	Victim abandonment rate	114
4.6	Support for the predictions of the ideational theory of tactical violence	125
5.1	First behaviour exhibited by insurgents	159
5.2	Number of bullets fired by insurgents	159
5.3	Number of explosive rounds/devices used by insurgents	160
5.4	Insurgent attacks per city	162
5.5	Support for the predictions of the ideational theory of tactical violence	164
7.1	Support for the predictions of the ideational theory of tactical violence	214

Acknowledgements

I would like to acknowledge the invaluable help provided by Dick Price of the University of British Columbia's Department of Political Science, who served as my postdoctoral research supervisor during the early stages of this study. I would also like to recognize the gracious financial support provided by the Social Sciences and Humanities Research Council of Canada.

I wish to thank my editor, Andrew Humphrys, for his guidance and patience in shepherding this book through the publication process at Routledge. Along with the anonymous reviewers he selected, Andrew devoted considerable time to carefully reading my manuscript and identified several ways to improve it.

Moreover, this book would not have been possible without the support and encouragement of my parents, Laura and Roger Bourque and Gerry and Claudette Fitzsimmons, and my brother and fellow scholar, Dan Fitzsimmons.

Finally, I owe my deepest appreciation to my friends and colleagues, including Allan Craigie, Marc André Bodet, Owen Worth, Andrew Shorten, Neil Robinson, Rory Costello, Frank Häge, Karina Sangha and Stacia Beiniks, for not only sitting through my innumerable formal and informal presentations on this research over the past three years but also asking plenty of insightful questions that helped me clarify and enhance several aspects of this book.

Abbreviations

AT	advance team
BVA	Blackwater Veterans Association
CAT	counter assault team
CAV	counter assault vehicle
CIA	Central Intelligence Agency
CPA	Coalition Provision Authority
DDM	designated defensive marksman
DGSD	DynCorp Government Services Division
DSS	Diplomatic Security Service
EFP	explosively-formed penetrator
EOF	escalation of force
FBI	Federal Bureau of Investigation
HMMWV	high mobility multipurpose wheeled vehicle
ICDC	Iraqi Civil Defence Corps
IED	improvised explosive device
ISIS	Islamic State of Iraq and Syria
LRMT	long-range marksmen team
LZ	landing zone
MEJA	Military Extraterritorial Jurisdiction Act
MOA	memorandum of agreement
NATO	North Atlantic Treaty Organization
OSCE	Organization for Security and Cooperation in Europe
PLSC	private logistical support company
PMC	private military company
PSC	private security company
PSCVID	Private Security Company Violent Incident Dataset
PSD	protective/personal security detail
PTCC	private training and consultancy company
QRF	quick reaction force
REO	Regional Embassy Office
RPG	rocket-propelled grenade
SAS	Special Air Service (British Army)
SEAL	Sea, Air and Land (US Navy)

SOAR	Special Operations Aviation Regiment (US Army)
SOFA	Status of Forces Agreement
SUV	sports utility vehicle
SWAT	Special Weapons and Tactics
TST	tactical support team
UCMJ	Uniform Code of Military Justice
UN	United Nations
US	United States
USAID	US Agency for International Development
VBIED	vehicle-based improvised explosive device
WPPS	Worldwide Personnel Protective Services

Introduction

The morning of 23 May 2007 saw multiple teams of Blackwater security personnel, the chief guardians of US Department of State employees in Iraq at that time, embroiled in one of their largest firefights of the Iraq War.[1] While providing security for a diplomatic meeting at Amanat City Hall in the centre of Baghdad, the firm's personnel came under heavy small-arms fire from numerous insurgents in nearby buildings. They quickly suppressed the threat to themselves and their clients by engaging the gunmen with hundreds of rounds of ammunition; they then abandoned the dead and wounded insurgents and escorted their clients to safety. A few months later, on 16 September 2007, another Blackwater security team opened fire on pedestrians and motorists in Baghdad's bustling Nisour Square.[2] This brief but ferocious use of violence against unarmed Iraqi civilians, which came to be known as the "Nisour Square incident", left 17 people dead and two dozen wounded. These events were among the most violent incidents involving Blackwater's personnel, but they were also characteristic of the firm's record of belligerent actions against civilians and insurgents during the Iraq War.

Blackwater's security personnel displayed behaviour that stands in particularly stark relief to the actions exhibited by their counterparts in DynCorp, one of the other major private security companies (PSCs) that provided protective security services for the US Department of State during the Iraq War. Indeed, despite sharing several important characteristics – drawing personnel from the same general population of military and police veterans, working for the same primary client during the same time period, performing the same tasks under the same client-imposed rules of engagement, and facing the same kinds of threats in the same general operating environment – Blackwater's personnel fired their weapons far more often and killed and seriously injured far more people than DynCorp's personnel (as shown in Table I.1).[3] Between 2003 and 2009, Blackwater's security personnel were involved in at least 428 violent incidents, meaning incidents where violence was used by them and/or against them, while their counterparts in DynCorp were involved in 78 violent incidents. During this period, Blackwater's employees used violence in at least 353 incidents and inflicted

2 Introduction

Table I.1 Casualties inflicted by Blackwater and DynCorp, 2003–2009

	Blackwater	DynCorp
Violent incidents	428	78
Incidents in which firms used violence	353	60
Incidents in which firms fired weapons	342	59
Non-insurgent deaths	38	3
Insurgent deaths	33*	8
Total deaths	71*	11
Serious non-insurgent injuries	64*	1
Serious insurgent injuries	58*	4
Total serious injuries	122*	5

Note
* Blackwater's personnel are known to have inflicted 26 insurgent deaths and 45 serious insurgent injuries. However, the firm's personnel also inflicted an unknown number of insurgent deaths during 7 incidents and an unknown number of serious insurgent injuries during 13 incidents. Likewise, Blackwater's personnel are known to have inflicted 61 non-insurgent serious injuries, but the firm's personnel inflicted an unknown number of non-insurgent injuries during three incidents. This table is based on the assumption that Blackwater's personnel killed or seriously injured at least one person during these incidents. By this reckoning, Blackwater's personnel inflicted a total of 64 deaths and a total of 106 serious injuries. The vast majority of the non-insurgent deaths and serious injuries inflicted by the firms' personnel were on civilians. However, Blackwater's personnel also killed three employees of another PSC and seriously injured three Iraqi soldiers and one employee of another PSC, and, by this count, inflicted a total of at least 71 deaths and 122 serious injuries during the 2003 to 2009 period of the Iraq War. Blackwater's personnel are known to have inflicted 35 of the 38 non-insurgent deaths and 58 of the 64 serious non-insurgent injuries against suspected threats. They inflicted the remaining three non-insurgent deaths and six serious non-insurgent injuries upon civilian bystanders.

at least 71 deaths and 122 serious injuries, while their counterparts in DynCorp used violence in only 60 incidents, killed 11 people and caused only five serious injuries. The figures on the casualties inflicted by Blackwater's personnel should be viewed as a floor, not a ceiling. As explained later in this chapter, they actually inflicted a far higher – though ultimately unknown – number of deaths and serious injuries during their security operations in Iraq.

At the same time, while neither firm lost any clients to enemy fire, Blackwater's personnel in Iraq enjoyed a considerably lower casualty rate than their counterparts in DynCorp (see Table I.2).[4] Some readers may be surprised by this claim, given that 20 of Blackwater's security personnel died in insurgent attacks during the Iraq War while DynCorp lost only 14 security personnel to hostile fire during the conflict. However, Blackwater suffered its 20 deaths during eight out of the 118 total incidents where its personnel were attacked by insurgents, which means that it suffered deaths in 6.8 per cent of these engagements and lost, on average, 0.17 employees per attack. On the other hand, DynCorp suffered its 14 deaths during eight out of just 22 total incidents where insurgents attacked its personnel, which means that fully 36 per cent of these engagements proved deadly

Table I.2 Casualties suffered by Blackwater and DynCorp, 2003–2009

	Blackwater	DynCorp
Encounters with insurgents	131	26
Attacks by insurgents	118	22
Security personnel deaths	20	14
Security personnel deaths per insurgent attack	0.17	0.64
Client deaths	0	0

and that it lost, on average, 0.64 employees per attack – a casualty rate almost four times higher than Blackwater's. In other words, if and when insurgents chose to attack Blackwater's security teams, they were much less likely to inflict casualties than when they attacked DynCorp's teams.

Blackwater's relatively low casualty rate is all the more remarkable when one considers that its personnel were tasked with protecting many of the most hated people in Iraq – including Coalition Provision Authority (CPA) chief Paul Bremer, US ambassadors and other employees of the Department of State, visiting US congressmen and senators, and other foreign government officials – from well-armed and committed insurgents who managed to kill and injure thousands of American troops during the 2003 to 2009 period of the Iraq War. In his memoirs, Bremer stated that "the US Secret Service had done a survey of my security (in Iraq) and concluded that I was the most threatened American official anywhere in the world", but Blackwater ensured that he completed his 11-month term as proconsul of Iraq without suffering a scratch.[5] Ryan Crocker, a later US Ambassador to Iraq, stated that the firm's personnel protected him "extremely well" and that he had "high regard for the individuals who work for Blackwater".[6] Likewise, US President George W. Bush stated that "Blackwater provides a valuable service. They protect people's lives, and I appreciate the sacrifice and service that the Blackwater employees have made".[7] US Congressmen Patrick McHenry and Chris Shays similarly highlighted Blackwater's "perfect record" of protecting the lives of its clients in Iraq.[8] Moreover, an arms-length review conducted for the Department of State in 2007, at the height of insurgent violence in Iraq, concluded that "The Department's security operations in Iraq have been highly effective in ensuring the safety of mission personnel".[9] Even the firm's most ardent critic, Jeremy Scahill, acknowledged that "Blackwater had done its job in Iraq: to keep the most hated US occupation official alive by any means necessary".[10] Therefore, Blackwater's executives spoke the truth when they boasted that their firm did not experience "a single loss of life or serious injury to our clients" in Iraq.[11] However, as is discussed throughout this book, Blackwater's methods for achieving this "100 per cent survival rate" inflicted a terrible humanitarian cost that, in turn, sparked a host of legal and political scandals that undermined Blackwater's ability to compete in the contemporary market for private armed forces.

By undertaking the most comprehensive study ever attempted of the use of violence by private security personnel in Iraq, this book provides a credible answer to the following questions: Why did Blackwater's personnel inflict much higher casualties during their security operations? Why did Blackwater's personnel suffer a far lower casualty rate during their security operations? Utilizing the ideational theory of tactical violence, the central argument put forward here is that Blackwater's personnel killed and seriously injured many more people in Iraq than their counterparts in DynCorp, and achieved a far lower friendly casualty rate, because Blackwater maintained a relatively bellicose military culture that placed strong emphasis on norms encouraging its personnel to exercise personal initiative, a proactive use of force and an exclusive approach to security, which, together, motivated its personnel to use violence quite freely against anyone they suspected of posing a threat. Indeed, Blackwater's military culture motivated its personnel to employ violence against suspected threats more quickly, at greater distances and with a greater number of bullets and to more readily abandon the people they attacked when compared to DynCorp's personnel, who maintained a military culture that encouraged far less violent behaviour. These actions, in turn, contributed to the significant disparity in both the number of deaths and serious injuries inflicted by these private armed forces during the Iraq War and the rate of casualties they suffered from hostile fire.

In spite of the fact that variations in the use of violence by different PSCs in Iraq constitute one of the most widely discussed, condemned and glorified topics in the literature on contemporary PSCs, this book constitutes the first comprehensive, empirically-grounded study of this phenomenon.[12] To be clear, this book is not intended to glorify or condemn the behaviour of either firm's security personnel. Rather, it is intended to serve as a sober, scholarly account of private security operations during the Iraq War.

Developing a coherent explanation for the use of violence by private security personnel is important for several reasons. Given that PSCs are currently being used by Western and local governments to provide protective security services in Iraq, Afghanistan and several other countries around the world, it is important for the governments contracting with these firms and those working alongside them to understand the factors that influence their propensity to use violence during their security operations. Likewise, since PSCs may someday be contracted for peacekeeping and counterinsurgency operations, it is important to determine whether these actors would be suitable for these missions. In the absence of this knowledge, governments cannot form reliable expectations about how PSCs may influence the course of conflicts, nor can governments form reliable expectations about whether PSCs can significantly supplement or even supplant national armed forces in situations where deploying a large number of citizen-soldiers is not politically feasible. Moreover, people seeking to manage the development of private armed forces will benefit from knowledge of how an armed force's military culture can influence the tactical behaviour exhibited by its personnel.

The ideational theory of tactical violence

The central claims of the ideational theory of tactical violence, the primary theoretical contribution of this book, are that the behavioural norms that make up a PSC's military culture have a strong influence on the degree of violence employed by that firm's personnel and that, in turn, the degree of violence employed by these personnel strongly affects two security outcomes. These are, first, the degree of security enjoyed by the people under the firm's protection, such as the firm's personnel and clients, and, second, the degree of security enjoyed by other actors in the firm's operating environment, such as insurgents, civilians, the personnel of other PSCs, and the members of national security and military forces.

The theory reasons that, if a PSC's military culture is made up of norms that actively encourage its personnel to employ violence quite freely against suspected threats, then its personnel should, indeed, tend to do so during their security operations. It further reasons that, if a firm's personnel tend to employ a great deal of violence during their security operations, then they should also tend to enhance the security of themselves and the people under their protection and to undermine the security of other actors in their operating environment. This is because, when a PSC uses violence in this manner by, for instance, firing off great numbers of bullets at suspected threats, this increases the chance that it will harm not only legitimate threats, such as insurgents, but also civilians and other non-threatening actors in a conflict zone. Therefore, the theory posits that the very same behavioural norms that can help make a PSC's personnel very good at protecting themselves and their clients can also help make them a menace to the society they operate in.

The ideational theory of tactical violence offers specific, testable predictions about how the behavioural norms contained in a PSC's military culture should influence the tactical behaviour exhibited by its security personnel. Specifically, this book examines the relationship between particular cultural norms – encouraging security personnel to exercise personal initiative, proactive use of force and an exclusive approach to security – with the speed and distance at which these personnel tended to engage suspected threats, the number of bullets they tended to fire and the rate at which they tended to abandon the people they fired at. This book also examines how the particular patterns of tactical behaviour exhibited by different PSCs led to significant disparities in the casualties they inflicted and suffered during the Iraq War.

Furthermore, this book examines a number of alternative explanations for the disparity in the number of deaths and serious injuries the personnel of different PSCs inflicted during their security operations as well as the casualties they suffered during the Iraq War. On the first topic, due to the fact that Blackwater assigned a larger security force to its Department of State operations than DynCorp did during the 2003 to 2009 period, it is possible that Blackwater's personnel simply encountered a greater number of suspected threats and were, consequently, forced to use violence on a more regular basis than their counterparts in DynCorp. Moreover, it is possible that Blackwater's personnel inflicted more deaths and serious injuries than their counterparts in DynCorp because they were undisciplined and were granted too much autonomy over how they conducted their security operations. Furthermore, given that Blackwater and DynCorp had different primary operating areas and also that Blackwater's personnel had access to a unique type of equipment – helicopters – that they used in several incidents to inflict harm on suspected threats, it is possible to question whether these factors may have skewed the results of this study. Finally, given that accounts of violent incidents provided by the firms' employees constitute a key source of empirical data in this study, it is possible to question whether the evidence discussed in this study reflects the actual behaviour exhibited by these personnel. With respect to the casualties suffered by the firms' personnel during the war, it is possible that Blackwater's personnel simply faced less potent security threats in Iraq. Likewise, it is possible that Blackwater's personnel tended to operate in safer areas of Iraq. Finally, it is possible that Blackwater's personnel had access to significantly better equipment than that available to DynCorp's security teams. A careful examination of the empirical evidence on the firms' private security operations in Iraq indicates that none of these alternative explanations is well-supported and that the ideational theory of tactical violence provides a much more plausible explanation for the observed patterns of violence and casualties.

Literature review

Scholarship on private armed forces has increased dramatically since the beginning of the wars in Iraq and Afghanistan. However, most of the leading works on PSCs are long on narrative and short on theory and explanation. Significantly, few works have sought to study the very reason why PSCs exist, which is their willingness to use violence to protect people, places and things in dangerous environments. Instead, most of these works offer overviews of specific PSCs or the broader private military industry. Peter Singer's *Corporate Warriors*, which was published in 2003 but remains one of the leading texts in the field, is a typical example of the existing literature on these actors in that it provided an overview of the then-current state of the private military industry.[13] Singer's primary contribution was to put forward an organizational scheme, the "tip-of-the-spear" typology, to assist in differentiating between three broad categories of firms in the private military industry: military provider firms (most other scholars refer to these firms as PSCs), which provide their clients with combat services, such as fighting wars and protecting convoys of goods and people from attack; military consulting firms, which provide training for other security forces and analysis on threats to their clients; and military supply firms, which provide their clients with intelligence and logistical support.[14]

A host of books published since the release of *Corporate Warriors*, such as James Jay Carafano's *Private Sector, Public Wars*, David Isenberg's *Shadow Force*, Robert Young Pelton's *Licensed to Kill*, Shawn Engbrecht's *America's Covert Warriors*, and Steve Fainaru's *Big Boy Rules* essentially adopted Singer's approach by providing more up-to-date overviews of the private military industry.[15] Moreover, as with *Corporate Warriors*, these more recent books also drew attention to the use of violence by PSCs; however, none sought to explain this behaviour. The existing book-length published works on Blackwater itself, including Jeremy Scahill's *Blackwater* and Suzanne Simons' *Master of War*, are even less helpful in this respect.[16] Rather than explaining the behaviour of Blackwater's personnel, or even describing this behaviour in detail, these books largely focus on highlighting genuine and suspected political connections between Blackwater's founder, Erik Prince, and the administration of President George W. Bush. Ultimately, most of the leading works on PSCs offer little insight into the factors that may influence how these firms interact with a range of other armed and unarmed actors in conflict zones. This is significant because, in the absence of knowledge on the factors that may influence the behaviour of PSCs, it is difficult to develop reliable expectations about how such actors may in future influence the course of conflicts and the degree of security and insecurity experienced by themselves, their clients and other actors who live and work inside conflict zones.

Most of the major theoretical works on private armed forces have likewise failed to offer much insight into the use of violence by these actors. For instance, although Deborah Avant's *The Market for Force* puts forward arguments grounded in economic and sociological institutionalist theories, it focuses on the possibility that the growing use of PSCs could undermine the degree of control that governments can exercise over the use of deadly force in modern conflict zones.[17] This book does not explain why different PSCs, even those with the very same government clients, have employed vastly different amounts of deadly force during their security operations. Further, although Sarah Percy's *Mercenaries* is grounded in the constructivist approach to international relations, it is primarily a historical work in that it traces the evolution of the norm discouraging the use of mercenaries and other private armed forces from the medieval era to the present day.[18] Given its sweeping focus, it is understandable that this book devotes little attention to the behaviour of contemporary PSCs.

A few scholars have recently conducted serious studies of the use of violence by private armed forces, but they generally do not share the empirical focus of this book. Building on earlier work by Michael Ross as well as Dina Rasor and Robert Bauman, Ulrich Petersohn's "The Impact of Mercenaries and Private Military and Security Companies on Civil War Severity between 1946 and 2002" examines whether the presence of private armed forces in a civil war influences the number of combat-related deaths seen in the conflict.[19] It finds that the presence of mercenaries correlates with a 65 per cent increase in the number of combat-related deaths and concludes that "mercenaries in general are brutal and trigger-happy actors".[20] This pioneering study makes a valuable contribution to knowledge about the potential roles played by private armed forces in modern conflicts, but it only establishes a correlation between the mere presence of these actors and the number of deaths resulting from a conflict. It does not determine whether these actors actually contributed to the increased number of deaths. This book, in contrast, focuses specifically on the relationship between the actual tactical behaviour exhibited by private security personnel and the casualties they inflicted and suffered during their security operations. Moreover, while Petersohn's article focuses on the role of private armed forces in civil wars, this book examines their role in private security operations.

In *Victory for Hire*, Molly Dunigan concludes that private armed forces "tend to decrease military effectiveness ... in modern cases of PSC–military co-deployment", such as during the Iraq War, due to a combination of poor structural integration with state-based armed forces, a clash of identities, and disparate adherence to ethical standards and norms.[21] In a similar vein, in "The Effectiveness of Contracted Coalitions", Petersohn conducts a comparative analysis of certain aspects of the combat effectiveness of PSCs along with the US and Iraqi militaries.[22] He concludes that PSCs in Iraq generally behaved less aggressively than their counterparts in the two state-based armed forces and also generally inflicted fewer casualties per friendly fire incident. Although the present book shares Dunigan and Petersohn's focus on effectiveness, it focuses specifically on private security personnel's effectiveness at protecting themselves and their clients from harm. On the other hand, Dunigan and Petersohn's works focus, respectively, on how the presence of private armed forces impacts on the effectiveness of state-based armed forces and how adept various public and private armed forces are at avoiding friendly-fire incidents and casualties. Moreover, while this book examines incidents where private security personnel used violence against insurgents and civilians, Petersohn's article largely focuses on incidents where friendly armed forces inadvertently fired at each other.[23] Beyond this, some of my own studies, such as *Mercenaries in Asymmetric Conflict*s and "When Few Stood against Many", argue that the military cultures maintained by mercenary forces and their opponents in a number of African civil wars shaped their tactical behaviour, which, in combination, largely determined which side won each conflict.[24] However, while this book explains patterns of violence and casualties during private security operations, these other works explain the outcome of civil wars.

Besides my own "Wheeled Warriors", no published studies have put forward a theoretical explanation for the relationship between the military cultures maintained by different PSCs, the violent tactical behaviour exhibited by their personnel, and the casualties they inflicted and suffered during their security operations.[25] This book improves upon my "Wheeled Warriors" article in several notable respects. For instance, this book examines a much longer period of the Iraq War (2003 to 2009) than that covered in "Wheeled Warriors" (2005 to 2007) and is informed by a greater range of data sources. In addition, while the article largely focuses on the firms' use of violence against civilians, this book adopts a more balanced approach by also discussing how well the firms were able to protect their own personnel and clients in Iraq against insurgent attacks. This is significant because protecting people, places and things is the primary reason why PSCs exist and it forms one of the key criteria on which clients, journalists, scholars, human rights activists, government officials and the general public can judge their activities. In addition, while "Wheeled Warriors" examined only incidents where the firms' personnel fired their weapons, this book also examines incidents where their personnel employed different modes of violence, such as ramming a suspected threat with a vehicle.

Moreover, this book also provides a significantly more thorough analysis of the firms' military cultures and use of violence during the Iraq War than that contained in the article. In addition to including a more comprehensive range of statistics, this book contains richly detailed narrative accounts of the tactical behaviour exhibited by the private security personnel under study during violent incidents. Furthermore, Chapter 1 of this book provides a detailed, original discussion of the origins, structure and organization, personnel, mission types and equipment for each of the two firms, and also the various kinds of threats they faced during their security operations in Iraq. This material is intended to provide readers with a comprehensive understanding of the nature of these firms and the work they performed during the war. Finally, in Chapters 6 and 7, this book discusses the myriad legal, regulatory, political, corporate and operational implications that flow from the behaviour exhibited by these firms during the Iraq War. "Wheeled Warriors", in contrast, only touches briefly on two policy implications related to my findings. To summarize, this book offers a much more thorough explanation of not merely the use of violence by the firms' personnel, but also how the United States has managed and monitored its use of PSCs in Iraq, how the behaviour exhibited by these PSCs affected diplomatic relations between the governments of the United States and Iraq and their own corporate health, and how policymakers can best engage with PSCs in the future.

Methodology

To test the predictions made by the ideational theory of tactical violence, this study examines empirical evidence on the security operations of Blackwater and DynCorp during the Iraq War. The available information on these operations is quite rich and extensive. Of greatest importance, this study draws upon data contained in over 4,000 pages of recently-declassified incident reports prepared by the private security personnel involved and investigators from the Department of State's Diplomatic Security Service (DSS). In response to a Freedom of Information Act request submitted by Gawker Media, in December 2011 the Department of State declassified reports covering the 2005 to 2007 period of the Iraq War. In 2012, I submitted successful requests to obtain reports covering the 2003–2004 and 2008–2009 periods. These reports contain exclusive information about how the firms' security personnel engaged unarmed civilians and also the genuine threats they encountered during their security operations, such as insurgent gunmen, improvised explosive devices (IEDs) and vehicle-based improvised explosive devices (VBIEDs). As a result, to the extent that the data reveal patterns in the behaviour of either firm that readers may deem praiseworthy or contemptible, it is important to note that these firms and their chief client provided much of the empirical basis on which to make these assessments.

In addition, this study also examines a great deal of information from classified diplomatic cables and US military incident reports released by Wikileaks. Besides identifying several dozen additional violent incidents, these documents provided information on how Department of State staff and numerous officials in the government of Iraq viewed the firms' behaviour and also offered considerable insight into the tense political, legal, and regulatory conflicts sparked by this behaviour. Moreover, this study also derives information from investigative reports on the firms' activities, such as reports produced by US House and Senate committees, government departments and agencies, and non-governmental organizations. Furthermore, this study draws upon books and other publications written by the firms' executives and employees as well as journalists, news coverage of the firms' activities, and the existing academic literature on these actors. Utilizing this diverse array of sources allows this study to frequently cross-check and corroborate important information on the firms' private security operations in Iraq.

Finally, this study not only tests the theory's predictions against narrative accounts of the behaviour exhibited by the firms' personnel but also makes a significant empirical and methodological contribution to the study of PSCs by utilizing a dataset I developed to quantify the behaviour of private security personnel and the suspected threats they encountered during their operations: the Private Security Company Violent Incident Dataset (PSCVID). Virtually all of the existing works on PSCs, including

Introduction 11

most of those discussed earlier in this chapter, have limited their discussion of the use of violence by private security personnel to only about a dozen incidents. These incidents received considerable media attention, which made it relatively easy for scholars to discuss them in their work. However, they do not constitute a sufficiently robust empirical foundation on which to test theories of the behaviour of these actors because, when taken as a whole, they present a biased and grossly incomplete account of the behaviour of private security personnel in Iraq. For example, few of the commonly discussed incidents involved the use of violence by private security personnel against unambiguous threats, such as insurgent gunmen; rather, most of the commonly discussed incidents involved the use of violence by private security personnel against unarmed civilians. Moreover, scholars of PSCs have usually discussed these incidents as disparate anecdotes, and have not attempted to either identify trends in the behaviour of any firm's personnel or draw comparisons between the behaviour exhibited by the personnel of different firms.

Bearing these limitations in mind, utilizing a statistical dataset containing information on hundreds of incidents where the firms' personnel used violence allows this study to evaluate the predictions of the ideational theory of tactical violence against a more diverse array of data than that used by any other scholar. This dataset provides a much more comprehensive and less biased empirical record of the use of violence by both firms' personnel, and, through the use of comparative bivariate statistical analysis, also permits identification of clear trends in the behaviour exhibited by these employees. Of particular importance, this dataset includes information on how often the firms' personnel used violence against insurgents and civilians, how quickly these personnel employed violence after noticing a suspected threat, how often these personnel issued nonviolent warnings before employing deadly force, the distances at which these personnel attacked suspected threats, the number of bullets they fired, their propensity to abandon the people they attacked, and, of course, the deaths and serious injuries they inflicted and suffered during their security operations. Likewise, this dataset includes a host of information on the behaviour exhibited by the suspected threats the firms encountered in Iraq. By utilizing this dataset, along with a great deal of qualitative information, this study not only conducts a rigorous test of the ideational theory of tactical violence but also provides the most comprehensive account ever written of private security operations during the Iraq War. Except where noted, all of the information contained in the tables presented in this study is derived from the PSCVID.

Readers familiar with the October 2007 report issued by the US House Committee on Oversight and Government Reform on violent incidents involving private security personnel working for the Department of State will no doubt notice that it identifies far fewer violent incidents, deaths and serious injuries than are discussed in this book.[26] This report stated that Blackwater's personnel fired their weapons during 195 incidents between 1 January 2005 and 12 September 2007.[27] I, on the other hand, found that the firm's personnel fired their weapons during 328 incidents during this period (out of a total of 342 during the entire 2003 to 2009 period). Besides the fact that I had access to a greater range of sources on violent incidents involving the firm's personnel, the primary reason for this disparity is that the authors of the October 2007 report considered all violent incidents occurring on a given day to be a single incident, even though these incidents may have occurred at different times and involved different security teams and different suspected threats. In contrast, I distinguished these events from each other and counted them as separate incidents. For instance, if a particular security team fired at a red car at 10:00 a.m., a blue van at 10:45 a.m., and a white car at 11:00 a.m., I counted these as three separate violent incidents, while the report's authors counted them as one incident. My counting method is more accurate and allowed me to record precise information on the behaviour exhibited by a security team toward nearly every suspected threat it faced. This would not have been possible if I had amalgamated numerous incidents together. Moreover, this disparity is also due in part to the fact that the report's authors mistakenly counted several of Blackwater's violent incidents as DynCorp incidents, which made Blackwater's personnel appear less violent and DynCorp's personnel more violent than was actually the case. Many of the records provided by the firms and the Department of State contain redactions that may have confused or misled the authors, who had only two weeks to analyze the records and prepare their report. Haste may also explain why the authors were only able to attribute 16 Iraqi deaths to Blackwater's security teams during this period, while I found a minimum of 49 deaths (out of a total of at least 71).

At this point, it is valuable to highlight the fact that Blackwater's personnel actually killed and seriously injured far more people in Iraq than is reflected in the quantitative analysis contained in this book. During seven incidents, the firm's personnel killed an unknown number of people; they likewise seriously injured an unknown number of people during 16 incidents. Since it is not possible to determine how many casualties they inflicted in each of these incidents, I assumed that they killed and/or seriously injured at least one person per incident in order to include these incidents in the quantitative analysis. However, during some of these incidents, including a multi-hour defence of a CPA compound in Najaf on 4 April 2004 and a series of incidents on 23 January 2007, which saw dozens of the firm's personnel attempt to rescue a beleaguered security team and a downed helicopter crew, Blackwater's employees killed and seriously injured several hundred insurgents.[28] Taking this into account, the figures on the casualties inflicted by Blackwater's personnel discussed in this study should be viewed as a numerical minimum, not a maximum, and they do not convey the full extent of the disparity in the casualties inflicted by the firms.

I drew on a range of sources to determine the number of deaths suffered by the firms' security personnel. The Blackwater Veterans Association maintains a publicly-available record for every one of the firm's employees that died in Iraq and Afghanistan. These contain information on the date and cause of death, which I cross-checked against information derived from other sources on violent incidents contained in the PSCVID in order to link the deaths to particular incidents. Tracking the deaths of DynCorp's security personnel proved more challenging, but I developed an accurate count by analyzing the firm's incident reports as well as news media accounts and attempts by other scholars to compile casualty lists. It is of critical importance that this study focuses only on the deaths of security personnel who died in circumstances where they could plausibly be deemed responsible for their own safety. Therefore, if a turret gunner in a DynCorp security team died while undertaking a security mission in Iraq, then I included his death in the analysis. On the other hand, I did not include the deaths of Dyn-Corp's police trainers because they were not employed as security personnel and are not otherwise discussed in this study. Likewise, the Blackwater personnel that died on 21 April 2005, when the Skylink helicopter they were flying in was shot down, are not included in this analysis because the helicopter was operated by another firm and Blackwater was not responsible for their safety, as passengers, during the flight.[29] Finally, only deaths caused by hostile acts, such as insurgent gunfire or IEDs, are included in this analysis, since deaths from other sources, such as traffic accidents, are not a plausible reflection of the firms' ability to defend their employees and clients from harm in a conflict zone.

A diverse array of data sources informs the portrayal of the firms' military cultures in Chapter 3. Among these are memoirs written by former Blackwater personnel, including Erik Prince; Frank Gallagher, who headed Bremer's security detail and later served as an instructor at the firm's headquarters in Moyock, North Carolina; Tim Beckman, who worked in multiple Blackwater ground-based security teams in Iraq before becoming an instructor for the firm; and Dan Laguna, a senior pilot and director of Blackwater's flight operations in Iraq. In addition, since Blackwater derived its military culture from the US Navy's Sea, Air and Land (SEAL) teams, this chapter also draws on memoirs written by several SEAL veterans to further explain the nature and origins of particular aspects of the firm's military culture. Moreover, this chapter draws information from internal DynCorp documents pertaining to its security operations in Iraq, such as its "DI Rules for the Use of Force (RUF) for DI Programs in Iraq". Furthermore, these sources are supplemented with information derived from interviews and testimonies provided by the firms' personnel. Finally, this chapter also draws information from existing studies and media accounts of the firms.

It is, of course, possible that any of these data sources could be biased in favour of or against one or both firms. It is also possible to question how much weight should be placed on information provided by "insider" sources, such as the internal documents and the memoirs and statements of former employees, and "outsider" sources, such as scholarly and media accounts. To mitigate these risks, Chapter 3 utilizes multiple independent data sources to illustrate each characteristic of the firms' military cultures. It should be clear to readers of this chapter that a remarkable degree of consistency exists across a range of sources on the nature of both firms' military cultures. Moreover, like all of the other chapters in this book, Chapter 3 includes a large number of citations to allow readers to determine the source of each piece of information and to judge for themselves whether they consider the source reliable. Finally, it should be noted that the data sources used in this chapter were not intended to be clear-cut discussions of either firm's military culture. Rather, among voluminous irrelevant material, they contain snippets of information that hint at the dominant behavioural norms that the firms encouraged their employees to adhere to. As a result, while some of these sources may have been produced to push a particular agenda, it is not likely that their authors intended them to present a slanted or otherwise inaccurate take on the firms' military cultures.

Some readers may question why this book focuses on Blackwater and DynCorp alone rather than including other PSCs. One reason why it focuses on these two particular firms is because they are inherently important. For instance, these firms undertook the most significant function of any private armed forces during the Iraq War, which was to ensure that officials working for the government of the United States could safely carry out their government's occupation of Iraq. In addition, their behaviour while working for the Department of State provoked a variety of political and legal scandals that, in turn, prompted the government of the United States to alter how it managed and monitored its use of PSCs. Moreover, I also chose to focus on these particular firms because, as Chapters 4 and 5 illustrate, I have access to rich sources of data on the behaviour exhibited by their employees.

Furthermore, I chose to compare the behaviour exhibited by the employees of these particular firms because they share several important characteristics – they fielded employees with similar backgrounds, worked for the same primary client during the same time period, performed the same tasks (i.e. operating convoys of armoured vehicles in Iraqi cities and highways) under the same client-imposed rules of engagement, and faced the same kinds of threats in the same general operating environment. This made it reasonable to focus on a characteristic on which they differed markedly – their military culture – to explain why their employees behaved quite differently in Iraq and why, in turn, they also differed in terms of the casualties they inflicted and suffered during this conflict. Other firms do not share all of these core characteristics. For example, a firm called Triple Canopy also worked for the Department of State in Iraq but, during the period under study, its primary task was to guard fixed installations from occasional mortar and machine gun attacks. As a result, the behaviour its personnel exhibited during their operations is quite different from that exhibited by DynCorp and Blackwater's personnel and difficult to compare. Since Triple Canopy's primary threat was mortar attacks, it tended to fire at threats that were many hundreds of metres away. Blackwater and DynCorp's violent incidents, on the other hand, tended to take place at much closer ranges, on busy streets and highways, against civilians and gunmen in cars or nearby buildings. Likewise, since most of Triple Canopy's security teams were stationary, it is not reasonable to include them in a comparative analysis of how frequently each firm's personnel chose to abandon (i.e. leave behind) the people they attacked. With this in mind, running a comparative statistical analysis of all three firms' behaviour would yield highly misleading results. Other major PSCs, such as the British firm Hart, have not released the kinds of detailed incident reports that I would need in order to compile statistics on the behaviour exhibited by their personnel. This makes it impossible, at present, to include them in a comparative analysis with Blackwater and DynCorp. Moreover, even if the required data were available, comparing firms working for different clients, or in different locations, or during different time periods could yield unreliable results since it would likely be very challenging to definitively explain away the possible influence of differing client preferences and threat environments on the tactical behaviour exhibited by their employees.

Organization of the book

Chapter 1 of this book provides a detailed overview of the firms' origins, the threats they faced in Iraq, the types of operations they mounted to address these threats, their structures and organizations, and the equipment they used during their security operations. Chapter 2 discusses in detail the ideational theory of tactical violence and offers predictions regarding how a PSC's military culture should influence the tactical behaviour exhibited by its personnel. Chapter 3 discusses the origins and relevant characteristics of the firms' military cultures. Chapters 4 and 5 evaluate the theoretical propositions introduced in Chapter 2 against the empirical record of the firms' security operations during the Iraq War. Chapter 6 discusses the legal, regulatory, political and corporate implications of the firms' behaviour during the Iraq War. Finally, Chapter 7 provides a summary of the book's findings and discusses the implications of these findings for the use and development of private armed forces.

Notes

1 Blackwater changed its name to Xe in 2009, to Academi in 2011 and to Constellis Holdings in 2014. However, since the firm is almost invariably referred to by its original name, this book follows the same usage.

16 Introduction

2 Carafano, *Private Sector*, 107; Dunigan, *Victory for Hire*, 71–72; Fainaru, *Big Boy Rules*, 88; Simons, *Master of War*, 176 and 262; Scahill, *Blackwater*, 2nd edn, 8.
3 US Department of State Diplomatic Security Service, "High Threat Protective Operations", 7–9; Coalition Provisional Authority, "Memorandum Number 17", 10–11.
4 Prince, *Civilian Warriors*, 81.
5 Bremer and McConnell, *My Year in Iraq*, 149; Prince, *Civilian Warriors*, 77. This assertion was confirmed by the head of Bremer's Blackwater security detail, Frank Gallagher. Gallagher and Del Vecchio, *The Bremer Detail*, Loc. 31.
6 Associated Press, "US Ambassador".
7 Sands, "Bush lauds security firm".
8 House Committee on Oversight and Government Reform, "Hearing on Blackwater USA", 56 and 68.
9 Boswell *et al.*, "Secretary of State's Panel", 5.
10 Scahill, *Blackwater*, 2nd edn, 16.
11 Quoted in Dunning, "Heroes or Mercenaries", 7. See also Prince's testimony in House Committee on Oversight and Government Reform, "Hearing on Blackwater USA", 56.
12 See, for example, the extensive discussion of this topic in Scahill, *Blackwater*, 2nd edn; Carafano, *Private Sector, Public Wars*; Simons, *Master of War*; Dunigan, *Victory for Hire*.
13 Singer, *Corporate Warriors*, 4–6.
14 Ibid., 88–100.
15 Carafano, *Private Sector, Public Wars*; Engbrecht, *America's Covert Warriors*; Fainaru, *Big Boy Rules*; Isenberg, *Shadow Force*; Pelton, *Licensed to Kill*.
16 Scahill, *Blackwater*, 1st edn, Simons, *Master of War*.
17 Avant, *The Market for Force*, 5–7.
18 Percy, *Mercenaries*.
19 Petersohn, "Impact of Mercenaries"; Rasor and Bauman, *Betraying Our Troops*; Ross, "Natural Resources".
20 Petersohn, "Impact of Mercenaries", 205.
21 Dunigan, *Victory for Hire*, 3–4.
22 Petersohn, "Effectiveness of Contracted Coalitions".
23 Petersohn, "The Effectiveness of Contracted Coalitions", 479–482.
24 Fitzsimmons, *Mercenaries in Asymmetric Conflicts*; Fitzsimmons, "When Few Stood against Many".
25 This book is derived in part from an article titled "Wheeled Warriors: Explaining Variations in the Use of Violence by Private Security Companies in Iraq", which was published in *Security Studies*: Fitzsimmons, "Wheeled Warriors".
26 Majority Staff, "Memorandum".
27 Ibid., 7.
28 Chatterjee, *Iraq, Inc.*, 129–130; Human Rights First, "Private Security Contractors at War", 24; Sizemore and Kimberlin, "Blackwater: On the Front Lines"; Majority Staff, "Memorandum", 8; Barstow, "Security Firm Says"; Miller, *Blood Money*, 165; Scahill, *Blackwater*, 1st edn, 125–130; US Embassy, Baghdad, "Spot Report – 012307–02"; Kimberlin, "Blackwater's 'Little Birds'"; Laguna, *You Have to Live Hard*, Loc. 350, 432–433, 442–443, 476,477, 496–522, 531–556, 564–565, 585–595, 604–667, 675–690, 696–728, 3559–3561 and 3570–3581; Simons, *Master of War*, 154–157; Associated Press, "US Helicopter Crashes"; Staff, "Five Killed"; BVA Honor Roll; Batty, "Rock Stars of Baghdad".
29 BVA Honor Roll, "Robert Jason Gore"; "Steven Matthew McGovern"; "Jason Edward Obert"; "David Michael 'Pat' Patterson"; "Luke Adam Petrik"; "Eric Smith".

References

Associated Press. "US Ambassador Calls Blackwater Shooting Horrific, but Still Feels High Regard for Guards". 25 October 2007.
Associated Press. "US Helicopter Crashes in Iraq in the Past 6 Months". 7 February 2007.
Avant, Deborah. *The Market for Force: The Consequences of Privatizing Security*. Cambridge: Cambridge University Press, 2005.
Barstow, David. "Security Firm says its Workers were Lured into Iraqi Ambush". *New York Times*, 9 April 2004.
Batty, Roy. "Rock Stars of Baghdad". *Military.com*, 8 February 2007.
BVA Honor Roll (Blackwater Veterans Association. "Honor Roll – Blackwater Personnel Killed in Action". 6 January 2013. Available at https://bwvets.com/index.php?forums/honor-roll-blackwater-personnel-killed-in-action.63/).
BVA Honor Roll. "David Michael 'Pat' Patterson".
BVA Honor Roll. "Eric Smith".
BVA Honor Roll. "Jason Edward Obert".
BVA Honor Roll. "Luke Adam Petrik".
BVA Honor Roll. "Robert Jason Gore".
BVA Honor Roll. "Steven Matthew McGovern".
Boswell, Eric J., George A. Joulwan, J. Stapleton Roy and Patrick F. Kennedy. "Report of the Secretary of State's Panel on Personal Protective Services in Iraq". Washington, DC: US Department of State, October 2007.
Bremer, L. Paul, and Malcolm McConnell. *My Year in Iraq: The Struggle to Build a Future of Hope*. Kindle edn. New York: Simon & Schuster, 2006.
Carafano, James Jay. *Private Sector, Public Wars: Contractors in Combat – Afghanistan, Iraq, and Future Conflicts*. Westport, CT: Praeger Security International, 2008.
Chatterjee, Pratap. *Iraq, Inc.: A Profitable Occupation*. New York: Seven Stories Press, 2004.
Coalition Provisional Authority. "Coalition Provisional Authority Memorandum Number 17". Baghdad: Coalition Provisional Authority, 26 June 2004.
Dunigan, Molly. *Victory for Hire: Private Security Companies' Impact on Military Effectiveness*. Stanford, CA: Stanford Security Studies, 2011.
Dunning, Rebecca. "Heroes or Mercenaries? Blackwater, Private Security Companies, and the US Military". Case study. Durham, NC: The Kenan Institute for Ethics, Duke University, 2010.
Engbrecht, Shawn. *America's Covert Warriors: Inside the World of Private Military Contractors*. Washington, DC: Potomac Books, 2011.
Fainaru, Steve. *Big Boy Rules: America's Mercenaries Fighting in Iraq*. Philadelphia: Da Capo Press, 2008.
Fitzsimmons, Scott. *Mercenaries in Asymmetric Conflicts*. New York: Cambridge University Press, 2012.
Fitzsimmons, Scott. "Wheeled Warriors: Explaining Variations in the Use of Violence by Private Security Companies in Iraq". *Security Studies* 22, no. 4 (2013): 707–739. Available at: www.tandfonline.com/doi/pdf/10.1080/09636412.2013.844521.
Fitzsimmons, Scott. "When Few Stood against Many: Explaining Executive Outcomes' Victory in the Sierra Leonean Civil War". *Defence Studies* 13, no. 2 (2013): 245–269.
Gallagher, Frank, and John M. Del Vecchio. *The Bremer Detail: Protecting the Most Threatened Man in the World*. Kindle edn. New York: Open Road Media, 2014.

House Committee on Oversight and Government Reform. "Hearing on Blackwater USA". Washington, DC: House of Representatives, Congress of the United States, 2 October 2007.
Human Rights First. "Private Security Contractors at War: Ending the Culture of Impunity". New York: Human Rights First, 2008.
Isenberg, David. *Shadow Force: Private Security Contractors in Iraq*. Westport, CT: Praeger Security International, 2009.
Kimberlin, Joanne. "Blackwater's 'Little Birds' of Baghdad Pack Quite a Sting". *Virginian-Pilot*, 1 March 2007.
Laguna, Dan. *You Have to Live Hard to Be Hard: One Man's Life in Special Operations*. Kindle edn. Bloomington, IN: Authorhouse, 2010.
Majority Staff. "Memorandum – Additional Information about Blackwater USA". Washington, DC: Congress of the United States, 1 October 2007.
Miller, T. Christian. *Blood Money: Wasted Billions, Lost Lives, and Corporate Greed in Iraq*. New York: Little Brown and Company, 2006.
Pelton, Robert Young. *Licensed to Kill: Hired Guns in the War on Terror*. New York: Crown Publishers, 2006.
Percy, Sarah. *Mercenaries: The History of a Norm of International Relations*. New York: Oxford University Press, 2007.
Petersohn, Ulrich. "The Effectiveness of Contracted Coalitions: Private Security Contractors in Iraq". *Armed Forces and Society* 39, no. 3 (2013): 467–488.
Petersohn, Ulrich. "The Impact of Mercenaries and Private Military and Security Companies on Civil War Severity between 1946 and 2002". *International Interactions* 40, no. 2 (2014): 191–215.
Prince, Erik. *Civilian Warriors: The Inside Story of Blackwater and the Unsung Heroes of the War on Terror*. Kindle edn. New York: Portfolio, 2013.
Rasor, Dina, and Robert Bauman. *Betraying Our Troops: The Destructive Results of Privatizing War*. New York: Palgrave Macmillan, 2007.
Ross, M. L. "How Do Natural Resources Influence Civil War? Evidence from Thirteen Cases". *International Organization* 58, no. 1 (2004): 35–67.
Sands, David R. "Bush Lauds Security Firm; Blackwater Chief Sought Defense". *Washington Times*, 18 October 2007.
Scahill, Jeremy. *Blackwater: The Rise of the World's Most Powerful Mercenary Army*. 1st edn. New York: Nation Books, 2007.
Scahill, Jeremy. *Blackwater: The Rise of the World's Most Powerful Mercenary Army*. 2nd edn. New York: Nation Books, 2008.
Simons, Suzanne. *Master of War: Blackwater USA's Erik Prince and the Business of War*. New York: Harper, 2009.
Singer, Peter W. *Corporate Warriors: The Rise of the Privatized Military Industry*. Ithaca, NY: Cornell University Press, 2003.
Sizemore, Bill, and Joanne Kimberlin. "Blackwater: On the Front Lines". *Virginian-Pilot*, 25 July 2006.
Staff. "Five Killed in Attack on 2 Blackwater Helicopters". *Virginian-Pilot*, 24 January 2007.
US Department of State Diplomatic Security Service. "High Threat Protective Operations in Baghdad: General Information and Standard Operating Procedures for WPPS Contract Personnel". Baghdad: US Department of State, August 2005.
US Embassy, Baghdad. "Spot Report – 012307–02 – Complex Attack on COM PSD Resulting in Five KIA". Baghdad: US Department of State, 23 January 2007.

1 The nature of Blackwater and DynCorp's security operations during the Iraq War

This chapter provides essential background information on private armed forces in general and Blackwater and DynCorp in particular. It introduces the concept of PSCs, differentiates these actors from other firms in the private military industry and traces the development of the contemporary market for private armed forces. It then discusses the origins and early development of Blackwater and DynCorp. Finally, it provides a detailed overview of their security operations in Iraq between 2003 and 2009, including information on the insurgent threats they faced, the kinds of security missions they undertook to address these threats, the structure and organization of their security forces and the equipment they used during their security operations.

What is a private security company?

A private security company (PSC) is a legally-established commercial firm offering services that could involve the use of deadly force to support the needs of its clients. These services can include fielding personnel, weapons and other equipment to defend a client's staff and facilities from potential threats. According to this definition, Blackwater and DynCorp should be considered PSCs during the period under study because they conducted static security operations, in which they deployed teams of armed personnel to defend the US Embassy to Iraq and other fixed sites, and mobile security operations, in which they deployed armed security teams in convoys of armoured vehicles to ensure that their clients could safely travel through unstable territory.

PSCs are but one of several types of firms in the contemporary private military industry. Private training and consulting companies (PTCC) focus on training armed forces and providing advice on, for instance, how to organize a military force, which weapons to purchase and how to conduct military and security operations. For example, Military Professional Resources Incorporated (MPRI), an American company founded and run by retired US military officers, earned its reputation as the world's premier military consulting firm in 1995, during the Bosnian War, when it conducted an extensive training operation to vastly improve the combat capabilities of the Croatian armed forces. The firm also provided advice to the Croatian military regarding how to defeat their Serb opponents in that conflict. After years of bloody stalemates, the retrained Croatian armed forces launched an offensive on 4 August 1995 that, along with a North Atlantic Treaty Organization (NATO) aerial bombing campaign against Serb targets, ended the Bosnian War and allowed both Bosnia and Croatia to become fully independent states.[1] Such firms generally do not employ deadly force in their work.

As their name implies, private logistical support companies (PLSCs) offer services ranging from constructing military bases to maintaining weapons systems, cooking food, doing laundry, collecting and analyzing intelligence, and transporting supplies. KBR and Halliburton, both based in the United States, are among the largest PLSCs. PLSCs tend to have more employees and generate greater revenue than other any other type of firm in the private military industry. They are also the most important type of firm to highly developed military forces, such as the US and British armed forces, because they provide the logistical and other support functions that these developed military forces have not been able to provide for themselves since downsizing or eliminating many of their own logistical support units during the 1980s and 1990s. PLSCs rarely, if ever, employ deadly force in their work.

Finally, private military companies (PMCs) directly take part in sustained violent operations against other armed forces. Like some PSCs, firms in this category also use deadly force, but they tend to do so on a larger scale because they tend to be hired to accomplish highly ambitious objectives. For example, such firms may be hired to win a civil war on behalf of a government or rebel faction, or to launch or prevent coup attempts against the government of a state. The now-defunct South African firm Executive Outcomes, which won the Angolan and Sierra Leonean civil wars during the 1990s on behalf of the governments of these states, was among the most successful PMCs.[2] At present, there are few active PMCs due to their questionable legality and the comparatively high risks involved in their work and because of the greater stability and financial rewards associated with the work performed by other types of firms.

Although this typology relies on ideal types that may not perfectly reflect the nature of any particular real-world firm, it has advantages over most other categorization schemes. It is a relatively simple and straightforward scheme because it distinguishes firms purely on the basis of their functional behaviour – that is, on the basis of what they actually do. Most other typologies add other criteria, such as attempting to differentiate firms by the nature of their clients and their proximity to the front line of a battlefield. As discussed throughout this section, adding additional classification criteria makes it difficult for scholars to classify real-world firms. Furthermore, unlike most other typologies, which lack a means for deciding which category multi-service firms should be placed in, this typology sorts firms on the basis of the most lethal service they provided during the period under study. Therefore, even though Blackwater and DynCorp offered a variety of other services during the period under study, including training and support services, they are classified as PSCs under this scheme because they provided lethal security services for some of their clients. A firm such as Halliburton, on the other hand, which provided logistical and support services but did not provide lethal security services during the period under study, is rightly classified as a PLSC.

Other scholars of international relations have put forward alternative typologies to try to make sense of the private military industry. In 2002, Robert Mandel developed one of the first typologies. It differentiated firms on the basis of their geographic scope (inside or outside of their home state), client (a state government or a non-state actor such as a corporation, gang, militia, NGO or terrorist group), purpose (maintaining the status quo or significantly modifying it) and the nature of the services they provided (armed combat support, training, logistics, etc.).[3] As with some of the more recently-developed typologies, Mandel's scheme is best suited to classifying highly-focused firms that serve a single client in a single country and provide a single type of service – few of which exist – but cannot adequately categorize the diversified major players in the industry. For example, Blackwater started as a domestically-focused training and supply firm with an almost exclusively government (local, state and federal) client base. Within a few years, however, it began supplementing its original services and client base by providing armed security details and designing armoured vehicles and by maintaining several government and non-governmental clients.[4] It is difficult to determine where Blackwater should fit in Mandel's typology because he does not provide clearly-defined rules for deciding how complex firms should be categorized.

Peter Singer put forward perhaps the best-known typology of firms in the private military industry in his 2003 book *Corporate Warriors*.[5] His "tip-of-the-spear" typology distinguishes firms on the basis of how close their operations are to the front line in conflicts. Military provider firms operate on the front-line tactical battlefield; military consulting firms operate within conflict zones, but not quite on the front lines; finally, military support firms operate within conflict zones but are usually far back from the front lines. Singer presumed that the firms in each of these categories offer a distinct set of services. Military provider firms offer front-line tactical combat services. In other words, these firms provide services that are directly related to fighting and winning a conflict. This can involve taking a direct part in fighting enemy military forces on behalf of a client by, for instance, providing ground troops or specialists to undertake certain tasks that their clients cannot handle themselves, such as flying helicopters. For example, Executive Outcomes provided both ground troops and specialist pilots when it helped the governments of Angola and Sierra Leone win civil wars against determined rebel forces during the 1990s. Although Singer developed his scheme before the outbreak of the Iraq War and the rise to prominence of the current generation of PSCs, he later placed Blackwater in this category.[6] Military consulting firms, in contrast, provide advice and training services to help enhance their client's own military or security forces. They offer the benefit of their years of experience and expertise in how to properly structure a military force, train its personnel and fight and defeat enemy military forces. MPRI, introduced earlier in this chapter, is the best-known firm in this category. Finally, military support firms, such as Halliburton and KBR, provide supporting services for their clients such as distributing food, ammunition and fuel supplies and performing maintenance, transportation and intelligence analysis.

The chief contribution of Singer's typology is that, in his words,

> one can ... explore not only the variations within the industry but also the variations in firms' organization, their operations, and impact. Broader statements can be made about overall firm types, rather than being forced to rely on simple judgments that only apply to one specific firm.[7]

Besides the fact that this typology does not clearly differentiate between PMCs, such as Executive Outcomes, and PSCs, such as Blackwater, the most oft-noted problem is that it fails to account for the fact that most firms in the private military industry offer multiple kinds of services at the same time. As noted earlier, a firm may simultaneously offer a military provider firm's security services, a military consulting firm's training and advice services, and a military support firm's logistical services. For example, during the period under study, DynCorp not only mounted security operations for the US Department of State and other clients in Iraq but also helped train the Iraqi police service and maintained numerous weapons systems for the US armed forces.[8] Therefore, it is unclear how this firm should be properly classified in Singer's scheme. If one were to presume, as the typology presented in this book does, that firms should be categorized on the basis of the most lethal service they offer, then the fact that DynCorp provided security services means it should be considered a military provider firm. Singer's typology does not allow for such determinations. Finally, Singer's typology also fails to account for the fact that contemporary conflicts do not always have a clearly defined "front line", since violence can occur virtually anywhere within the conflict zone at any time. With this in mind, using proximity to a nonexistent front line is not a useful way to differentiate between firms.

Deborah Avant's typology, which she outlined in her 2005 *Market for Force*, draws inspiration from Singer's scheme but distinguishes between what Avant labels "military" and "police" functions.[9] The categories in Avant's scheme are based on the various kinds of contracted functions a firm may fulfill rather than ideal types of firms. As a result, her scheme allows for a single firm to be placed in multiple functional categories. Within the military functions, Avant includes "armed operational support", "unarmed operational support on the battlefield", "unarmed military advice and training" and "logistical support". Police functions include "armed site security", "unarmed site security", "police advice and training", "crime prevention" and "intelligence". Therefore, using this scheme, scholars can highlight the fact that, during the 2003 to 2009 period, Blackwater and DynCorp carried out certain "military" functions, such as "unarmed military advice and training" and "logistical support", and also some "police" functions such as "armed site security" and "police advice and training". Perplexingly, this typology does not include "armed mobile security", the activity that contemporary PSCs are best known for. In addition, it is unclear why "intelligence" should constitute only a police function and why "logistical support" should constitute only a military function. Of greatest importance, since this scheme eschews ideal-type categories, it fails to provide a simple way for scholars to distinguish between different firms or attempt to make generalizations about certain parts of the private military industry. It merely highlights the fact that firms can be contracted to perform a range of different functions.

Rather than trying to categorize the firms that make up the private military industry into ideal types or on the basis of their contracted functions, Christopher Kinsey differentiated firms and related actors, such as national military forces, on the basis of two criteria: the object of their protection (ranging from public entities/the state to private entities) and the means they use to secure the object (ranging from lethal to non-lethal).[10] According to this typology, a national military force would be placed at the public end of the public–private axis and at the lethal end of the lethal–non-lethal axis. Those PSCs, such as Blackwater and DynCorp, that regularly used deadly force in defence of Department of State personnel and facilities would, in contrast, be placed further away from the public end of the public–private axis and further away from the lethal end of the lethal–non-lethal axis since they did not exclusively serve national governments and tended to employ less deadly force than national military forces in wartime. Less violent PSCs, such as Hart and Group 4 Securicor, and firms that derive most of their income from non-governmental clients would be placed still further away from the public and lethal ends of these respective axes. Firms that focus largely on training and logistics, such as MPRI and Halliburton, would be placed quite close to the non-lethal end of the lethal–non-lethal axis.

Kinsey's typology has certain advantages over those put forward by Mandel, Singer and Avant. Among these are its ability to distinguish different firms from each other on the basis of their actual behaviour and client base rather than merely on how well they conform to overly complex ideal types. In other words, Kinsey's scheme allows scholars to illustrate that, although firms like Blackwater and Hart are both, to use Singer's terminology, "military provider firms", and both, to use Avant's terminology, have undertaken "armed site security" operations, they differ markedly in the amount of deadly force they employ during their security operations. In addition, unlike the other schemes, Kinsey's typology also allows scholars to distinguish PSCs from other security-related actors such as national military forces and conventional police forces.

This typology does, however, suffer from some of the same drawbacks of the other schemes. For instance, since firms offer a diverse range of services, some much more lethal than others, it is unclear where they should be placed on the lethal–non-lethal axis. For example, Blackwater's private security operations were often quite violent and deadly but its target manufacturing and vehicle design divisions were completely non-lethal. Likewise, since firms can have multiple public and private clients at the same time, it is unclear where exactly they should be placed on the public–private axis. For example, although Blackwater and DynCorp both conducted private security operations to protect Department of State personnel and facilities, they also worked for other elements of the US government, such as the Central Intelligence Agency (CIA) and Department of Defense, and maintained private clients, such as the catering company Eurest Support Services.[11] Finally, these first two issues are compounded by the fact that a firm's behaviour and client base will likely change over time.

The development of the contemporary market for private armed forces

The notion that the market for private armed forces has long been driven by patterns of military downsizing is quite popular among scholars. They argue, for example, that the end of the decades-long Peloponnesian War in 404 BCE motivated thousands of veteran soldiers to work as mercenaries for warring leaders throughout the Mediterranean world.[12] In addition, scholars suggest that the periods of peace amidst the series of conflicts between the English and French nobility known as the Hundred Years War (1337–1453) allowed groups of demobilized soldiers to form "free" and "great" companies and sell their services throughout Europe.[13] Scholars have similarly argued that the unprecedented demobilization of millions of soldiers from the Allied and Axis militaries after the end of the Second World War led to the rise of numerous mercenary groups during the Cold War period. Among these were 5 Commando, which defeated the 7,000 strong Simba insurgent force in the Congo in 1964–65, and the rag-tag group known simply as "Callan's Mercenaries" that was crushed by a combined Angolan–Cuban army unit numbering about 2,000 in 1976.[14] Likewise, scholars frequently point to the downsizing or elimination of Apartheid-era South African military and police units, such as 32 Battalion and Koevoet, when explaining the origins of the best-known post–Cold War PMC, Executive Outcomes.[15]

In contrast, the development of the current generation of PSCs was driven largely by a combination of three unplanned processes and unintended circumstances. While some scholars still favour the notion that downsizing led directly to a rise of private armed forces, they have not presented evidence to support the assertion that the military downsizing that occurred in the United States and Western Europe after the end of the Cold War directly led to the development of firms such as Blackwater, Triple Canopy, DynCorp, Hart and the other notable PSCs of the current era.[16] Most downsizing initiatives actually concentrated on logistical and support personnel – the soldiers and marines who served as clerks, secretaries and cooks – rather than combat units. The growth of PLSCs such as Halliburton and KBR can therefore be attributed in part to post–Cold War downsizing efforts, but the role of this process in the growth of contemporary PSCs is more indirect. Indeed, downsizing and then outsourcing well over 100,000 support roles to PLSCs helped promote the widespread acceptance of private companies in conflict zones.[17] This, in turn, allowed governments to consider the possibility that companies offering combat-related services should also have a place on the battlefield. In other words, if the United States and other Western governments had not downsized and outsourced many of the support roles in their armed forces, then they probably would not have deemed it acceptable and legitimate to extensively outsource security roles to private firms.

The growth of the current generation of PSCs was also facilitated by a highly permissive legal and regulatory environment in the firms' home countries and also in Iraq and Afghanistan. On paper, the owners and employees of US-based firms such as Blackwater and DynCorp are subject to several federal laws that allow them to be punished for harming or killing people during their security operations. These include the Military Extraterritorial Jurisdiction Act of 2000, the Uniform Code of Military Justice, the Special Maritime and Territorial Jurisdiction Act, the US Arms Export Control Act of 1976, the War Crimes Act of 1996 and certain provisions of National Defense Authorization Acts from 2008 onward. Other Western countries have enacted similar legislation. However, these laws are rarely applied to prosecute Western private security personnel, even those that have been implicated in the deaths of unarmed civilians in Iraq and Afghanistan.[18] Prosecutions of Western private security personnel by the governments of Iraq and Afghanistan are likewise very rare. This largely hands-off approach to PSCs allowed these actors to undertake operations that could see them utilize deadly force on a regular basis, with little fear that their actions would ever come under serious legal scrutiny.

Finally, the rise of the current generation of PSCs was driven in part by the demand for large numbers of extra combat personnel to support the US-led stabilization efforts in Iraq and Afghanistan. Put simply, the United

States and its allies declined to provide sufficient military personnel to accomplish their security objectives in Iraq and Afghanistan and this, in turn, created an opportunity for the private sector to offer security services to governments, private businesses and international and non-governmental organizations so that their employees could work safely in these unstable conflict zones. Moreover, by taking on roles such as protecting pipelines, VIPs and numerous public and private facilities, PSCs allowed Western and local military forces to devote a greater proportion of their soldiers to counterinsurgency and stability operations. Most of the more than 90 PSCs that provided security services in these countries, such as Triple Canopy, DynCorp, Blackwater, Hart, Control Risks and Erinys, were either founded or motivated to greatly expand their security services divisions in order to meet this demand.[19]

The origins of Blackwater

Erik Prince, a former US Navy SEAL, founded Blackwater on 26 December 1996 in Moyock, North Carolina. Located just a few hours' drive from Washington, DC, the firm's headquarters was also close to several military bases, such as the US Marine's Camp Lejeune and the US Army's Fort Bragg, and the CIA's main training facility, known as "The Farm".[20] Taking its name from the dark, tannin-stained water of the nearby Great Dismal Swamp, Blackwater began as a manufacturer of metal shooting targets but soon branched out into tactical weapons training for soldiers and police SWAT (Special Weapons and Tactics) units.[21] In 2002, Prince established the security and aviation services divisions that would later reap unprecedented revenue but also sully the Blackwater name to such an extent that the firm has rebranded three times since 2009 – to Xe Services, then Academi and, finally, Constellis Holdings – to try to outrun its past.[22] Blackwater joined the private military industry because Prince genuinely believed that a private armed force could be more responsive and efficient than the enormously powerful but bureaucratic and over-tasked US military: "We are trying to do for the national security apparatus what FedEx did for the Postal Service".[23] His timing could not have been better since, with the onset of the War in Afghanistan in October 2001 and the Iraq War in March 2003, the government of the United States found itself in desperate need of additional troops to protect people, places and things in overseas warzones.

The firm undertook its first security operation in 2002 for the CIA, which sought contractors to guard its Afghan headquarters in Kabul.[24] During the following year, Blackwater embarked on one of the most dangerous missions of the Iraq War: protecting US and other Western diplomats and politicians from insurgent attacks.[25] This came about because the US military, already stretched thin on the ground in Iraq, felt that it could not afford to assign enough soldiers to provide protection for CPA and

Department of State officials at all times.[26] Its chief protectees, or "principals", in Iraq included Paul Bremer, who served as the CPA administrator from May 2003 to June 2004, US ambassadors to Iraq and numerous Department of State staff.[27] The firm also protected visiting US secretaries of state, other members of the US federal cabinet, several members of congress, and British Prime Minister Tony Blair.[28] To do their jobs effectively, these dignitaries needed to move freely throughout Iraq to meet political and religious leaders, military personnel and community organizers.[29] This, in turn, required a sizeable protection force that could watch over dozens of people and facilities throughout Iraq, 24 hours a day. Although it shared some of its responsibilities with other PSCs, Blackwater quickly emerged as the primary security provider for both the CPA and Department of State in Iraq.[30] Besides these organizations and the CIA, the firm also protected the Iraq Survey Group, which was hunting weapons of mass destruction, and United Nations (UN) humanitarian workers that stayed behind in Iraq after their organization removed most of its staff from the country in 2003.[31] Blackwater also undertook work for the US Department of Defense in several countries around the world. The firm's work for the CIA is, as of this writing, largely classified, but it included providing static security details around the agency's facilities in Afghanistan, serving as bodyguards for its officers in the field, assisting in the operation of Predators and other remotely piloted aircraft, and planning and carrying out covert special operations such as "snatch-and-grab" missions targeting suspected terrorists inside Afghanistan and Pakistan.[32] The activities accounted for approximately 15 per cent of the firm's revenue during the first decade of the twenty-first century.[33] The firm also worked for a few foreign armed forces, such as the Azerbaijan Navy, and offered counter-piracy services for shipping companies operating in the waters near Somalia and the Gulf of Aden.[34]

The origins of DynCorp

Relative to Blackwater, DynCorp, based in Falls Church, Virginia, is a much older company. It was founded in 1946 as two firms, Land–Air Inc. and California Eastern Airways.[35] The latter company acquired the former in 1951, renamed itself Dynalectron Corporation and, in 1987, rebranded again to DynCorp. DynCorp was acquired by Computer Sciences Corporation in 2003 and by Cerberus Capital Management in 2010.[36] Therefore, unlike the standalone Blackwater, DynCorp was merely one part of a much larger cooperate entity during the Iraq War.

Throughout its history, the firm has provided a wide range of services – from infrastructure development to logistics, maintenance, facility management, training, engineering solutions and security – to dozens of departments and agencies of the US and foreign governments as well as private companies.[37] Prior to the Iraq War, it was perhaps best known for deploying contract field teams, made up of civilian technicians, outside the United States to maintain weapons, aircraft and other complex military systems.[38] Through these and other services, the firm has played a supporting role in every major American military operation since the Korean War.[39] Reflecting on this legacy, the firm's then CEO stated in 2003 that the US military "could fight without us, but it would be difficult. Because we're so involved, it's difficult to extricate us from the process".[40]

In the security sphere, DynCorp has deployed police forces to overseas conflict and post-conflict zones in Bosnia, Haiti and Afghanistan and pilots to take part in counter-narcotics operations in Afghanistan and Columbia.[41] In the latter role, its employees sprayed herbicides in an attempt to reduce the yield of cocaine and opium crops and, more controversially, flew armed helicopter gunships to protect its crop-dusting aircraft. The firm also fielded armed search-and-rescue teams to find and extract their colleagues in the event of a crash. It also deployed police trainers to help reconstitute Iraqi police units after the fall of the Hussein regime.[42] Finally, the firm fielded private security teams in Iraq, Afghanistan and other conflict zones to protect Department of State facilities and personnel. Although its private security operations in Iraq generated only about 2 per cent of the firm's revenue during the 2003 to 2009 period, this proved to be its most controversial business line.[43]

Blackwater and DynCorp in Iraq

Operating from 2003 to 2009 under a contract with the CPA and, later, the Department of State's first and second Worldwide Personnel Protective Services Contracts (WPPS-1 and -2), Blackwater and DynCorp shared responsibility for protecting American officials with a PSC called Triple Canopy, based in Reston, Virginia.[44] Blackwater operated in the most unstable areas of Iraq, such as Baghdad, Ramadi, Najaf, Karbala and Al Hillah, and provided close air support for Department of State security operations throughout the country.[45] DynCorp, on the other hand, largely focused on relatively safe cities in northern Iraq, such as Erbil and Kirkuk, while Triple Canopy's main area of operations was southern Iraq, including the cities of Basra and Tallil.[46] The firms did, however, frequently conduct operations in each others' area of responsibility. Reflecting its comparatively extensive responsibilities, Blackwater fielded far more security personnel than either DynCorp or Triple Canopy, at 987 of the 1,395 total private security personnel working for the Department of State in Iraq in 2007, and also commanded the lion's share of the revenue from the WPPS contracts.[47] For comparison, DynCorp fielded 151 security personnel in Iraq in 2007 and Triple Canopy's force numbered 257.[48] A 2007 report on the WPPS-2 contract concluded that Blackwater earned over US$472 million in revenue during the previous year, while Triple Canopy earned just over US$59 million and DynCorp received approximately

US$39 million.[49] This corresponds with Prince's claim that his firm received approximately 85 per cent of the total revenue earned by the three firms during the peak years of the WPPS-2 contract.[50] In 2007, at the height of its operations in Iraq, the Department of State considered Blackwater virtually indispensable. When asked, in the aftermath of the September 2007 Nisour Square shootings, why they did not immediately cancel the firm's contracts and transfer its responsibilities to DynCorp and Triple Canopy, a Department of State official told a reporter for the *New York Times* that the department "did not believe they had any alternative to Blackwater. ... (O)nly three companies in the world meet their requirements for protective services in Iraq, and the other two do not have the capability to assume Blackwater's role in Baghdad" or take over its air support role.[51]

Threats faced and basic mission types

The Iraqi insurgency differed in many respects from the classic guerrilla-type campaigns experienced in many parts of Africa, Asia and Latin America during the twentieth century.[52] With the exception of Muqtada al-Sadr's Shiite Mahdi Army, which fiercely defended the Sadr City area of Baghdad, the insurgent groups lacked a strong leadership component, operated in a highly decentralized manner and made few attempts to capture and control territory.[53] Sunni insurgent groups, made up largely of Iraqis but supplemented with foreign fighters, pursued a diverse array of objectives.[54] However, like the many Shiite insurgent groups, the Sunni groups shared an interest in driving the government of the United States out of Iraq by harming its personnel, damaging its facilities and disrupting its attempts to maintain order.[55] Facing these threats, American officials, as living symbols of their country's occupation of Iraq, required robust protection at all times, but particularly whenever they travelled outside the heavily fortified area of central Baghdad containing the CPA's headquarters and US Embassy to Iraq, known as the Green Zone.

Insurgent groups attempted to harm the firms' personnel and clients in various ways.[56] The most common insurgent attacks involved small groups of gunmen armed with AK-47s, AK-74s and other kinds of Soviet-designed assault rifles, RPK, RPD and PKM machine guns, and rocket-propelled grenades (RPGs).[57] The vast majority of these assaults were brief, hit-and-run affairs, during which gunmen staged an ambush along a stretch of road, fired their weapons and threw grenades at a security convoy and then attempted to melt back into the civilian populace.[58] Less often, gunmen fired at convoys from moving vehicles.[59] The first four deaths suffered by Blackwater personnel in Iraq, which occurred in Fallujah on 31 March 2004, vividly illustrated the danger posed by insurgent gunmen.[60] The security team involved in that day's operation, known as November 1, was made up of four contractors in two unarmoured Mitsubishi Pajeros. The team was tasked with providing mobile security for a small convoy of Iraqi trucks carrying kitchen supplies from Camp Taji, located to the north-east of Fallujah, to Camp Ridgeway, located to the west of the city.[61] Wesley Batalona and Jerry Zovko staffed the lead SUV (sports utility vehicle), while Scott Helvenston and Michael Teague's vehicle served as the tail end of the convoy.[62] All the personnel were seated in the front seats of their vehicles; therefore, unlike most Blackwater convoys, November 1 lacked rear-facing gunners with belt-fed machine guns. The team could have taken either of two possible routes to Camp Ridgeway: circumventing Fallujah using a northern road, known as Route Mobile, or driving directly through the city. Although Fallujah was well-known as a hotbed of insurgent activity, the team opted to drive through the city because this route was about three hours shorter and because travelers on Route Mobile still faced the possibility of ambushes and sudden road closures.[63]

The team picked up an escort of two Iraqi Civil Defence Corps (ICDC) trucks when it passed the ICDC checkpoint at the eastern edge of Fallujah.[64] About 2.5 kilometres into the city, travelling on Highway 10, the lead Iraqi transport truck came to an abrupt halt, which, in turn, forced all the vehicles behind it to stop.[65] Within moments, at least five insurgents armed with AK-47s and hiding their faces with keffiyehs rushed out of nearby stores and began firing at the rearmost SUV. Their bullets passed right through the vehicle's unarmoured windows and side panels.[66] Helvenston and Teague did not have enough time to fire back before being incapacitated. While an Iraqi filmed the carnage, Batalona and Zovko attempted to make a U-turn across a median in the road and rush to help their beleaguered colleagues, destroying the vehicle's rear tyres in the process. They too were incapacitated before firing a shot.[67] Meanwhile, the civilian Iraqi truck drivers and the ICDC personnel drove off without a scratch. The insurgents, now joined by a large crowd of civilians, chanted "God is great" and "Fallujah is the graveyard of Americans" as they dragged the bloodstained contractors' still-warm bodies out of their vehicles, dismembered them, set the vehicles on fire, and then strung up the human remains on a bridge spanning the Euphrates River.[68] All four of Blackwater's personnel were killed or otherwise incapacitated within seconds of the first shots being fired.[69]

In a much more successful security operation, Blackwater's personnel saved Ambassador Bremer's life from insurgent gunmen on 6 December 2003.[70] On the return trip from seeing off US Secretary of Defense Donald Rumsfeld at the Baghdad International Airport, Bremer's convoy of lightly armoured HMMWVs (high mobility multipurpose wheeled vehicles) and GMC Suburbans encountered an insurgent ambush.[71] According to firsthand accounts provided by Bremer and the leader of his security team, Frank Gallagher, the attack began when an IED made up of multiple artillery shells exploded next to the convoy's lead vehicle, damaged its tyres and shattered the bulletproof rear window of Bremer's limousine.[72]

Nearby insurgents then launched a barrage of AK-47 fire at the convoy. The door gunners in an attached air team, made up of two escorting MD-530 Little Bird helicopters, responded immediately with suppressive fire, which allowed the ground team to quickly extract the ambassador back to the Green Zone.[73] Although multiple vehicles in the convoy were damaged in the attack, neither Bremer nor any of the security personnel were seriously injured.[74] DynCorp likewise engaged in deadly firefights with insurgent gunmen. For example, an employee named Christian Kilpatrick died instantly when insurgents armed with assault rifles and RPGs attacked his security team on 1 May 2004 in Tikrit.[75]

Less common, though even more dangerous, were sustained assaults mounted by up to several hundred gunmen against a convoy or venue. One such incident occurred on 4 April 2004, when a force of eight Blackwater personnel, along with one US Marine, three US Army military police and three Salvadorian soldiers, defended a CPA compound in Najaf against a multi-hour siege mounted by several hundred insurgent gunmen.[76] Similarly, on 23 January 2007, multiple Blackwater security teams and air crews deployed to rescue a protective security detail (PSD) that came under attack from close to a thousand insurgent gunmen near the Iraqi Public Works Annex in Baghdad.[77]

Insurgent snipers, operating alone or in small teams with scoped rifles, constituted another potent threat to the firm's personnel and clients.[78] Although most insurgent snipers lacked the skill or firepower to pose a serious threat to a moving convoy of armoured vehicles, they could direct harassing fire at stationary personnel, such as those staffing a security perimeter around the venue for a meeting. At these locations, snipers could also kill or seriously injure one of the firm's employees or clients with a single well-aimed shot. A Blackwater employee named Thomas W. "Bama" Jaichner was killed when a sniper's bullet hit him in the throat as his PSD and their client dismounted from their vehicles at a venue in Baghdad on 10 May 2005.[79] Another sniper fired two bullets at a Blackwater team at the Provincial Council Building in Tikrit.[80] The first round missed a team member's head by just 15 cm. Yet another sniper, firing from a building in Baghdad, hit a moving Blackwater Mamba with a 7.62 mm bullet that skidded along the vehicle's armoured roof, ricocheted off the raised turret, and entered the cabin, where it grazed a crew member's cheek.[81] To mitigate this threat, Blackwater deployed long-range marksmen teams (LRMTs) and designated defensive marksmen (DDMs) to spot and neutralize potential snipers.

Landmines and IEDs posed the single greatest threat to the firms' security convoys.[82] These weapons were often well-camouflaged and difficult to spot, especially from inside a moving vehicle. For example, some insurgents covered their IEDs with bits of the rubble and garbage that could be found almost anywhere on Iraq's poorly-maintained roads. Others placed the explosives inside rubbish bins and animal carcasses.[83]

Of even greater importance, they were far more powerful than any of the firearms fielded by the insurgents and could rapidly disable even a well-armoured vehicle by tearing off one of its wheels, breaking its axles, destroying its engine, flipping it onto its side or incapacitating its crew. Consequently, even in instances where security personnel survived the initial shrapnel and concussive blast produced by these weapons, they might find themselves saddled with an immobile vehicle and thus highly vulnerable to follow-on attacks by insurgent gunmen.[84]

A Blackwater PSD was hit by an IED as it approached a highway cloverleaf junction in Karbala on 12 March 2005.[85] The team had recently departed Baghdad International Airport when a device on the side of the highway exploded next to the convoy's rear vehicle. The blast spun the vehicle around with such force that two employees sitting in the front and rear seats on its right hand side, Bruce T. "Bee" Durr and James E. "Tracker" Cantrell, were killed instantly and ejected onto the road.[86] Another crew member in the vehicle suffered serious shrapnel injuries in his upper body and neck but survived and received on-site medical treatment from the team's medics. Another Blackwater employee, Curtis L. "Sparky" Hundley, died near the city of Ramallah on 21 April 2005, when an IED struck his armoured vehicle.[87]

DynCorp's security teams also suffered losses to IEDs. Three members of a DynCorp PSD were killed and two others seriously wounded in Baghdad on 14 November 2005, when an IED struck the rear vehicle in their convoy.[88] The team had just passed through the Assassin's Gate on Haifa Street, en route to the Iraqi Ministry of Justice, when the explosion hit the vehicle on the driver's side and set it on fire. Johannes Potgieter, the vehicle's driver, died instantly. His fellow South African, Ignatius Du Preez, who was seated in the front passenger seat, died on his way to the 86th Combat Support Hospital. Two other team members sustained burns on close to 90 per cent of their bodies and a third lost his right foot in the blast. Miguel Tablai, one of the severely burned personnel, died of his injuries five days later.

The firms' security personnel also encountered VBIEDs.[89] These were civilian cars and trucks loaded with explosives and driven by suicide bombers who sought to detonate their payloads close to a security convoy or venue.[90] Few VBIEDs exploded in close proximity to the firms' personnel but those that did could prove highly destructive. For example, a DynCorp employee named José Mauricio Mena Puerto was killed by a VBIED on 30 November, 2004.[91] A DynCorp convoy made up of SUVs was attacked by a pickup truck filled with explosives on 5 October 2004.[92] The blast tore the truck apart and spread body parts and its cargo of dates all over a Baghdad street, but the contractors survived. Still another DynCorp team was attacked by a van-based VBIED while travelling in a tunnel in Baghdad on 4 January 2006.[93] The blast disabled the lead vehicle in the convoy and, while the team stopped to change the disabled vehicle's tyres, they were attacked with another explosive. However, like the first, this blast failed to inflict any casualties. On the other hand, Blackwater lost three of its security personnel during a VBIED attack on one of its convoys in Mosul on 19 September 2005.[94] The VBIED threat was complicated by the fact that these weapons looked little different from a normal civilian vehicle, meaning that the firms' personnel were regularly in close proximity to dozens, if not hundreds, of *potential* VBIEDs during their security operations.

Finally, as "foreign occupiers" in the eyes of the insurgents, both firms' personnel and clients also faced a constant threat of being kidnapped and executed.[95]

The firms conducted two general types of security operations. The first, known as "static" or "site" security, involved protecting fixed locations, such as the US Embassy in Baghdad and other CPA and Department of State facilities throughout Iraq, from insurgent attacks.[96] Besides maintaining a security perimeter and helping to process visitors to their particular venue, the main role of static security personnel was to shepherd their clients into shelters during insurgent attacks. The firms' incident reports make clear that most of their static security operations were relatively safe, since the personnel assigned to these operations rarely suffered or inflicted casualties.

The firms also conducted "mobile" security operations, which involved protecting armoured convoys of goods and people from insurgent attacks as they travelled between venues through unsecured areas such as the streets of Baghdad and Kirkuk and the highways connecting Iraq's cities and towns, establishing temporary security perimeters at venues, and providing close protection for clients for the duration of their stay at venues.[97] Between 2004 and 2008, the firms were responsible for protecting well over 100 high-risk individuals at any given time.[98] Mobile security operations were much more dangerous than static security operations since insurgents could plant IEDs, prepare ambushes or field VBIEDs at any point along a convoy's route. Most attacks against the firms' personnel and clients occurred during these operations.[99] As discussed later in this chapter, the firms fielded several different kinds of security teams to address the myriad challenges posed by mobile security operations.

Many scholars of PSCs, along with self-interested members of the private security industry, argue that, because these operations involved "defensive" uses of force, they did not constitute combat. For instance, Tony Geraghty argued that "In Iraq, the freelance function was not – as in the Congo, Angola, Sierra Leone, Yemen and elsewhere – to wage war against other professional soldiers or to seize ground. It was essentially defensive, protective and reactive."[100] Sarah Percy similarly argued that PSCs can be differentiated from earlier kinds of private soldiers by "their active avoidance of combat".[101] In addition, Molly Dunigan noted that "modern private security companies are adamant that they provide only defensive services and will not fight offensively".[102] Finally, in testimony before The House Committee on Oversight and Government Reform in October 2007, Prince stated that "Blackwater does not engage in offensive or military missions, but performs only defensive security functions".[103] This assessment of the Department of State's security operations is not, however, supported by the empirical evidence on the tactical behaviour exhibited by the firms' personnel.

Chapters 4 and 5 discuss the firms' tactical behaviour in detail. For now, it is sufficient to point out that their personnel frequently shot at suspected threats that had not attacked them or their clients.[104] In fact, both firms acted as the initiator of violence against suspected threats approximately 70 per cent of the time. For example, after utilizing hand and smoke signals to try to ward off an approaching car in Al Hillah on 2 November 2005, the well gunner and both rear gunners of a Blackwater counter assault vehicle simultaneously fired into the vehicle's engine grille.[105] A similar incident occurred in Al Hillah on 21 April 2007, when the well gunner of a Blackwater vehicle directed first a spot light and pen flare and then two three-round bursts of fire at an approaching SUV.[106] After employing hand signals, the turret gunner of a stationary DynCorp vehicle fired one round into the grille of an approaching van in Baghdad on 24 October 2005.[107] A DynCorp team in Erbil similarly issued non-violent warnings before firing a single round at an approaching Mercedes car on 16 May 2007.[108] All of the civilian victims in these incidents stopped their vehicles shortly after being fired upon. Blackwater's personnel also suffered and inflicted casualties during a number of multi-hour firefights against insurgents armed with assault rifles, machine guns and rocket-propelled grenades.[109]

It is certainly reasonable to argue that the firms' personnel fired their weapons in order to defend themselves or their clients from genuine or suspected threats, but it is also reasonable to argue that they frequently engaged in behaviour that would be likely to cause the death or serious injury of the people they targeted. In other words, by most traditional conceptions of warfare, the behaviour exhibited by the firms' personnel constitutes a form of combat. Scholars who share this view include Marcus Hedahl who, referring to Blackwater's personnel in Iraq, argued that "these contractors appear to be conducting combat operations in addition to the support functions they have performed in the past".[110] Paul Verkui similarly argued that "assignments such as securing convoys or protecting Paul Bremer or even the Secretary of State often involves indirect or even direct combat confrontations".[111] Gallagher likewise characterized what his firm did in Iraq as "Combat PSD protective operations".[112] Finally, Chris Taylor, a one-time vice president of Blackwater, acknowledged that his firm's personnel undertook combat operations in defence of Bremer and subsequent US ambassadors to Iraq. He described the firm's successful efforts to protect Bremer as no ordinary executive protection requirement; it really amounted to a hybrid personal security detail (PSD) solution that had yet to be used elsewhere. In response, Blackwater developed an innovative combat PSD program to ensure Ambassador Bremer's safety and that of any ambassador who followed.[113]

Taking this into account, it is not surprising that Blackwater's personnel inflicted numerous casualties during their security operations.

Force structure

The firms' security forces steadily increased from 2004 to 2007 as the Department of State expanded its presence in Iraq and the overall security of the country deteriorated. Blackwater fielded approximately 100 security personnel in Iraq in June 2004 but quickly increased this to 390 by 2005.[114] At that time, DynCorp and Triple Canopy assigned 157 and 130 personnel, respectively, to Department of State operations.[115] By the beginning of 2007, Blackwater's force in Iraq had increased to 900 armed personnel, and this further increased to a peak of close to 1,000 personnel that lasted from mid-2007 to mid-2008.[116] In contrast, DynCorp fielded 151 in 2007 and 78 in 2008.[117] Relative to the total number of private security personnel in Iraq at that time, which scholars estimate at about 30,000 troops spread across dozens of firms, Blackwater's peak force size was quite substantial.[118] Its force in Iraq gradually shrank, however, following the Department of State's decision, in the aftermath of the Nisour Square incident, to stop using the firm for security operations.[119]

Americans made up approximately three-quarters of Blackwater's security personnel in Iraq; almost all the rest were "third country nationals", meaning citizens from any country other than the United States or Iraq.[120] This ratio set Blackwater apart from most of its competitors in Iraq, since Americans made up only 10 per cent of the total number of private security contractors in that country, with Iraqis accounting for 6 per cent and third country nationals accounting for the remaining 84 per cent.[121] Although Blackwater favoured former US Navy SEALs, it also sought out veteran officers and non-commissioned officers of other American special operations units, such as the US Army's Rangers, Special Forces, Delta Force and Special Operations Aviation Regiment (SOAR) and also the US Marine Corps's Force Recon, and supplemented these with recruits from regular US Army, Marine, Navy, Air Force and civilian law enforcement units.[122]

According to Prince, US Army veterans made up two-thirds of his American security personnel, former US Marines made up another quarter, and the remainder had served in the US Navy, US Air Force, US Federal Bureau of Investigation (FBI), US Secret Service and civilian police SWAT units.[123] Prince also noted that more than half of his American security personnel were combat veterans.[124] The firm also drew military veterans from Chile and other Latin American countries and employed a number of British, Australian and South African personnel.[125] As with its American recruiting efforts, the firm focused on attracting third country nationals with experience in elite or special operations units, such as the British and Australian Special Air Service, the Polish armed forces' JW GROM, and Pinochet-era Chilean commando units.[126] The firm somewhat segregated its employees by country of origin, with the Americans and other Western personnel concentrating on the comparatively dangerous mobile security operations and non-Western personnel focusing on static security operations such as guarding the US Embassy in Baghdad.[127] The firm also paid its American and Western employees considerably more than its non-Western personnel, with the former group earning between US$450 and US$675 on the days they conducted missions and the latter group averaging less than US$100 per mission day.[128] Since mission days in Iraq frequently lasted 12 hours, the former group's hourly wage ranged from US$37.5 to US$54.2 and the latter averaged less than US$8.33.[129] On "standby" days, when they were not expected to conduct missions, American and other Western employees earned approximately US$150.[130] DynCorp offered salaries comparable to Blackwater's and drew personnel with similar backgrounds, though it employed a greater proportion of non-American employees on its mobile security teams.[131] Numerous employees worked for both firms during the Iraq War.

Personnel assigned to undertake mobile security operations could expect to serve on any one of several different kinds of security teams. Employees assigned to protective security details (PSDs), also known as personal security details, were tasked with transporting the firm's clients – referred to as "principals" during these operations – to and from destinations throughout Iraq in convoys made up of multiple armoured vehicles and with protecting the principals at the venues.[132] Since the purpose of most of their missions was to ensure that their principal could attend meetings, often with the media present, the firm's security personnel had to engage in what one employee called "a kabuki dance of the highest order" to keep possible threats away from the principal while still allowing them to have face-to-face interactions with people.[133] Bremer being perhaps the most high-profile target in Iraq from 2003 to 2004, his PSD could feature as many as 36 security personnel, 17 ground vehicles and three helicopters, though most of the time his PSD was far smaller, at just three vehicles and 11 security personnel.[134] Convoys could be made up of as few as two vehicles, with four being the average. The lead vehicle in a typical four vehicle PSD convoy was often a lightly-armoured HMMWV or a more robust armoured personnel carrier.[135] Although the crews of these vehicles were not always well-positioned to engage suspected threats to the convoy, which frequently approached from the rear, they were still expected to support the rest of the convoy with firepower as best they could.[136] Next came the limousine – often a lightly armoured GMC Suburban – carrying the principal.[137] In non-PSD teams, which generally did not contain limousines, a command vehicle frequently took up the second position in a convoy. Close behind was the appropriately named "follow car" that could be a staffed by a standard squad of infantry or a squad of bomb-sniffing dogs and their armed handlers.[138] The personnel assigned to the follow car were expected not only to use their vehicle to block threats to the limousine but to also transfer the principal from the limousine and get him to safety if the limousine became disabled.[139] Finally, another HMMWV, up-armoured civilian pickup truck or SUV, or armoured personnel carrier completed the convoy as rear vehicle.[140] Serving in the rear vehicle was the most dangerous assignment in most security teams since most suspected threats, both insurgents and aggressive civilians, approached convoys from the rear. Rear vehicle personnel were also the most likely members of a typical security team to have reported shooting at suspect threats.

If a moving PSD encountered a suspected threat, it was expected to quickly get its principal to a secure location such as a Department of State compound. To facilitate this task, PSDs often contained a counter assault team (CAT).[141] These squads of infantry travelled in counter assault vehicles (CAVs), or "hate trucks".[142] Although these vehicles were usually the same models of HMMWVs, SUVs and armoured personnel carriers as those used for other roles in a convoy, they were particularly well-armed, with assault rifles, shotguns and multiple machine guns, often positioned on swivel mounts or in turrets.[143] They usually travelled behind the rest of the convoy so that they could easily spot and attack potential threats for a sufficiently long period of time for the rest of the convoy to escape.[144] In taking on this role, the personnel who operated the CAVs not only aggressively pursued and used deadly force against suspected threats but also, on their own initiative, exposed themselves to greater threat of harm in order to reduce the threat posed to their colleagues and clients. A Blackwater CAT in Al Hillah proved its worth during an operation in 2004 when insurgents armed with PKM machine guns ambushed the PSD it was travelling with.[145] In response, the tail gunner in the hate truck, who usually faced backwards, quickly dismounted his light machine gun and began firing forward at the insurgents' vehicles. Within seconds, the gunner neutralized the threat to the convoy by killing one attacker and forcing the others to flee.[146]

At most venues, such as Iraqi government buildings, some members of the PSD served as bodyguards for the clients while others maintained a security perimeter around the venue.[147] If the venue came under threat, the PSD could "hard point" the principal – that is, attempt to protect them at the venue – or return the principal to the convoy and attempt to make a rapid escape back to the Green Zone.[148] When confronted with a potential threat, PSDs could request backup from other kinds of security teams.

However, they carried sufficient firepower to mount a forceful defence on their own.[149]

As its name implies, the personnel who served on tactical support teams (TSTs) were tasked with providing tactical support – that is, armed backup – for other teams whenever a team believed it was under threat of attack.[150] Tim Beckman, a long-time Blackwater TST member, rightly argued that these teams sought to be "faster than anything the US military could put together" at short notice.[151] Some TSTs were assigned to shadow a specific PSD, as when a PSD was transporting a particularly important principal such as the US Ambassador to Iraq, or a visiting member of congress.[152] Other TSTs drove around an area of a city that other teams intended to travel through so that they could respond very quickly to distress calls. When called upon, TSTs could act as an entire convoy of CAVs by attacking and attempting to neutralize a suspected threat in order to allow another team to escape to safety. Operating under the assumption that their colleagues faced genuine deadly threats, TSTs frequently behaved in a highly aggressive manner. In Prince's words, these teams "could bulldoze a path" through traffic to reach a PSD and help it escape.[153] For example, while speeding to rescue a PSD that had been attacked by insurgents, Beckman's TST fired a "stream" of bullets at the driver of a civilian pickup truck that was travelling through a traffic circle ahead of the team's vehicles.[154] When the driver failed to stop, Beckman rammed the truck with his HMMWV, causing the civilian vehicle to break in half right behind the driver's seat.[155]

In a separate incident, the driver of one of the HMMWVs in Beckman's TST decided to use a "pitting" maneuver against a large tractor-trailer on a highway just outside Baghdad.[156] Suspecting that the truck could be a gigantic VBIED, the HMMWV's driver positioned the front axle of his vehicle so that it was parallel to the rear axle of the truck, and then turned into the truck to force it to fishtail and spin out of control.[157] According to Beckman, this "worked like a champ, with the truck jackknifing and sliding off the highway".[158] Moreover, a TST was involved in Blackwater's deadliest incident of the Iraq War, which saw members of the Raven 23 team kill 17 Iraqis and seriously injure 24 others in Baghdad's Nisour Square on 16 September 2007.[159] A member of a DynCorp TST disabled an approaching civilian vehicle with a single shot to the grille on 1 February 2006 in Baghdad.[160] Multiple members of another DynCorp TST also injured an Iraqi judge in Erbil on 16 July 2007 when they fired at his approaching SUV.[161]

The personnel assigned to the firm's quick reaction forces (QRFs) operated in a similar manner to their counterparts in the TSTs in that they too provided armed backup for other teams.[162] However, while TSTs tended to forward deploy into the Red Zone – that is, any part of Baghdad outside the Green Zone – so that they were relatively close to the PSDs they might need to assist, QRFs tended to wait inside a Department of

State compound to deploy into the Red Zone after receiving a distress signal.[163] QRFs and TSTs could assume each other's roles at any time, however. QRFs sought to put their weapons and other gear on and be on the road within five minutes.[164] Beckman recounted an incident where his QRF received a distress call from another team that had lost two armoured Suburbans to an IED.[165] His team was so committed to responding in a timely fashion that they arrived at the blast site in shorts, body-armour and flip-flops. Tommy Vargas, who served as a turret gunner in a QRF that sped toward the site of a Blackwater helicopter crash on 23 January 2007, conveyed the importance of getting to the site of an incident very quickly:

> I just wanted to get boots on the ground either to recover or help my brothers. Knowing the pilots and gunners, what weapons capabilities they had and that they would always make their rounds count; however, all being equal, time was not on their side. Once again, all I could think about is getting there and supporting our brothers on the ground, knowing they will fight until their guns went dry.[166]

As with the other kinds of teams, both firms' QRFs could employ deadly force during their operations. For example, a gunner in a Blackwater QRF shot at the grille of an approaching bus in Baghdad on 15 March 2005.[167] On 18 July of the same year, a gunner in another Blackwater QRF shot and injured the driver of an approaching Kia minivan in Baghdad.[168] A rear gunner from yet another Blackwater QRF, manning a perimeter around a PSD that had been hit by an IED, shot at the driver of an approaching passenger van in Baghdad on 2 January 2006.[169] A member of a DynCorp QRF en route to the Ministry of Transportation headquarters in Baghdad fired two bullets at an approaching civilian SUV.[170] The turret gunner in another DynCorp QRF fired at an approaching civilian car on 8 September 2005 in Baghdad.[171]

Personnel assigned to Blackwater's LRMTs served as observers and snipers in support of other teams.[172] They were equipped with long-range scoped rifles, binoculars and night vision goggles; their primary role was to spot and engage potential threats that were either not visible to the other teams or beyond the effective range of the carbines and machine guns carried by the firm's other security personnel.[173] As Gallagher recalled:

> Many times these men would be placed on buildings across the street from the event or down the block from the event. They had no additional support. They worked alone on unsecured rooftops, endured the heat and the dust, and watched our backs. Truly a daunting task.[174]

Members of an LRMT saved the lives of one of the firm's air crews on 23 January 2007 by killing multiple insurgents who were attempting to shoot down a helicopter.[175] Although snipers were frequently attached to other Blackwater or DynCorp security teams, where they were referred to as designated defensive marksmen (DDMs), Blackwater's LRMTs operated independently.[176] In contrast to the firms' other ground-based teams, which tended to travel in highly conspicuous convoys of armoured vehicles, Blackwater's LRMTs often adopted a more covert approach by travelling in the same models of unarmoured Japanese cars favoured by many Iraqi civilians.

A typical Blackwater DDM operation occurred in Baghdad in 2004. Shortly after arriving at their destination, a dog from one of the firm's K9 units indicated that a nearby car contained explosives; a US Army Explosives Ordinance Disposal team later confirmed that the car was, indeed, loaded with ammonium-nitrate-based explosives.[177] In response, Beckman and another DDM took up positions to scan for potential threats. Within a few minutes, they spotted a small group of men on the far side of the Tigris River, approximately 350 metres away, setting up a banner and video camera. Fearing an imminent VBIED attack, Beckman recalled that "the other sniper and I split the targets in case it comes to a shooting event".[178] Neither DDM fired his weapon during the incident because, after reporting the suspected VBIED threat, they were recalled to the Embassy. However, Beckman stated that he and the other DDM were prepared to shoot the suspicious men. Beckman, who was armed with a semi-automatic rifle, specifically claimed he intended to shoot anyone who attempted to run, while the other DDM, who was armed with a slower-firing, bolt-action rifle, intended to engage the stationary targets.[179]

Advance teams (ATs) tended to be smaller than and not as well-armed as other ground teams. They conducted reconnaissance of the intended routes and destinations of PSDs travelling later in the day and set up concentric rings of security around the venue prior to the arrival of the principal's PSD to force would-be threats to keep their distance.[180] The information they gathered was used by PSDs and other teams to plan their operations, anticipate possible threats and decide whether they should actually conduct a PSD operation or reschedule for another day. Of critical importance, ATs used K9 squads to sweep for explosives at venues and gathered information on road closures to help other teams avoid routes on which they could be easily boxed in and trapped by insurgents.[181] The value of advance reconnaissance was made clear on 31 March 2004, when a small Blackwater convoy was ambushed and trapped by a roadblock in Fallujah and then surrounded and killed by a mixed force of insurgents and civilians.[182]

Although one of their chief purposes was to determine how to avoid confrontations with insurgents, ATs were sometimes attacked during their operations. For example, on 27 January 2004 the Bremer detail's AT was shot at by a group of insurgents armed with AK-47s as it crossed a road junction in Baghdad.[183] The team quickly drove out of the killing zone and did not suffer any casualties, but the attack forced the ambassador's PSD to cancel an upcoming trip. This AT was also attacked as it crossed a Baghdad junction in February 2004 by an insurgent who threw an IED under the vehicles' wheels. By chance, the bomb exploded in between rather than under the vehicles and merely burst some of the middle vehicle's tyres.[184] ATs were sometimes involved in controversial incidents. For example, on 14 December 2007 a Blackwater AT's dog handler kicked and then shot a guard dog outside a building occupied by reporters for the *New York Times* after the dog allegedly attacked the handler's own bomb-sniffing K9.[185]

Finally, the personnel assigned to Blackwater's air teams, which began flying missions in October 2003, operated as airborne ATs, TSTs and QRFs.[186] Indeed, the pilots and door gunners who served on these teams not only performed reconnaissance of the routes and destinations that were to be used by Blackwater's ground teams but also conducted medical evacuation operations and provided close air support for the firm's ground teams, other PSCs and even US military units.[187] As Dan Laguna, one of Blackwater's senior pilots and an air operations commander, put it, the firm's air crews would "typically ... fly immediately to the ambush site, provide enough firepower to help the convoy disengage, then escort them back into the Green Zone".[188] Gallagher similarly recalled that, "If something happened, they would hover over the action and make life miserable for whomever was trying to kill us".[189] Joanne Kimberlin likewise argued in a 2007 article in the *Virginia-Pilot* that

> the Little Birds can symbolize all that's right or wrong with the war. To the enemy, they are an evil to be struck from the sky. To an ally in trouble, their inbound buzz is the blessed sound of a second chance.[190]

For example, two of the firm's air crews flew their Little Bird helicopters to rescue a low-profile Blackwater PSD that had been attacked on Route Irish in April 2004.[191] The ground team's car was destroyed in the attack but the insurgents fled shortly after the helicopters arrived.

The air crews' most celebrated operation took place on 3 October 2007, when, with the help of one of the firm's QRFs, they rescued Edward Pietrzyk, the Polish Ambassador to Iraq, from certain death.[192] Insurgents attacked Pietrzyk's three vehicle convoy with three closely coordinated IEDs in the Red Zone while it traveled from the Ambassador's residence to the Polish Embassy.[193] The convoy then came under attack from insurgent gunmen.[194] Pietrzyk was not a Blackwater client; the firm therefore bore no responsibility for rescuing him. However, the US military informed the US Embassy to Iraq that it could not conduct a rapid airborne rescue because its UH-60 Blackhawk helicopters were too large to land on the narrow street where the IED attack took place. As a result,

Ryan Crocker, the US Ambassador to Iraq, asked Blackwater to conduct the rescue.[195] At 8.3 metres, the rotor diameter of a Blackwater Little Bird helicopter is just over half that of a US Army Blackhawk; consequently, the firm's pilots were able to land very close to the devastated motorcade less than 10 minutes after receiving Crocker's call.[196] Pietrzyk suffered severe burns in the IED attack and would have died if Blackwater had not rescued him.[197] In gratitude for actions that, in Pietrzyk's words, granted him "a second life", he arranged for Dan Laguna, the pilot who led the rescue mission, to receive the first Silver Star awarded by Poland to an American since the end of the Second World War.[198] The other Blackwater personnel who took part in the mission received Polish Bronze Stars.[199] The Polish Permanent Representative to NATO also expressed his government's gratitude for the rescue at the 17 October 2007 meeting of the North Atlantic Council.[200]

Another unplanned air operation occurred on 18 January 2005, when, after hearing gunfire emanating from an area behind the US Embassy in Baghdad, two Blackwater Little Birds crews opted to investigate the suspected threat.[201] They soon spotted a squad of US soldiers that were pinned down by a group of nine insurgents firing from the top floor of a nearby four-storey apartment building. Despite being under no obligation to place their lives at risk for the American servicemen, one of the air crews decided to circle around and approach the apartment building from the rear of the insurgents' position.[202] Flying only about 12 metres above the ground, where they were highly vulnerable to insurgent gunfire, the air crews fired "several magazines" of M4 ammunition at the insurgents' position.[203] Taking advantage of the firm's suppressive fire, the US Army squad rushed into the building and captured the insurgents. Four of the nine detainees tested positive for TNT residue, which indicates that they were manufacturing IEDs.

The firms' ground vehicle crews operated much like the crews of Second World War bombers, since each employee was primarily responsible for a particular task and field of fire but had to coordinate with his colleagues in order to ensure maximum effectiveness. A nominal hierarchy existed within the ground crews, with certain personnel bearing such titles as "team leader", "detail leader", "shift leader", "tactical commander", "vehicle commander" or "operations chief".[204] They usually sat next to the driver of their vehicle; they were expected to handle communications between the vehicles in the convoy and any supporting assets such as other ground and air teams, call out suspected threats, and engage threats emanating from the front-right of their vehicle with their M4 carbines.[205] They received higher pay than their subordinates – the drivers, rear gunners, turret gunners and well gunners – and they could issue orders to their subordinates; they could also write up disciplinary reports that could result in a subordinate being fired or otherwise punished by the firm. However, as discussed in Chapter 3, Blackwater's military culture encouraged every member of its security teams to demonstrate personal initiative by taking it upon themselves to engage suspected threats without being ordered to. It is clear from that firm's incident reports that the personnel serving in its various gunner positions frequently decided on their own to fire at suspected threats and only afterwards informed a more senior employee that they had done so.[206]

Turret gunners were also known as "up" or "top" gunners because they operated weapons in a turret on top of their vehicle. Their exposed position afforded a much better view of the surrounding area than their colleagues had from inside the vehicle, and so they were expected to continuously scan for potential threats emanating from any direction. However, because a vehicle's driver could not accurately shoot and drive at the same time, the turret gunners were expected to devote particular attention to potential threats emanating from the front-left side of the vehicle. These employees could also direct more firepower at suspected threats than most of their colleagues because they were equipped with belt-fed M240 or M249 machine guns that could sustain high rates of fire. Rear, or "hatch", gunners rode inside their vehicle at the left- and right-side rear doors and were usually equipped with M4s. Their role was to spot and engage potential threats emanating from the left-rear and right-rear of the vehicle respectively. If travelling in a limousine, these gunners were positioned on either side of the principal and served as the principal's last line of defence during an insurgent attack. As Gallagher put it, "When all our rings of security have been breached and the protectee is actually under fire or attack, the detail team must become the Praetorian Guards and be prepared to stand and fight and die".[207] Finally, well gunners were positioned in the boot area of their vehicle and, like the turret gunners, equipped with belt-fed M240 or M249 machine guns that were either positioned on tripods or suspended from the vehicle's ceiling. They faced backwards at all times and were responsible for spotting and engaging potential threats emanating from directly behind their vehicle, such as approaching cars.

Equipment

The firms' security teams were equipped with body armour and a range of American, European and Russian small arms. Much like US soldiers in Iraq, most of the firms' personnel utilized M4 carbines, M240 and M249 machine guns, SR-25 sniper rifles, Glock 19 pistols and M203 grenade launchers.[208] Some teams were, however, equipped with German-made G3 assault rifles and MP5 submachine guns and with Russian-made PKM machine guns.[209] One list of the equipment used by the Department of State security contractors in Iraq included Level III close-quarters battle ballistic helmets, Level IV body armour capable of sustaining multiple hits from assault rifle or pistol rounds, 14 30-round magazines of 5.56mm ammunition suitable for M4 carbines, two M67 fragmentation grenades, a smoke grenade, a radio and a cell phone.[210] A DynCorp security contractor deemed his equipment "state of the art" and noted that "each operator is issued roughly ten thousand dollars' worth of gear".[211]

A Department of State report noted that convoy configurations varied "depending on the individual being protected, the threat environment, and the availability of personnel and vehicles".[212] Many of the firms' PSDs, TSTs, ATs or QRFs fielded armoured personnel carriers or, to use the Department of State's description, "military-style fighting vehicles".[213] These included South African-made Mambas, Cougars and Pumas, British-made Saxons and American-made Bearcats.[214] These vehicles, fitted with mounts and ports for machine guns and assault rifles, allowed the firms' security personnel to confront suspected threats with potent firepower. As Robert Young Pelton rightly observed, "a typical Blackwater Mamba security convoy could, within moments, unleash upward of seven thousand bullets against an attacker".[215] These vehicles also offered much greater protection against landmines, IEDs and small-arms fire than the firms' other ground vehicles, but they were slower, more costly to operate, and harder to shoot from because they featured very small gun ports in their windows that greatly constrained most of the gunners' ability to aim their weapons at suspected threats. Gunners consequently often resorted to opening the vehicles' doors to increase their effective field of fire. This simultaneously compromised the vehicles' armour by providing a clear path for bullets, shrapnel, flames and blast waves to enter the cabin. These vehicles were usually painted white, which made the firms' convoys stand out like a herd of "white circus elephants" among civilian Iraqi vehicles.[216] Their ability to protect their occupants from harm was, therefore, partially offset by the fact that their appearance made it easy for insurgents to spot and attack them. Moreover, although these vehicles were armoured, they were hardly invulnerable. Their armour and V-shaped hulls were designed to stop or deflect small-arms fire and the blasts from landmines and small IEDs, but they could not withstand sustained heavy machine gun fire, rocket-propelled grenades, large IEDs or explosively-formed penetrators (EFPs).[217] An EFP is a particularly powerful type of IED that uses an explosive charge to create a molten spike- or cone-shaped copper projectile that can burn through the armour of most vehicles, including main battle tanks.

The firms also utilized lightly armoured HMMWVs and civilian SUVs, such as GMC Suburbans and Yukons, Ford Excursions and Toyota Land Cruisers, in their convoys.[218] Due to their superior comfort, both firms tended to use SUVs as limousines to transport their clients throughout Iraq. Despite being equipped with hundreds of kilograms of aftermarket armour, including "bulletproof" windows, side panels and floor panels, these vehicles were not nearly as well-protected as the firms' armoured personnel carriers. For instance, while the firms' SUVs were equipped to stop a few short bursts of bullets from an assault rifle or light machine gun, insurgents could quickly pound through their armour with sustained small-arms fire or a small explosive device.[219] Moreover, since they lacked the weight of the firms' more heavily armoured vehicles, the SUVs were particularly vulnerable to rolling over if struck by a landmine, IED or VBIED. This vulnerability was tragically illustrated on 19 September 2005, when a VBIED explosion launched a Blackwater SUV across a multi-lane highway.[220] All of the vehicle's occupants, including three of the firm's personnel and one member of the Department of State's DSS, were killed in the attack along with a civilian Iraqi driver whose vehicle was crushed when the SUV landed on top of it. The firms, along with the Department of State, attempted to compensate for these vulnerabilities by placing some of their SUVs in the middle of multi-vehicle convoys so that the more robust HMMWVs and armoured personnel carriers at the front and rear could block and absorb the brunt of insurgent attacks.[221]

Most of Blackwater's air crews flew Boeing MD-530 Little Bird helicopters.[222] Some commentators have erroneously mislabeled these assets AH-6s because the aircraft share the same airframe and therefore look very similar.[223] However, AH-6s feature armoured side panels and mounted weapons, such as 12.7 mm GAU-19 Gatling guns, 7.62 mm M134 Miniguns, LAU-68D/A rocket pods containing 70 mm rockets or AGM-114 Hellfire anti-tank missiles.[224] MD-530s, in contrast, lack side armour, or even side windows, and do not carry integrated armament.[225] Blackwater did, however, operate its MD-530s and unarmoured Bell 412 helicopters with two door gunners armed with 5.56 mm M4 carbines or M249 machine guns, which were powerful enough to neutralize suspected threats traveling on foot or in unarmoured vehicles.[226] On the other hand, virtually every weapon fielded by the Iraqi insurgents, including the ubiquitous AK-47, could easily damage the firm's helicopters and harm their crews.[227] In Gallagher's words, "What a lot of people don't realize is that the Little Birds are not armoured helos. A round as small as a .22 could easily take one down. The margin for error in the Little Birds was extremely small."[228] The firm's door gunners were particularly vulnerable because they operated outside the helicopters in "monkey harnesses" and were, therefore, completely exposed to enemy fire.[229] Blackwater's air crews attempted to make up for the vulnerabilities of their aircraft through a combination of firepower and intentionally erratic flying.[230] They also laid personal body armour on the floor and seats of their helicopters in an effort to add some protection from enemy fire. Despite their efforts, the firm lost multiple helicopters to enemy fire during the Iraq War.

Conclusion

Reflecting on Blackwater's personnel and equipment, a US Congressperson concluded in 2006 that "in terms of military might, the company could single-handedly take down many of the world's governments".[231] This firm's material capabilities undoubtedly contributed to its ability to use violence during its operations in Iraq. However, the mere presence of these instruments of destruction did not mean that they had to be used as tools of foul play. Rather, these capabilities were only as harmful as the organization tasked with using them. With this in mind, Chapter 3 discusses the nature of Blackwater's bellicose military culture and contrasts it against the much more passive culture that guided the behaviour of DynCorp's personnel.

Notes

1. Singer, *Corporate Warriors*, 126; Dunigan, *Victory for Hire*, 93; Avant, *Market for Force*, 103.
2. Fitzsimmons, *Mercenaries in Asymmetric Conflicts*; Fitzsimmons, "When Few Stood against Many".
3. Mandel, *Armies Without States*, 100–105.
4. Uesseler, *Servants of War*, 27 and 85–87; US Government Accountability Office, "Rebuilding Iraq", 7; Dahl, "Soldiers of Fortune", 121; Scahill, *Blackwater*, 1st edn, xix and 25–26; Prince, *Civilian Warriors*, 57, 70, 81, 92–93 and 153–154; Verkuil, *Outsourcing Sovereignty*, 27; Bremer and McConnell, *My Year in Iraq*, 319; Cotton *et al.*, *Hired Guns*, 13–14; Carafano, *Private Sector, Public Wars*, 67; House Committee on Oversight and Government Reform, "Hearing on Blackwater USA", 18.
5. Singer, *Corporate Warriors*, 88–100.
6. Ibid., 248.
7. Ibid., 91.
8. Krahmann, *States, Citizens*, 7; Alabarda and Lisowiec, "Private Military Firms", 59, 60 and 67–70; Isenberg, *Shadow Force*, xii, 2 and 91–92; Kinsey, *Corporate Soldiers*, 25, 88 and 100; De Nevers, "Looking Beyond Iraq", 65–67; Singer, *Corporate Warriors*, 207–208; Dunigan, *Victory for Hire*, 58; Chatterjee, *Iraq, Inc.*, 111; Geraghty, *Soldiers of Fortune*, 30–31 and 250–252; Elsea, Schwartz and Nakamura, "Private Security Contractors", 8; Cole and Hogan, *Under the Gun*; Kramer, "Does History Repeat Itself?", 30; Box Cox, "DynCorp is no Blackwater"; Falconer, "IPOA Smackdown"; Pelton, *Licensed to Kill*, 72–73 and 110–111; Carafano, *Private Sector, Public Wars*, 93; Rosen, *Contract Warriors*, 6, 154 and 164.
9. Avant, *The Market for Force*, 16–21.
10. Kinsey, *Corporate Soldiers*, 8–13.
11. The CIA's Blackwater contingent in Iraq was known as "The Dirty 30". Gallagher and Del Vecchio, *The Bremer Detail*, Loc. 801–802.
12. Singer, *Corporate Warriors*, 20.
13. Ortiz, *Private Armed Forces*, 14–15; Tonkin, *State Control*, 8–9.
14. Ortiz, *Private Armed Forces*, 34; Kinsey, *Corporate Soldiers*, 49–50 and 61–63; Tickler, *The Modern Mercenary*, 17–96; Geraghty, *Soldiers of Fortune*, 46–78; Rogers, *Someone Else's War*, 11–36 and 67–93; Fitzsimmons, *Mercenaries in Asymmetric Conflicts*, 47–166.
15. Tonkin, *State Control*, 14; Howe, *Ambiguous Order*, 187–241; Geraghty, *Soldiers of Fortune*, 55–78 and 153–170; Rogers, *Someone Else's War*, 283–286; Carafano, *Private Sector, Public Wars*, 57–60; Fitzsimmons, *Mercenaries in Asymmetric Conflicts*, 167–230; Fitzsimmons, "When Few Stood against Many".

16 Ortiz, "New Public Management", 36; Terlikowski, "Private Military Companies", 36; Nimkar, "From Bosnia to Baghdad", 6.
17 Kidwell, "Public War, Private Fight?", 16 and 21.
18 Doyle, "Civilian Extraterritorial Jurisdiction Act", 1–2; Terlikowski, "Private Military Companies", 47–48; Kidwell, "Public War, Private Fight", 4; Human Rights First, "Private Security Contractors", 3.
19 Bruneau, *Patriots for Profit*, Loc. 2400; Schwartz, "Department of Defense's Use", 5; Schumacher, *A Bloody Business*, 26; Percy, *Mercenaries*, 62–63.
20 Uesseler, *Servants of War*, 86; Scahill, *Blackwater*, 1st edn, 11; Dahl, "Soldiers of Fortune", 121; Miller, *Blood Money*, 135; Prince, *Civilian Warriors*, 32–33.
21 Uesseler, *Servants of War*, 86–87; Dahl, "Soldiers of Fortune", 121; Scahill, *Blackwater*, 1st edn, 25–26.
22 Uesseler, *Servants of War*, 86–87; Dahl, "Soldiers of Fortune", 121; Scahill, *Blackwater*, 1st edn, 25–26; Prince, *Civilian Warriors*, 57.
23 House Committee on Oversight and Government Reform, "Hearing on Blackwater USA", 2; Prince, *Civilian Warriors*, 57.
24 Prince, *Civilian Warriors*, 57.
25 Ibid., 70.
26 Ibid., 153–154.
27 Verkuil, *Outsourcing Sovereignty*, 27; US Government Accountability Office, "Rebuilding Iraq", 7; Bremer and McConnell, *My Year in Iraq*, 319; Uesseler, *Servants of War*, 27 and 85–86; Cotton et al., *Hired Guns*, 13–14; Scahill, *Blackwater*, 1st edn, xix; Carafano, *Private Sector, Public Wars*, 67; Prince, *Civilian Warriors*, 70.
28 House Committee on Oversight and Government Reform, "Hearing on Blackwater USA", 18.
29 Loeffler, "Fortress America".
30 Geraghty, *Soldiers of Fortune*, 186; Dunning, "Heroes or Mercenaries?", 8; Stanger, *One Nation Under Contract*, 99; Schreier and Caparini, "Privatizing Security", 33; Carafano, *Private Sector, Public Wars*, 67; Bremer and McConnell, *My Year in Iraq*, 146 and 157–158.
31 Prince, *Civilian Warriors*, 81.
32 Boot, "The CIA and Erik Prince", 333–351.
33 Prince, *Civilian Warriors*, 92.
34 Ibid., 92–93.
35 Paulou-Loverdos and Armendariz, *Privatization of Warfare*, 38, 62 and 137; Kinsey, *Corporate Soldiers*, 99; Elsea, Schwartz and Nakamura, "Private Security Contractors", 8; Alabarda and Lisowiec, "Private Military Firms", 61–62; Chatterjee, *Iraq, Inc.*, 110.
36 Paulou-Loverdos and Armendariz, *Privatization of Warfare*, 38.
37 Alabarda and Lisowiec, "Private Military Firms", 59; Krahmann, *States, Citizens*, 7.
38 Alabarda and Lisowiec, "Private Military Firms", 59 and 67–70; Isenberg, *Shadow Force*, 2.
39 Isenberg, *Shadow Force*, 2.
40 Ibid., xii.
41 Kinsey, *Corporate Soldiers*, 25 and 100; Alabarda and Lisowiec, "Private Military Firms", 60; De Nevers, "Looking Beyond Iraq", 65–67; Singer, *Corporate Warriors*, 207–208; Dunigan, *Victory for Hire*, 58; Chatterjee, *Iraq, Inc.*, 111; Geraghty, *Soldiers of Fortune*, 30–31 and 250–252.
42 Elsea, Schwartz and Nakamura, "Private Security Contractors", 8; Isenberg, *Shadow Force*, 91–93; Cole and Hogan, *Under the Gun*.
43 Kramer, "Does History Repeat Itself?", 30; Kinsey, *Corporate Soldiers*, 25 and 88; Box Cox, "DynCorp is no Blackwater"; Falconer, "IPOA Smackdown"; Pelton,

Licensed to Kill, 72–73 and 110–111; Carafano, *Private Sector, Public Wars*, 93; Geraghty, *Soldiers of Fortune*, 250; Rosen, *Contract Warriors*, 6, 154 and 164.
44 Cotton *et al.*, *Hired Guns*, 14; Majority Staff, "Memorandum", 2–5; Scahill, *Blackwater*, 1st edn, 165; Boswell *et al.*, "Secretary of State's Panel", 4; Fainaru, *Big Boy Rules*, 18 and 137; House Committee on Oversight and Government Reform, "Hearing on Blackwater USA", 54 and 131; US Department of State and the Broadcasting Board of Governors Office of the Inspector General, "Review of Security Programs", 29; Carafano, *Private Sector, Public Wars*, 67; US Department of State and the Broadcasting Board of Governors Office of the Inspector General, "Joint Audit", 1; Prince, *Civilian Warriors*, 153–155 and 169; Isenberg, *Shadow Force*, 30; Pelton, *Licensed to Kill*, 110–111.
45 Uesseler, *Servants of War*, 86; Dunning, "Heroes or Mercenaries?", 8; Prince, *Civilian Warriors*, 169; US Department of State and the Broadcasting Board of Governors Office of the Inspector General, "Joint Audit", 7.
46 Majority Staff, "Memorandum", 4; Prince, *Civilian Warriors*, 169.
47 Uesseler, *Servants of War*, 86; Dunning, "Heroes or Mercenaries?", 8; House Committee on Oversight and Government Reform, "Hearing on Blackwater USA", 133 and 141; Elsea and Serafino, "Private Security Contractors", 7.
48 Elsea and Serafino, "Private Security Contractors", 7.
49 House Committee on Oversight and Government Reform, "Hearing on Blackwater USA", 133.
50 Prince, *Civilian Warriors*, 169–170.
51 Risen, "Iraq Contractor".
52 Hoffman, *Insurgency and Counterinsurgency*, Loc. 365–367; Record, *Beating Goliath*, 68.
53 Hoffman, *Insurgency and Counterinsurgency*, Loc. 365–367; Record, *Beating Goliath*, 68.
54 Record, *Beating Goliath*, 68–76.
55 Hoffman, *Insurgency and Counterinsurgency*, Loc. 341–343; Record, *Beating Goliath*, 68.
56 US Department of State and the Broadcasting Board of Governors Office of the Inspector General, "Review of Security Programs", 5 and 35.
57 House Committee on Oversight and Government Reform, "Hearing on Blackwater USA", 54–55.
58 Lonsdale, "Convoy Security", 5.
59 Gallagher and Del Vecchio, *The Bremer Detail*, Loc.341.
60 Fainaru, *Big Boy Rules*, 137; Kachejian, *SUVs Suck in Combat*, Loc. 3184–3254; Gallagher and Del Vecchio, *The Bremer Detail*, Loc. 2110–2122.
61 Prince, *Civilian Warriors*, 106–107; Scahill, *Blackwater*, 2nd edn, 162.
62 Prince, *Civilian Warriors*, 106–108; Simons, *Master of War*, 84–89; Scahill, *Blackwater*, 2nd edn, 162 and 165.
63 Prince, *Civilian Warriors*, 110.
64 Pelton, *Licensed to Kill*, 131–133; Prince, *Civilian Warriors*, 110.
65 Simons, *Master of War*, 89.
66 Pelton, *Licensed to Kill*, 131–133; Simons, *Master of War*, 89–99; Prince, *Civilian Warriors*, 111; Scahill, *Blackwater*, 166.
67 Prince, *Civilian Warriors*, 111.
68 Pelton, *Licensed to Kill*, 131–133; Simons, *Master of War*, 89; Scahill, *Blackwater*, 2nd edn, 166–167.
69 Prince, *Civilian Warriors*, 111.
70 Sipress, "Bremer Survived"; Faul, "Bremer Escaped Injury".
71 Scahill, *Blackwater*, 1st edn, 74–75; Bremer and McConnell, *My Year in Iraq*, 243–245; Prince, *Civilian Warriors*, 1–3.

72 Scahill, *Blackwater*, 1st edn, 74–75; Bremer and McConnell, *My Year in Iraq*, 243–245; Gallagher and Del Vecchio, *The Bremer Detail*, Loc. 1265–1317; Prince, *Civilian Warriors*, 2.
73 Sipress, "Bremer Survived"; Bremer and McConnell, *My Year in Iraq*, 243–245; Prince, *Civilian Warriors*, 3.
74 Prince, *Civilian Warriors*, 3.
75 Associated Press, "News in Brief"; McClintock, "Ranger Christian Kilpatrick"; Fimrite, "Tears Flow".
76 Chatterjee, *Iraq, Inc.*, 129–130; Human Rights First, "Private Security Contractors", 24; Sizemore and Kimberlin, "Blackwater"; Majority Staff, "Memorandum", 8; Miller, *Blood Money*, 165; Rosen, *Contract Warriors*, 38–39; Priest, "Private Guards"; Scahill, *Blackwater*, 1st edn, 118–130; Wiltrout, "If I Had to Die"; Barstow, "Security Firm Says"; *US Fed News*, "True Grit".
77 Laguna, *You Have to Live Hard*, Loc. 318–741; Blackwater, PSD Incident Report, 23 January 2007; US Embassy, Baghdad, "Spot Report – 012307–02".
78 Lonsdale, "Convoy Security", 5.
79 BVA Honor Roll; US Embassy, Baghdad, "Spot Report – 051005–03".
80 US Embassy, Baghdad, "Spot Report – 053106–02"; Blackwater, PSD Incident Report, 31 May 2006.
81 Blackwater, PSD Incident Report, 17 January 2007; US Embassy, Baghdad, "Spot Report – 011707–03".
82 Lonsdale, "Convoy Security", 5; Wilson, "Improvised Explosive Devices"; US Army, "Improvised Explosive Device Found".
83 Gallagher and Del Vecchio, *The Bremer Detail*, Loc. 341 and 818.
84 House Committee on Oversight and Government Reform, "Hearing on Blackwater USA", 54–55.
85 Blackwater, PSD Incident Report, 12 March 2005.
86 BVA Honor Roll.
87 BVA Honor Roll; Burns, "Video"; Scahill, *Blackwater*, 2nd edn, 362.
88 US Embassy, Baghdad, "Spot Repot – DynCorp Contractors Killed"; Semple and Wong, "US–Iraqi Assault"; Anderson, "US Widens Offensive"; DGSD, "Two Dead"; DGSD, "South African Man Dies".
89 House Committee on Oversight and Government Reform, "Hearing on Blackwater USA", 54–55; US Army, "(Explosive Hazard) IED Explosion Rpt"; Gallagher and Del Vecchio, *The Bremer Detail*, Loc. 818.
90 Lonsdale, "Convoy Security", 5.
91 Martinez, "Soldado Hondureno Muere".
92 Vick and Fekeiki, "Car Bombs Kill".
93 US Embassy, Baghdad, "Spot Report – 010406–02"; DGSD, PSD Incident Report, 4 January 2006.
94 Blackwater, PSD Incident Report, 19 September 2005; Oppel and Tavernise, "Attacks in Iraq"; House Committee on Oversight and Government Reform, "Hearing on Blackwater USA", 78–79; US Embassy, Baghdad, "Spot Report – 091905–01"; US Department of State Diplomatic Security Service, "DS Report Number 2005–0092".
95 Lonsdale, "Convoy Security", 5.
96 US Government Accountability Office, "Rebuilding Iraq", 7; Simons, *Master of War*, 84–85 and 113; Schwartz, "Department of Defense's Use", 2; Office of the Special Inspector General for Iraq Reconstruction, "Investigation and Remediation Records", 6; Office of Inspector General, "Audit of USAID/Iraq's Oversight", 14; Commission on Wartime Contracting in Iraq and Afghanistan, "Transforming Wartime Contracting", 52; Schreier and Caparini, "Privatizing Security", 32; Cotton *et al.*, *Hired Guns*, 13.

97 Fainaru, *Big Boy Rules*, 131; Schwartz, "Department of Defense's Use", 2; Cotton *et al.*, *Hired Guns*, 13; Office of the Special Inspector General for Iraq Reconstruction, "Investigation and Remediation Records", 6.
98 Beckman, *Blackwater from the Inside Out*, Loc. 1029–1030.
99 Gallagher and Del Vecchio, *The Bremer Detail*, Loc. 500.
100 Geraghty, *Soldiers of Fortune*, 186.
101 Percy, *Mercenaries*, 231.
102 Dunigan, *Victory for Hire*, 3.
103 House Committee on Oversight and Government Reform, "Hearing on Blackwater USA", 24.
104 Schumacher, *A Bloody Business*, 170, 177–178 and 207; Pelton, *Licensed to Kill*, 145 and 202; Jennings, "Armed Services", 15; Holmqvist, "Private Security Companies", 5.
105 US Embassy, Baghdad, "Spot Report – 110205–03".
106 US Embassy, Baghdad, "Spot Report – 042107–03".
107 DGSD, PSD Incident Report, 24 October 2005; US Embassy, Baghdad, "Spot Report – 102405–03".
108 US Department of State Diplomatic Security Service, "WPPS Incident Casualty Report 17–07".
109 Chatterjee, *Iraq, Inc.*, 129–130; Human Rights First, "Private Security Contractors", 24; Sizemore and Kimberlin, "Blackwater"; Majority Staff, "Memorandum", 8; Laguna, *You Have to Live Hard*, Loc. 318–741; Blackwater, PSD Incident Report, 23 January 2007; US Embassy, Baghdad, "Spot Report – 012307–02"; Miller, *Blood Money*, 165; Rosen, *Contract Warriors*, 38–39; Priest, "Private Guards"; Scahill, *Blackwater*, 1st edn, 118–130; Wiltrout, "If I Had to Die"; Barstow, "Security Firm Says"; *US Fed News*, "True Grit".
110 Hedahl, "Blood and Blackwaters", 20.
111 Verkuil, *Outsourcing Sovereignty*, 28.
112 Gallagher and Del Vecchio, *The Bremer Detail*, Loc. 3052.
113 Scahill, *Blackwater*, 1st edn, 70; Taylor, "Contractors on The Battlefield".
114 Prince, *Civilian Warriors*, 160; US Department of State and the Broadcasting Board of Governors Office of the Inspector General, "Review of Security Programs", 30.
115 US Department of State and the Broadcasting Board of Governors Office of the Inspector General, "Review of Security Programs", 30.
116 Prince, *Civilian Warriors*, 169–170.
117 Middle East Regional Office, "Performance Evaluation", 12.
118 Dunigan, *Victory for Hire*, 1.
119 Scahill, *Blackwater*, 2nd edn, 462; Fainaru, *Big Boy Rules*, 137; House Committee on Oversight and Government Reform, "Hearing on Blackwater USA", 24 and 98; Uesseler, *Servants of War*, 87.
120 Nimkar, "From Bosnia to Baghdad", 5; Schwartz, "Department of Defense's Use", 3; Geraghty, *Soldiers of Fortune*, 187; Isenberg, *Shadow Force*, 37; Brathwaite, *Impact of Private Security*, 4; Uesseler, *Servants of War*, 87; House Committee on Oversight and Government Reform, "Hearing on Blackwater USA", 110.
121 Schwartz, "Department of Defense's Use", 11; Prince, *Civilian Warriors*, 179.
122 Laguna, *You Have to Live Hard*, Loc. 326–342; Pelton, *Licensed to Kill*, 221; Prince, *Civilian Warriors*, 177; Beckman, *Blackwater from the Inside Out*, Loc. 54 and 254; Blackwater, PSD Incident Reports, 16 February 2005, 11 September 2005, 7 February 2006, 18 May 2006, 28 May 2006, 30 May 2006, 17 August 2006, 6 September 2006, 31 January 2007, 12 August 2007; BVA Honor Roll, "Wesley 'Wes' J. K. Batalona"; "Stephen Scotten 'Scott' Helvenston"; "Mike 'Iron Mike' Teague"; "Jerko Gerland 'Jerry' Zovko"; "Richard Allen 'Kato'

Bruce"; "Krzysztof Tadeusz 'Kaska' Kaskos"; "Jarrod Christopher "J.C." Little"; "Christopher E. Neidrich"; "Artur S. 'Zuku' Zukowski"; "James E. 'Jim' 'Tracker' Cantrell"; "Bruce T. 'Bee' Durr"; "Robert Jason Gore"; "Curtis 'Sparky' Hundley"; "Steven Matthew McGovern"; "Jason Edward Obert"; "David Michael 'Pat' Patterson"; "Luke Adam Petrik"; "Eric Smith"; "Thomas Walter 'Bama' Jaichner"; "David R. Shephard"; "Peter J. Tocci"; "Kenneth Webb"; "Casey 'Rooster' Casavant"; "Steve 'G-Man' Gernet"; "Ron 'Cat Daddy' Johnson"; "Arthur 'Art' Laguna"; "Shane 'War Baby' Stanfield"; "William F. 'Sonny' Hinchman"; "Roland 'Jonny Quest' Tressler"; "Nicholas William 'Nick' Leotti".

123 Prince, *Civilian Warriors*, 177.
124 Ibid., 177.
125 Kimberlin and Sizemore, "Blackwater: New Horizons", 32; Stoner, "Outsourcing the Iraq War"; Human Rights First, "Private Security Contractors", 7; Avant *et al.*, "The Mercenary Debate: Three Views", 32–33; Isenberg, *Shadow Force*, 37.
126 Scahill, *Blackwater*, 1st edn, 160–161.
127 House Committee on Oversight and Government Reform, "Hearing on Blackwater USA", 91; Prince, *Civilian Warriors*, 175 and 179.
128 Scahill, *Blackwater*, 1st edn, xx, 70 and 160–161; House Committee on Oversight and Government Reform, "Hearing on Blackwater USA", 89; Prince, *Civilian Warriors*, 78 and 184; Gallagher and Del Vecchio, *The Bremer Detail*, 675.
129 Prince, *Civilian Warriors*, 184.
130 Ibid., 108.
131 DGSD, PSD Incident Report, 6 March 2006; Blackwater, PSD Incident Reports, 6 March 2006, 17 August 2006, 10 January 2007, 12 August 2007; Schumacher, *A Bloody Business*, 169; DGSD, "South African Man Dies"; Martinez, "Soldado Hondureno Muere"; *Hemel Gazette*, "Guard Killed in 'Random Attack'"; BBC, "Iraq Bomb Blast"; *The Herald*, "Scot Killed in Attack"; Pelton, *Licensed to Kill*, 76.
132 Commission on Wartime Contracting in Iraq and Afghanistan, "Transforming Wartime Contracting", 52; House Committee on Oversight and Government Reform, "Hearing on Blackwater USA", 14; Congressional Budget Office, "Contractors' Support", 13; Office of Inspector General, "Audit of USAID/Iraq's Oversight", 14; US Government Accountability Office, "Rebuilding Iraq", 7; Schreier and Caparini, "Privatizing Security", 33; Fainaru, *Big Boy Rules*, 131; Beckman, *Blackwater from the Inside Out*, Loc. 912–913; Simons, *Master of War*, 84; Pelton, *Licensed to Kill*, 7, 74 and 111; Dunigan, *Victory for Hire*, 52; US Embassy, Baghdad, "Spot Report – 041905-1"; US Embassy, Baghdad, "Spot Report – 090907-01"; US Embassy, Baghdad, "Spot Report – 041906-01": Blackwater, PSD Incident Report, 18 July 2007.
133 Gallagher and Del Vecchio, *The Bremer Detail*, Loc. 2674.
134 Geraghty, *Soldiers of Fortune*, 186; Bremer and McConnell, *My Year in Iraq*, 381; Engbrecht, *America's Covert Warriors*, 96; Uesseler, *Servants of War*, 85; Scahill, *Blackwater*, 1st edn, 80; Dunning, "Heroes or Mercenaries?", 8; Prince, *Civilian Warriors*, 78–80; Gallagher and Del Vecchio, *The Bremer Detail*, Loc. 402, 538 and 585.
135 Prince, *Civilian Warriors*, 92; Blackwater, PSD Incident Report, 19 September 2005; US Department of State Diplomatic Security Service, "DS Report Number 2005–0092"; US Embassy, Baghdad, "Spot Report – 041405-4".
136 Gallagher and Del Vecchio, *The Bremer Detail*, Loc. 544.
137 Prince, *Civilian Warriors*, 92; Blackwater, PSD Incident Report, 19 September 2005; US Department of State Diplomatic Security Service, "DS Report Number 2005–0092"; DGSD, PSD Incident Report, 6 July 2007.

52 *Blackwater and DynCorp's Iraq operations*

138 Prince, *Civilian Warriors*, 92; Blackwater, PSD Incident Report, 19 September 2005; US Department of State Diplomatic Security Service, "DS Report Number 2005–0092"; US Embassy, Baghdad, "Spot Report – 040405–2".
139 Gallagher and Del Vecchio, *The Bremer Detail*, Loc. 544.
140 Prince, *Civilian Warriors*, 92; Blackwater, PSD Incident Report, 19 September 2005; US Department of State Diplomatic Security Service, "DS Report Number 2005–0092"; DGSD, PSD Incident Report, 6 March 2006.
141 US Embassy, Baghdad, "Spot Report – 071405–3"; Blackwater, PSD Incident Reports, 18 August 2005, 15 January 2006, 17 July 2007. Most of the firm's convoys provided their own CATs but a team of US Army military police served in this role for the Bremer detail in 2003 and 2004. Gallagher and Del Vecchio, *The Bremer Detail*, 548.
142 Nguyen, "IED and Small Arms Fire"; US Embassy, Baghdad, "Spot Report – 091507–01"; US Embassy, Baghdad, "Spot Report – 071405–3"; Blackwater, PSD Incident Reports, 21 February 2007; 26 October 2005.
143 Lonsdale, "Convoy Security", 10; Beckman, *Blackwater from the Inside Out*, Loc. 872–880; Pelton, *Licensed to Kill*, 220.
144 Schumacher, *A Bloody Business*, 172; Beckman, *Blackwater from the Inside Out*, Loc. 872–880; Pelton, *Licensed to Kill*, 201 and 220–221; Lonsdale, "Convoy Security", 10; Yeager, *High Risk Civilian Contracting*, Loc. 2200–2203; US Embassy, Baghdad, "Spot Report – 051905–01"; Blackwater, PSD Incident Report, 18 August 2005; US Embassy, Baghdad, "Spot Report – 091207–02".
145 Pelton, *Licensed to Kill*, 222.
146 Ibid.
147 Bruneau, *Patriots for Profit*, Loc. 2286; Pelton, *Licensed to Kill*, 74.
148 Prince, *Civilian Warriors*, 208.
149 US Embassy, Baghdad, "Spot Report – 041405–3"; US Embassy, Baghdad, "Spot Report – 060506–01".
150 Beckman, *Blackwater from the Inside Out*, Loc. 887–890; Simons, *Master of War*, 261; US Embassy, Baghdad, "Spot Report – 050905–01"; Pelton, *Licensed to Kill*, 201; Blackwater, PSD Incident Report, 9 September 2007; US Department of State Diplomatic Security Service, "DS Report Number 2007–00096"; US Embassy, Baghdad, "Spot Report – 090907–01"; DGSD, PSD Incident Report, 16 July 2007; Blackwater, PSD Incident Report, 2 May 2006.
151 Beckman, *Blackwater from the Inside Out*, Loc. 889.
152 US Embassy, Baghdad, "Spot Report – 030606–01"; US Embassy, Baghdad, "Spot Report – 082905–01"; Blackwater, PSD Incident Reports, 2 August 2005, 29 August 2005, US Embassy, Baghdad, "Spot Report".
153 Prince, *Civilian Warriors*, 208.
154 Beckman, *Blackwater from the Inside Out*, Loc. 790–792.
155 Ibid., Loc. 794.
156 Ibid., Loc. 357–376.
157 Ibid., Loc. 335–336.
158 Ibid., Loc. 375–376.
159 Fainaru, *Big Boy Rules*, 88; Carafano, *Private Sector, Public Wars*, 107; Simons, *Master of War*, 176 and 262; Dunigan, *Victory for Hire*, 71–72; Scahill, *Blackwater*, 2nd edn, 8.
160 DGSD, PSD Incident Report, 1 February 2006.
161 DGSD, PSD Incident Report, 16 July 2007; US Embassy, Baghdad, "Spot Report – 071607–07"; US Department of State Diplomatic Security Service, "DS Report Number 7/16/2007".
162 House Committee on Oversight and Government Reform, "Private Military Contractors", 13; Pelton, *Licensed to Kill*, 201; Commission on Wartime Contracting in Iraq and Afghanistan, "Transforming Wartime Contracting", 47;

US Embassy, Baghdad, "Spot Report – 031505–1"; Prince, *Civilian Warriors*, 160; US Embassy, Baghdad, "Spot Report – 041405–4"; US Embassy, Baghdad, "Spot Report – 031307–01".
163 Blackwater, PSD Incident Report, 1 February 2006; Yeager, *High Risk Civilian Contracting*, Loc. 2207–2210; US Embassy, Baghdad, "Spot Report – 031505–1"; US Embassy, Baghdad, "Spot Report – 062505–1"; US Embassy, Baghdad, "Spot Report – 080205–1"; US Embassy, Baghdad, "Spot Report – 031307–01"; Gallagher and Del Vecchio, *The Bremer Detail*, Loc. 934.
164 Laguna, *You Have to Live Hard*, Loc. 3541–3543.
165 Beckman, *Blackwater from the Inside Out*, Loc. 760–800.
166 Quoted in Laguna, *You Have to Live Hard*, Loc. 3553–3555.
167 US Embassy, Baghdad, "Spot Report – 031505–1".
168 Blackwater, PSD Incident Report, 18 July 2005.
169 US Embassy, Baghdad, "Spot Report – 010406–01".
170 DGSD, PSD Incident Report, 6 March 2006.
171 US Embassy, Baghdad, "Spot Report – 090805–01".
172 Blackwater, PSD Incident Report, 18 February 2007; US Government Accountability Office, "Rebuilding Iraq", 7; Scahill, *Blackwater*, 1st edn, 165; Blackwater, PSD Incident Reports, 8 February 2007, 23 June 2007.
173 Beckman, *Blackwater from the Inside Out*, Loc. 74–85 and 981–985; Gallagher and Del Vecchio, *The Bremer Detail*, Loc. 468–469.
174 Ibid.
175 Laguna, *You Have to Live Hard*, Loc. 556–564.
176 Beckman, *Blackwater from the Inside Out*, Loc. 74–85; Blackwater, PSD Incident Reports, 13 June 2005, 15 March 2006; Gallagher and Del Vecchio, *The Bremer Detail*, Loc. 452.
177 Beckman, *Blackwater from the Inside Out*, Loc. 73–115.
178 Ibid., Loc. 99–100.
179 Ibid.
180 Blackwater, PSD Incident Report, 9 September 2007; US Department of State Diplomatic Security Service, "DS Report Number 2007–00096"; US Embassy, Baghdad, "Spot Report – 090907–01"; Beckman, *Blackwater from the Inside Out*, Loc. 73–85, 407–411 and 776–780; Simons, *Master of War*, 176, 179 and 183; US Embassy, Baghdad, "Spot Report – 053006–01"; Pelton, *Licensed to Kill*, 181; US Embassy, Baghdad, "Spot Report – 071507–09"; US Embassy, Baghdad, "Spot Report – 090907"; US Embassy, Baghdad, "Spot Report – [Redacted] Fires"; US Embassy, Baghdad, "Spot Report – 081206–01"; US Embassy, Baghdad, "Spot Report – 051205–01"; Blackwater, PSD Incident Report, 25 June 2006; Gallagher and Del Vecchio, *The Bremer Detail*, Loc. 452 and 609.
181 Prince, *Civilian Warriors*, 160; US Embassy, Baghdad, "Spot Report – 121407–01"; Gallagher and Del Vecchio, *The Bremer Detail*, Loc. 472–475.
182 Schmitt, "Test in a Tinderbox"; Chan and Vick, "U.S. Vows".
183 Gallagher and Del Vecchio, *The Bremer Detail*, Loc. 1718.
184 Gallagher and Del Vecchio, *The Bremer Detail*, Loc. 1962–1968.
185 US Embassy, Baghdad, "Spot Report – 121407–01"; Reuters, "New York Times in Iraq".
186 Laguna, *You Have to Live Hard*, Loc. 318–741, 3152, 3160–3161 and 3732; US Embassy, Baghdad, "Spot Report – 012307–02"; Blackwater, PSD Incident Report, 23 January 2007; Burke *et al.*, "Second Amended Complaint", 10–11; Scahill, *Blackwater*, 2nd edn, 12; Partlow and Raghavan, "Iraq Probe"; US Embassy, Baghdad, "Spot Report – 090907–01"; Blackwater, PSD Incident Report, 9 September 2007; US Department of State Diplomatic Security Service, "DS Report Number 2007–00096"; Kimberlin, "Blackwater's 'Little

Birds'"; Simons, *Master of War*, 154–155; Dunigan, *Victory for Hire*, 145; Gallagher and Del Vecchio, *The Bremer Detail*, Loc. 761 and 1786.
187 Laguna, *You Have to Live Hard*, Loc. 467 and 474; Prince, *Civilian Warriors*, 78 and 160.
188 Laguna, *You Have to Live Hard*, Loc. 438–439.
189 Gallagher and Del Vecchio, *The Bremer Detail*, Loc. 1786.
190 Kimberlin, "Blackwater's 'Little Birds'".
191 Gallagher and Del Vecchio, *The Bremer Detail*, Loc. 2383–2392.
192 North Atlantic Council, "North Atlantic Council Readout"; Prince, *Civilian Warriors*, 261.
193 US Department of State, "North Atlantic Council Readout"; Prince, *Civilian Warriors*, 261.
194 US Department of State, "North Atlantic Council Readout"; Kimberlin, "Blackwater's 'Little Birds'".
195 Laguna, *You Have to Live Hard*, Loc. 3150–3159; Price and Kadhim, "Blackwater flies injured Polish diplomat"; Simons, *Master of War*, 202; *State Magazine*, "To the Rescue", 3.
196 Harding, "McDonnell-Douglas H-6"; Gunston, *Encyclopedia of Modern Warplanes*; Simons, *Master of War*, 202; Wilson, "Improvised Explosive Devices"; Grant, "Aerial IEDs"; Price and Kadhim, "Blackwater flies injured Polish diplomat".
197 Simons, *Master of War*, 202; US Department of State, "North Atlantic Council Readout".
198 Laguna, *You Have to Live Hard*, Loc. 3181, 3222 and 3227–3143; US Department of State, "North Atlantic Council Readout"; *State Magazine*, "To the Rescue", 3.
199 Laguna, *You Have to Live Hard*, Loc. 3181, 3222 and 3227–3143; US Department of State, "North Atlantic Council Readout"; *State Magazine*, "To the Rescue", 3.
200 North Atlantic Council, "North Atlantic Council Readout".
201 Laguna, *You Have to Live Hard*, Loc. 3092–3095; Blackwater, PSD Incident Report, 18 January 2005.
202 Laguna, *You Have to Live Hard*, Loc. 3095–3112; Blackwater, PSD Incident Report, 18 January 2005.
203 Laguna, *You Have to Live Hard*, Loc. 3095–3112; Blackwater, PSD Incident Report, 18 January 2005.
204 Blackwater, PSD Incident Report, 9 September 2007; US Department of State Diplomatic Security Service, "High Threat Protective Operations", 17; US Department of State Diplomatic Security Service, "DS Report Number 2007–00096"; US Embassy, Baghdad, "Spot Report – 090907–01"; US Embassy, Baghdad, "Spot Report – COM PSD Fires"; US Embassy, Baghdad, "Spot Report – 042205–1"; US Department of State Diplomatic Security Service, "DS Report Number 2005–0005"; Blackwater, PSD Incident Reports, 16 February 2005, 19 May 2005, 15 March 2006, 18 May 2006; Gallagher and Del Vecchio, *The Bremer Detail*, Loc. 520, 538 and 1685.
205 Gallagher and Del Vecchio, *The Bremer Detail*, Loc. 513–544.
206 Blackwater, PSD Incident Reports, 10 May 2005, 15 March 2006, 21 February 2007, 17 July 2007; US Department of State Diplomatic Security Service, "DS Report Number 2006–003"; Blackwater, PSD Incident Reports, 24 October 2005, 30 May 2006, 5 June 2006, 19 February 2007.
207 Gallagher and Del Vecchio, *The Bremer Detail*, Loc. 513–515.
208 US Department of Justice, "Transcript", 2–3; Schumacher, *A Bloody Business*, 74.
209 Beckman, *Blackwater from the Inside Out*, Loc. 492–496; Thurner, "Drowning in Blackwater", 64.

210 Schumacher, *A Bloody Business*, 74–75.
211 Ibid., 74.
212 US Department of State and the Broadcasting Board of Governors Office of the Inspector General, "Review of Security Programs", 29.
213 Beckman, *Blackwater from the Inside Out*, Loc. 887–890; US Department of State and the Broadcasting Board of Governors Office of the Inspector General, "Review of Security Programs", 2, 29 and 34.
214 Beckman, *Blackwater from the Inside Out*, Loc. 492–496 and 981–985; Simons, *Master of War*, 243; Pelton, *Licensed to Kill*, 9; US Department of State and the Broadcasting Board of Governors Office of the Inspector General, "Review of Security Programs", 34; Thurner, "Drowning in Blackwater", 64; Prince, *Civilian Warriors*, 159; Fainaru, *Big Boy Rules*, 52; DGSD, PSD Incident Report, 15 August 2008; Blackwater, PSD Incident Report, 8 May 2008; US Embassy, Baghdad, "Spot Report – 091207–01"; US Embassy, Baghdad, "Spot Report – 050905–01"; Blackwater, PSD Incident Reports, 20 June 2005, 24 September 2006.
215 Pelton, *Licensed to Kill*, 202.
216 Ibid., 9.
217 Wilson, "Improvised Explosive Devices", 3; Fainaru, *Big Boy Rules*, 52.
218 Beckman, *Blackwater from the Inside Out*, Loc. 343 and 640–642; US Department of State and the Broadcasting Board of Governors Office of the Inspector General, "Review of Security Programs", 33; Thurner, "Drowning in Blackwater", 64; Schumacher, *A Bloody Business*, 74; US Embassy, Baghdad, "Spot Report – 091507–01"; DGSD, PSD Incident Report, 1 February 2006, Blackwater, PSD Incident Reports, 17 July 2007, 15 June 2008, 15 January 2009.
219 Lonsdale, "Convoy Security", 7.
220 Blackwater, PSD Incident Report, 19 September 2005; Oppel and Tavernise, "Attacks in Iraq"; House Committee on Oversight and Government Reform, "Hearing on Blackwater USA", 78–79; US Embassy, Baghdad, "Spot Report – 091905–01"; US Department of State Diplomatic Security Service, "DS Report Number 2005–0092".
221 US Department of State and the Broadcasting Board of Governors Office of the Inspector General, "Review of Security Programs", 2, 29 and 34.
222 Beckman, *Blackwater from the Inside Out*, Loc. 354–355; Simons, *Master of War*, 72; Prince, *Civilian Warriors*, 78.
223 Fainaru, *Big Boy Rules*, 163; Hurst and Abdul-Zahra, "Pieces Emerge"; Gibbons-Neff, "Blackwater Back Under Scrutiny".
224 Fainaru, *Big Boy Rules*, 163.
225 Gallagher and Del Vecchio, *The Bremer Detail*, Loc. 1786.
226 Pelton, *Licensed to Kill*, 145.
227 Simons, *Master of War*, 157.
228 Gallagher and Del Vecchio, *The Bremer Detail*, Loc. 1786.
229 Laguna, *You Have to Live Hard*, Loc. 3695–3698.
230 Laguna, *You Have to Live Hard*, Loc. 381; Kimberlin, "Blackwater's 'Little Birds'"; Batty, "Rock Stars of Baghdad".
231 Scahill, *Blackwater*, 1st edn, 343.

References

Alabarda, Yusuf, and Rafal Lisowiec. "The Private Military Firms – Historical Evolution and Industry Analysis". Monterey, California: Naval Postgraduate School, United States Navy, June 2007.

Anderson, John Ward. "US Widens Offensive in Far Western Iraq". *Washington Post*, 15 November 2005.
Associated Press. "News in Brief from California's North Coast". 21 May 2004.
Avant, Deborah. *The Market for Force: The Consequences of Privatizing Security*. Cambridge: Cambridge University Press, 2005.
Avant, Deborah, Max Boot, Jorg Friedrichs and Cornelius Friesendorf. "The Mercenary Debate: Three Views". *American Interest* May/June 2009, 32–48.
Barstow, David. "Security Firm says its Workers were Lured into Iraqi Ambush". *New York Times*, 9 April 2004.
Batty, Roy. "Rock Stars of Baghdad". *Military.com*, 8 February 2007.
BBC. "Iraq Bomb Blast Killed UK Workers". *BBC News*, 26 February 2007.
Beckman, Tim. *Blackwater from the Inside Out*. Kindle edn. New York: HDTI, 2010.
Blackwater. PSD Incident Reports and Sworn Statements. Baghdad: Blackwater, 2005–2009.
Boot, Max. "The CIA and Erik Prince". In *Civilian Warriors: The Inside Story of Blackwater and the Unsung Heroes of the War on Terror*, edited by Erik Prince. New York: Portfolio, 2013, 333–351.
Boswell, Eric J., George A. Joulwan, J. Stapleton Roy and Patrick F. Kennedy. "Report of the Secretary of State's Panel on Personal Protective Services in Iraq". Washington, DC: US Department of State, October 2007.
Brathwaite, Robert. *The Impact of Private Security on U.S. Foreign Policy*. Washington, DC: The Center for Security Policy, 2007.
Bremer, L. Paul, and Malcolm McConnell. *My Year in Iraq: The Struggle to Build a Future of Hope*. Kindle edn. New York: Simon & Schuster, 2006.
Bruneau, Thomas. *Patriots for Profit: Contractors and the Military in US National Security*. Kindle edn. Stanford, CA: Stanford Security Studies, 2011.
Burke, Susan L., William T. O'Neil, Elizabeth M. Burke, Rosemary B. Healy and Katherine B. Hawkins. "Second Amended Complaint in Abtan v. Blackwater". Washington, DC: The United States District Court for the District of Columbia, 28 March 2008.
Burns, John F. "Video Appears to Show Insurgents Kill a Downed Pilot". *New York Times*, 23 April 2005.
BVA Honor Roll (Blackwater Veterans Association. "Honor Roll – Blackwater Personnel Killed in Action". 6 January 2013. Available at https://bwvets.com/index.php?forums/honor-roll-blackwater-personnel-killed-in-action.63/).
BVA Honor Roll. "Arthur 'Art' Laguna".
BVA Honor Roll. "Artur S. 'Zuku' Zukowski".
BVA Honor Roll. "Bruce T. 'Bee' Durr".
BVA Honor Roll. "Casey 'Rooster' Casavant".
BVA Honor Roll. "Christopher E. Neidrich".
BVA Honor Roll. "Curtis 'Sparky' Hundley".
BVA Honor Roll. "David Michael 'Pat' Patterson".
BVA Honor Roll. "David R. Shephard".
BVA Honor Roll. "Eric Smith".
BVA Honor Roll. "James E. 'Jim' 'Tracker' Cantrell".
BVA Honor Roll. "Jarrod Christopher "J.C." Little".
BVA Honor Roll. "Jason Edward Obert".
BVA Honor Roll. "Jerko Gerland 'Jerry' Zovko".
BVA Honor Roll. "Kenneth Webb".

BVA Honor Roll. "Krzysztof Tadeusz 'Kaska' Kaskos".
BVA Honor Roll. "Luke Adam Petrik".
BVA Honor Roll. "Mike 'Iron Mike' Teague".
BVA Honor Roll. "Nicholas William 'Nick' Leotti".
BVA Honor Roll. "Peter J. Tocci".
BVA Honor Roll. "Richard Allen 'Kato' Bruce".
BVA Honor Roll. "Robert Jason Gore".
BVA Honor Roll. "Roland 'Jonny Quest' Tressler".
BVA Honor Roll. "Ron 'Cat Daddy' Johnson".
BVA Honor Roll. "Shane 'War Baby' Stanfield".
BVA Honor Roll. "Stephen Scotten 'Scott' Helvenston".
BVA Honor Roll. "Steve 'G-Man' Gernet".
BVA Honor Roll. "Steven Matthew McGovern".
BVA Honor Roll. "Thomas Walter 'Bama' Jaichner".
BVA Honor Roll. "Wesley 'Wes' J. K. Batalona".
BVA Honor Roll. "William F. 'Sonny' Hinchman".
Carafano, James Jay. *Private Sector, Public Wars: Contractors in Combat – Afghanistan, Iraq, and Future Conflicts*. Westport, CT: Praeger Security International, 2008.
Chan, Sewell, and Karl Vick. "U.S. Vows to Find Civilians' Killers". *Washington Post*, 2 April 2004, A01.
Chatterjee, Pratap. *Iraq, Inc.: A Profitable Occupation*. New York: Seven Stories Press, 2004.
Cole, Robert, and Jan Hogan. *Under the Gun in Iraq: My Year Training the Iraqi Police*. Amherst, NY: Prometheus Books, 2007.
Commission on Wartime Contracting in Iraq and Afghanistan. "Transforming Wartime Contracting: Controlling Costs, Reducing Risks". Washington, DC: Commission on Wartime Contracting in Iraq and Afghanistan, August 2001.
Congressional Budget Office. "Contractors' Support of US Operations in Iraq". Washington, DC: Congress of the United States, August 2008.
Cotton, Sarah K., Ulrich Petersohn, Molly Dunigan, Q. Burkhart, Megan Zander-Cotugno, Edward O'Connell and Michael Webber. *Hired Guns: Views About Armed Contractors in Operation Iraqi Freedom*. Santa Monica, CA: The Rand Corporation, 2010.
Cox, Box. "DynCorp is no Blackwater, says Chief Executive". *Fort Worth Star-Telegram*, 24 December 2007.
Dahl, Matthew C. "Soldiers of Fortune – Holding Private Security Contractors Accountable: The Alien Tort Claims Act and its Potential Application to *Abtan, et al. v. Blackwater Lodge and Training Center, Inc., et al.*". *Denver Journal of International Law and Policy* 37 (2008): 119–134.
De Nevers, Renée. "Looking Beyond Iraq: Contractors in US Global Activities". In *Contractors and War: The Transformation of United States' Expeditionary Operations*, edited by Christopher Kinsey and Malcolm Hugh Patterson. Stanford, CA: Stanford Security Studies, 2012, 60–82.
DGSD (DynCorp Government Services Division). PSD Incident Reports and Sworn Statements. Falls Church, VA: DynCorp, 2005–2008.
Doyle, Charles. "Civilian Extraterritorial Jurisdiction Act: Federal Contractor Criminal Liability Overseas". Washington, DC: Congressional Research Service, United States Congress, 15 February 2012.

Dunigan, Molly. *Victory for Hire: Private Security Companies' Impact on Military Effectiveness*. Stanford, CA: Stanford Security Studies, 2011.

Dunning, Rebecca. "Heroes or Mercenaries? Blackwater, Private Security Companies, and the US Military". Durham, NC: The Kenan Institute for Ethics, Duke University, 2010.

Elsea, Jennifer K., and Nina M. Serafino. "Private Security Contractors in Iraq: Background, Legal Status, and Other Issues". Washington, DC: Congressional Research Service, 21 June 2007.

Elsea, Jennifer K., Moshe Schwartz and Kennon H. Nakamura. "Private Security Contractors in Iraq: Background, Legal Status, and Other Issues". Washington, DC: Congressional Research Service, 25 August 2008.

Engbrecht, Shawn. *America's Covert Warriors: Inside the World of Private Military Contractors*. Washington, DC: Potomac Books, 2011.

Fainaru, Steve. *Big Boy Rules: America's Mercenaries Fighting in Iraq*. Philadelphia: Da Capo Press, 2008.

Falconer, Bruce. "IPOA Smackdown: DynCorp vs. Blackwater". *Mother Jones*, 12 November 2007.

Faul, Michele. "Bremer Escaped Injury in Ambush on Convoy; Iraqi Woman Killed by Blast at Shiite Party Office". Associated Press, 19 December 2003.

Fimrite, Peter. "Tears Flow in Santa Rosa for Civilian Slain in Iraq". *San Francisco Chronicle*, 5 May 2004.

Fitzsimmons, Scott. *Mercenaries in Asymmetric Conflicts*. New York: Cambridge University Press, 2012.

Fitzsimmons, Scott. "When Few Stood against Many: Explaining Executive Outcomes' Victory in the Sierra Leonean Civil War". *Defence Studies* 13, no. 2 (2013): 245–269.

Gallagher, Frank, and John M. Del Vecchio. *The Bremer Detail: Protecting the Most Threatened Man in the World*. Kindle edn. New York: Open Road Media, 2014.

Geraghty, Tony. *Soldiers of Fortune: A History of the Mercenary in Modern Warfare*. New York: Pegasus Books, 2009.

Gibbons-Neff, Thomas. "Blackwater Back Under Scrutiny". *Washington Post*, 30 June 2014.

Grant, Greg. "Aerial IEDs Target US Copters". *Defense News*, 16 January 2006.

Gunston, Bill. *The Encyclopedia of Modern Warplanes*. London: Aerospace Publishing Ltd., 1995.

Harding, Stephen. "McDonnell-Douglas H-6 Cayuse/Little Bird". In *US Army Aircraft Since 1947*. Atglen, PA: Schiffer Publishing Ltd., 1997.

Hedahl, Marcus. "Blood and Blackwaters: A Call to Arms for the Profession of Arms". *Journal of Military Ethics* 8, no. 1 (2009): 19–33.

Hemel Gazette. "Guard Killed in 'Random Attack' by Iraqi Bomber". *Hemel Gazette*, 28 February 2007.

Hoffman, Bruce. *Insurgency and Counterinsurgency in Iraq*. Kindle edn. Santa Monica, CA: The Rand Corporation, 2004.

Holmqvist, Caroline. "Private Security Companies: The Case for Regulation". Stockholm: Stockholm International Peace Research Institute, January 2005.

House Committee on Oversight and Government Reform. "Hearing on Blackwater USA". Washington, DC: House of Representatives, Congress of the United States, 2 October 2007.

House Committee on Oversight and Government Reform. "Private Military Contractors in Iraq: An Examination of Blackwater's Actions in Fallujah". Washington, DC: House of Representatives, Congress of the United States, September 2007.

Howe, Herbert. *Ambiguous Order: Military Forces in African States*. London: Lynne Rienner, 2001.

Human Rights First. "Private Security Contractors at War: Ending the Culture of Impunity". New York: Human Rights First, 2008.

Hurst, Steven R., and Qassim Abdul-Zahra. "Pieces Emerge in Blackwater Shooting". *USA Today*, 8 October 2007.

Isenberg, David. *Shadow Force: Private Security Contractors in Iraq*. Westport, CT: Praeger Security International, 2009.

Jennings, Kathleen M. "Armed Services: Regulating the Private Military Industry". Oslo: Fafo Foundation, 2006.

Kachejian, Kerry C. *SUVs Suck in Combat: Chaos and Valor – The Rebuilding of Iraq during a Raging Insurgency*. Kindle edn. Jacksonville, FL: Fortis Publishing, 2010.

Kidwell, Deborah C. "Public War, Private Fight? The United States and Private Military Companies". Fort Leavenworth, KS: Combat Studies Institute Press, 2005.

Kimberlin, Joanne. "Blackwater's 'Little Birds' of Baghdad Pack Quite a Sting". *Virginian-Pilot*, 1 March 2007.

Kimberlin, Joanne, and Bill Sizemore. "Blackwater: New Horizons". *Virginian-Pilot*, 28 July 2006.

Kinsey, Christopher. *Corporate Soldiers and International Security: The Rise of Private Military Companies*. London: Routledge, 2006.

Krahmann, Elke. *States, Citizens and the Privatization of Security*. Cambridge: Cambridge University Press, 2010.

Kramer, Daniel. "Does History Repeat Itself? A Comparative Analysis of Private Military Entities". In *Private Military and Security Companies: Chances, Problems, Pitfalls and Prospects*, edited by Thomas Jäger and Gerhard Kümmel. Wiesbaden: Vs Verlag für Sozialwissenschaften, 2007, 23–35.

Laguna, Dan. *You Have to Live Hard to Be Hard: One Man's Life in Special Operations*. Kindle edn. Bloomington, IN: Authorhouse, 2010.

Loeffler, Jane C. "Fortress America". *Foreign Policy*, September/October 2007, 54–57.

Lonsdale, Mark V. "Convoy Security in Semi-permissive War Zones (Iraq and Afghanistan)". Washington, DC: Operational Studies, 2007.

Majority Staff. "Memorandum – Additional Information about Blackwater USA". Washington, DC: Congress of the United States, 1 October 2007.

Mandel, Robert. *Armies Without States: The Privatization of Security*. Boulder, CO: Lynne Rienner Publishers, 2002.

Martinez, Renan. "Soldado Hondureno Muere en Irak Opciones". *La Prensa*, 12 December 2004.

McClintock, Mike. "Ranger Christian Kilpatrick Remembered". *Ranger Register XI-4*, 6–7.

Middle East Regional Office. "Performance Evaluation of the DynCorp Contract for Personal Protective Services in Iraq". US Department of State and the Broadcasting Board of Governors Office of Inspector General, June 2009.

Miller, T. Christian. *Blood Money: Wasted Billions, Lost Lives, and Corporate Greed in Iraq*. New York: Little, Brown and Company, 2006.

Nguyen, Ed. "IED and Small Arms Fire (SAF) Attack on USAID/DynCorp Erbil PSD Motorcade". Erbil, Iraq: US Department of State, 20 June 2005.

Nimkar, Ruta. "From Bosnia to Baghdad: The Case for Regulating Private Military and Security Companies". *Journal of Public and International Affairs* 20 (Spring 2009): 1–24.

North Atlantic Council. "North Atlantic Council Readout – 17 October 2007". North Atlantic Treaty Organization, 17 October 2007.

Office of Inspector General. "Audit of USAID/Iraq's Oversight of Private Security Contractors in Iraq". Baghdad: US Agency for International Development, 4 March 2009.

Office of the Special Inspector General for Iraq Reconstruction. "Investigation and Remediation Records Concerning Incidents of Weapons Discharges by Private Security Contractors can be Improved". Washington, DC: Special Inspector General for Iraq Reconstruction, 28 July 2009.

Oppel, Richard A., and Sabrina Tavernise. "Attacks in Iraq Kill 9 Americans, Including State Dept. Aide". *New York Times*, 21 September 2005.

Ortiz, Carlos. "The New Public Management of Security: The Contracting and Managerial State and the Private Military Industry". *Public Money and Management* 30, no. 1 (January 2010): 35–41.

Ortiz, Carlos. *Private Armed Forces and Global Security: A Guide to the Issues*. Santa Barbara, CA: Praeger, 2010.

Partlow, Joshua, and Sudarsan Raghavan. "Iraq Probe of US Security Firm Grows; Blackwater, Accused of Killing 11 on Sunday, Cited in Earlier Deaths". *Washington Post*, 22 September 2007.

Paulou-Loverdos, Jordi, and Leticia Armendariz. *The Privatization of Warfare, Violence and Private Military and Security Companies: A Factual and Legal Approach to Human Rights Abuses by PMSC Iraq*. Barcelona: NOVA, 2011.

Pelton, Robert Young. *Licensed to Kill: Hired Guns in the War on Terror*. New York: Crown Publishers, 2006.

Percy, Sarah. *Mercenaries: The History of a Norm of International Relations*. New York: Oxford University Press, 2007.

Price, Jay, and Hussein Kadhim. "Blackwater Flies Injured Polish Diplomat to Hospital". *McClatchy Newspapers*, 3 October 2007.

Priest, Dana. "Private Guards Repel Attack on US Headquarters". *Washington Post*, 6 April 2004.

Prince, Erik. *Civilian Warriors: The Inside Story of Blackwater and the Unsung Heroes of the War on Terror*. Kindle edn. New York: Portfolio, 2013.

Record, Jeffrey. *Beating Goliath: Why Insurgencies Win*. Kindle edn. Washington, DC: Potomac Books, 2007.

Reuters. "New York Times in Iraq: 'Blackwater Shot Our Dog'". Reuters, 18 December 2007.

Risen, James. "Iraq Contractor in Shooting Case Makes Comeback". *New York Times*, 10 May 2008.

Rogers, Anthony. *Someone Else's War: Mercenaries from 1960 to the Present*. London: HarperCollins, 1998.

Rosen, Fred. *Contract Warriors: How Mercenaries Changed History and the War on Terrorism*. New York: Alpha, 2005.

Scahill, Jeremy. *Blackwater: The Rise of the World's Most Powerful Mercenary Army*. 1st edn. New York: Nation Books, 2007.

Scahill, Jeremy. *Blackwater: The Rise of the World's Most Powerful Mercenary Army*. 2nd edn. New York: Nation Books, 2008.

Schmitt, Eric. "Test in a Tinderbox". *New York Times*, 28 April 2004, A1.
Schreier, Fred, and Marina Caparini. "Privatizing Security: Law, Practice and Governance of Private Military and Security Companies". Geneva: Geneva Centre for the Democratic Control of Armed Forces, 2005.
Schumacher, Gerald. *A Bloody Business: America's War Zone Contractors and the Occupation of Iraq*. St. Paul, MN: Zenith Press, 2006.
Schwartz, Moshe. "The Department of Defense's Use of Private Security Contractors in Iraq and Afghanistan: Background, Analysis, and Options for Congress". Washington, DC: Congressional Research Service, United States Congress, 22 June 2010.
Schwartz, Moshe. "The Department of Defense's Use of Private Security Contractors in Afghanistan and Iraq: Background, Analysis, and Options for Congress". Washington, DC: Congressional Research Service, 13 May 2011.
Semple, Kirk, and Edward Wong. "US–Iraqi Assault Meets Resistance Near Syrian Border". *New York Times*, 15 November 2005.
Simons, Suzanne. *Master of War: Blackwater USA's Erik Prince and the Business of War*. New York: Harper, 2009.
Singer, Peter W. *Corporate Warriors: The Rise of the Privatized Military Industry*. Kindle edn. Ithaca, NY: Cornell University Press, 2007.
Sipress, Alan. "Bremer Survived Ambush Outside Baghdad; Officials Don't See Attack as Attempt at Assassination". *Washington Post*, 20 December 2003.
Sizemore, Bill, and Joanne Kimberlin. "Blackwater: On the Front Lines". *Virginian-Pilot*, 25 July 2006.
Stanger, Allison. *One Nation Under Contract: The Outsourcing of American Power and the Future of Foreign Policy*. New Haven, CT: Yale University Press, 2009.
State Magazine. "To the Rescue: Embassy's Contract Security Staff Saves Polish Ambassador". *State Magazine*, April 2008, 3.
Stoner, Eric. "Outsourcing the Iraq War: Mercenary Recruiters Turn to Latin America". *NACLA Report on the Americas*, July/August 2008, 9–12.
Taylor, Chris. "Contractors on The Battlefield: Learning from The Experience in Iraq". Washington, DC: George Washington University, 28 January 2005.
Terlikowski, Marcin. "Private Military Companies in the US Stabilization Operation in Iraq". Warsaw: The Polish Institute of International Affairs, 2008.
The Herald. "Scot Killed in Attack Just Hours after Arriving in Iraq, Inquest Told". *The Herald*, 27 February 2007.
Thurner, Jeffrey S. "Drowning in Blackwater: How Weak Accountability over Private Security Contractors Significantly Undermines Counterinsurgency Efforts". *Army Lawyer* (July 2008): 64–90.
Tickler, Peter. *The Modern Mercenary: Dog of War, or Soldier of Honour?* Wellingborough, UK: Patrick Stephens, 1987.
Tonkin, Hannah. *State Control over Private Military and Security Companies in Armed Conflict*. New York: Cambridge University Press, 2011.
Uesseler, Rolf. *Servants of War: Private Military Corporations and the Profit of Conflict*. Translated by Jefferson Chase. Berkeley, CA: Soft Skull Press, 2008.
US Army. "Improvised Explosive Device Found/Cleared by Blackwater Security in the Vicinity of Baghdad (Zone 10)". Baghdad: Wikileaks, 19 December 2004.
US Army. "(Explosive Hazard) IED Explosion Rpt (Vehicle-Borne Ied (Vbied)) 4–25 Abct: 5 Civ KIA 44 Civ WIA". Karbala, Iraq: Wikileaks, 9 December 2006.

US Department of Justice. "Transcript of Blackwater Press Conference". Washington, DC: US Department of Justice, 8 December 2008.

US Department of State. "North Atlantic Council Readout – 17 October 2007". Washington, DC: US Department of State, 17 October 2007.

US Department of State and the Broadcasting Board of Governors Office of the Inspector General. "Review of Security Programs at US Embassy Baghdad". Washington, DC: US Department of State and the Broadcasting Board of Governors Office of Inspector General, July 2005.

US Department of State and the Broadcasting Board of Governors Office of the Inspector General. "Joint Audit of Blackwater Contract and Task Orders for Worldwide Personal Protective Services in Iraq". Washington, DC: US Department of State and the Broadcasting Board of Governors Office of Inspector General, June 2009.

US Department of State Diplomatic Security Service. "DS Report Number 7/16/2007 – Kirkuk". Baghdad: US Department of State, 16 September 2007.

US Department of State Diplomatic Security Service. "DS Report Number 2005–0005". Baghdad: US Department of State, 16 February 2005.

US Department of State Diplomatic Security Service. "DS Report Number 2005–0092". Baghdad: US Department of State, 19 September 2005.

US Department of State Diplomatic Security Service. "High Threat Protective Operations in Baghdad: General Information and Standard Operating Procedures for WPPS Contract Personnel". Baghdad: US Department of State, August 2005.

US Department of State Diplomatic Security Service. "DS Report Number 2006–003". Baghdad: US Department of State, 20 January 2006.

US Department of State Diplomatic Security Service. "DS Report Number 2007–00096". Baghdad: US Department of State, 9 September 2007.

US Department of State Diplomatic Security Service. "WPPS Incident Casualty Report Number 17–07". Baghdad: US Department of State, 16 May 2007.

US Embassy, Baghdad. "Spot Report – 010406–01 – COM PSD Motorcade Attacked by IED". Baghdad: US Department of State, 4 January 2006.

US Embassy, Baghdad. "Spot Report – 010406–02 – International Narcotics and Law Enforcement (INL) Convoy Attacked by IED". Baghdad: US Department of State, 4 January 2006.

US Embassy, Baghdad. "Spot Report – 011707–03 – COM TST Attacked by SAF". Baghdad: US Department of State, 17 January 2007.

US Embassy, Baghdad. "Spot Report – 012307–02 – Complex Attack on COM PSD Resulting in Five KIA". Baghdad: US Department of State, 23 January 2007.

US Embassy, Baghdad. "Spot Report – 030606–01 – COM PSD Team Fires Two Rounds into an Aggressive Vehicle". Baghdad: US Department of State, 6 March 2006.

US Embassy, Baghdad. "Spot Report – 031307–01 – IED Attack on COM PSD Team". Baghdad: US Department of State, 13 March 2007.

US Embassy, Baghdad. "Spot Report – 031505–1 – PSD Engaged Threatening Vehicle". Baghdad: US Department of State, 15 March 2005.

US Embassy, Baghdad. "Spot Report – 040405–2 – Shots Fired by DynCorp Team". Baghdad: US Department of State, 4 April 2005.

US Embassy, Baghdad. "Spot Report – 041405–3 – Shot Fired by Blackwater Team Member". Baghdad: US Department of State, 14 April 2005.

US Embassy, Baghdad. "Spot Report – 041405–4 – Shot Fired by DynCorp Team Member". Baghdad: US Department of State, 14 April 2005.
US Embassy, Baghdad. "Spot Report – 041905–1 – Shots Fired by Blackwater Team Member". Baghdad: US Department of State, 19 April 2005.
US Embassy, Baghdad. "Spot Report – 041906–01 – IED/SAF Attack on Com Convoy". Baghdad: US Department of State, 19 April 2006.
US Embassy, Baghdad. "Spot Report – 042107–03 – COM PSD Escalation of Force". Baghdad: US Department of State, 21 April 2007.
US Embassy, Baghdad. "Spot Report – 042205–1 – Attack on Chief of Mission Motorcade". Baghdad: US Department of State, 22 April 2005.
US Embassy, Baghdad. "Spot Report – 043007–05 – COM Tactical Support Team (TST) Attacked by Small Arms Fire (SAF) and Rocket Propelled Grenades (RPGs)". Baghdad: US Department of State, 30 April 2007.
US Embassy, Baghdad. "Spot Report – 050905–01 – Tactical Support Team Fires on Vehicle". Baghdad: US Department of State, 9 May 2005.
US Embassy, Baghdad. "Spot Report – 051005–03 – Blackwater DOD PSD Team-member Killed". Baghdad: US Department of State, 10 May 2005.
US Embassy, Baghdad. "Spot Report – 051205–01 – DynCorp/COM PSD Advance Team". Baghdad: US Department of State, 12 May 2005.
US Embassy, Baghdad. "Spot Report – 051905–01 – CAV Engages Aggressive Vehicle". Baghdad: US Department of State, 19 May 2005.
US Embassy, Baghdad. "Spot Report – 053006–01 – COM PSD Team Fires Eleven Rounds into Aggressive Vehicle". Baghdad: US Department of State, 30 May 2006.
US Embassy, Baghdad. "Spot Report – 053106–02 – Sniper Attack on COM PSD in Tikrit". Baghdad: US Department of State, 31 May 2006.
US Embassy, Baghdad. "Spot Report – 060506–01 – COM PSD Fires on Aggressive Vehicle". Baghdad: US Department of State, 5 June 2006.
US Embassy, Baghdad. "Spot Report – 062505–1 – COM PSD Team Fires on Aggressive Vehicle". Baghdad: US Department of State, 25 June 2005.
US Embassy, Baghdad. "Spot Report – 071405–3 – Ramadi PSD Team Involved in Motor Vehicle Accident/Use of Force". Baghdad: US Department of State, 15 July 2005.
US Embassy, Baghdad. "Spot Report – 071507–09 – COM PSD Advance Team Fires on an Aggressive Vehicle". Baghdad: US Department of State, 15 July 2007.
US Embassy, Baghdad. "Spot Report – 071607–07 – COM PSD Team Fires on Aggressive Vehicle". Baghdad: US Department of State, 16 July 2007.
US Embassy, Baghdad. "Spot Report – 080205–1 – COM PSD Engaged Vehicle with Small Arms Fire". Baghdad: US Department of State, 2 August 2005.
US Embassy, Baghdad. "Spot Report – 081206–01 – COM PSD Team Fires on an Aggressive Vehicle". Baghdad: US Department of State, 12 August 2006.
US Embassy, Baghdad. "Spot Report – 082905–01 – COM PSD Team Fires on Aggressive Vehicle". Baghdad: US Department of State, 29 August 2005.
US Embassy, Baghdad. "Spot Report – 090805–01 – COM PSD Team Fires on Aggressive Vehicle". Baghdad: US Department of State, 8 September 2005.
US Embassy, Baghdad. "Spot Report – 090907–01 – Complex Attack Against COM PSD Teams". Baghdad: US Department of State, 9 September 2007.
US Embassy, Baghdad. "Spot Report – 091207–01 – Complex Attack against COM Team". Baghdad: US Department of State, 12 September 2007.

US Embassy, Baghdad. "Spot Report – 091207–02 – Complex TST Team Attacked by SAF". Baghdad: US Department of State, 12 September 2007.
US Embassy, Baghdad. "Spot Report – 091507–01 – PSD Team EOF on Aggressive Vehicle". Baghdad: US Department of State, 15 September 2007.
US Embassy, Baghdad. "Spot Report – 091905–01 – COM PSD Team Attacked by VBIED Causing Fatal Injuries to Four US Citizens". Baghdad: US Department of State, 19 September 2005.
US Embassy, Baghdad. "Spot Report – 102405–03 – COM PSD Team Fires on Aggressive Vehicle". Baghdad: US Department of State, 24 October 2005.
US Embassy, Baghdad. "Spot Report – 110205–03 – COM PSD – Fires on Aggressive Vehicle". Baghdad: US Department of State, 2 November 2005.
US Embassy, Baghdad. "Spot Report – 121407–01 – EOF Involving Stray Dog". Baghdad: US Department of State, 14 December 2007.
US Embassy, Baghdad. "Spot Report – [Redacted] Fires on Armed Individual Near Venue". Baghdad: US Department of State, 12 November 2005.
US Embassy, Baghdad. "Spot Report – COM PSD Fires to Disable Aggressive Vehicles". Baghdad: US Department of State, 15 March 2006.
US Embassy, Baghdad. "Spot Report – DynCorp Contractors Killed and Wounded in IED Attack on INL Convoy". Baghdad: US Department of State, 14 November 2005.
US Fed News. "True Grit: Real-Life Account of Combat Readiness". *US Fed News*, 2 September 2004.
US Government Accountability Office. "Rebuilding Iraq: DOD and State Department Have Improved Oversight and Coordination of Private Security Contractors in Iraq, but Further Actions are Needed to Sustain Improvements". Washington, DC: US Government Accountability Office, July 2008.
Verkuil, Paul R. *Outsourcing Sovereignty: Why Privatizing of Government Functions Threatens Democracy and What We can Do About It*. New York: Cambridge University Press, 2007.
Vick, Karl, and Omar Fekeiki. "Car Bombs Kill at Least 22 in Iraq". *Washington Post*, 5 October 2004.
Wilson, Clay. "Improvised Explosive Devices in Iraq: Effects and Countermeasures". Washington, DC: Congressional Research Service, 23 November 2005.
Wiltrout, Kate. "If I Had to Die, It Would Be Defending My Country". *Virginian-Pilot*, 18 September 2004.
Yeager, James. *High Risk Civilian Contracting: Working in a War Torn World*. Kindle edn. New York: Tactical Response, 2011.

2 The ideational theory of tactical violence

This chapter introduces the ideational theory of tactical violence, which is utilized in Chapters 4 and 5 to explain the behaviour of Blackwater and DynCorp's security personnel during the Iraq War. This theory, which shares many assumptions with the leading ideational approach to the study of international politics, constructivism, is intended to explain the use of violence by PSCs operating in mixed combatant–civilian environments. This chapter begins by introducing the theory's major assumptions. It then discusses the theory's central claims, positing that the behavioural norms that make up a PSC's military culture have a strong influence on the degree of violence employed by that company's personnel and that, in turn, the degree of violence employed by these personnel can significantly affect the security enjoyed by themselves, their clients and also the insurgents and non-insurgents that live and work in their operating environment. Following this, it outlines the theory's predictions regarding how certain aspects of a PSC's military culture should influence the use of violence by its personnel and, in turn, influence the degree of security enjoyed by themselves and their clients and also the degree of security enjoyed by insurgents, civilians and other actors in their operating environment. It concludes with a discussion of how these predictions will be tested against the empirical record of private security operations during the Iraq War.

Theoretical foundations of the ideational theory of tactical violence

The ideational theory of tactical violence shares the constructivist assumption that the behaviour of actors is influenced by the structuralist "logic of appropriateness". In contrast to the agent-centric "logic of consequences", where political actors are assumed to make rational decisions based on their expected results, James March and Johan Olsen's conception of the "logic of appropriateness" assumes that the behaviour of states and non-state actors is influenced by shared understandings of whether a particular kind of behaviour is considered to be appropriate, acceptable and legitimate within the society or organization to which they belong.[1] Moreover, the logic of appropriateness also assumes that these shared understandings are conveyed to actors by encouraging them to believe in and adjust their behaviour to conform to particular behavioural norms.[2] Multiple studies of inter- and intra-state conflict have demonstrated that behavioural norms can influence the degree of violence employed by states and non-state actors by encouraging them to believe it is acceptable and legitimate to employ a great deal of violence in particular circumstances and against particular kinds of suspected threats.[3]

Constructivist scholars tend to agree that behavioural norms should be considered an institutional form specifying standards of appropriate and inappropriate behaviour for actors in specific situations.[4] As Martha Finnemore put it, "norms, by definition, concern behaviour. One could say that they are collectively held ideas about behaviour".[5] Theo Farrell similarly argues that "beliefs that inform behaviour are called norms" and that "norms regulate action by defining what is appropriate".[6] Peter Katzenstein likewise argues that behavioural norms "define standards of appropriate behaviour".[7] Taking these definitions of norms into account, and given the empirical focus of this book, the ideational theory of tactical violence considers behavioural norms to be collectively held ideas that set standards of appropriate and inappropriate tactical behaviour for the members of a society or organization such as a state-based military force or PSC.

Building on this understanding of behavioural norms, the ideational theory of tactical violence considers a military culture to be a *collection* of behavioural norms that set standards of appropriate and inappropriate behaviour for the members of an armed force. The concept of military culture, like the broader concept of culture, is deeply contested; it is defined and used in significantly different ways by different scholars.[8] The definition utilized in this book is a hybrid derived from multiple published works on military culture.[9] Following the logic of appropriateness, the theory reasons that an armed force's military culture helps guide the behaviour of its personnel by encouraging them to adhere to these behavioural standards.[10] Moreover, by influencing the behaviour undertaken by the members of an armed force, the behavioural norms that make up an armed force's military culture can help that force affect tangible security outcomes.[11]

Put differently, the norms that make up a PSC's military culture are the components of its identity that guide the tactical behaviour exhibited by its personnel.[12] Other scholars have recently published studies examining other aspects of firms' identities. For instance, after examining information displayed on the websites of several PSCs, Joachim and Schneiker concluded that the public "personas" that different major firms attempt to market to potential clients are highly homogenous, emphasizing broadly similar combinations of their credentials as military actors, business managers and humanitarians.[13] These authors, as well as Chisholm and Higate, have also suggested that hyper-masculinity is a common aspect of the identities of several firms, especially American firms such as Blackwater.[14] Higate also delved into identity formation when he analyzed memoirs published by multiple British private security personnel and concluded that these individuals developed their self-identity as competent professionals in part by reflecting on their perceived superiority over their counterparts in the American military and American PSCs.[15] Taken as a whole, this scholarship has largely focused on aspects of firms' identities that have little or nothing to do with how they do their jobs – that is, protecting people, places and things from possible threats. This book, in contrast, focuses on how differences in the degree of emphasis placed on particular behavioural norms in the military cultures maintained by different firms may have affected the tactical behaviour exhibited by their personnel during their security operations.

Of critical importance, the conceptualization of behavioural norms and military culture utilized in this theory refers to *ideas* that can influence tactical *behaviour*; norms are distinct from tactical behaviour itself.[16] As Terriff explains, "The normative approach to conceptualizing military culture is very useful for it provides a means for understanding how beliefs ... influence the ... activities of an organization and its individual members".[17] Therefore, the ideational theory of tactical violence assumes that the particular behavioural norms introduced later in this chapter *encourage* a PSC's personnel to behave in specific ways, but the theory does not assume that these norms are expressions of their actual behaviour. In Terriff's words, the behavioural norms that make up an armed force's military culture tell the force's members "what they *should* do", but will not necessarily reflect the members' actual behaviour.[18]

The ideational theory of tactical violence is also premised on the assumption that the norms that make up an armed force's military culture are merely one of several plausible influences on the behaviour of its members. Jepperson, Wendt and Katzenstein rightly argue that "norms make new types of action possible, while neither guaranteeing action nor determining its results".[19] A PSC's military culture may, therefore, greatly constrain the range of tactical behaviour that its employees are likely to engage in and, through this, increase the consistency of their tactical behaviour, but a company's military culture cannot and likely will not precisely determine the tactical behaviour exhibited by every employee at all times.[20] Taking this into account, when this theory offers claims about how certain aspects of a PSC's military cultures should influence the use of violence by its personnel, it is merely suggesting that these norms should encourage the personnel to display general behavioural tendencies; it is not suggesting that every employee will behave in precisely the same way throughout their tenure with a firm.[21]

Furthermore, the ideational theory of tactical violence also shares the constructivist assumption that behavioural norms do not necessarily encourage actors to perform useful or effective behaviour.[22] Therefore, when a PSC's military culture encourages its personnel to adhere to particular standards of appropriate behaviour, this may not bring about effective tactical behaviour. As Pierson puts it, "particular arrangements may well be adopted because they are perceived to be appropriate, not because they serve a means–end instrumentality. If so, such arrangements may not work all that well in a particular local context".[23] That is, if an individual adheres to a particular behavioural norm, they will think more about whether a possible course of action conforms to that norm than about what the consequences will be for him- or herself or for other actors in his or her operating environment. Goldstein and Keohane argue similarly that "the uncertainties that confront political actors can lead to reliance on beliefs as guides to action even if those ideas do not lead to benefits".[24] Reflecting this assumption, Terriff likewise argues that "military culture can ... provide a compelling explanation for why specific military organizations may continue to pursue ways of warfare that are incompatible with emerging or prevailing strategic and operational realities".[25] Indeed, as explained further below, the ideational theory of tactical violence predicts that when a PSC's personnel adhere to norms encouraging the use of a great deal of violence, they may sometimes engage in highly ineffective tactical behaviour that, for instance, inflicts unnecessary harm on civilians and other innocent victims.

The core logic of the ideational theory of tactical violence

The central claims of the ideational theory of tactical violence are that the behavioural norms that make up a PSC's military culture have a strong influence on the degree of violence employed by that firm's personnel and that, in turn, the degree of violence employed by these personnel strongly affects two security outcomes. These include, first, the degree of security enjoyed by the people under the firm's protection, such as the firm's personnel and clients, and, second, the degree of security enjoyed by other actors in the firm's operating environment, such as insurgents, civilians, the personnel of other PSCs and the members of state-based security and military forces.

The theory reasons that, if a PSC's military culture is made up of norms that strongly encourage its personnel to employ a great deal of violence against suspected threats, then its personnel should, indeed, tend to do so during their security operations. It further reasons that, if a firm's personnel tend to employ a great deal of violence during their security operations, then they and the clients under their protection are less likely to suffer casualties, and these employees are also more likely to kill or seriously injure other actors in their operating environment than are security personnel who behave in a less violent manner. This is because, when a PSC uses violence in this manner by, for instance, firing off great numbers of bullets at suspected threats, this increases the chance that it will harm not only genuine threats, such as insurgents, but also civilians and other non-threatening actors in a conflict zone. This assumption is well supported in the literature on the use of violence in armed conflicts.[26] Therefore, the theory posits that the very same behavioural norms that can help make a PSC's personnel very good at protecting themselves and their clients can also help make them a menace to the society they operate in. The theory likewise reasons that, if a PSC's military culture is made up of norms that do not strongly encourage its personnel to employ a great deal of violence, then these personnel should tend to employ considerably less violence during their security operations when compared to the personnel of firms that do strongly emphasize these norms. It further reasons that, if the employees of a PSC tend to refrain from using a great deal of violence during their security operations, then they and the clients under their protection are more likely to suffer casualties, and these employees are also less likely to kill or seriously injure other actors in their operating environment than are security personnel who behave in a more violent manner.

The ideational theory of tactical violence assumes that the use of a great deal of violence by a security force is an effective means of harming insurgents and reducing the risk that the force will suffer casualties.[27] Given that many PSCs employed during the Iraq War were chiefly concerned with protecting convoys of armoured and unarmoured vehicles, and given that IEDs and insurgent gunmen posed the deadliest threats to security forces during this conflict, there are good reasons to think that employing a great deal of violence in the face of suspected threats would help reduce the risk of casualties among the convoys' personnel and passengers.[28] For instance, employing a great deal of violence should encourage non-suicidal attackers, such as an insurgent armed with an assault rifle or rocket-propelled grenade, to quickly halt if not abandon their attack against a security convoy. In addition, using a great deal of violence should reduce the chance that a suicidal attacker, such as an insurgent wearing an explosive vest or driving a vehicle-based IED, can get close enough to harm a security convoy's personnel by carrying out his or her attack. Moreover, bearing these first two mechanisms in mind, as insurgents come to recognize a security force's propensity to use a great deal of violence, their willingness to mount attacks against that force should decrease over time due to concerns about suffering harm and concerns that such attacks will not likely succeed.[29] The use of a great deal of violence should, therefore, help deter attacks and motivate insurgents to, instead, launch attacks against targets that are not known to use a great deal of violence against suspected threats, since these targets should be easier to attack successfully.[30] Finally, employing a great deal of violence should discourage would-be "insurgents of the moment", who are not part of an organized insurgent group and who otherwise live their lives as civilians, from approaching a security convoy to try to throw stones, set fires or otherwise inflict harm on its personnel or clients.

The perceived utility of employing a great deal of violence to harm insurgents and reduce friendly casualties has found considerable support from scholars and practitioners of violence.[31] For instance, during the Korean War, American General James Van Fleet informed his subordinates that "We must expend steel and fire, not men. I want so many artillery holes that a man can step from one to the other".[32] Robert Cassidy similarly pointed to more recent American conflicts in Panama in 1989 and the Persian Gulf in 1990–1991 to support the notion that the use of a great deal of violence, which has been dubbed the "sledgehammer approach", can cause significant harm to enemy forces while simultaneously minimizing friendly casualties.[33] Reflecting on his analysis of Israeli uses of violence in Lebanon, Yigal Levy likewise concluded that employing a great deal of violence is an effective means of inflicting losses upon enemy combatants while reducing friendly casualties.[34]

From this it is clear that an armed force can harm insurgents and reduce its risk of suffering casualties by employing a great deal of violence. Nevertheless, as mentioned earlier in this chapter, the ideational theory of tactical violence also assumes that the use of a great deal of violence by an armed force should increase the risk of casualties among civilians and other innocents in a conflict zone. The logic underpinning this assumption is straightforward: employing a great deal of violence by, for instance, firing off great numbers of bullets at suspected threats is inevitably going to increase the probability that some of this violence will be inflected upon innocents who intended no harm to the armed force's personnel.[35] This assumption is well supported in the literature on the use of violence in armed conflicts.[36] For instance, Michael Reisman rightly argues that employing a great deal of violence can provide "more safety ... for your forces" but will also likely cause "regrettable injury to civilians".[37] John Lynn similarly argues that the use of violence "works best when it identifies an enemy and concentrates only on him".[38] In contrast, armed forces that tend to employ considerably less violence than their counterparts in the same conflict zone are less likely to inflict harm upon insurgents or innocents but are more likely to suffer casualties among their personnel and clients.

The relationship between norms, tactical behaviour and security outcomes in the ideational theory of tactical violence

As with a state-based military force, a PSC's military culture is made up of multiple norms that guide the behaviour of its personnel in a range of areas, from ceremonial decorum to dealing with the news media. The ideational theory of tactical violence focuses on the particular behavioural norms in a PSC's military culture that influence how its personnel use violence during their security operations. The theory thus assumes that when a PSC strongly emphasizes norms encouraging personal initiative, it encourages its personnel to take it upon themselves to engage suspected threats rather than wait for an order to do so. Moreover, the theory assumes that, when a PSC strongly emphasizes norms encouraging proactive use of force, it strongly encourages its personnel to employ force against suspected threats before such threats have used force against the security personnel or their clients. Strongly encouraging the proactive use of force tells a firm's personnel that it is acceptable and legitimate to try to harm a person, such as a pedestrian or the driver of a vehicle, on the mere *suspicion* that such a person *could* inflict harm on the firm's personnel or clients in the near future.

Finally, the theory assumes that, when a PSC strongly emphasizes norms encouraging its personnel to exercise an exclusive approach to security, it strongly encourages its personnel to care only about the security of themselves and their clients and, as a result, to discount the security of insurgents, civilians and other actors in their operating environment.[39] Several studies of inter-group violence indicate that attempts to aggravate existing in-group/out-group hostility, which is likely to be present in cases involving a largely Western private security force operating in a Middle Eastern country, can increase the probability that violence will break out between members of the in-group and members of the out-group. [40] As Dutton *et al.* put it, if the members of a particular group, such as a security force, come to believe that they should do whatever they need to do to protect their fellow group members from potential threats posed by actors outside the group, then "Behaviour towards ... [actors outside the group] ... that would previously have been considered inconceivable now becomes acceptable".[41] When this norm is accepted by the personnel of a PSC (the in-group), they should be quite willing to harm members of the out-group in order to reduce the probability that harm will befall members of the in-group.[42]

Norms encouraging the members of an armed force to exercise personal initiative, proactive use of force and an exclusive approach to security are present in the military cultures of many public and private armed forces. However, armed forces differ in the degree of emphasis they place on these norms, which, in turn, should influence the amount of violence exhibited by their personnel. The ideational theory of tactical violence is thus not intended to be merely a "theory of Blackwater and DynCorp" that can apply only to these particular PSCs. Rather, it offers a general explanation for the degree of violence employed by private security personnel in conflict zones.

These behavioural norms serve as the independent variables in the ideational theory of tactical violence; tactical behaviour serves as an intervening variable; and security outcomes serve as the theory's dependent variable. The theory's specific predictions, which are introduced later in this chapter, regarding how emphasis on these norms should influence the tactical behaviour exhibited by the employees of PSCs are structured as follows: if a PSC strongly emphasizes norms of behaviour that encourage the use of a great deal of violence, then the theory predicts that the firm's personnel should tend to exhibit relatively violent tactical behaviour. If, on the other hand, the PSC does not strongly emphasize norms of behaviour that encourage the use of a great deal of violence, then the theory predicts that the firm's personnel should tend to exhibit considerably less violent tactical behaviour. The theory's broad predictions, which are introduced after the specific predictions, follow a similar structure: if the employees of a PSC tend to employ a great deal of violence during their security operations, then they and the clients under their protection will likely suffer a lower casualty rate, and these employees are also more likely to kill or seriously injure other actors in their operating environment than are security personnel who behave in a less violent manner. If, in contrast, the employees of a PSC tend to refrain from employing a great deal of violence during their security operations, then they and the clients under their protection are likely to suffer a higher casualty rate, and these employees are also less likely to kill or seriously injure other actors in their operating environment than are security personnel who behave in a more violent manner.

Predictions of the ideational theory of tactical violence

The ideational theory of tactical violence offers specific, testable predictions about how the behavioural norms contained in a PSC's military culture should influence the tactical behaviour exhibited by its security personnel (Table 2.1).

Engagement time

The theory predicts that the security personnel of PSCs that place strong emphasis on norms encouraging personal initiative, proactive use of force and an exclusive approach to security should tend to employ violence more quickly after observing a suspected threat than the security personnel of firms that do not place strong emphasis on these norms. For instance, although the security personnel of firms that strongly emphasize these norms should often issue non-violent warnings to suspected threats before firing their weapons, they should escalate to using deadly force more quickly than their counterparts in firms that do not strongly emphasize these norms. Security personnel who behave in this manner in effect reduce the amount of time available for a suspected threat to alter its behaviour and attempt to convince the security personnel that it means them no harm by, for example, dropping a weapon, halting its approach or altering its course away from the security personnel and their clients before they engage the suspected threat with deadly force. This, in turn,

Ideational theory of tactical violence 73

Table 2.1 Summary of predictions of the ideational theory of tactical violence

The security personnel of PSCs that place strong emphasis on norms encouraging personal initiative, proactive use of force and an exclusive approach to security should tend to employ violence more quickly after observing a suspected threat than the security personnel of firms that do not place strong emphasis on these norms.

The security personnel of PSCs that place strong emphasis on norms encouraging personal initiative, proactive use of force and an exclusive approach to security should tend to employ violence against suspected threats at greater distances than the security personnel of firms that do not place strong emphasis on these norms.

The security personnel of PSCs that place strong emphasis on norms encouraging personal initiative, proactive use of force and an exclusive approach to security should tend to fire a greater number of bullets at suspected threats than the security personnel of firms that do not place strong emphasis on these norms.

The security personnel of PSCs that place strong emphasis on norms encouraging personal initiative, proactive use of force and an exclusive approach to security should tend to abandon a greater proportion of the victims they produce through their use of violence, rather than offer them assistance, when compared to the security personnel of firms that do not place strong emphasis on these norms.

The security personnel and clients of PSCs that tend to employ a great deal of violence during their security operations should suffer a lower casualty rate than their counterparts in firms that behave in a less violent manner.

The security personnel of PSCs that tend to employ a great deal of violence during their security operations should kill and seriously injure a greater number of suspected threats and innocent bystanders than their counterparts in firms that behave in a less violent manner.

means that security personnel who behave in this manner are more likely to kill or seriously injure a suspected threat during an incident than are security personnel who behave in a less violent manner.

Engagement distance

The theory predicts that the security personnel of PSCs that place strong emphasis on norms encouraging personal initiative, proactive use of force and an exclusive approach to security should tend to employ violence against suspected threats at greater distances than the security personnel of firms that do not place strong emphasis on these norms. Employing the assumption that the suspected threats encountered by various firms travel, on average, at the same speed, security personnel who behave in this manner again reduce the amount of time available for a suspected threat to alter its behaviour and attempt to convince the security personnel that it means them no harm before they engage the suspected threat with deadly force. This, in turn, means that security personnel who behave in this manner are more likely to kill or seriously injure a suspected threat during an incident than are security personnel who behave in a less violent manner.

Number of bullets fired

The theory predicts that the security personnel of PSCs that place strong emphasis on norms encouraging personal initiative, proactive use of force and an exclusive approach to security should tend to fire a greater number of bullets at suspected threats than the security personnel of firms that do not place strong emphasis on these norms. Since each bullet fired could, of course, hit a suspected threat, security personnel who behave in this manner are more likely to kill or seriously injure a suspected threat during an incident than are security personnel who behave in a less violent manner.

Propensity to abandon the victims of violence

The theory predicts that the security personnel of PSCs that place strong emphasis on norms encouraging personal initiative, proactive use of force and an exclusive approach to security should tend to abandon a greater proportion of the victims they produce through their use of violence, rather than offer them assistance, than the security personnel of firms that do not place strong emphasis on these norms. Since the security personnel of these firms have been strongly encouraged to care only about the security of their own colleagues and clients, they should feel no obligation to assist any insurgents, civilians or other actors they harm through their use of violence. Moreover, since abandoning wounded victims could allow their injuries to worsen or even allow them to die, security personnel who behave in this manner are more likely to kill or seriously injure a suspected threat during an incident than security personnel who behave in a less violent manner.

Broad predictions regarding the relationship between military culture, tactical behaviour and security outcomes

These specific predictions outline observable, testable causal relationships between the military cultures maintained by PSCs and the tactical behaviour exhibited by their personnel. The ideational theory of tactical violence also makes two predictions about how the tactical behaviour exhibited by a PSC's personnel should affect two security outcomes, including, first, the degree of security enjoyed by the people under the firm's protection, such as the firm's employees and clients, and, second, the degree of security enjoyed by other actors in their operating environment, such as insurgents and civilians. The theory predicts that, if the employees of a PSC tend to employ a great deal of violence during their security operations, then they and the clients under their protection should suffer a lower casualty rate than their counterparts in firms that behave in a less violent manner. It also predicts that, if the employees of a PSC tend to employ a great deal of violence during their security operations, then they should kill and seriously injure a greater number of suspected threats and innocent bystanders than the security personnel of firms that behave in a less violent manner.

Conclusion: assessing the theory's predictions

Chapters 4 and 5 evaluate the ideational theory of tactical violence's predictions against evidence on the behaviour of Blackwater and DynCorp's security personnel in Iraq in order to establish the level of support that this behaviour provides for the theory. If the evidence on the behaviour of a firm's personnel closely conforms to a stated prediction, then that prediction is deemed "supported". If some evidence on the behaviour of a firm's personnel closely conforms to a stated prediction, but other evidence does not, then that prediction is deemed "partially supported". If little or no evidence on the behaviour of a firm's personnel conforms to a stated prediction, then that prediction is deemed "not supported". If insufficient available evidence exists to evaluate a stated prediction, then this is noted. If a stated prediction does not apply to the behaviour of a firm's personnel, then that prediction is deemed "not applicable". Chapter 7 provides a summary of how well the theory's predictions are supported by the behaviour studied.

Testing the theory's specific predictions against the behaviour of the firms' personnel involves examining evidence of how these personnel *actually behaved* during the Iraq War. For example, to evaluate the prediction that the security personnel of PSCs that place strong emphasis on norms encouraging personal initiative, proactive use of force and an exclusive approach to security should tend to fire a greater number of bullets at suspected threats than the security personnel of firms that do not place strong emphasis on these norms, this book examines empirical evidence on how many bullets the firms' personnel actually fired toward suspected threats during violent incidents. Testing the theory's broad predictions likewise involves examining quantitative and qualitative evidence pertaining to the degree of security enjoyed by the firms' own personnel and clients in Iraq and the degree of security enjoyed by other actors in the firms' operating environment, and then evaluating these security outcomes against the tactical behaviour exhibited by the firms' personnel to determine how, if at all, their use of violence affected these security outcomes.

76 *Ideational theory of tactical violence*

Notes

1 Lecours, *New Institutionalism*, 10; March and Olsen, "Institutional Dynamic", 951–952.
2 Dueck, "Realism, Culture and Grand Strategy", 200–201.
3 Peterson and Graham, "Shared Human Rights Norms", 248–249; Meyer, "Convergence", 529–530; Bhavnani, "Ethnic Norms", 652; Caprioli and Trumbore, "Identifying 'Rogue' States", 379–380.
4 March and Olsen, "Institutional Dynamic"; Klotz, *Norms in International Relations*; Finnemore, *National Interests*, 22; Finnemore and Sikkink, "International Norm Dynamics", 891.
5 Finnemore, *National Interests*, 23.
6 Farrell, "Constructivist Security Studies", 50; Farrell, "Global Norms", 136.
7 Katzenstein, *Cultural Norms*, 18–19. Katzenstein refers to this particular type of norm as "regulatory norms". Some other scholars have adopted this label, while still others prefer the term "behavioural norms". This book adopts the latter phrase. Katzenstein distinguishes this type of norm from constitutive norms, which, in his words, "express actor identities". Katzenstein, *Cultural Norms*, 18–19.
8 King, "Towards a European Military Culture?", 258.
9 Legro, "Military Culture and Inadvertent Escalation", 109; Vardi, "Pounding Their Feet", 296; Dueck, "Realism", 200; Schein, "Organizational Culture", 110; Stulberg, "Managing Military Transformations", 495; Snider, "Uninformed Debate", 13; Rosen, "New Ways of War", 141; Kier, "Culture and Military Doctrine", 69–70; Wilson, "Defining Military Culture", 11–12; Farrell, "Global Norms", 136; Terriff, "Warriors and Innovators", 215–216.
10 Vardi, "Pounding Their Feet", 296; Dueck, "Realism", 200–201; Brooks, "Introduction", 16; Vardi, "Pounding Their Feet", 296; Kier, "Culture and Military Doctrine", 69; March and Olsen, "Institutional Dynamic", 951.
11 Wendt, "Collective Identity Formation"; Wendt, "Anarchy"; Kower and Legro, "Norms, Identity", 463; Dessler, "Constructivism"; Goldstein and Keohane, *Ideas and Foreign Policy*, 4; Keohane, "International Institutions"; Finnemore, *National Interests*, 15; Terriff, "Warriors and Innovators", 218.
12 Terriff, "Warriors and Innovators", 216.
13 Joachim and Schneiker, "All for One".
14 Joachim and Schneiker, "Of 'True Professional'"; Chisholm, "The Silenced and Indispensable".
15 Higate, "'Cowboys and Professionals'".
16 This assumption helps distinguish this work from that of scholars, such as Johnston, Siegl and Meilinger, who have included behaviour in their conceptualizations of culture. Johnston, *Cultural Realism*, 5–7; Meilinger, "American Military Culture", 80; Siegl, "Military Culture", 103. Conflating behaviour and culture undermines one's ability to use culture as an independent variable to explain the behaviour of states and other actors. As a result, many cultural theorists in political science have long argued that culture and other ideational factors should be conceptualized apart from behaviour. Desch, "Culture Clash"; Duffield, "Political Culture" 769; Johnston, *Cultural Realism*, 19; Kupchan, *The Vulnerability of Empire*, 26.
17 Terriff, "Warriors and Innovators", 216.
18 Terriff, "'Innovate or Die'", 479.
19 Jepperson, Wendt, and Katzenstein, "Norms, Identity, and Culture", 56.
20 Duffield, "Political Culture and State Behavior", 772; Dueck, "Realism", 201; Terriff, "'Innovate or Die'", 498–500; Wilson, "Defining Military Culture", 14; Hall and Taylor, "Political Science", 951; Goldstein and Keohane, *Ideas and Foreign Policy*, 13.

21 Hamady, *Temperament and Character*, 23; Pollack, "Influence of Arab Culture", 39; Caprioli and Trumbore, "Human Rights Rogues", 134.
22 Miller and Banaszrak-Holl, "Cognitive and Normative Determinants", 195; Pierson, *Politics in Time*, 110 and 112.
23 Pierson, *Politics in Time*, 112.
24 Goldstein and Keohane, *Ideas and Foreign Policy*, 17.
25 Terriff, "Warriors and Innovators", 215.
26 Levy, "Tradeoff", 387; Hawkins, "Costs of Artillery", 92–93 and 96; Downes, "Introduction", 318.
27 Downes, "Draining the Sea", 425; Kalyvas, "Wanton and Senseless", 251; Kalyvas, "Logic of Terrorism", 105; Koc-Menard, "Switching", 332; Vardi, "Pounding Their Feet", 295.
28 Smith, "Protecting Civilians", 148.
29 Condra and Shapiro, "Who Takes the Blame?", 169; Downes, "Draining the Sea".
30 Lonsdale, "Convoy Security", 8.
31 Gilmore, "Kinder, Gentler Counter-Terrorism", 23–25; Lyall and Wilson, "Rage Against the Machines", 100–101; Chin, "Examining the Application", 6; Smith, "Protecting Civilians", 145–146 and 151; Reisman, "Lessons of Qana", 397; Ricks, *Fiasco*, 266; Cassidy, *Counterinsurgency*, 123; Kramer, "Perils of Counterinsurgency", 22.
32 Quoted in Cassidy, *Counterinsurgency*, 29; Gray, "National Style", 38.
33 Cassidy, *Counterinsurgency*, 29.
34 Levy, "Tradeoff", 386–387; Levy, "Unbearable Price", 72.
35 Eck and Hultman, "One-Sided Violence", 235.
36 Levy, "Tradeoff", 387; Hawkins, "Costs of Artillery", 92–93 and 96; Downes, "Draining the Sea", 420–421; Downes, "Introduction", 318; Chin, "Examining the Application", 4; Dixon, "'Hearts and Minds'?", 375.
37 Reisman, "Lessons of Qana", 397.
38 Lynn, "Patterns of Insurgency", 24.
39 Duffy and Lindstrom, "Conflicting Identities", 76.
40 Kaufman, "Escaping", 202; Bakke, "Beslan", 17; Dutton, Boyanowsky and Bond, "Extreme Mass Homicide", 457.
41 Dutton, Boyanowsky and Bond, "Extreme Mass Homicide", 456.
42 Bakke, "Beslan", 17.

References

Bakke, Kristin M. "Beslan and the Study of Violence". *Political Geography* 28, no. 1 (January 2009): 16–18.
Bhavnani, Ravi. "Ethnic Norms and Interethnic Violence: Accounting for Mass Participating in the Rwandan Genocide". *Journal of Peace Research* 43, no. 6 (November 2006): 651–669.
Brooks, Risa. "Introduction: The Impact of Culture, Society, Institutions, and International Forces on Military Effectiveness". In *Creating Military Power: The Sources of Military Effectiveness*, edited by Risa A. Brooks and Elizabeth A. Stanley. Stanford, CA: Stanford University Press, 2007, 1–26.
Caprioli, Mary, and Peter F. Trumbore. "Human Rights Rogues in Interstate Disputes, 1980–2001". *Journal of Peace Research* 43, no. 2 (2006): 131–148.
Caprioli, Mary, and Peter F. Trumbore. "Identifying 'Rogue' States and Testing their Interstate Conflict Behavior". *European Journal of International Relations* 9, no. 3 (2003): 377–406.

Cassidy, Robert M. *Counterinsurgency and the Global War on Terror: Military Culture and Irregular War.* Westport, CT: Praeger Security International, 2006.

Chin, Warren. "Examining the Application of British Counterinsurgency Doctrine by the American Army in Iraq". *Small Wars and Insurgencies* 18, no. 1 (March 2007): 1–26.

Chisholm, Amanda. "The Silenced and Indispensable". *International Feminist Journal of Politics* 16, no. 1 (2014): 26–47.

Condra, Luke N., and Jacob N. Shapiro. "Who Takes the Blame? The Strategic Effects of Collateral Damage". *American Journal of Political Science* 56, no. 1 (January 2012): 167–187.

Desch, Michael. "Culture Clash: Assessing the Importance of Ideas in Security Studies". *International Security* 23, no. 1 (Summer 1998): 141–170.

Dessler, David. "Constructivism within a Positivist Social Science". *Review of International Studies* 25, no. 1 (January 1999): 123–137.

Dixon, Paul. "'Hearts and Minds'? British Counter-Insurgency from Malaya to Iraq". *The Journal of Strategic Studies* 32, no. 3 (June 2009): 353–381.

Downes, Alexander B. "Draining the Sea by Filling the Graves: Investigating the Effectiveness of Indiscriminate Violence as a Counterinsurgency Strategy". *Civil Wars* 9, no. 4 (December 2007): 420–444.

Downes, Alexander B. "Introduction: Modern Insurgency and Counterinsurgency in Comparative Perspective". *Civil Wars* 9, no. 4 (December 2007): 313–323.

Dueck, Colin. "Realism, Culture and Grand Strategy: Explaining America's Peculiar Path to World Power". *Security Studies* 14, no. 2 (April–June 2005): 195–231.

Duffield, John S. "Political Culture and State Behavior: Why Germany Confounds Neorealism". *International Organization* 53, no. 4 (Autumn 1999): 765–803.

Duffy, Gavin, and Nicole Lindstrom. "Conflicting Identities: Solidarity Incentives in the Serbo-Croatian War". *Journal of Peace Research* 39, no. 1 (2002): 69–90.

Dutton, Donald G., Ehor O. Boyanowsky and Michael Harris Bond. "Extreme Mass Homicide: From Military Massacre to Genocide". *Aggression and Violent Behavior* 10 (2005): 437–473.

Eck, Kristine, and Lisa Hultman. "One-Sided Violence Against Civilians in War: Insights from New Fatality Data". *Journal of Peace Research* 44, no. 2 (2007): 233–246.

Farrell, Theo. "Constructivist Security Studies: Portrait of a Research Program". *International Studies Review* 4, no. 1 (Spring 2002): 49–72.

Farrell, Theo. "Global Norms and Military Effectiveness: The Army in Early Twentieth-century Ireland". In *Creating Military Power: The Sources of Military Effectiveness*, edited by Risa A. Brooks and Elizabeth A. Stanley. Stanford, CA: Stanford University Press, 2007, 136–157.

Finnemore, Martha. *National Interests in International Society.* Ithaca, NY: Cornell University Press, 1996.

Finnemore, Martha, and Katheryn Sikkink. "International Norm Dynamics and Political Change". *International Organization* 52, no. 4 (August 1998): 887–917.

Gilmore, Jonathan. "A Kinder, Gentler Counter-terrorism: Counterinsurgency, Human Security and the War on Terror". *Security Dialogue* 42, no. 1 (February 2011): 21–37.

Goldstein, Judith, and Robert Keohane. *Ideas and Foreign Policy: Beliefs, Institutions, and Political Change.* Ithaca, NY: Cornell University Press, 1993.

Gray, Colin S. "National Style in Strategy: The American Example". *International Security* 6, no. 2 (Fall 1981): 21–47.

Hall, Peter A., and Rosemary C. R. Taylor. "Political Science and the Three New Institutionalisms". *Political Studies* 44, no. 5 (December 1996): 936–957.

Hamady, Sania. *The Temperament and Character of the Arabs.* New York: Twayne, 1960.

Hawkins, John M. "The Costs of Artillery: Eliminating Harassment and Interdiction Fire During the Vietnam War". *The Journal of Military History* 70, no. 1 (January 2006): 91–122.

Higate, Paul. "'Cowboys and Professionals': The Politics of Identity Work in the Private and Military Security Company". *Millennium: Journal of International Studies* 40, no. 2 (2012): 321–341.

Jepperson, Ronald L., Alexander Wendt, and Peter J. Katzenstein. "Norms, Identity, and Culture in National Security". In *The Culture of National Security: Norms and Identity in World Politics*, edited by Peter J. Katzenstein. New York: Columbia University Press, 1996, 33–75.

Joachim, Jutta, and Andrea Schneiker. "All for One and One in All: Private Military Security Companies as Soldiers, Business Managers and Humanitarians". *Cambridge Review of International Affairs* 27, no. 2 (2014): 246–267.

Joachim, Jutta, and Andrea Schneiker. "Of 'True Professional' and 'Ethical Hero Warriors': A Gender-discourse Analysis of Private Military and Security Companies". *Security Dialogue* 43, no. 6 (2012): 495–512.

Johnston, Alastair. *Cultural Realism: Strategic Culture and Grand Strategy in Chinese History.* Princeton, NJ: Princeton University Press, 1995.

Kalyvas, Stathis N. "Wanton and Senseless? The Logic of Massacres in Algeria". *Rationality and Society* 11, no. 3 (1999): 243–285.

Kalyvas, Stathis N. "The Logic of Terrorism in Civil War". *Journal of Ethics* 8, no. 1 (2004): 98–137.

Katzenstein, Peter J. *Cultural Norms and National Security: Police and Military Power in Postwar Japan.* Ithaca, NY: Cornell University Press, 1996.

Kaufman, Stuart J. "Escaping the Symbolic Politics Trap: Reconciliation Initiatives and Conflict Resolution in Ethnic Wars". *Journal of Peace Research* 43, no. 2 (2006): 201–218.

Keohane, Robert O. "International Institutions: Two Approaches". *International Studies Quarterly* 32, no. 4 (December 1988): 379–396.

Kier, Elizabeth. "Culture and Military Doctrine: France between the Wars". *International Security* 19, no. 4 (Spring 1995): 65–93.

King, Anthony. "Towards a European Military Culture?" *Defence Studies* 6, no. 3 (September 2006): 257–277.

Klotz, Audie. *Norms in International Relations.* Ithaca, NY: Cornell University Press, 1995.

Koc-Menard, Sergio. "Switching from Indiscriminate to Selective Violence: The Case of the Peruvian Military 1980–95". *Civil Wars* 8, no. 3–4 (September–December 2006): 332–354.

Kower, Paul, and Legro, Jeffrey. "Norms, Identity, and their Limits: A Theoretical Reprise". In *The Culture of National Security: Norms and Identity in World Politics*, edited by Peter J. Katzenstein. New York: Columbia University Press, 1996, 451–497.

Kramer, Mark. "The Perils of Counterinsurgency: Russia's War in Chechnya". *International Security* 29, no. 3 (Winter 2004–2005): 5–63.

Kupchan, Charles. *The Vulnerability of Empire.* Ithaca, NY: Cornell University Press, 1994.

Lecours, Andre. *New Institutionalism: Theory and Analysis*. Toronto: University of Toronto Press, 2005.

Legro, Jeffrey. "Military Culture and Inadvertent Escalation in World War II". *International Security* 18, no. 4 (Spring 1994): 108–142.

Levy, Yagil. "An Unbearable Price: War Casualties and Warring Democracies". *International Journal of Politics, Culture, and Society* 22, no. 1 (2009): 69–82.

Levy, Yagil. "The Tradeoff between Force and Casualties: Israel's Wars in Gaza, 1987–2009". *Conflict Management and Peace Science* 27, no. 4 (2010): 386–405.

Lonsdale, Mark V. "Convoy Security in Semi-permissive War Zones (Iraq and Afghanistan)". Washington, DC: Operational Studies, 2007.

Lyall, Jason, and Isaiah Wilson. "Rage Against the Machines: Explaining Outcomes in Counterinsurgency Wars". *International Organization* 63, no. 1 (Winter 2009): 67–106.

Lynn, John A. "Patterns of Insurgency and Counterinsurgency". *Military Review* 87, no. 4 (July–August 2005): 22–27.

March, James, and Johan P. Olsen. "The Institutional Dynamic of International Political Orders". *International Organization* 52, no. 4 (Autumn 1998): 943–969.

Meilinger, Phillip S. "American Military Culture and Strategy". *Joint Forces Quarterly* 46 (2007): 80–86.

Meyer, Christopher O. "Convergence Toward a European Strategic Culture? A Constructivist Framework for Explaining Changing Norms". *European Journal of International Relations* 11, no. 4 (2005): 523–549.

Miller, Edward Alan, and Jane Banaszrak-Holl. "Cognitive and Normative Determinants of State Policymaking Behaviour: Lessons from the Sociological Institutionalism". *Publius: The Journal of Federalism* 35, no. 2 (Spring 2005): 191–216.

Peterson, Timothy M., and Leah Graham. "Shared Human Rights Norms and Military Conflict". *Journal of Conflict Resolution* 55, no. 2 (2011): 248–273.

Pierson, Paul. *Politics in Time: History, Institutions and Social Analysis*. Princeton, NJ: Princeton University Press, 2004.

Pollack, Kenneth M. "The Influence of Arab Culture on Arab Military Effectiveness". Cambridge, MA: Massachusetts Institute of Technology, 1996.

Reisman, W. Michael. "The Lessons of Qana". *Yale Journal of International Law* 22, no. 2 (Summer 1997): 381–399.

Ricks, Thomas E. *Fiasco: The American Military Adventure in Iraq*. New York: Penguin Press, 2006.

Rosen, Stephen Peter. "New Ways of War: Understanding Military Innovation". *International Security* 13, no. 1 (Summer 1998): 134–168.

Schein, Edgar. "Organizational Culture". *American Psychologist* 45, no. 2 (February 1990): 109–119.

Siegl, Michael B. "Military Culture and Transformation". *Joint Forces Quarterly* 49 (2008): 103–106.

Smith, Thomas W. "Protecting Civilians ... or Soldiers? Humanitarian Law and the Economic of Risk in Iraq". *International Studies Perspectives* 9, no. 2 (May 2008): 144–164.

Snider, Don. "An Uninformed Debate on Military Culture". *Orbis* 43, no. 1 (Winter 1999): 11–26.

Stulberg, Adam. "Managing Military Transformations: Agency, Culture, and the U.S. Carrier Revolution". *Security Studies* 14, no. 3 (July–September 2005): 489–528.

Terriff, Terry. "'Innovate or Die': Organizational Culture and the Origins of Maneuver Warfare in the United States Marine Corps". *The Journal of Strategic Studies* 29, no. 3 (June 2006): 475–503.

Terriff, Terry. "Warriors and Innovators: Military Change and Organizational Culture in the US Marine Corps". *Defence Studies* 6, no. 2 (June 2006): 215–247.

Vardi, Gil-Li. "Pounding Their Feet: Israeli Military Culture as Reflected in Early IDF Combat History". *The Journal of Strategic Studies* 31, no. 2 (April 2008): 295–324.

Wendt, Alexander. "Anarchy is What States Make of It". *International Organization* 46, no. 2 (Spring 1992): 391–425.

Wendt, Alexander. "Collective Identity Formation and the International State". *American Political Science Review* 88, no. 2 (June 1994): 384–396.

Wilson, Peter H. "Defining Military Culture". *The Journal of Military History* 72, no. 1 (January 2008): 11–41.

3 The military cultures of Blackwater and DynCorp

This chapter examines the nature of the military cultures maintained by Blackwater and DynCorp during the Iraq War. As discussed in Chapter 2, a military's culture is a collection of behavioural norms that set standards of appropriate and inappropriate behaviour for the members of that armed force. Military cultures serve critical functions for a PSC. For instance, in her work on PSCs, Kateri Carmola argued that firms that adopted their military culture from a particular state-based military unit, such as the US Army's Special Forces (the "Green Berets") or the British Army's Special Air Service (SAS), hold a competitive advantage since they can market themselves as a for-hire version of the unit. Paraphrasing individuals involved in the private security industry, Carmola noted that they "stress the benefits of the military culture inherited from those they hire, and argue that this military background will extend to procedures and operating attitudes on the ground in war zones" such as Iraq and Afghanistan.[1]

Of greater importance, a PSC's military culture can also help provide its employees with a sense of direction by informing them how they should behave as they undertake assigned tasks. This function is particularly important because PSCs tend to draw their security personnel from a diverse array of backgrounds. For instance, some of their personnel will have served in state-based special operations military units, others will have spent their entire military career in regular units, others will have served in police forces, and still others will have no formal experience with any state-based or private security forces. Blackwater and DynCorp exhibited similar recruiting patterns, with veterans of American and other Western special operations units, such as the US Navy SEALs, the US Army Rangers and Special Forces, and the British SAS being the most sought-after personnel.[2] Both firms also, however, hired veterans of regular US Army and Marine and civilian police units. With this in mind, maintaining a specific military culture helps PSCs reshape their employees' preexisting beliefs about how they should behave in a conflict zone.[3] In the absence of such a culture, a firm's personnel are likely to act at cross-purposes as each employee opts to behave in accordance with their preexisting cultural tenets. As a result, a PSC that lacks a military culture will likely resemble a heavily armed rabble.

A military's culture is, therefore, one of the most important means of shaping the behaviour of its personnel. In fact, military cultures may have an even stronger influence on the behaviour of private security personnel than they do on soldiers serving in state-based armed forces.[4] Besides indoctrinating their soldiers into the military culture of the unit they are serving in, state-based armed forces also shape the behaviour of their soldiers through a variety of other means, such as issuing ranks with clearly defined privileges and responsibilities and maintaining both a system of military laws and an authoritative hierarchical structure. In contrast, PSCs, which Carmola characterizes as "informal organizations", usually lack most of these supplementary means of directing the behaviour of their personnel and must rely largely, if not exclusively, on their military culture.[5] Making a closely related point, Pelton rightly argued that "The ultimate moral leash on ... [private security personnel] is how they view themselves, not how the world views them".[6] As Chapters 4 and 5 illustrate, the nature of the military cultures maintained by Blackwater and DynCorp had a powerful influence on how their personnel behaved during their security operations in Iraq.

Although it has never been discussed in detail, both former employees and scholars who have studied the firm share the belief that Blackwater's military culture influenced the behaviour of its personnel.[7] Shawn Engbrecht, for example, argued that the firm maintained a "group mind-set" that strongly influenced the behaviour of its personnel in Iraq.[8] While referring to it as "the Blackwater system", Gary Jackson, who served as the firm's president until 2009, acknowledged that it maintained a culture that every employee was strongly encouraged to adopt and adhere to; the firm accomplished this through a brief (approximately 164 hours) but rigorous training and indoctrination program at the firm's facility in Moyock, North Carolina.[9] This culture placed strong emphasis on norms encouraging the firm's personnel to exercise personal initiative, proactive use of force and an exclusive approach to security. In other words, the firm strongly encouraged its personnel to believe that they should take it upon themselves to engage suspected threats, to use deadly force against suspected threats before those threats had used force against them and their clients, and to simultaneously prioritize the security of themselves and their clients and discount the security concerns of suspected threats.

Blackwater's military culture was strongly influenced by the military culture maintained by the US Navy's elite special operations force, the SEAL teams.[10] Blackwater was not unique in this respect. For example, Triple Canopy's military culture was derived from the US Army's 1st Special Forces Operational Detachment–Delta. Likewise, Hart, one of the largest British PSCs, derived its military culture from the British Army's Special Air Service.[11] Dick Couch, a former SEAL, who has written multiple books on the SEALs' training and indoctrination programs, confirmed that the SEALs have a "unique culture".[12] SEAL veteran Chuck Pharrer argued that the SEALs' *raison d'être* "is hurting the enemy" and that the unit's military culture strongly encouraged its personnel to accomplish this task.[13] Chris Kyle, another SEAL veteran, likewise contrasted the US Army Special Forces' emphasis on "training foreign forces" with the SEALs' emphasis on direct action missions, wherein SEALs are expected to "strike hard and fast before the enemy knows what's going on".[14] In addition to Blackwater's founder, Erik Prince, who served as a lieutenant with the SEALs, several other key Blackwater personnel were also SEAL veterans.[15] These included Jackson; Brian Berry, director of the firm's security operations division; Jim Sierawski and Al Clark, directors of training; Ken Viera, the firm's general manager; and Jim Dehart, the firm's director of facilities and chief design officer, who oversaw development of the training system used by its security personnel.[16] Combined, these senior personnel possess more than a century's worth of experience serving in the SEAL teams, so it is unsurprising that they sought to pass on much of the SEALs' "warrior" culture to Blackwater's other employees.[17]

In contrast to Blackwater, combat services has never been one of DynCorp's central business lines.[18] Overseas security operations generated only about 2 per cent of the firm's total revenue during the 2003 to 2009 period, with the remainder produced by such services as aircraft maintenance, logistical support, information systems management and police training.[19] It therefore makes good sense that the firm's military culture did not share Blackwater's strong emphasis on norms encouraging its personnel to exercise personal initiative, proactive use of force and an exclusive approach to security. Rather, in a conscious effort to safeguard the lives of Iraqi civilians and hold its security personnel to, in the words of one-time CEO Herb Lanese, "higher ethical and behavioural standards" that should shield the firm's more lucrative divisions, and their clients, from bad press, the firm developed a military culture that discouraged the use of violence by its security personnel.[20] The firm's executives understood that their chief client, the government of the United States, might attempt to sever ties in response to bad behaviour on the part of the private security personnel assigned to protect US Department of State employees in Iraq.[21] Reflecting on this concern, Gary Schumacher, a retired US Special Forces officer, rightly argued that

> If you do things quiet enough, you'll continue to get more business from the US government. If you don't, you'll see fewer and fewer contracts. DynCorp has been one of the more effective organizations in attempting to keep their operations quiet.[22]

In written testimony presented to the US House of Representatives' Subcommittee on National Security, Emerging Threats, and International

Relations on 13 June 2006, the firm stated that it has "its own set of established standards ... that we expect our employees to follow".[23] Lanese subsequently argued that his firm adopted a more "conservative" approach to the use of deadly force than that sought by the Department of State or the CPA by developing its "own rules of the use of force that are more detailed than those issued by the US government".[24] The nature of DynCorp's military culture was made explicit in a document produced by the firm's Government Services division titled "DI Rules for the Use of Force (RUF) for DI Programs in Iraq", which all of the firm's security personnel had to read and sign before they were allowed to undertake security operations in Iraq.[25] These rules surpassed those put forward by either the CPA or the Department of State in terms of their length, inflexibility and emphasis on passivity over belligerence.[26]

Personal initiative

Blackwater's military culture strongly encouraged its personnel to demonstrate personal initiative, meaning they were encouraged to take it upon themselves to engage the suspected threats they might encounter during their security operations rather than wait for a more senior employee to order them to engage.[27] In his memoirs, Prince described "our company culture" as "aggressively proactive".[28] According to one of the firm's security personnel, Prince encouraged his employees to "to do whatever it takes" to accomplish their missions.[29] Frank Gallagher, who headed Bremer's security detail in Iraq, confirmed that one of the firm's "big boy rules" was that "We do what we want as long as it does not affect the mission or mission readiness".[30] Tim Beckman, who worked as a security contractor and trainer for Blackwater from 2004 to 2009, recalled that the firm's training and indoctrination program ran new employees through "full spectrum scenarios, where we learned to address situations", such as insurgent attacks and vehicles that failed to stay away from the firm's security convoys.[31] For example, the firm had its personnel undertake a variety of simulated tactical drills on roadways and a mockup village, complete with training assistants posing as armed insurgents, to indoctrinate them to believe that they should take it upon themselves to engage possible threats.[32] Reflecting on this aspect of the firm's military culture, Suzanne Simons rightly argued that "Blackwater, in a lot of ways, reflects Prince's own personality: stubborn, driven, and obsessed with finding ways to make things happen".[33] Sierawski, one of Blackwater's directors of training during the period under study, likewise noted that his firm encouraged all of its security personnel to believe that they should simply "do what they have to do" to accomplish their security operations.[34] One of the firm's lead pilots in Iraq reflected this belief when he told Gallagher "That's what we do. We make shit happen. Let's go", before embarking on an unauthorized mission to rescue some of his colleagues.[35]

This aspect of Blackwater's military culture echoed the SEALs' strong emphasis on exercising personal initiative.[36] As Couch put it, "leadership is taught and expected at all levels" within the SEALs, not simply from the senior leader of a SEAL unit. Put differently, although officers and senior enlisted men in the SEALs are expected to have overall authority for major decisions, the unit's military culture holds that "every man is a leader" and every SEAL is expected to take it upon themselves to carry out orders as general as "Here's our objective. Okay, guys, make it happen".[37] John Lindsay likewise argued that the SEALs' military culture emphasizes "mission-accomplishment at all costs" and values showing "competence and initiative over rank and position".[38] He also noted that "SEALs are brought up to believe that a frogman can and must be able to do anything himself".[39] Couch went on to argue that SEALs are indoctrinated to believe that, "individually and collectively", they should "tak(e) the action to resolve" tasks very quickly, and to ensure that their actions reflect the SEALs' "hard-core, get-it-done" attitude.[40]

DynCorp's military culture, in contrast, did not place strong emphasis on personal initiative. Rather than encourage its personnel to take it upon themselves to engage suspected threats, the firm encouraged them to follow, in Engbrecht's words, "a mandatory procedural checklist" before deciding whether they should pull their trigger.[41] This checklist, known as the "Special Procedures for Convoys and Vehicle Threats to Compounds", was far more detailed than the Department of State's procedures for the use of force in Iraq. For example, unlike the Department of State's procedures, DynCorp told its personnel precisely how close they should allow a suspected threat to approach before taking certain violent or non-violent actions against it.[42] Moreover, the firm's personnel were also informed that, if they fired their weapons at a suspected threat, a review board would scrutinize their actions and that their employment would be terminated if the board determined that they fired without adequate cause.[43] Furthermore, the firm informed its security personnel to restrict their use of deadly force to "specifically identified" threats, which implied that they should not take it upon themselves to, say, fire at a building or vehicle simply because a hostile gunshot emanated from its general direction.[44] By explicitly telling its security personnel that all of these procedures "will be employed" before using deadly force, it is clear that this aspect of the firm's military culture encouraged its personnel to believe that they should not take it upon themselves to decide when and how to use deadly force against a suspected threat.[45]

Proactive use of force

Blackwater's military culture strongly encouraged its personnel to use force proactively when they encountered a possible threat.[46] The firm encouraged its security personnel, who were known as "shooters" within the firm's military culture, to use force if they believed that a suspected threat *might* try to harm them or their clients in the near future.[47] As Prince put it, "Blackwater's contractors understood that letting their guards down while on duty, even for a moment, could be fatal".[48] Beckman reflected this belief when he stated that "Adults get what they get when it's game time", meaning that he and his colleagues believed it was acceptable to inflict serious harm upon any adults who might pose a threat to them.[49] Prince conveyed this aspect of the firm's military culture during his testimony before a congressional committee in October 2007. When asked by Congressmen John Tierney why Blackwater personnel "fire first, ask questions later" when they encounter a suspected threat, such as an approaching vehicle, Prince made the following statement:

> Sir, like I said, the bad guys have made a precision weapon (a vehicle-based improvised explosive device). The Air Force has a system called a DIRCM, Directional Infrared Countermeasures. It is used to break the lock of incoming surface-to-air missiles. It shines a laser in the seeker head. The missile breaks lock, and it veers away. We have to go through a use of force continuum to try to break the lock of this potential deadly suicide weapon.[50]

This statement suggests that Prince wanted his employees to view any approaching unidentified vehicle, regardless of whether it was overtly carrying weapons or had attempted to inflict harm, as a probable deadly threat that simply had to be stopped before it could harm a security team or its clients. Clark, one of the chief designers of Blackwater's training and indoctrination program, likewise argued that the firm's personnel were encouraged to "get over" any reservations they may otherwise have had about using their armoured vehicles as weapons in Iraq to disable unidentified vehicles or their drivers whenever they approached a security convoy or failed to quickly get out of its way.[51]

Highlighting this aspect of the firm's military culture, Robert Young Pelton argued that "if they do come under attack, Blackwater has a policy of using overwhelming firepower to break contact".[52] Human Rights First likewise argued that Blackwater's employees maintained a "'shoot-first, ask questions later – or never' attitude".[53] Furthermore, Pelton also argued that Blackwater's "brash" and "aggressive persona" set it apart from other PSCs, such as the British firm Hart, which encouraged its employees to refrain from using force whenever possible.[54]

This aspect of Blackwater's military culture paralleled the SEALs' strong emphasis on the proactive use of force. For example, Couch and Robert Gormly, both SEAL veterans, argued that SEALs are encouraged to "drain their magazines" when they encounter a suspected threat in order "to get as much continuous fire as possible" directed at the threat.[55] Couch went on to argue that the written code of tactical behaviour that newly minted

SEALs receive at the conclusion of their formal training encourages them to believe that "There is no second place in a gunfight. Winners kill, losers get killed. Fight to win".[56] Couch also argued that the SEALs' "warrior culture ... instills them with a relentless desire to fight and win".[57] Pharrer similarly argued that the SEALs sought to develop warriors that would strike "with a ferocity far out of proportion to their number".[58] Kyle likewise stated that SEALs are "trained to go out and kill people".[59] Furthermore, Lindsay argued that the SEALs' military culture "actively construes direct action as a path to glory", while non-violent "indirect missions, by contrast, have lower prestige ... and are usually performed only grudgingly by operators".[60] Finally, Billy Waugh, a veteran of the US Army Special Forces and CIA special operations forces, characterized SEALs as soldiers that "just want to go in, blow a lot of people away" and quickly move on to their next operation.[61]

DynCorp's military culture, in contrast, did not strongly encourage its security personnel to use force proactively when they encountered a suspected threat. Although the firm did permit its personnel to use deadly force against a suspected threat that had not attacked them first, it also encouraged its personnel to refrain from using deadly force before issuing multiple non-violent warnings to a suspected threat and making multiple attempts to disable it, such as by shooting out the tyres or engine of an approaching vehicle with "the fewest possible number of [well-aimed] shots necessary in order to achieve the desired security effect".[62] Moreover, the firm also encouraged its personnel to refrain from using deadly force against a suspected threat until it approached quite close (well under 40 metres) to them and their clients.[63] Furthermore, the firm encouraged its security personnel to try to flee to a secure location, such as a military or Department of State compound, "whenever a situation occurs in which deadly force is deemed necessary ... in order to minimize the necessity of having to use deadly force".[64] In written testimony presented to the US House of Representatives' Subcommittee on National Security, Emerging Threats, and International Relations on 13 June 2006, the firm likewise stated that the "basic approach" it asked its security teams to take in Iraq was "to ensure security for its protectee(s) by avoiding danger, hostile elements, and attack at all costs, as opposed to 'moving into and securing an area,' where hostile activity may have been detected".[65] The firm therefore discouraged its personnel from exhibiting proactive violent behaviour such as shooting suspected threats on sight. Front-line personnel appear to have accepted and understood this aspect of the firm's military culture. For example, a reporter embedded with a DynCorp team in Iraq in 2004 observed one of the firm's American employees tell some Iraqi subcontractors "Don't shoot anybody unless somebody shoots at you" before sending them to investigate a group of suspected insurgents.[66]

Exclusive approach to security

Finally, Blackwater's military culture strongly encouraged the firm's personnel to exercise an exclusive approach to security, meaning they were encouraged to prioritize the security of themselves and their clients far above that of any other actor they might encounter in their operating environment, such as insurgents, civilians, the employees of other PSCs, Iraqi security personnel or soldiers serving with the US-led military coalition.[67] In Prince's words, his firm wanted its personnel "to create ... a 'high-visibility deterrent' to attackers and keep State's personnel safe no matter what", and went on to state that "It didn't matter if it was probably the worst approach for the department actually achieving its diplomatic objectives in Iraq".[68] According to Prince, his firm "drilled" its personnel to believe that they should quickly "get off the X" when they encountered a suspected threat, meaning they were encouraged to use whatever means they deemed necessary to escape a threatening situation, including firing their weapons in fully automatic mode or employing their armoured vehicles as battering rams to smash through unarmoured civilian vehicles.[69] Moreover, Clark argued that the firm's personnel were encouraged to believe that they should not concern themselves with the probable consequences of using deadly force during their security operations: "Your car can be a 3,000 pound weapon when you need it. Hit and run. Trust me. The police aren't coming to your house because you left the scene of an accident".[70] By instilling this belief among the firm's security personnel, the firm was, in effect, telling its employees that the victims of their violence did not "matter".

These beliefs were accepted and adhered to by the firm's employees. A private security contractor who worked for one of Blackwater's competitors argued that one of the defining characteristics of the firm's personnel was that they had an inflated sense of their own and their clients' security concerns and, simultaneously, discounted the security concerns of everyone else they encountered in Iraq.[71] For example, Ann Exline Starr, an American who travelled under the protection of Blackwater personnel while working as an advisor for the CPA in Iraq, recalled that the Blackwater personnel assigned to her stated that "'Our mission is to protect the principal at all costs. If that means pissing off the Iraqis, too bad.'"[72] Starr went on to argue that the firm's security personnel understood that they "are going to be judged by their bosses solely on whether they get their client from point A to point B, not whether they win Iraqi hearts and minds along the way".[73] Finally, multiple Blackwater employees such as Dan Laguna, a senior pilot and director of Blackwater's flight operations in Iraq, and Tommy Vargas, one of the firm's ground personnel in Iraq, have argued that all of the firm's personnel believed that "Your own survival is the ultimate monkey" and that their colleagues would, in Laguna's words, "never leave them behind no matter what happened" during a security operation.[74]

Contrasting Blackwater's military culture against the "low-key SAS culture of assimilation" maintained by the British security company Hart, Pelton described Blackwater's culture as "almost xenophobic" because of its exclusive focus on the security of its own personnel and clients and lack of concern for anyone else in its operating environment.[75] Referring to Blackwater's personnel, Max Boot similarly suggested that they cared only about protecting themselves and their clients and criticized them for "not caring that they leave hatred in their wake".[76] Steve Fainaru, a *Washington Post* reporter who spent several months covering the activities of PSCs in Iraq, likewise argued that Blackwater's personnel believed that the safety concerns of "Whoever held the contract ruled".[77] Finally, Thomas Hammes, a military analyst, argued that Blackwater likely felt it was necessary to impart this part of its military culture since the safety of its clients determined its future business prospects:

> If Blackwater loses a principal, they're out of business, aren't they? Can you imagine being Blackwater, trying to sell your next contract, saying, "Well, we did pretty well in Iraq for about four months, and then he got killed." And you're the CEO who's going to hire and protect your guys. You'll say, "I think I'll find somebody else." ... The problem for Blackwater [is] if the primary gets killed, what happens to Blackwater is they're out of business. For the military, if the primary gets killed, that's a very bad thing. There will be after-action reviews, etc., but nobody's going out of business.[78]

As with the other norms that made up Blackwater's military culture, the firm's strong emphasis on maintaining an exclusive approach to security reflected the military culture of the SEALs.[79] New SEAL recruits are "immediately immersed in the culture of the teams" by being assigned to a small team throughout their training and indoctrination process to help instill a sense of loyalty to the other members of the team, who, to a large extent, succeed or fail as a team.[80] Pharrer recalled that "the SEAL Teams are not looking for loners. The instructors watch carefully to see that each man is pulling his own weight and functioning as a member of the team".[81] Lindsay likewise argued that SEAL training "forges a powerful in-group dynamic".[82] This aspect of the SEALs' culture is intended to turn the teams into a "fraternity".[83] Describing the SEALs' military culture, Couch stated that the "SEALs are all about teammates and commitment to team. We're pack animals".[84] He also argued that SEALs are encouraged to believe that they should "never leave a teammate" behind, whether in training or in a firefight.[85] SEAL veteran Howard E. Wasdin similarly argued that trainee SEALs are taught to "look out for each other" and to "leave no man behind".[86] Wasdin, who highlighted the fact that no SEAL have ever been held as a prisoner of war, also argued:

> As SEALs ... we believe our surrender [to enemy forces] would be giving in, and giving in is never an option.... Ours is an unwritten code: It's better to burn out than to fade away – and with our last breaths we'll take as many of the enemy with us as possible.[87]

Furthermore, Pharrer argued that SEALs are taught to believe that, when a comrade comes under threat of harm,

> you will move without thinking and without hesitation. You will break cover, expose yourself to enemy fire, and drag this person to safety. Anything less than your full commitment, any hesitation whatsoever, any unwillingness, any fear or backtalk will disqualify you instantly and forever from continuing with the Teams.[88]

He went on to argue that, "in the (SEAL) Teams", attempts to save the life of a comrade "are not seen as heroic acts" but, rather, are simply "expected" from every single member of the unit.[89]

DynCorp's military culture, in contrast, did not strongly encourage its security personnel to exercise an exclusive approach to security. On the contrary, DynCorp's military culture strongly encouraged the firm's personnel to exercise an inclusive approach to security, meaning they were encouraged to prioritize the security of not only themselves and their clients but also every non-insurgent they might encounter in their operating environment. In addition to explicitly encouraging their security personnel to "make every effort to avoid civilian casualties" and admonishing them to believe that "civilians will ALWAYS be treated humanely", the firm also informed them that it "recognizes and respects the paramount value of all human life".[90] In written testimony presented to the US House of Representatives' Subcommittee on National Security, Emerging Threats, and International Relations on 13 June 2006, the firm similarly stated that "our security services ... can best be described as passive.... Our primary objective is to protect the asset, not destroy the threat".[91] Moreover, in its "Special Procedures for Convoys and Vehicle Threats to Compounds", the firm informed its security personnel that the purpose of adhering to these procedures is "to prevent loss of life".[92] Although DynCorp certainly valued the safety of its principals and personnel, it did not consider this objective to be its sole concern for, as discussed earlier, the firm had to balance the safety of the principals under its protection against the public image and financial interests of the non-security divisions that generated most of its revenue. Therefore, while Blackwater's security personnel were encouraged to protect their principals (and primary sources of revenue) at all costs, DynCorp's emphasis on maintaining an inclusive approach to security reflected the relative unimportance of security services to its overall financial health.

Conclusion

It is clear that Blackwater's security personnel were immersed in a much more belligerent military culture than their counterparts in DynCorp were. By placing strong emphasis on norms encouraging its personnel to exercise personal initiative, proactive use of force and an exclusive approach to security, Blackwater strongly encouraged its personnel to believe that they should take it upon themselves to engage suspected threats, to use deadly force against suspected threats before those threats had used force against them and their clients, and to simultaneously prioritize the security of themselves and their clients and discount the security concerns of suspected threats. DynCorp's military culture, in contrast, did not strongly emphasize any of these norms. Chapters 4 and 5 analyze the predicted relationships between each firm's military culture, the tactical behaviour exhibited by their personnel and the casualties they inflicted and suffered during their security operations.

Notes

1 Carmola, *Private Security Contractors*, 31.
2 Isenberg, *Shadow Force*, 37; Fainaru, *Big Boy Rules*, 52; Singer, *Corporate Warriors*, 17; Engbrecht, *America's Covert Warriors*, 20; Laguna, *You Have to Live Hard*, Loc. 326–342; Pelton, *Licensed to Kill*, 221; Middle East Regional Office, "Performance Evaluation", 5 and 17.
3 Pelton, *Licensed to Kill*, 178.
4 Dunigan, *Victory for Hire*, 81.
5 Carmola, *Private Security Contractors*, 10, 34 and 38–39.
6 Pelton, *Licensed to Kill*, 6.
7 Simons, *Master of War*, 237; Prince, *Civilian Warriors*, 58.
8 Engbrecht, *America's Covert Warriors*, 16.
9 Simons, *Master of War*, 84; Beckman, *Blackwater from the Inside Out*, Loc. 287–289; House Committee on Oversight and Government Reform, "Hearing on Blackwater USA", 94; Rosen, *Contract Warriors*, 34; Prince, *Civilian Warriors*, 178.
10 Chatterjee, *Iraq, Inc.*, 129; Rosen, *Contract Warriors*, 33; Simons, *Master of War*, 37; Pelton, *Licensed to Kill*, 166 and 184; Gallagher and Del Vecchio, *The Bremer Detail*, Loc. 1124.
11 Pelton, *Licensed to Kill*, 166.
12 Couch, *Warrior Elite*, 19; Couch, *Finishing School*, 6, 9 and 12.
13 Pfarrer, *Seal Target Geronimo*, Loc. 272–273.
14 Kyle, McEwen and DeFelice, *American Sniper*, Loc. 779–780 and 782–786.
15 Scahill, *Blackwater*, 11 and 13; House Committee on Oversight and Government Reform, "Hearing on Blackwater USA", 23; Prince, *Civilian Warriors*, 22–27; Gallagher and Del Vecchio, *The Bremer Detail*, Loc. 187–188.
16 Simons, *Master of War*, 46, 52 and 61; Uesseler, *Servants of War*, 87; Pelton, *Licensed to Kill*, 125; Prince, *Civilian Warriors*, 32–34.
17 Simons, *Master of War*, 84; Beckman, *Blackwater from the Inside Out*, Loc. 287–289; House Committee on Oversight and Government Reform, "Hearing on Blackwater USA", 94 and 108; Couch, *Warrior Elite*, 11; Engbrecht, *America's Covert Warriors*, 19.
18 Kramer, "Does History Repeat Itself?", 30.
19 Ibid., 30; Kinsey, *Corporate Soldiers*, 25 and 88; Box Cox, "DynCorp is no Blackwater"; Falconer, "IPOA Smackdown".

20 Engbrecht, *America's Covert Warriors*, 9–10 and 18–19; Box Cox, "DynCorp is no Blackwater".
21 Carlson, "Hired Guns".
22 Robberson, "DynCorp: Shadows".
23 Subcommittee on National Security, Emerging Threats, and International Relations, "Private Security Firms", 107.
24 Falconer, "IPOA Smackdown".
25 DGSD, "DI Rules".
26 US Department of State Diplomatic Security Service, "High Threat Protective Operations", 7–9; House Committee on Oversight and Government Reform, "Hearing on Blackwater USA", 134–136 and 144–145; Coalition Provisional Authority, "Memorandum Number 17", 10–11; DGSD, "DI Rules", 1–9.
27 Simons, *Master of War*, 56 and 237.
28 Prince, *Civilian Warriors*, 45.
29 Risen and Mazzetti, "Blackwater Guards"; Prince, *Civilian Warriors*, 343.
30 Gallagher and Del Vecchio, *The Bremer Detail*, Loc. 346 and 624.
31 Beckman, *Blackwater from the Inside Out*, Loc. 377–378.
32 Beckman, *Blackwater from the Inside Out*, Loc. 385–386.
33 Simons, *Master of War*, 265.
34 Scahill, *Blackwater*, 1st edn, 198.
35 Gallagher and Del Vecchio, *The Bremer Detail*, Loc. 2182.
36 Couch, *Finishing School*, 30.
37 Ibid., 31.
38 Lindsay, "Information Friction", 219 and 243.
39 Ibid., 243.
40 Couch, *Finishing School*, 31; Couch, *Warrior Elite*, 314.
41 Engbrecht, *America's Covert Warriors*, 19.
42 US Department of State Diplomatic Security Service, "High Threat Protective Operations", 7–9; House Committee on Oversight and Government Reform, "Hearing on Blackwater USA", 134–136 and 144–145; Coalition Provisional Authority, "Memorandum Number 17", 10–11; DGSD, "DI Rules", 6–8.
43 Engbrecht, *America's Covert Warriors*, 19; DGSD, "DI Rules", 2 and 5–6.
44 DGSD, "DI Rules", 6.
45 DGSD, "DI Rules", 6.
46 Beckman, *Blackwater from the Inside Out*, Loc. 287–289, 295–296, 303, 304 and 307.
47 Laguna, *You Have to Live Hard*, Loc. 3475; Beckman, *Blackwater from the Inside Out*, Loc. 65; Prince, *Civilian Warriors*, 39–42 and 80.
48 Prince, *Civilian Warriors*, 208.
49 Beckman, *Blackwater from the Inside Out*, Loc. 724.
50 House Committee on Oversight and Government Reform, "Hearing on Blackwater USA", 78–79.
51 Scahill, *Blackwater*, 1st edn, 72.
52 Pelton, *Licensed to Kill*, 111 and 201.
53 Human Rights First, "Private Security Contractors", 3.
54 Pelton, *Licensed to Kill*, 111, 201 and 296–297. Pelton supported his argument with a statement from Hart's CEO, who argued that "It's abhorrent to shoot a warning shot. It's never nice to discharge your weapon". Pelton, *Licensed to Kill*, 297.
55 Couch, *Finishing School*, 114; Gormly, *Combat Swimmer*, 57.
56 Couch, *Finishing School*, 161.
57 Couch, *Warrior Elite*, 11.
58 Pfarrer, *Seal Target Geronimo*, Loc. 284–285.
59 Kyle, McEwen and DeFelice, *American Sniper*, Loc. 865–867.

60 Lindsay, "Information Friction", 219.
61 Pelton, *Licensed to Kill*, 17 and 31.
62 DGSD, "DI Rules", 7; Subcommittee on National Security, Emerging Threats, and International Relations, "Private Security Firms", 94.
63 DGSD, "DI Rules", 7.
64 DGSD, "DI Rules", 5.
65 Subcommittee on National Security, Emerging Threats, and International Relations, "Private Security Firms", 125.
66 Carlson, "Hired Guns".
67 Avant et al., "Mercenary Debate"; Pelton, *Licensed to Kill*, 296; Fainaru, *Big Boy Rules*, 163–164; Prince, *Civilian Warriors*, 259.
68 Prince, *Civilian Warriors*, 157.
69 Ricks, *Fiasco*, 332; House Committee on Oversight and Government Reform, "Hearing on Blackwater USA", 61; Prince, *Civilian Warriors*, 135.
70 Scahill, *Blackwater*, 1st edn, 72.
71 Engbrecht, *America's Covert Warriors*, 35.
72 Fainaru, *Big Boy Rules*, 139.
73 Quoted in House Committee on Oversight and Government Reform, "Hearing on Blackwater USA", 77.
74 Laguna, *You Have to Live Hard*, Loc. 671–672 and 3585; Ricks, *Fiasco*, 332.
75 Pelton, *Licensed to Kill*, 296.
76 Avant et al., "The Mercenary Debate".
77 Fainaru, *Big Boy Rules*, 163–164.
78 Gaviria and Smith, "Interview".
79 Couch, *Finishing School*, 56.
80 Couch, *Warrior Elite*, 11–12, 76 and 98; Couch, *Finishing School*, 12; Pfarrer, *Seal Target Geronimo*, Loc. 388–391 and 408–411; Wasdin and Templin, *Seal Team Six*, 51 and 54; Kyle, McEwen and DeFelice, *American Sniper*, Loc. 500–502; Mann and Pezzullo, *Inside Seal Team Six*, 79 and 83.
81 Pfarrer, *Seal Target Geronimo*, Loc. 352–353.
82 Lindsay, "Information Friction", 219.
83 Couch, *Warrior Elite*, 96.
84 Couch, *Finishing School*, 6.
85 Couch, *Warrior Elite*, 287.
86 Wasdin and Templin, *Seal Team Six*, 83.
87 Ibid., 83.
88 Pfarrer, *Seal Target Geronimo*, Loc. 476–478.
89 Ibid., Loc. 481–482.
90 DGSD, "DI Rules", 3–4; Coalition Provisional Authority, "Memorandum Number 17", 10.
91 Subcommittee on National Security, Emerging Threats, and International Relations, "Private Security Firms", 105.
92 DGSD, "DI Rules", 7.

References

Avant, Deborah, Max Boot, Jorg Friedrichs and Cornelius Friesendorf. "The Mercenary Debate: Three Views". *The American Interest* May/June 2009, 32–48.
Beckman, Tim. *Blackwater from the Inside Out*. Kindle edn. New York: HDTI, 2010.
Carlson, Tucker. "Hired Guns". *Esquire*, 29 February 2004.
Carmola, Kateri. *Private Security Contractors and New Wars: Risk, Law, and Ethics*. New York: Routledge Press, 2010.

Chatterjee, Pratap. *Iraq, Inc.: A Profitable Occupation*. New York: Seven Stories Press, 2004.
Coalition Provisional Authority. "Coalition Provisional Authority Memorandum Number 17". Baghdad: Coalition Provisional Authority, 26 June 2004.
Couch, Dick. *The Warrior Elite: The Forging of Seal Class 228*. New York: Crown Publishers, 2001.
Couch, Dick. *The Finishing School: Earning the Navy SEAL Trident*. New York: Crown Publishers, 2004.
Cox, Box. "DynCorp is no Blackwater, says Chief Executive". *Fort Worth Star-Telegram*, 24 December 2007.
DGSD (DynCorp Government Services Division). "DI Rules for the Use of Force (RUF) for DI Programs in Iraq". Falls Church, VA: DynCorp, 13 August 2007.
Dunigan, Molly. *Victory for Hire: Private Security Companies' Impact on Military Effectiveness*. Stanford, CA: Stanford Security Studies, 2011.
Engbrecht, Shawn. *America's Covert Warriors: Inside the World of Private Military Contractors*. Washington, DC: Potomac Books, 2011.
Fainaru, Steve. *Big Boy Rules: America's Mercenaries Fighting in Iraq*. Philadelphia: Da Capo Press, 2008.
Falconer, Bruce. "IPOA Smackdown: DynCorp vs. Blackwater". *Mother Jones*, 12 November 2007.
Gallagher, Frank, and John M. Del Vecchio. *The Bremer Detail: Protecting the Most Threatened Man in the World*. Kindle edn. New York: Open Road Media, 2014.
Gaviria, Marcela, and Martin Smith. "Interview with Thomas Hammes". *PBS Frontline*, 21 June 2005.
Gormly, Robert A. *Combat Swimmer: Memoirs of a Navy SEAL*. New York: Dutton, 1998.
House Committee on Oversight and Government Reform. "Hearing on Blackwater USA". Washington, DC: House of Representatives, Congress of the United States, 2 October 2007.
Human Rights First. "Private Security Contractors at War: Ending the Culture of Impunity". New York: Human Rights First, 2008.
Isenberg, David. *Shadow Force: Private Security Contractors in Iraq*. Westport, CT: Praeger Security International, 2009.
Kinsey, Christopher. *Corporate Soldiers and International Security: The Rise of Private Military Companies*. London: Routledge, 2006.
Kramer, Daniel. "Does History Repeat Itself? A Comparative Analysis of Private Military Entities". In *Private Military and Security Companies: Chances, Problems, Pitfalls and Prospects*, edited by Thomas Jäger and Gerhard Kümmel. Wiesbaden: Vs Verlag für Sozialwissenschaften, 2007, 23–35.
Kyle, Chris, Scott McEwen and Jim DeFelice. *American Sniper: The Autobiography of the Most Lethal Sniper in US Military History*. Kindle edn. New York: W. Morrow, 2012.
Laguna, Dan. *You Have to Live Hard to Be Hard: One Man's Life in Special Operations*. Kindle edn. Bloomington, IN: Authorhouse, 2010.
Lindsay, John Randall. "Information Friction: Information Technology and Military Performance". Cambridge, MA: Massachusetts Institute of Technology, February 2011.
Mann, Don, and Ralph Pezzullo. *Inside Seal Team Six: My Life and Missions with America's Elite Warriors*. Kindle edn. New York: Little, Brown & Co., 2011.

Middle East Regional Office. "Performance Evaluation of the DynCorp Contract for Personal Protective Services in Iraq". US Department of State and the Broadcasting Board of Governors Office of Inspector General, June 2009.

Pelton, Robert Young. *Licensed to Kill: Hired Guns in the War on Terror.* New York: Crown Publishers, 2006.

Pfarrer, Chuck. *Seal Target Geronimo: The Inside Story of the Mission to Kill Osama bin Laden.* Kindle edn. New York: St. Martin's Press, 2011.

Prince, Erik. *Civilian Warriors: The Inside Story of Blackwater and the Unsung Heroes of the War on Terror.* Kindle edn. New York: Portfolio, 2013.

Ricks, Thomas E. *Fiasco: The American Military Adventure in Iraq.* New York: Penguin Press, 2006.

Risen, James, and Mark Mazzetti. "Blackwater Guards Tied to Secret C.I.A. Raids". *New York Times*, 11 December 2009.

Robberson, Tod. "DynCorp: In the Shadows of War". *Dallas Morning News*, 24 December 2006.

Rosen, Fred. *Contract Warriors: How Mercenaries Changed History and the War on Terrorism.* New York: Alpha, 2005.

Scahill, Jeremy. *Blackwater: The Rise of the World's Most Powerful Mercenary Army.* 1st edn. New York: Nation Books, 2007.

Simons, Suzanne. *Master of War: Blackwater USA's Erik Prince and the Business of War.* New York: Harper, 2009.

Singer, Peter W. *Corporate Warriors: The Rise of the Privatized Military Industry.* Ithaca, NY: Cornell University Press, 2003.

Subcommittee on National Security, Emerging Threats, and International Relations. "Private Security Firms: Standards, Cooperation and Coordination on the Battlefield". Washington, DC: House of Representatives, Congress of the United States, 13 June 2006.

Uesseler, Rolf. *Servants of War: Private Military Corporations and the Profit of Conflict.* Translated by Jefferson Chase. Berkeley, CA: Soft Skull Press, 2008.

US Department of State Diplomatic Security Service. "High Threat Protective Operations in Baghdad: General Information and Standard Operating Procedures for WPPS Contract Personnel". Baghdad: US Department of State, August 2005.

Wasdin, Howard E., and Stephen Templin. *Seal Team Six: Memoirs of an Elite Navy Seal Sniper.* Kindle edn. New York: St. Martin's Press, 2011.

4 The relationship between military culture, tactical behaviour and casualties inflicted on suspected threats

This chapter examines the relationship between the firms' military cultures, the use of violence by their security personnel and the casualties they inflicted during their security operations. It focuses, in particular, on the casualties they inflicted against civilians, while Chapter 5 concentrates on the deaths and serious injuries they inflicted on the insurgents they encountered in Iraq and also the casualties they suffered during their security operations. This chapter consists of three main parts. It first analyzes the predictions of the ideational theory of tactical violence regarding the relationship between military culture, tactical behaviour and the casualties inflicted by each firm's personnel. Second, it discusses a number of possible alternative explanations for these findings. Finally, it concludes with a summary of the findings of this analysis.

Predictions of the ideational theory of tactical violence

The ideational theory of tactical violence offers specific, testable predictions about how the behavioural norms contained in a PSC's military culture should influence the tactical behaviour exhibited by its security personnel.

Engagement time

The theory predicts that the security personnel of PSCs that place strong emphasis on norms encouraging personal initiative, proactive use of force and an exclusive approach to security should tend to employ violence more quickly after observing a suspected threat than the security personnel of firms that do not place strong emphasis on these norms. For instance, although the security personnel of firms that strongly emphasize these norms should often issue non-violent warnings to suspected threats before firing their weapons, they should escalate to using deadly force more quickly than their counterparts in firms that do not strongly emphasize these norms. Security personnel who behave in this manner in effect reduce the amount of time available for a suspected threat to alter its behaviour and attempt to convince the security personnel that it means them no harm by, for example, dropping a weapon, halting its approach or altering its course away from the security personnel and their clients before they engage the suspected threat with deadly force. This, in turn, means that security personnel who behave in this manner are more likely to kill or seriously injure a suspected threat during an incident than are security personnel who behave in a less violent manner.

This prediction was supported by the behaviour exhibited by both Blackwater and DynCorp's personnel. Blackwater's security teams frequently employed violence before exhausting the non-violent courses of action in the US Department of State's "escalation of force" continuum, which included directing hand signals, bright lights or shouts toward the suspected threat; firing a flare at the suspected threat; and pointing weapons at the suspected threat.[1] Of critical importance, the Department of State's use of force policy states that "the touchstone of the policy is necessity; deadly force can only be used in situations where there is no safe alternative to using such force".[2] However, it allows security contractors to decide for themselves as to whether this criterion has been met, noting that "deadly force can be immediately applied provided that it is necessary under the specific situation's circumstances".[3] Therefore, the probability that deadly force will be used is determined by how quickly, if at all, a PSC's personnel decide that this "necessity" criterion has been met.

These provisions provide ample room for the personnel of different PSCs to respond to similar situations in markedly different ways. As illustrated throughout this chapter, Blackwater's military culture, with its strong emphasis on norms encouraging personal initiative, the proactive use of deadly force and an exclusive approach to security, encouraged its personnel to resort to deadly force very quickly after encountering what they deemed to be potential threats. Therefore, when employees such as Dan Laguna and Tim Beckman argue that the firm's personnel "fired their weapons only when their lives or the lives of the diplomat they were protecting was threatened", or claim that their colleagues followed their assigned escalation of force continuum and rules of engagement, they are providing an honest assessment of their colleagues' beliefs and behaviour that is, at the same time, heavily influenced by the military culture they were operating within.[4]

Beckman argued plainly that he and his colleagues in Blackwater reacted very quickly – "like a machine" – when they spotted suspected threats (see Table 4.1).[5] This firm's personnel fired their weapons as their initial response to a suspected threat during 44 incidents, representing 12 per cent of the incidents where they employed violence. To be clear, although the firm's personnel first issued a non-violent warning in 81 per cent of all the incidents where they also fired their weapons, the firm's incident reports indicate that, in more than one out of every 10 incidents, its personnel did not issue a non-violent warning before engaging a

Table 4.1 First behavioural responses to suspected threats

	Issue non-violent warning	Ram suspected threat	Fire at suspected threat	Attempt to flee location of incident	Stop moving
Blackwater	285 80.74%	6 1.70%	44 12.46%	11 3.12%	7 1.98%
DynCorp	56 93.33%	0 0.00%	0 0.00%	3 5.00%	1 1.67%

suspected threat with deadly force. In many of these incidents, Blackwater's fire probably took the suspected threat by complete surprise and thus provided no time for the suspected threat to alter its behaviour and attempt to convince the security personnel that it meant them no harm. DynCorp's employees, in contrast, initially offered non-violent warnings in 93 per cent of all the incidents where they fired their weapons and never initiated an engagement with a suspected threat by firing their weapons. Therefore, all of the suspected threats that DynCorp attacked were afforded at least some time to alter their behaviour before being engaged with deadly force.

Moreover, Blackwater's personnel fired at suspected threats considerably more often (30 per cent of the time) during the second stage of a violent incident than their counterparts in DynCorp, who fired during this stage in just 18 per cent of the incidents where they employed violence (Table 4.2). DynCorp's personnel were much more likely to issue another non-violent warning as their second behavioural response to a suspected threat, doing so in 78 per cent of the incidents where they ultimately fired their weapons, than were Blackwater's personnel, who did so in only in 63 per cent of the incidents where they employed violence at some point.

As the theory predicts, Blackwater's personnel killed and seriously injured numerous suspected threats relatively quickly during incidents where they used violence, and thus they afforded very little time for the suspected threats to alter their behaviour. In fact, virtually all of the known

Table 4.2 Second behavioural responses to suspected threats

	Issue non-violent warning	Ram suspected threat	Fire at suspected threat	Attempt to flee location of incident	Stop moving
Blackwater	221 62.96%	7 1.99%	107 30.48%	12 3.42%	4 1.14%
DynCorp	47 78.33%	1 1.67%	11 18.33%	0 0.00%	1 1.67%

deaths inflicted by Blackwater's security teams occurred during incidents where the firm's personnel chose to fire their weapons as their first and/or second behavioural response to a suspected threat. Specifically, at least 63 out of the 71 known deaths of suspected threats (89 per cent) inflicted by the firm's personnel occurred during these incidents. Moreover, 31 out of the 38 known deaths of non-insurgent suspected threats inflicted by the firm's personnel (82 per cent) occurred during these incidents.

For example, on 12 May 2005, while transporting US Embassy spokesman Robert J. Callahan, Blackwater personnel in a five-vehicle PSD convoy reportedly sped out of a side street in Baghdad and immediately fired two bursts of bullets at an Iraqi taxi as they crossed in front of it.[6] These shots wounded the taxi's driver, Mohammed Nouri Hattab, in the shoulder and fatally stuck one of Hattab's passengers in the chest. An American official, who declined to be named, reportedly told a correspondent for the *Los Angeles Times* that the two Blackwater employees who fired at the taxi failed to issue a non-violent warning to its driver to stay back from the convoy.[7] However, since mere seconds elapsed between the time when the speeding Blackwater convoy emerged from a side street and fired at the taxi, it seems unlikely that Hattab could have responded to a non-violent warning, even if one had been issued.

In a highly controversial incident, which occurred on 24 May 2007, a rear gunner attached to one of Blackwater's TSTs issued a brief warning before firing at and killing the driver of a maroon car near the Baghdad headquarters of the Iraqi Ministry of Interior.[8] The driver accelerated toward the convoy from the rear. The shooter later stated that "From past experience", the driver's unwillingness to immediately comply with his warning to stop "was a clear indicator ... that he could be driving a possible VBIED".[9] The shooter also acknowledged firing two bursts at the car, one at the grille and the second, longer burst directly at the driver, and stated that he was "reasonably sure that I had hit the driver with at least 1 round".[10] One of the convoy's turret gunners stated that the rear gunner started firing a mere "two or three seconds" after issuing a verbal warning to stop.[11] The incident was also witnessed by Ministry of Interior personnel who attempted, unsuccessfully, to detain the team.[12]

The most widely discussed and controversial example of the rapid resort to deadly force by Blackwater personnel occurred shortly after noon on 16 September 2007 in Baghdad's Nisour Square.[13] Prior to the incident, Blackwater's PSD Team 4 had escorted Kerry Pelzman, an official with the US Agency for International Development (USAID), to a meeting approximately three kilometres outside the Green Zone concerning a joint US–Iraqi infrastructure project called Izdihar.[14] During the meeting, an explosion – likely a VBIED – occurred approximately 200 metres away from the venue.[15] Fearing subsequent attacks, Team 4 requested backup. Two of the firm's TSTs, Raven 22 and 23, each of which had close to 20 armed personnel and four armoured vehicles, some of which were equipped with 7.62 mm mounted M240 machine guns, soon arrived to help get Pelzman to safety.[16] During the extraction, Raven 23 drove ahead of the other Backwater security details and stopped in Nisour Square, a traffic circle in the Mansour district of Baghdad, to try to temporarily halt the flow of civilian traffic so that the other security details could quickly pass through the square and proceed toward the Green Zone.[17] According to written testimony submitted by Prince to the House Committee on Oversight and Government Reform, Raven 23 "came under small-arms fire" from "men with AK-47s" and informed Teams 4 and 22 that they should take an alternative route back to the Green Zone.[18]

Although it is not possible to fully reconcile the conflicting accounts of what happened that day, there is some agreement that, shortly after Raven 23 entered the traffic circle, some of its gunners used verbal and hand signals to direct civilian vehicles to stop and, moments later, began firing at the windscreen of a white Kia car containing an Iraqi doctor named Mahasin al-Rubaie and her medical student son, Ahmed.[19] Ahmed's skull exploded instantly, but his lifeless foot applied sufficient pressure to the vehicle's accelerator to move it slowly into the traffic circle.[20] Still viewing the Kia, or its occupants, as a potential threat – Prince's testimony referred to "approaching vehicles that appeared to be suicide car bombers" – members of Raven 23 fired another burst of bullets and an M203 grenade into the vehicle's engine and windscreen, shattering the elder al-Rubaie's head and torso and setting the vehicle aflame.[21] At this point, at least six members of Raven 23 began firing "randomly" and "indiscriminately" "in all directions", including at the rear windows of civilian vehicles that were attempting to flee the "bloody" and "chaotic" scene.[22] The firm's personnel also immediately shot at anyone who stepped out of a vehicle.[23] A young boy was allegedly shot in the head while leaping from a minibus; his mother reportedly suffered the same fate moments later.[24] Multiple Iraqi witnesses and a Blackwater employee, who was not present during the incident, alleged that the door gunners of one of the firm's Little Bird helicopters also fired into the square.[25] Prince acknowledged that "Blackwater air assets did assist in directing the teams to safety" but resolutely denied that any door gunners fired their weapons during the incident.[26]

Members of Raven 23 continued to shoot, even after one of their colleagues allegedly pointed his weapon at them while shouting "cease fire!", "no! no!" and "stop shooting!"[27] This attempt to stop the violence was doomed to failure, however, since the shooters almost certainly could not hear what he was saying over their own gunfire and would have assumed that he drew his weapon to fire at the very same "threats" they were engaging. The team's assault in Nisour Square lasted approximately 15 minutes and resulted in 17 deaths and 24 serious injuries.[28] In addition, at least 18 civilian vehicles were damaged by gunfire during the incident.[29] Raven 23 did not suffer any deaths or injuries during the incident but claimed that one of its armoured vehicles was disabled by hostile fire and had to be towed away by one of the other vehicles in the convoy.[30]

Numerous Blackwater personnel, including Prince, and all but one of the security personnel who took part in the shootings at Nisour Square, as well as several security personnel who were not directly involved, are adamant that the shooters in Raven 23 attempted to engage armed gunmen in the square.[31] Paul A. Slough, one of the Blackwater personnel who fired his weapon during the incident, claimed that not only had the driver of the white Kia continued toward the firm's convoy after Slough and others had employed shouts and hand signals directing him to stop, but also that a "uniformed individual started pushing the vehicle" toward the convoy after its driver had been killed by the team's initial bursts of fire.[32] Slough stated that he suspected the vehicle of being a VBIED and that he feared for his own life and that of his comrades. The accounts reflected in the Department of State's initial spot report, which was actually written by a Blackwater employee named Darren Hanner, indicated that "8–10 persons fired from multiple nearby locations, with some aggressors dressed in civilian apparel and others in Iraqi Police uniforms" and that "The team returned defensive fire".[33] Prince's written statement to the House Committee on Oversight and Government Reform likewise stated that "some of those firing on this Blackwater team appeared to be wearing Iraqi National Police uniforms, or portions of such uniforms".[34] In interviews conducted after the incident, some of the Blackwater personnel who fired their weapons in Nisour Square stated that they felt threatened by a vehicle that failed to stop after they entered the traffic circle, presumably the white Kia, and fired at it in an attempt to neutralize the threat.[35] At least one account of the incident, citing Iraqi witnesses, claims that Iraqi security forces opened fire on Blackwater's convoy from a watchtower.[36] If true, this could have contributed to the contractors' perception that they were under attack.

Five of the Blackwater personnel who took part in the shootings – Slough, Dustin Heard, Evan Liberty, Nicholas Slatten and Donald Ball – were later charged by the US Department of Justice with multiple counts of voluntary manslaughter, attempts to commit manslaughter, and using and discharging a firearm and a destructive device during and in relation to a crime of violence.[37] Slatten was eventually charged with premeditated murder. A sixth shooter, Jeremy Ridgeway, pled guilty to lesser charges.[38] Iraqi witnesses of the incident said these personnel "started firing without reason".[39] An assessment by Human Rights First similarly concluded that the firm's personnel fired "with no justification".[40] Finally, the US Commission on Wartime Contracting in Iraq and Afghanistan alleged that Blackwater's use of violence in Nisour Square lacked "justification or provocation".[41]

Subsequent investigations by the US military, the Department of State, the FBI and the Iraqi government did not deem any of the individuals who were killed or injured during the incident, who included men, women and children, to be insurgents.[42] This does not rule out the possibility that that the shooters in Raven 23 *believed* they were under threat, nor does it mean that no threat was present; what this does mean is that insufficient evidence was found to prove that the team faced a genuine threat that day.[43] Of perhaps greater importance for understanding why Blackwater's personnel behaved as they did is that, regardless of whether a genuine threat was present in Nisour Square that day, the firm's military culture motivated its personnel to employ deadly force very quickly against *suspected* threats.[44] Indeed, the firm's personnel launched a vociferous and indiscriminate assault in a crowded traffic circle after issuing a single nonviolent warning. As Shawn Engbrecht put it, if somewhat theatrically,

> the group mind-set ... (prevalent within Blackwater) allowed intelligent, law-abiding young American men to become killers in the same way that that SS inducted sharp, outstanding Germans under the Nazi reign. These Germans, similar to the Americans in Iraq, would have balked at any thought of transgressing the law except the all-powerful atmosphere at the time not only permitted it but also encouraged it.[45]

The personnel of a PSC that maintained a less belligerent military culture, one that did not encourage the rapid resort to deadly force, likely would have provided more time to the drivers and pedestrians in Nisour Square to demonstrate their passivity. Likewise, the personnel of a PSC with a less belligerent military culture might have attempted to use deadly force in a more discriminating manner to engage the suspected threats by, again, providing more time for the people who were not fired upon in the initial barrage to demonstrate their passivity, rather than, in the manner of Blackwater's personnel, "firing in all directions".[46] More than any of the hundreds of other violent incidents that the firm's personnel were involved in during the Iraq War, the Nisour Square incident demonstrates the terrible costs of resorting to deadly force very quickly.

In half of the incidents where DynCorp shot and killed someone, their personnel fired their weapons as their second behavioural response to a suspected threat. In both of these incidents, which took place in Baghdad and saw the deaths of a man in an Opel car on 24 January 2005 and a man in a Hyundai taxi on 11 November 2007, the firm's personnel issued nonviolent warnings before firing their weapons.[47] During the first incident, the PSD allowed the suspected threat to approach within 15 metres of the convoy before firing first two and then three additional bullets at the vehicle's bonnet and grille. The team then allowed the suspected threat to start overtaking the rearmost vehicle in the convoy and approach one of the limousines containing their clients before finally firing into the passenger compartment. The wounded driver continued to approach the limousine, at which point two team members in a vehicle further up in the convoy leapt from their seats and fired additional bursts of bullets at the driver, fatally striking him in the head.[48] Although the team eventually stopped the suspected threat, they allowed it to get well within the destructive range of a car-based VBIED (30–38 metres) before initially firing on it, let alone neutralizing it. In doing so, they exposed themselves and their clients to undue risk.[49] The DynCorp team during the second incident, which saw at least one bullet enter the taxi's windscreen and strike Mohamad Khalil Khudair in the chest, seemingly did not intend to even wound the driver when they fired in front of his car, since a company spokesmen stated it was "kind of surprised that there was a death" during the incident.[50] Khudair was pulled alive from his car but died on the way to hospital.

At least 102 of the 122 known serious injuries (84 per cent) known to have been inflicted by Blackwater's security teams during the 2003 to 2009 period occurred during incidents where the firm's personnel chose to fire their weapons as their first and/or their second behavioural response to a suspected threat. Moreover, 45 of the 64 non-insurgents (70 per cent) who were seriously injured by the firm's personnel suffered their injuries during these incidents. Besides the serious injuries that occurred during the incidents discussed earlier in this section, the firm's security teams inflicted serious injuries on suspected threats during several other incidents that saw them quickly resort to deadly force. For example, on 29 August 2005 one of the firm's TSTs fired at and seriously injured the driver of an approaching Volkswagen Golf in Baghdad within two seconds of issuing a non-violent warning to the driver.[51] According to the team's personnel, a turret gunner riding in a Mamba fired three bullets as the driver was heading straight toward the limousine in the PSD convoy they were accompanying. The first two hit the Golf's grille while the third ricocheted off the vehicle's bonnet, struck the driver on the top of his head and exited through the rear windscreen. The driver then slumped sideways into the passenger seat as his vehicle slowly came to a halt.

In a particularly bizarre incident, a Blackwater team made up of two black cars burst through an Iraqi Army checkpoint in Baghdad and, without warning, proceeded to shoot and throw grenades at Iraqi soldiers before splitting up and heading in different directions.[52] One car fled into the Green Zone while the other parked outside a building. At this point, the occupants of the latter vehicle got out, threw thermite grenades into their car to set it on fire, and entered the building. Two minutes later, one of the firm's QRFs, made up of two white cars, arrived and fired at Iraqi soldiers in a nearby guard tower. In response, the Iraqi soldiers fired approximately 30 rounds of M240 machine gun ammunition at this team. Following this, one of the firm's air teams arrived and, together with the QRF, extracted the remaining members of the PSD from the building and returned to the Green Zone. The firm's personnel seriously injured three Iraqi soldiers during the incident.

From this it is clear that, by firing at suspected threats relatively quickly, Blackwater's personnel provided little time for the suspected threats that meant no harm to demonstrate this by dropping their weapons, halting their approach or altering their course away from the firm's personnel and clients. As a result, the behaviour exhibited by Blackwater's personnel likely inflicted several deaths and serious injurious to non-insurgents that could have been avoided if they had simply reacted more slowly, although this behaviour also probably reduced the likelihood of casualties being suffered by themselves and their clients.

One of the incidents where DynCorp's personnel seriously injured a suspected threat occurred near Erbil on 16 July 2007.[53] The PSD involved made two separate attempts to issue non-violent warnings to the driver of an approaching red Isuzu SUV before firing as their third behavioural response to the suspected threat. As the SUV closed with the convoy from the rear, both rear gunners of the trailing vehicle opening their doors and issued simultaneous verbal and hand signals to the driver; when that failed, they motioned with their gun barrels. The well gunner of the trailing vehicle then fired one round into the SUV's grille; this was followed shortly by a second round fired into the grille by the right rear gunner. The SUV then swerved to the left and received two more rounds in its grille fired by the left rear gunner before swerving back to the right and receiving a fifth round in the grille from the well gunner. One of these bullets went through the engine block and struck the driver, an Iraqi judge, in the leg, which forced him to bring his SUV to a stop at the side of the road. Although the Department of State authorized a US$2,500 payment to compensate the judge for his injury and the damage to his vehicle, emails written by DSS personnel also praised the controlled manner in which DynCorp handled the situation.[54]

Engagement distance[55]

The ideational theory of tactical violence predicts that the security personnel of PSCs that place strong emphasis on norms encouraging personal initiative, proactive use of force and an exclusive approach to security should tend to employ violence against suspected threats at greater distances than the security personnel of firms that do not place strong emphasis on these norms. On the assumption that the suspected threats encountered by various firms travel, on average, at the same speed, security personnel who behave in this manner again reduce the amount of time available for a suspected threat to alter its behaviour and attempt to convince the security personnel that it means them no harm before they engage the suspected threat with deadly force. This, in turn, means that security personnel who behave in this manner are more likely to kill or seriously injure a suspected threat during an incident than are security personnel who behave in a less violent manner.

This prediction was supported by the evidence in this case. Regardless of whether Blackwater's personnel fired their weapons immediately after observing a suspected threat or at a later stage of an incident, they tended to engage suspected threats at far greater average distances than their counterparts in DynCorp (Table 4.3).[56] For example, during the incidents where Blackwater's personnel fired immediately after observing a suspected threat, they engaged the suspected threats at an average distance of 126 metres. As mentioned earlier, DynCorp's personnel never initiated an incident by firing their weapons. When Blackwater's personnel fired their weapons during the second stage of an incident, they tended to do so when the suspected threat was, on average, 67 metres away, which is over twice as far as the average engagement distance of DynCorp's personnel (28 metres) during this stage of an incident. This is a particularly interesting finding because it suggests that DynCorp's personnel tended to refrain from firing their weapons during an early stage of an incident unless a suspected threat was very close and could therefore have easily caused a great deal of harm if it fired upon the private security team or detonated a bomb. Blackwater's personnel, on the other hand, were frequently willing to fire upon threats that were much farther away.

In addition, when Blackwater's personnel fired their weapons during the third stage of an incident, they tended to engage suspected threats at an average distance of 47 metres, while DynCorp's personnel tended to fire at suspected threats that were, on average, 38 metres away during this stage. Finally, Blackwater's personnel tended to fire their weapons at suspected threats that were an average of 35 metres away during the fourth stage of an incident, while DynCorp's personnel, in contrast, tended to fire their weapons at suspected threat that were, on average, 26 metres away during this stage. This is another particularly interesting finding since the fourth stage of an incident was usually the stage during which private security teams fired their lengthiest bursts of bullets in a final attempt to neutralize a suspected threat. Consequently, this finding suggests that Blackwater's personnel were not willing to let a suspected threat get as close to themselves or their clients as DynCorp's personnel were before using sufficient deadly force to ensure they neutralized it.

If one assumes that the suspected threats engaged by Blackwater's security teams approached the firm's personnel at approximately the same speed, on average, as those that approached DynCorp's security teams, the

Table 4.3 Mean engagement distances during first four stages of incidents

	First stage	Second stage	Third stage	Fourth stage
Blackwater	126 metres	67 metres	47 metres	35 metres
DynCorp	—	28 metres	38 metres	26 metres

tendency of Blackwater's personnel to engage suspected threats at greater distances reduced the amount of time available for suspected threats to alter their behaviour and attempt to convince the security personnel that they meant no harm. For example, during incidents where the firms' security teams chose to fire as their second behavioural response to a suspected threat, if a suspected threat was first observed when it was 100 metres away from a security team and traveled at the moderate speed of 50 kilometres per hour (14 metres per second), then it would have been afforded only two seconds to alter its behaviour before being fired upon by an average Blackwater security team but would have been afforded more than five seconds to alter its behaviour before being shot at by an average DynCorp team. Similarly, during incidents where the firms' security teams chose to fire as their third behavioural response to a suspected threat, a suspected threat travelling at this speed would, on average, have been afforded less than four seconds to alter its behaviour before being fired upon by a Blackwater security team, while, in contrast, the average DynCorp team would have afforded about a five-second grace period before firing their weapons. Finally, during incidents where the firms' security teams chose to fire as their fourth behavioural response to a suspected threat, a suspected threat travelling at this speed would have been afforded less than five seconds to alter its behaviour by the average Blackwater security team but would have been granted more than five seconds to alter its behaviour by the average DynCorp security team.

Although these time differences may seem small, they represent crucial extra seconds during which a suspected threat, particularly a civilian who intended no harm to a security team or its clients, could alter its behaviour and demonstrate that it did not in fact pose any danger to the security team or its clients. Therefore, by engaging suspected threats at considerably greater distances than their counterparts in DynCorp, Blackwater's personnel in effect denied suspected threats crucial time to alter their behaviour and attempt to avoid being fired upon.

As the theory predicts, by engaging suspected threats at much greater distances on average, Blackwater's security teams were more likely to kill or seriously injure a suspected threat during an incident than their counterparts in DynCorp. For instance, an analysis of incidents where Blackwater's security teams fired at suspected threats at distances exceeding the mean engagement distance of DynCorp's personnel during each of the first four stages of an incident indicates that Blackwater's personnel inflicted at least 39 deaths during relatively long-distance engagements.[57] It is important to note that this number may not reflect all of the deaths inflicted by the firm's personnel during relatively long-distance engagements because information on engagement distances is, unfortunately, not available for several of the firm's incidents. Any incident for which information on engagement distances was not available was not included in the analysis contained in this section. Regardless, since these 39 deaths represent 55 per cent of the 71 known deaths inflicted by Blackwater's personnel during the 2003 to 2009 period, it is clear that a substantial proportion of the total deaths inflicted by the firm's personnel during this period occurred during relatively long-distance engagements. Moreover, 18 out of the 38 known deaths of non-insurgent suspected threats inflicted by the firm's personnel (47 per cent) occurred during these incidents.

In a high-profile incident that took place on 7 February 2007, DDMs attached to a Blackwater team providing security for a meeting at the Iraqi Ministry of Justice's headquarters building in Baghdad shot and killed three armed Iraqi guards, whom the team wrongly assumed were insurgents, at a distance of 137 metres.[58] Just prior to the shooting, a guard named Nabras Mohammed Hadi, who was stationed on a balcony at the state-funded Iraqi Media Network building, apparently rose from a seated position while holding his AK-47 assault rifle and began shouting at drivers to remove their vehicles from a traffic circle located below him.[59] Within seconds, the Blackwater DDMs, who claimed they were fired upon by the guards, shot Hadi in the head.[60] Azhar Abdullah al-Maliki, another guard, crawled over to Hadi to offer assistance. While crawling, he was shielded from gunfire by a one-metre-high wall. But when he momentarily raised his head above the wall while attempting to drag Hadi's body to safety, a Blackwater DDM shot him in the neck.[61] The firm's personnel shot a third guard a few minutes later when he attempted to retrieve the other guards' weapons from the balcony.[62] An Iraqi government investigation into the incident concluded that the DDMs fired "without provocation".[63] In contrast, Anne E. Tyrrell, a Blackwater spokeswoman, argued that "This was absolutely a provoked incident" because the firm's snipers claimed to have come under "precision small-arms fire" and merely employed deadly force in self-defence.[64] Moreover, on 11 and 20 September 2005 two of the firm's PSDs initially fired at approaching cars when the vehicles were 75 and 65 metres away, respectively, which is far in excess of the average engagement distances of their counterparts in DynCorp.[65] Blackwater's employees ensured that these suspected threats could not harm their personnel or clients but they also killed the drivers of both vehicles.

Although members of a DynCorp's PSD shot and killed a man in an approaching Opel car during an incident in Baghdad on 24 January 2005, they issued non-violent warnings and refrained from firing their weapons until the victim was fewer than 15 metres away from their motorcade.[66] This team also failed to stop the suspected threat with their first two bursts of close-range fire. While they wounded the driver, he still managed to pass the rearmost vehicle in the convoy and swerve between that vehicle and the limousine in front of it. The team fired several more bullets at the driver, ultimately killing him with a bullet to the head. At that point, he was only a few metres away from the limousine containing the firm's clients.

An analysis of incidents where Blackwater's security teams engaged suspected threats with their weapons at distances exceeding the mean engagement distance of DynCorp's personnel, during each of the first four stages of an incident, indicated that Blackwater's personnel inflicted at least 53 serious injuries during relatively long-distance engagements. As was the case for the analysis of suspected deaths that were inflicted during relatively long-term engagements, this figure may not reflect all of the serious injuries inflicted by the firm's personnel during relatively long-distance engagements because any incident for which the engagement distances were not known was excluded from this analysis. Nevertheless, this result suggests that at least 43 per cent of the 122 known serious injuries inflicted by Blackwater's personnel during the 2003 to 2009 period occurred during relatively long-distance engagements. Moreover, 27 of the 64 non-insurgents (42 per cent) who were seriously injured by the firm's personnel suffered their injuries during these incidents. For example, on 18 October 2005, near an Iraqi police checkpoint in Baqubah, one of the firm's PSDs initially fired upon an approaching Toyota Land Cruiser at a distance of 75 metres, which forced the vehicle to change course away from the convoy but seriously injured the vehicle's driver.[67] Similarly, another of the firm's PSDs seriously injured one of the occupants of a car near an Iraqi National Guard checkpoint in Al-Hillah on 25 February 2005, when the team engaged that approaching vehicle at a distance of 75 metres.[68]

Number of bullets fired

The ideational theory of tactical violence predicts that the security personnel of PSCs that place strong emphasis on norms encouraging personal initiative, proactive use of force and an exclusive approach to security should tend to fire a greater number of bullets at suspected threats than the security personnel of firms that do not place strong emphasis on these norms. Since each bullet fired could, of course, hit a suspected threat, security personnel who behave in this manner are more likely to kill or seriously injure a suspected threat during an incident than are security personnel who behave in a less violent manner.

This prediction was supported. Blackwater's personnel were much more prone to firing multiple bullets toward a suspected threat when compared to their counterparts in DynCorp (Table 4.4). Blackwater's personnel fired

Table 4.4 Number of bullets fired

	Unknown	No bullets	1 bullet	2–5 bullets	6–20 bullets	21–50 bullets	Over 50 bullets
Blackwater	14 3.27%	86 20.09%	84 19.63%	153 35.75%	50 11.68%	14 3.27%	27 6.31%
DynCorp	5 6.41%	19 24.36%	27 34.62%	22 28.21%	3 3.85%	1 1.28%	1 1.28%

one bullet during 20 per cent of the violent incidents they were involved in, between two and five bullets during 36 per cent of these incidents, between six and 20 bullets during 12 per cent of these incidents, between 21 and 50 bullets during 3 per cent of these incidents, and more than 50 bullets during 6 per cent of these incidents. DynCorp, in contrast, fired one bullet during 35 per cent of the violent incidents they were involved in, between two and five bullets during 28 per cent of these incidents, between six and 20 bullets during 4 per cent of these incidents, between 21 and 50 bullets during 1 per cent of these incidents, and more than 50 bullets in another 1 per cent of these incidents.

The disparity in the number of bullets fired by the personnel of these firms is particularly pronounced in the upper firing categories, for Blackwater's personnel reported firing more than five bullets during 21 per cent of the violent incidents they were involved in, while, in contrast, their counterparts in DynCorp reported firing more than five bullets during only 6 per cent of the incidents they were involved in. Therefore, Blackwater's personnel were more than three times as likely to have fired more than five bullets during an incident as their counterparts in DynCorp. This disparity is even more pronounced in absolute terms, since Blackwater's personnel reported firing more than five bullets during 91 incidents while DynCorp's personnel reported doing so in only five incidents. From this it is clear that virtually all of the suspected threats encountered by DynCorp's security teams faced, at most, a single burst of small-arms fire or a series of single shots. Over a fifth of the suspected threats encountered by Blackwater's security teams, on the other hand, faced multiple bursts of small-arms fire and in almost half of these incidents faced a much larger number of bullets.

Some of the incidents where Blackwater's personnel fired in excess of 50 bullets at suspected threats saw the use of "hurricane barrages". This tactic involves firing hundreds of rounds of ammunition in several directions at the same time in a wild attempt to neutralize or, at least, temporarily suppress a suspected threat. Based on his first-hand observations of the firm's operations in Iraq, Robert Young Pelton argued that:

> If they do come under attack, Blackwater has a policy of using overwhelming firepower to break contact.... The team can strike back in response to an onslaught, forcing the attackers to seek cover long enough for the convoy to begin a safe retreat from the scene. Or if one of the vehicles is disabled, the contractors can ... hunker down in a defensible position to wait for an additional counterassault team to arrive with more firepower.[69]

Pelton went on to argue that "a typical Blackwater Mamba security convoy could, within moments, unleash upward of seven thousand bullets against an attacker".[70] Beckman's accounts of Blackwater security operations indicate that lack of communication between the members of a security team and between different teams contributed to this behaviour. As he put it, when team members saw one of their colleagues firing at a suspected threat, they would often "fire at whatever you were firing at", which is known as "dog piling" on a target, rather than delay their own use of deadly force and question why their colleagues were engaging the target in the first place.[71]

As the theory predicts, the tendency of Blackwater's personnel to fire comparatively large numbers of bullets at suspected threats contributed to the numerous deaths and serious injuries they inflicted in Iraq. They killed and seriously injured the vast majority of their victims during incidents where they fired more than five bullets at a suspected threat. The numbers are quiet dramatic. At least 58 of the 71 deaths (82 per cent) known to have been inflicted by Blackwater's personnel between 2003 and 2009 occurred during incidents where the firm's personnel fired more than five bullets at a suspected threat. Moreover, 31 out of the 38 known deaths of non-insurgent suspected threats inflicted by the firm's personnel (82 per cent) occurred during these incidents.

A typical incident of this sort occurred on 13 April 2005, as a Blackwater PSD en route from Karbala to Al-Hillah was approached by a white Kia car with four male passengers.[72] After issuing non-violent warnings, which were ignored, the team fired a series of bursts at the vehicle, totaling between 6 and 20 bullets, which caused the death of one of the passengers. The Department of State ultimately paid US$3,000 in condolence money to the family of this victim who, like the other passengers, was an unarmed civilian. In addition, on 2 February 2006, one of the firm's PSDs fired more than 50 bullets at an Iraqi taxi in Kirkuk and caused the death of one person in the taxi and an innocent bystander.[73] Furthermore, all but one of the incidents where the firm's personnel are known to have inflicted more than two deaths saw them fire more than 50 bullets at a suspected threat. The 17 deaths that occurred in Nisour Square demonstrated the harm that this especially violent form of behaviour could inflict upon civilians better than any other incident, but this was not an isolated case.[74] For example, another dramatic incident occurred on the morning of 2 May 2006.[75] Shortly after departing the Green Zone, a Blackwater TST en route to the Iraqi Ministry of Finance was attacked with an EFP as it passed in front of the Turkish embassy. The weapon, designed to defeat heavy tank armour, sliced through the firm's more modestly armoured Mamba like a hot knife through butter. Entering largely through the vehicle's bulletproof driver's-side window, the stream of molten metal almost completed severed the driver's right hand, destroyed one of the tactical commander's eyes, and peppered both turret gunners with multiple shards of shrapnel, all in a fraction of a second.

Upon hearing the blast, the three remaining crews quickly established a 360-degree defensive perimeter around the disabled vehicle by stopping all civilian traffic and popping coloured smoke canisters to mark the site. Meanwhile, the firm's medics tended to the wounded and other personnel destroyed radios and other sensitive equipment. Within minutes of the attack, an Iraqi ambulance approached the site at high speed, ignoring the smoke. Presuming that this could be a follow-on VBIED attack, three Blackwater personnel forced the ambulance driver to stop by firing between six and 20 bullets in short bursts at the ambulance's grille, tyres and windscreen. The driver, an Iraqi named Jasem Abed Sarhan, and his passenger fled from their vehicle but Sarhan later died of injuries sustained during the incident.[76] A US Army report on the incident stated that Blackwater's security personnel engaged in "uncontrolled small arms firing" when they spotted the ambulance, and speculated that they may have killed Sarhan in reprisal for the EFP strike.[77] Ambulances were, however, sometimes used by Iraqi insurgents to conduct follow-on attacks at the scene of IED/EFP strikes. It is, therefore, conceivable that the security team genuinely feared for their safety when they spotted Sarhan's approaching vehicle. A few minutes later, Blackwater Little Bird helicopters arrived to transport the team's two most severely wounded personnel to hospital.

Turning to DynCorp, 10 out of the 11 total deaths inflicted by that firm's personnel occurred during incidents where they fired more than five bullets. For example, on 20 June 2005 in Kirkuk, during the sole incident where this firm's personnel fired more than 50 bullets toward a suspected threat, which was also the sole incident where the firm's personnel killed more than one person, the PSD involved faced a truly life-or-death situation. Indeed, the firm's personnel only responded with voluminous firepower after one of their vehicles was disabled by an IED and they were attacked by a party of at least eight insurgents.[78]

The pattern of the serious injuries inflicted by each firm's personnel is quite similar, since Blackwater's personnel inflicted at least 93 out of the 122 known serious injuries (76 per cent) attributed to their small-arms fire during the 2003 to 2009 period during incidents where they fired more than five bullets at a suspected threat. Moreover, 43 of the 64 non-insurgents (67 per cent) who were seriously injured by the firm's personnel suffered their injuries during these incidents. For example, three members of one of the firm's PSDs fired a total of 13 bullets at the grille and windscreen of an approaching ambulance during an incident near the Iraqi Ministry of Health's headquarters on 12 August 2006, which seriously injured the vehicle's driver and two medics.[79] Another of the firm's PSDs fired a similar number of bullets at a blue car they suspected of being a VBIED as it approached an Iraqi National Guard checkpoint in Al-Hillah on 25 February 2005.[80] After firing two bullets into the vehicle's grille, to no discernible effect, a team member fired approximately 10 rounds into its windscreen. An Iraqi man then rolled out of the driver's side door with apparent injuries to his thigh and stomach. Likewise, during an incident in Baghdad on 19 February 2007, one of the firm's TSTs fired a reported 32 bullets at an approaching gray car they suspected of being a VBIED.[81] After the front and rear turret gunners of a Mamba each fired three-round bursts at the car's grille, with no discernible effect, they each fired sustained, 10-round bursts directly at the driver. Another team member simultaneously fired another six rounds into the passenger compartment. After inflicting life-threatening injuries on the driver, the convoy proceeded to their destination.

All of the incidents where Blackwater's personnel injured four or more people saw them fire more than 50 bullets at a suspected threat. The Nisour Square incident, once again, saw the most serious injuries of any incident where the firm fired more than 50 bullets, with 24 serious injuries reported.[82] In contrast, DynCorp's personnel only fired five bullets during one of the incidents where they inflicted serious but non-fatal injuries on a suspected threat, and they fired an unknown number of bullets during the other incident of this kind.[83]

Propensity to abandon the victims of violence

The ideational theory of tactical violence predicts that the security personnel of PSCs that place strong emphasis on norms encouraging personal initiative, proactive use of force and an exclusive approach to security should tend to abandon a greater proportion of the victims they produce through their use of violence, rather than offer them assistance, than the security personnel of firms that do not place strong emphasis on these norms. Since the security personnel of these firms have been strongly encouraged to care only about the security of their own colleagues and clients, they should feel no obligation to assist any insurgents, civilians or other actors that they harm through their use of violence. Moreover, since abandoning wounded victims could allow their injuries to worsen or even allow them to die, security personnel who behave in this manner are more likely to kill or seriously injure a suspected threat during an incident than security personnel who behave in a less violent manner.

This prediction was supported by the behaviour exhibited by both firms' personnel. Blackwater's personnel consistently abandoned the suspected threats they used violence against by quickly driving away from the locations of violent incidents. Blackwater's incident reports indicate that the firm's personnel abandoned the suspected threats they attacked about 88 per cent of the time, which is a considerably higher rate of abandonment than DynCorp's post-attack abandonment rate of 68 per cent (Table 4.5). Moreover, virtually all of the incidents where Blackwater's personnel did not abandon a suspected threat were incidents where the suspected threat chose to flee the location of the incident. In contrast, during incidents where Blackwater's personnel could have decided to remain on-site and offer assistance to a suspected threat that that had stopped moving

Table 4.5 Victim abandonment rate

	Remained at location of incident until assistance provided to victim(s)	Left location of incident before assistance could be provided to victim(s)*
Blackwater	42 11.90%	311 88.10%
DynCorp	19 31.67%	41 68.33%

Note
* The firms' personnel are not deemed to have abandoned their victims if their victims chose to leave the location of the incident prior to the security team's departure.

after being fired upon, the firm's personnel almost always chose to abandon the suspected threat and drive away.

For example, a declassified email written by the Department of State's Regional Security Officer for the city of Al-Hillah confirmed that a Blackwater security detail not only fatally shot a civilian Iraqi father of six in the chest on 25 June 2005 but also failed to offer assistance or promptly report this incident to the Department of State.[84] Prince later told a Congressional committee that:

> I believe what happened, it was a car bomb or a potential car bomb had rapidly approached the convoy. I believe our guys shot rounds at the car, not at the driver, to warn them off. One of those rounds, as I understand, penetrated through the far side of the car, ricocheted, and injured that innocent or killed that innocent man.[85]

A Department of State regional security officer pressured the firm to issue a US$5,000 condolence payment to the victim's family.[86]

A particularly controversial incident occurred on 24 October 2005, as two of the firm's security convoys were leaving the Provincial Hall in Mosul.[87] While exiting the venue, members of the TST spotted a gold car attempting to cross through a road junction in front of one of the firm's PSDs. Fearing that the driver of the car might attempt to trap the PSD in the intersection or detonate a VBIED, the TST's turret gunner disabled the car with a burst of rifle fire. The vehicle's driver was unhurt but one of the bullets ricocheted and struck a pedestrian named Sebhan Ahmed, who was standing on a nearby traffic median, in the head and caused him to collapse to the ground.[88] Members of the TST witnessed this but did not stop or offer assistance to the innocent bystander, who died for simply being in the wrong place at the wrong time. In the shooter's words, "While proceeding through the intersection I noticed that there was a 1 Local National that appeared to be fatally wounded. Our motorcade proceeded through and made it back to FOB Courage safe and sound".[89] This statement reflects the team member's exclusive concern with the safety of himself and his colleagues.

Another controversial incident occurred on 24 September 2006, as a Blackwater PSD in Al-Hillah engaged in a "counter flowing" maneuver, which involved driving approximately 70 kilometres per hour on the wrong side of a road directly toward oncoming traffic.[90] An Iraqi driver lost control of his Opel while attempting to avoid a head-on collision with the firm's lead vehicle, locked the breaks, skidded into the convoy's armoured limousine, spun 180 degrees as a result of the impact with the armoured GMC Suburban, and then crashed into a telephone pole. Despite stopping to evacuate the Suburban, which was rendered inoperable when its airbags deployed during the crash, and destroy the vehicle's radio, and despite observing the Opel becoming engulfed in a "ball of flames", the security team chose to abandon their victim to the inferno.[91]

In an undated account, Beckman recalled employing a pitting maneuver to jack-knife a tractor-trailer he suspected of being a gigantic VBIED on an Iraqi highway.[92] He considered this maneuver to have been very effective because the truck was almost immediately disabled. However, jack-knifing the civilian vehicle not only severely injured its driver but also posed a considerable danger to other drivers on the highway, who could have been run over by the out-of-control truck, crashed into it, or, had the truck actually held an IED, been hurt or killed by an explosion. Beckman's account did not say whether this occurred since his security team rapidly sped away from the disabled truck. His account also failed to state whether the truck actually contained an IED but, given that he did not recount seeing an explosion when the truck crashed, it is quite possible that he attacked and then abandoned an innocent civilian driver. Rather than dwell on his probable error, Beckman noted that the "only problem" with jack-knifing the truck was that "we got stuck to the side of the fender of the truck and almost got drug off the road with it".[93] The firm's personnel also abandoned the three Iraqi guards they shot on 7 February 2007, repeatedly mocked an Iraqi army captain who attempted to speak with the team's commander, and employed smoke grenades to mask their escape and avoid being detained by Iraqi security forces.[94] A Blackwater TST also employed smoke grenades to help mask their exit from Nisour Square on 16 September 2007, where they left behind dozens of dead and seriously injured victims.[95] The firm's use of smoke grenades complicated the Iraqi government's rescue, recovery and treatment efforts by making it difficult for would-be rescuers to locate some of the victims. As a result, the firm's use of smoke in Nisour Square may have contributed to further civilian deaths and certainly prolonged the suffering of those they injured.

One of the firm's employees captured the behaviour of his colleagues quite well when he stated that "We shot to kill and didn't stop to check a pulse".[96] The data contained in the PSCVID lend considerable support to this statement. For example, the firm's personnel abandoned at least 59 out of the 71 people (83 per cent) that they are known to have killed during their security operations. Moreover, 35 out of the 38 known deaths of non-insurgent suspected threats inflicted by the firm's personnel (92 per cent) occurred during these incidents. Likewise, the firm's personnel abandoned at least 96 out of the 122 people (at least 79 per cent) that they are known to have shot and seriously injured during their security operations. Furthermore, 46 of the 64 non-insurgents (72 per cent) who were seriously injured by the firm's personnel suffered their injuries during these incidents. Finally, although DynCorp's security teams did not abandon the people they shot at as often as their counterparts in Blackwater, they abandoned their victims during all four of the incidents where their actions resulted in one or more deaths.[97]

Blackwater's incident reports indicate that its security teams usually contained at least one medic trained to deal with combat-related traumatic injuries, such as those produced by shrapnel and bullets, and that these medics could provide competent on-site assistance to severely injured patients.[98] For example, following an incident on 29 August 2005, the firm's personnel demonstrated that they could provide helpful on-site medical assistance to their victims when one of the team's medics applied a trauma dressing to a bleeding head wound suffered by an Iraqi civilian who was shot while approaching one of the firm's convoys.[99] This intervention stopped the bleeding and allowed the victim to drive himself home. The firm's personnel therefore likely could have offered life-saving assistance to many of the victims they chose to abandon.

Although it is difficult to determine precisely how many of the victims of Blackwater's violence would have survived if they had received prompt medical attention, accounts of the firm's incidents suggest that the behaviour of its security personnel likely sealed the fate of several people. For example, the driver of a car who was shot by a Blackwater PSD on Highway 4 between Kirkuk and Sulaymaniyah on 21 April 2005 did not immediately die: according to the firm's incident reports, he was observed gradually decelerating before stopping on the side of the road.[100] The incident reports provide few other details about his fate but he apparently succumbed to his wounds later that day.

In addition, during an incident on 24 October 2005, one of the firm's PSDs shot and quickly abandoned Munther Kadhum Abid Ali, the driver of a Daewoo Prince in Al-Hillah.[101] Ali, a 63-year-old elementary school teacher, reportedly wove around other civilian vehicles and braved several bursts of fire while accelerating toward the convoy before being shot in the abdomen. According the firm's incident reports and accounts from Iraqi eyewitnesses, the driver was alive, though "struggling for life", when the team left the area. He died of his injuries while being driven to a hospital by an Iraqi bystander. The Department of State paid US$5,000 in condolence money to his son.[102]

Furthermore, a Blackwater security team likely injured numerous people on 28 November 2005, when they intentionally pitted, rammed or otherwise struck six Iraqi vehicles while transporting a client on a short journey to the Iraqi Ministry of Oil's headquarters, and then proceeded to strike a further 12 vehicles on the way back to their compound.[103] A Blackwater employee who participated in this mission reported that the security convoy's commander "openly admitted giving clear direction to the primary driver to conduct these acts of random negligence for no apparent reason".[104] While speeding to rescue a PSD that had been attacked by insurgents, Beckman's QRF first fired a "stream" of bullets at the driver of a civilian pickup truck that was travelling though a traffic circle ahead of Beckman's vehicle.[105] When the driver failed to stop, Beckman rammed the truck with his HMMWV, causing it to break in half just behind the driver's seat.[106] Excited exclamations along the lines of "holy shit, did you see that hit?" reportedly followed from other Blackwater personnel as they quickly left what remained of the truck and its driver in their wake. An employed named Christopher Neidrich, who died in an insurgent attack on 5 June 2004, conveyed the firm's general lack of concern about the people they injured or killed during their security operations when he told friends that he could not remember "the last time I drove slow, stopped for a light, or stop sign, or even a person".[107] Moreover, it is plausible that at least some of the 17 deaths that resulted from the firm's actions during the Nisour Square incident could have been prevented if the security team involved had remained on-site to reassess the situation, determine whether they had severely injured any civilians and ensure that those victims received medical attention. Some of the victims died long after the shooting stopped.[108] For example, 10-year-old Ali Hafeez was struck in the head by one of the 30 bullets fired at his father's car that day but his heart continued to beat. He died in hospital an hour later.[109] Ali Khalil, a 54-year-old blacksmith and father of six children, likewise initially survived multiple bullet wounds but died in hospital later that day.[110] Mahdi Sahib, a taxi driver who supported a family of 10, died from internal bleeding over three hours after the attack.[111] It is, of course, possible that these victims would have died anyway, but they likely would have lost considerably less blood before reaching a hospital if they had received prompt treatment from the firm's medics.

Nevertheless, the members of Raven 23, the TST involved in the incident, not only refrained from offering any assistance but also shot at the civilians in the square that attempted to do so.[112] Moreover, Raven 23's turret gunners exacerbated the situation by continuing to fire at civilian vehicles as they were fleeing Nisour Square.[113] Ridgeway, one of the shooters, later confessed that he fired multiple rounds from his M4 carbine into the roof of a Chevrolet Celebrity car as his convoy passed by on its way out of the traffic circle. These rounds inflicted disfiguring and life-threatening injuries on Abdul Wahab Abdul Qadar as they passed through his shoulders, arms and legs. Finally, DynCorp's personnel abandoned their victim in one of the reported incidents where they seriously injured someone in Iraq; however, they did so only after observing the victim stopping his vehicle and getting out to inspect it for damage, which led them to believe that he had not been seriously harmed.[114]

Broad predictions regarding the relationship between military culture, tactical behaviour and security outcomes

The central claims of the ideational theory of tactical violence are that the behavioural norms that make up a PSC's military culture have a strong influence on the degree of violence employed by that firm's personnel and that, in turn, the degree of violence employed by these personnel strongly affects two security outcomes. These include, first, the degree of security enjoyed by the people under the firm's protection, such as the firm's personnel and clients, and, second, the degree of security enjoyed by other actors in the firm's operating environment, such as insurgents, civilians, the personnel of other PSCs and the members of state-based security and military forces.

The theory predicts that if the employees of a PSC tend to employ a great deal of violence during their security operations then they and the clients under their protection should suffer a lower casualty rate than their counterparts in firms that behave in a less violent manner. It also predicts that if the employees of a PSC tend to employ a great deal of violence during their security operations then they should kill and seriously injure a greater number of suspected threats and innocent bystanders than the security personnel of firms that behave in a less violent manner.

This chapter largely focused on the second prediction and demonstrated that Blackwater's military culture motivated its personnel to fire upon suspected threats more quickly, at greater distances and with a greater number of bullets and to abandon the people they shot at more readily when compared to DynCorp's personnel, who maintained a military culture that encouraged far less violent behaviour. These actions, in turn, contributed to the significant disparity in the number of deaths and serious injuries inflicted by these firms during the Iraq War. Taking this into account, this prediction was supported by the empirical evidence in this case.

Alternative explanations for the disparate number of violent incidents, deaths and serious injuries involving Blackwater and DynCorp personnel

A number of alternative explanations can be put forward to try to account for the disparity in the number of violent incidents, deaths and serious injuries involving Blackwater and DynCorp personnel during the 2003 to 2009 period of the Iraq War. For instance, since Blackwater fielded a

Military culture and threat casualties 119

larger security force during this period than DynCorp did, it is reasonable to assume that Blackwater's personnel encountered a greater number of suspected threats and were, consequently, forced to use violence more often than their counterparts in DynCorp. However, the available data tell a different story. The Department of State and the Broadcasting Board of Governors Office of the Inspector General compiled information on the number of Blackwater and DynCorp personnel assigned to conduct security operations in Iraq in 2005.[115] During this year, Blackwater's force of 390 security personnel was involved in 210 incidents where at least one employee used violence against a suspected threat, for an average of 0.54 such incidents per employee. During the same year, DynCorp's force of 157 security personnel was involved in 31 incidents where at least one employee used violence, for an average of 0.19 such incidents per employee. From this it is clear that, irrespective of the relative size of the firms' security forces, Blackwater's personnel were, on a per-employee basis, almost three times more likely to fire their weapons than their counterparts in DynCorp.

Promoting a somewhat similar alternative explanation, Prince argued that his personnel killed and seriously injured more people than their counterparts in other firms because they were attacked far more often than any other private security personnel and were, again, forced to employ violence against a much greater number of deadly threats.[116] Prince conveyed his views during a hearing before the House Committee on Oversight and Government Reform in October 2007, where he told the assembled members of Congress that much of the harm inflicted by his personnel was unavoidable because they were attacked almost every day and simply had to defend themselves:

> We don't even record all the times that our guys receive fire. The vehicles get shot at on a daily basis, multiple times a day.... An incident occurs typically when our men fear for their life. They are not able to extract themselves from the situation. They have to use sufficient defensive fire to off the X, to get off that place where the bad guys have tried to kill Americans that day.[117]

In written testimony to the committee, Prince further argued that:

> The areas of Iraq in which we operate are particularly dangerous and challenging. Blackwater personnel are subject to regular attacks by terrorists and other nefarious forces within Iraq. We are the targets of the same ruthless enemies that have killed more than 3,800 American military personnel and thousands of innocent Iraqis.[118]

This explanation is certainly reasonable, given that Blackwater's personnel were involved in a far greater number of violent incidents (428) than their counterparts in DynCorp (78) during the 2003 to 2009 period of the Iraq War. Moreover, Blackwater's personnel were physically attacked by insurgents during 118 of these incidents and it is therefore reasonable to conclude that, at least at times, they needed to use deadly force to neutralize or drive off an armed, unambiguous deadly threat to themselves and their clients. However, the records contained in the PSCVID indicate that Blackwater's personnel did not use violence at all during a majority (52 per cent) of the incidents where they encountered insurgents. For example, during an incident in the vicinity of Habbaniyah on 16 March 2004, a Blackwater team immediately fled from a VBIED attack rather than stop and possibly engage any nearby insurgent gunmen.[119] In contrast, the firm's personnel employed violence during 99 per cent of the violent incidents where they encountered unarmed civilians. In addition, the records also indicate that the firm's personnel reported employing violence *preemptively* in 70 of the violent incidents they were involved in. In other words, Blackwater's personnel usually employed violence before they had been fired upon or otherwise attacked by a suspected threat. Furthermore, according to the records, the firm's personnel were far less likely to employ violence preemptively when facing insurgents, since they did so in only 10 per cent of these incidents, than against non-insurgents, since they used preemptive violence in 99 per cent of these incidents. To highlight one of many dozens of examples, a Blackwater PSD preemptively fired approximately 50 rounds at a civilian vehicle in Baghdad on 12 December 2005, injuring an innocent civilian bystander in the process.[120]

Moreover, since insurgents were involved in only 118 of the 428 violent incidents that Blackwater's personnel took part in, this means that 72 per cent of the suspected threats encountered by the firm were non-insurgents. For example, a Blackwater TST shot and killed the civilian driver of an approaching pickup truck while en route to a USAID compound in Erbil on 1 November 2005, after he failed to heed non-violent warnings and continued to approach the PSD they were protecting.[121] Likewise, one of the firm's PSDs inflicted an unknown number of injuries during an incident in Baghdad on 25 February 2005, when its follow vehicle rammed and caused "a significant amount of damage to the right front quarter panel and driver side door area" of a civilian car that attempted to approach the convoy's limousine.[122]

Beyond this, 46 per cent of the incidents where Blackwater's personnel killed someone and 50 per cent of the incidents where they seriously injured someone involved non-insurgents. Taken together, these data suggest that Blackwater's employees not only inflicted a great deal of harm during the Iraq War but also inflicted much of this harm upon non-insurgents who posed little or no threat to the firm or its clients. In other words, Blackwater's personnel chose to inflict a great deal of unnecessary harm during their security operations in Iraq.

Other commentators have argued that Blackwater's personnel inflicted more deaths and serious injuries than their counterparts in DynCorp because they were undisciplined and were granted too much autonomy over how they conducted their security operations. One of the proponents of this view, Steve Fainaru, argued that the Department of State allowed Blackwater's personnel "to do whatever [they] ... pleased" during their security operations.[123] Moreover, commentators ranging from Fainaru and Jeremy Scahill to members of the US Congress have argued that the 24 December 2006 shooting of one of the Iraqi vice president's bodyguards by an intoxicated off-duty Blackwater employee indicated that its employees lacked discipline, as did the firm's personnel records, which note that it fired numerous employees for such offenses as "Drug and Alcohol Violations", "Inappropriate/Lewd Conduct", "Insubordination", "Aggressive/Violent Behaviour", and "Weapons Related Incidents".[124]

These alternative explanations are quite reasonable, and it is likely that at least some of Blackwater's personnel did, indeed, lack discipline or feel that they should be able to operate with complete autonomy. However, both Blackwater and DynCorp tended to recruit experienced veterans of Western military or police forces for their mobile security operations, who should not, as a group, be prone to ignoring directives or demonstrating ill-discipline during military-like operations, at least in the absence of encouragement.[125] Moreover, since both firms operated under the Department of State's rules of engagement for private security operations in Iraq, there is no reason to presume that Blackwater's personnel were granted greater autonomy by their primary client than their counterparts in DynCorp.[126] Rather, the evidence presented in this book suggests that Blackwater's military culture motivated its personnel to regularly exceed the constraints that the Department of State attempted to place on their behaviour.

Of even greater importance is the point that if these explanations are valid, Blackwater's security teams should not have exhibited clear patterns of behaviour since it is implausible that each undisciplined, autonomous team would decide, on its own, to behave in a fairly consistent way during each of their security operations and also behave in a way that is fairly consistent with the behaviour of the firm's other teams. In fact, as this book makes clear, precisely the opposite occurred in that the behaviour of Blackwater's security teams fell into clear patterns that are distinct from those demonstrated by their counterparts in DynCorp. Specifically, Blackwater's security teams tended to attack suspected threats more quickly, at greater distances and with a greater number of bullets and were also considerably more likely to abandon the people they used violence against when compared to DynCorp's personnel. This suggests that a characteristic that differed between the two firms, such as their particular military cultures, had a significant influence on the behaviour of their personnel.

Furthermore, given that Blackwater and DynCorp had different primary operating areas and also that Blackwater's personnel had access to a unique type of equipment – helicopters – that they used in several incidents to inflict harm on suspected threats, it is possible to question whether these factors may have skewed the results of this study. A more tightly controlled analysis that focuses exclusively on operations carried out by the firms' ground teams in a single city – Baghdad – should help address this concern. Blackwater's ground teams were involved in 241 violent incidents in this city and they utilized violence during 202 of these incidents, killed at least 42 people and seriously injured at least 85 people. DynCorp's ground teams, for their part, were involved in 54 violent incidents in Baghdad and they used violence during 40 of these incidents, killed only three people and did not seriously injure anyone.

The results of this analysis do not perfectly mirror those of the broader study, but the same trends in the firms' tactical behaviour and the results of this behaviour are readily apparent. With respect to the firms' engagement times, Blackwater's ground personnel in Baghdad fired their weapons as their first behavioural response during 8 per cent of the incidents where they used violence and fired their weapons as their second behavioural response during 32 per cent of these incidents. As indicated by the results of the broader study, DynCorp's personnel were more passive, since they never fired their weapons as their first response to a suspected threat and fired their weapons as their second response during just 23 per cent of the incidents where they used violence at some point. Blackwater's personnel inflicted at least 38 of the 42 deaths (90 per cent) during the incidents where they fired relatively quickly and inflicted at least 72 of the 85 serious injuries (85 per cent) during these incidents. DynCorp's personnel inflicted two out of the three deaths (67 per cent) during these incidents.

Blackwater's ground teams in Baghdad tended to attack firms at greater average distances than their counterparts in DynCorp. They employed deadly force at an average engagement distance of 86 metres during the first stage of an incident, 61 metres during the second stage, 51 metres during the third stage, and 31 metres during the fourth stage. DynCorp's personnel, in contrast, employed deadly force when their targets were an average of 28 metres away during the second stage of an incident, 38 metres away during the third stage, and 24 metres away during the fourth stage. Therefore, as indicated by the results of the broader study, it appears that Blackwater's ground personnel in Baghdad were not willing to let a suspected threat get as close to themselves or their clients as DynCorp's personnel were before using sufficient deadly force to neutralize it. Blackwater's personnel inflicted at least 16 of the 42 deaths (38 per cent) and at least 25 of the 85 serious injuries (29 per cent) during incidents where they fired at suspected threats at distances exceeding the mean engagement distance of DynCorp's personnel, during each of the first four stages of an incident. As with the broader study, it is important to note that these figures probably do not reflect all of the casualties inflicted by Blackwater's personnel during relatively long-distance engagements because information on engagement distances is, unfortunately, not available for several of the firm's ground-based incidents in Baghdad.

As was the case in the broader study, Blackwater's ground teams in Baghdad were more likely to fire relatively large numbers of bullets during their operations. They fired more than five bullets during 18 per cent of their incidents. DynCorp's more passive personnel, in contrast, fired more than five bullets in just 6 per cent of their incidents. Blackwater's ground teams in this city inflicted at least 34 of the 42 deaths (81 per cent) and at least 60 of the 85 serious injuries (71 per cent) during incidents where they fired more than five bullets. DynCorp's personnel inflicted two out of the three deaths (67 per cent) during these incidents.

Blackwater's ground teams in Baghdad were, once again, more likely to abandon the people they used violence against when compared to their counterparts in DynCorp. Blackwater's ground personnel abandoned 90 per cent of their victims in this city while DynCorp's ground personnel only abandoned 63 per cent of their victims. Blackwater's personnel abandoned at least 37 of the 42 people they are known to have killed (88 per cent) and at least 72 of the 85 people they are known to have seriously injured (85 per cent) in Baghdad. DynCorp's personnel abandoned all three of the people they killed in this city. As with the broader study, all of the results of this more tightly controlled analysis support the theory's specific predictions regarding the relationship between a firm's military culture and the tactical behaviour exhibited by its personnel as well as its broad prediction regarding the relationship between their tactical behaviour and the casualties they inflicted during their security operations.

Finally, given that many of the accounts of incidents contained in the PSCVID are based, at least in part, on information reported by the security personnel involved, it is possible to question whether the evidence discussed in this book reflects the actual behaviour exhibited by these personnel. For instance, it is possible that Blackwater's personnel simply reported a greater proportion of the violent incidents they were involved in than their counterparts in DynCorp. If true, this would mean that DynCorp's personnel actually used violence more often than their records indicate. This would also mean that the disparity in the use of violence by both firms' employees was, in reality, smaller than the information contained in the PSCVID indicates. In the absence of an equally comprehensive alternative source of information on the activities of these firms in Iraq, these concerns cannot be fully ruled out. However, there are multiple reasons to believe that the data contained in the PSCVID present an accurate account of the behaviour exhibited by these firms' personnel.

Of perhaps greatest importance, the firms' own records constitute merely one of several sources of information on the incidents contained in the PSCVID. As discussed in the introductory chapter of this book, this dataset is based not only on the incident reports produced by the firms involved but also incident reports produced by US military units in Iraq, scholarly books and articles, news media accounts, and reports produced by US House and Senate committees, US government departments and agencies, research institutes and non-governmental organizations. The incidents where the firms' personnel inflicted or suffered casualties, which are the primary focus of this book, were particularly likely to have been discussed in a range of independent data sources, such as news reports filed by Iraq-based correspondents for the *Washington Post* and the *New York Times* and detailed investigative reports produced by the Department of State's DSS. Therefore, the most important incidents discussed in this book also tended to be the best-corroborated.

In addition, internal Department of State documents make clear that, at least in the opinion of the DSS, which monitored the activities of both firms in Iraq, DynCorp's personnel behaved in a relatively passive manner. For example, in an email to his colleagues, John Hislop, the DSS Special Agent in charge of monitoring DynCorp's primary area of operations in 2007, the cities of Erbil and Kirkuk, wrote:

> As we all know PSD members operate under the same EOF (Escalation of Force) procedures through out theatre; however operating in Baghdad and here in the North are two separate animals. The PSD teams that drive in Irbil and Kirkuk operate in a manner that is quite docile compared to elsewhere in Iraq.[127]

Hislop's statements are enlightening because they indicate that, although all of the security personnel that protected Department of State personnel and facilities in Iraq operated under a common set of rules of engagement, the security personnel employed by the Baghdad-based firm, Blackwater, clearly behaved in a more violent manner than their counterparts in DynCorp. This, again, suggests that a characteristic that differed between these firms had a significant influence on the behaviour of their personnel. Finally, since Blackwater was subjected to considerably more criticism than DynCorp from prominent news organizations and the governments of the United States and Iraq, it had a much stronger incentive to under-report uses of violence by its personnel. Therefore, if anything, the PSCVID might underplay the actual disparity in the use of violence by these firms. Ultimately, no evidence indicates that the data contained in the PSCVID present an inaccurate account of the use of violence by either firm during the Iraq War.

Conclusion

All of the predictions put forward by the ideational theory of tactical violence were supported by the available evidence on the firms' private

Table 4.6 Support for the predictions of the ideational theory of tactical violence

The security personnel of PSCs that place strong emphasis on norms encouraging personal initiative, proactive use of force and an exclusive approach to security should tend to employ violence more quickly after observing a suspected threat than the security personnel of firms that do not place strong emphasis on these norms.	Supported
The security personnel of PSCs that place strong emphasis on norms encouraging personal initiative, proactive use of force and an exclusive approach to security should tend to employ violence against suspected threats at greater distances than the security personnel of firms that do not place strong emphasis on these norms.	Supported
The security personnel of PSCs that place strong emphasis on norms encouraging personal initiative, proactive use of force and an exclusive approach to security should tend to fire a greater number of bullets at suspected threats than the security personnel of firms that do not place strong emphasis on these norms.	Supported
The security personnel of PSCs that place strong emphasis on norms encouraging personal initiative, proactive use of force and an exclusive approach to security should tend to abandon a greater proportion of the victims they produce through their use of violence, rather than offer them assistance, when compared to the security personnel of firms that do not place strong emphasis on these norms.	Supported
The security personnel of PSCs that tend to employ a great deal of violence during their security operations should kill and seriously injure a greater number of suspected threats and innocent bystanders than their counterparts in firms that behave in a less violent manner.	Supported

security operations during the Iraq War (as shown in Table 4.6). As predicted, Blackwater's personnel placed strong emphasis on norms encouraging personal initiative, proactive use of force and an exclusive approach to security and also tended to fire upon suspected threats more quickly, at greater distances and with a greater number of bullets and to more readily abandon the people they shot at when compared to DynCorp's personnel, who maintained a military culture that encouraged far less violent behaviour. Moreover, as predicted, Blackwater's comparatively violent behaviour resulted in the death or serious injury of a comparatively large number of suspected threats during their security operations. Chapters 6 and 7 discussed the legal, political and corporate implications of these findings as well as their implications for the use and development of private armed forces.

Notes

1 House Committee on Oversight and Government Reform, "Hearing on Blackwater USA", 134.
2 Ibid.
3 Ibid.
4 Laguna, *You Have to Live Hard*, Loc. 340–342.
5 Beckman, *Blackwater from the Inside Out*, Loc. 732–738.
6 Scahill, *Blackwater*, 1st edn, 72–73; Miller, *Blood Money*, 169–171; Palmer, "Meeting".
7 Scahill, *Blackwater*, 1st edn, 72–73; Miller, *Blood Money*, 169–171.
8 Krugman, "Hired Gun Fetish"; Fainaru, *Big Boy Rules*, 173–175; Simons, *Master of War*, 163; Welch, "Fragmented Power", 354; Scahill, *Blackwater*, 2nd edn, 11–12; Fainaru, "Guards in Iraq"; Fainaru and al-Izzi, "US Security Contractors"; Blackwater, PSD Incident Report, 24 May 2007; Prince, *Civilian Warriors*, 214.
9 Blackwater, PSD Incident Report, 24 May 2007.
10 Ibid.
11 Ibid.
12 Welch, "Fragmented Power", 354; Krugman, "Hired Gun Fetish"; Fainaru and al-Izzi, "US Security Contractors".
13 Human Rights First, "Private Security Contractors", 1; House Committee on Oversight and Government Reform, "Hearing on Blackwater USA", 29; Uesseler, *Servants of War*, 88; US Department of State and the Broadcasting Board of Governors Office of the Inspector General, "Status of the Panel", 3; Dunning, "Heroes or Mercenaries?", 9; Burke *et al.*, "Second Amended Complaint", 3 and 8; Dunigan, *Victory for Hire*, 71; Ciralsky, "Tycoon"; Simons, *Master of War*, 261; Fainaru, *Big Boy Rules*, 177.
14 Fainaru, *Big Boy Rules*, 177; US Department of Justice, "Transcript", 2; Prince, *Civilian Warriors*, 208.
15 Fainaru, *Big Boy Rules*, 177; Simons, *Master of War*, 261; Welch, "Fragmented Power", 355; US Department of State, "Blackwater Personnel".
16 Fainaru, *Big Boy Rules*, 177 and 261; Simons, *Master of War*, 176; Human Rights First, "Private Security Contractors", 1; Thurner, "Drowning in Blackwater", 64; US Department of Justice, "Transcript", 2; Scahill, *Blackwater*, 2nd edn, 3; US Department of State, "Blackwater Personnel".
17 Fainaru, *Big Boy Rules*, 177; House Committee on Oversight and Government Reform, "Hearing on Blackwater USA", 29; US Department of State and the Broadcasting Board of Governors Office of the Inspector General, "Status of the Panel", 3; Simons, *Master of War*, 176 and 261; Welch, "Fragmented Power", 355; US Department of Justice, "Transcript", 2–3.
18 House Committee on Oversight and Government Reform, "Hearing on Blackwater USA", 29; Uesseler, *Servants of War*, 88.
19 Karadsheh and Duke, "Blackwater Incident Witness"; Fainaru, *Big Boy Rules*, 177; Cotton *et al.*, *Hired Guns*, 25–26; Simons, *Master of War*, 176 and 261; Welch, "Fragmented Power", 355; Thurner, "Drowning in Blackwater", 64–65; US Department of Justice, "Transcript", 2–3; Scahill, *Blackwater*, 2nd edn, 5 and 32–33; US Department of State, "Blackwater Personnel".
20 Fainaru, *Big Boy Rules*, 177; Uesseler, *Servants of War*, 88.
21 Fainaru, *Big Boy Rules*, 178; House Committee on Oversight and Government Reform, "Hearing on Blackwater USA", 29; Simons, *Master of War*, 261; Welch, "Fragmented Power", 355; US Department of Justice, "Transcript", 2–3.
22 Williams, "Iraqis Angered"; Fainaru, *Big Boy Rules*, 178; Dunning, "Heroes or Mercenaries?", 9; Cotton *et al.*, *Hired Guns*, 25–26; Simons, *Master of War*, 176

and 262; Thurner, "Drowning in Blackwater", 64–65; Scahill, *Blackwater*, 2nd edn, 4–5.
23 Raghavan, "Tracing the Paths"; Fainaru, *Big Boy Rules*, 178; Scahill, *Blackwater*, 2nd edn, 6–7.
24 Scahill, *Blackwater*, 2nd edn, 7; Sengupta, "The Real Story".
25 Fainaru, *Big Boy Rules*, 178; Beckman, *Blackwater from the Inside Out*, Loc. 683–686; Scahill, *Blackwater*, 2nd edn, 6; Daskal, "Blackwater in Baghdad".
26 House Committee on Oversight and Government Reform, "Hearing on Blackwater USA", 30; Thurner, "Drowning in Blackwater", 64–65.
27 Glanz and Rubin, "Errand to Fatal Shot"; Glanz and Tavernise, "Blackwater Shooting Scene"; Fainaru, *Big Boy Rules*, 179; Scahill, *Blackwater*, 2nd edn, 8; Engel, "Blackwater's Ugly Americans".
28 Tavernise, "US Contractor Banned"; Schwartz, "Department of Defense's Use", 15; Fainaru, *Big Boy Rules*, 88; Uesseler, *Servants of War*; Commission on Wartime Contracting in Iraq and Afghanistan, "At What Cost?"; Carafano, *Private Sector, Public Wars*, 107; US Department of State and the Broadcasting Board of Governors Office of the Inspector General, "Status of the Panel", 3; Stanger, *One Nation Under Contract*, 4; Dunning, "Heroes or Mercenaries?", 9; Cotton *et al.*, *Hired Guns*, 25–26; Simons, *Master of War*, 176 and 262; Dunigan, *Victory for Hire*, 71–72; Thurner, "Drowning in Blackwater", 64–65; Scahill, *Blackwater*, 2nd edn, 8.
29 Karadsheh and Duke, "Blackwater Incident Witness"; US Department of Justice, "Transcript", 2–3; Scahill, *Blackwater*, 2nd edn, 5; US Department of State, "Blackwater Personnel".
30 Fainaru, *Big Boy Rules*, 179–180; House Committee on Oversight and Government Reform, "Hearing on Blackwater USA", 29; US Department of State, "Blackwater Personnel".
31 Simons, *Master of War*, 261–262; Tiefer, "No More Nisour Squares", 754; Beckman, *Blackwater from the Inside Out*, Loc. 682–686; Prince, *Civilian Warriors*, 209.
32 Quoted in Scahill, *Blackwater*, 2nd edn, 32–33.
33 Quoted in Fainaru, *Big Boy Rules*, 179.
34 House Committee on Oversight and Government Reform, "Hearing on Blackwater USA", 29.
35 Dunning, "Heroes or Mercenaries?", 9.
36 Dunigan, *Victory for Hire*, 71–72.
37 US Department of Justice, "Transcript", 2–3; Ciralsky, "Tycoon".
38 Simons, *Master of War*, 261–263.
39 Uesseler, *Servants of War*, 88.
40 Human Rights First, "Private Security Contractors", 1.
41 Commission on Wartime Contracting in Iraq and Afghanistan, "At What Cost?", 61.
42 Johnston and Broder, "F.B.I. Says"; Fainaru, *Big Boy Rules*, 178; US Department of State and the Broadcasting Board of Governors Office of the Inspector General, "Status of the Panel"; Jordan, "FBI Finds"; Scahill, *Blackwater*, 2nd edn, 33–35.
43 US Department of State, "First Meeting".
44 US Department of State, "PM Malaki".
45 Engbrecht, *America's Covert Warriors*, 16.
46 Fainaru, *Big Boy Rules*, 178.
47 Partlow and Sabah, "US Security Firm"; US Department of State Diplomatic Security Service, "January 24, 2005"; Glanz, "Security Guard Fires".
48 US Department of State Diplomatic Security Service, "January 24, 2005".
49 Global Security.org, "Vehicle Borne IEDs".

50 Glanz, "Security Guard Fires".
51 US Embassy, Baghdad, "Spot Report – 082905–01"; US Department of State Diplomatic Security Service, "DS Report Number 2005–0076"; Blackwater, PSD Incident Report, 29 August 2005.
52 US Army, "Green on Green".
53 DGSD, PSD Incident Report, 16 July 2007; US Embassy, Baghdad, "Spot Report – 071607–07"; US Department of State Diplomatic Security Service, "DS Report Number 7/16/2007".
54 Zittle, "RE: OEF in Erbil"; Amin, "Statement"; Zittle, "Re: Claim filed".
55 Eight Blackwater incidents were intentionally excluded from this analysis of mean engagement distances. These incidents were extreme outliers, for they involved engagement distances of 482, 500, 550, 600, 800 and 1,300 metres, which are considerably longer than the firm's next-longest engagement distance of 350 metres. Including these incidents would have therefore increased the firm's mean engagement distances to a point where they would no longer accurately reflect the firm's general behaviour.
56 Given that most of the incidents where Blackwater and DynCorp's employees fired their weapons involved firing upon an approaching vehicle, the average engagement distance tends to decrease at each stage of an incident.
57 Since DynCorp's personnel never fired their weapons at suspected threat during the first stage of an incident, a conservative standard of "deaths and serious injuries inflicted during incidents with engagement distances in excess of 74 metres during the first stage of the incident" was selected to analyse the harm inflicted by Blackwater's personnel during this stage.
58 Fainaru, *Big Boy Rules*, 170; Fainaru, "Blackwater Sniper Fire"; Scahill, *Blackwater*, 1st edn, 11; US Embassy, Baghdad, "Spot Report – 020707–01"; Simons, *Master of War*, 163; Prince, *Civilian Warriors*, 214.
59 Fainaru, *Big Boy Rules*, 170.
60 Fainaru, *Big Boy Rules*, 170; Scahill, *Blackwater*, 2nd edn, 11; Fainaru, "Blackwater Sniper Fire".
61 Fainaru, *Big Boy Rules*, 170; Scahill, *Blackwater*, 2nd edn, 11; Fainaru, "Blackwater Sniper Fire".
62 Fainaru, *Big Boy Rules*, 170; Scahill, *Blackwater*, 2nd edn, 11; Fainaru, "Blackwater Sniper Fire".
63 Fainaru, "Blackwater Sniper Fire".
64 Ibid.
65 US Department of State Diplomatic Security Service, "DS Report Number 2005–0084"; US Embassy, Baghdad, "Spot Report – 091105–03"; Blackwater, PSD Incident Reports, 11 Septbember 2005, 20 September 2005; US Department of State Diplomatic Security Service, "DS Report Number 2005–0093"; US Embassy, Baghdad, "Spot Report – 092005–02".
66 US Department of State Diplomatic Security Service, "January 24, 2005".
67 Blackwater, PSD Incident Report, 18 October 2005; US Embassy, Baghdad, "Spot Report – 101805–02"; US Department of State Diplomatic Security Service, "DS Report Number 2005–0118".
68 Blackwater, PSD Incident Report, 25 March 2005; US Embassy, Baghdad, "Spot Report – 032505–1".
69 Pelton, *Licensed to Kill*, 201.
70 Pelton, *Licensed to Kill*, 202.
71 Beckman, *Blackwater from the Inside Out*, Loc. 682–686.
72 US Embassy, Baghdad, "Preliminary Spot Report"; US Embassy, Baghdad, "2005BAGHDA01554"; Bonfiglio, "BW SIR Karbala PSD".
73 US Army, "Escalation of Force Conducted"; Blackwater, PSD Incident Report, 2 February 2006; Fainaru, "Warnings Unheeded"; Finer, "State Department

Military culture and threat casualties 129

Contractors"; US Embassy, Baghdad, "Spot Report – 020706–02"; US Department of State Diplomatic Security Service, "DS Report Number 2006–0019"; Kirkuk Police, "Police Reports".
74 Fainaru, *Big Boy Rules*, 88; Carafano, *Private Sector, Public Wars*, 107; Simons, *Master of War*, 176 and 262; Dunigan, *Victory for Hire*, 71–72; Scahill, *Blackwater*, 2nd edn, 8.
75 Stein, "Wikileaks Files"; Prince, *Civilian Warriors*, 162.
76 Iraq Body Count, "Ambulance Driver Shot".
77 Joint Contracting Command – Iraq, "Blue (Blackwater) on White", 1.
78 US Embassy, Baghdad, "Spot Report – 062005–7"; US Department of State Diplomatic Security Service, "DS Report for June 20, 2005".
79 Blackwater, PSD Incident Report, 12 August 2006; US Embassy, Baghdad, "Spot Report – 081206–01"; US Department of State Diplomatic Security Service, "DS Report Number 2006–0095".
80 Blackwater, PSD Incident Report, 25 March 2005; US Embassy, Baghdad, "Spot Report – 032505–1".
81 US Department of State Diplomatic Security Service, "DS Report Number 2007–00025"; Blackwater, PSD Incident Report, 19 February 2007; US Embassy, Baghdad, "Spot Report – 021907–01".
82 Fainaru, *Big Boy Rules*, 88; Carafano, *Private Sector, Public Wars*, 107; Simons, *Master of War*, 176 and 262; Dunigan, *Victory for Hire*, 71–72; Scahill, *Blackwater*, 2nd edn, 8.
83 DGSD, PSD Incident Report, 16 July 2007; US Embassy, Baghdad, "Spot Report – 071607–07"; US Department of State Diplomatic Security Service, "DS Report Number 7/16/2007".
84 Human Rights First, "Private Security Contractors", 6–7; Majority Staff, "Memorandum", 8; House Committee on Oversight and Government Reform, "Hearing on Blackwater USA", 71; Ciralsky, "Tycoon".
85 House Committee on Oversight and Government Reform, "Hearing on Blackwater USA", 71.
86 Ibid., 117.
87 Blackwater, PSD Incident Report, 24 October 2005; US Embassy, Baghdad, "Spot Report – 1005–3".
88 Majority Staff, "Memorandum", 7; Iraq Body Count, "Man Shot Dead".
89 Blackwater, PSD Incident Report, 24 October 2005; US Embassy, Baghdad, "Spot Report – 1005–3".
90 Majority Staff, "Memorandum", 8; Fainaru, *Big Boy Rules*, 164–165; DeYoung, "Other Killings"; Blackwater, PSD Incident Report, 24 September 2006; US Embassy, Baghdad, "Spot Report – 092406–01".
91 Majority Staff, "Memorandum", 8; Fainaru, *Big Boy Rules*, 164–165; DeYoung, "Other Killings"; Blackwater, PSD Incident Report, 24 September 2006; US Embassy, Baghdad, "Spot Report – 092406–01".
92 Beckman, *Blackwater from the Inside Out*, Loc. 357–376.
93 Ibid., Loc. 376–377.
94 Fainaru, *Big Boy Rules*, 169–172; Fainaru, "Blackwater Sniper Fire"; Scahill, *Blackwater*, 1st edn, 11; US Embassy, Baghdad, "Spot Report – 020707–01"; Simons, *Master of War*, 163.
95 Scahill, *Blackwater*, 2nd edn, 8.
96 Fainaru, *Big Boy Rules*, 42; Prince, *Civilian Warriors*, 214.
97 US Department of State Diplomatic Security Service, "DS Report Number 2005–0028"; US Department of State Diplomatic Security Service, "January 24, 2005"; Glanz, "Security Guard Fires"; Partlow and Sabah, "US Security Firm Involved"; US Embassy, Baghdad, "Spot Report – 062005–7"; US Department of State Diplomatic Security Service, "DS Report for June 20, 2005"; US

130 *Military culture and threat casualties*

      Embassy, Baghdad, "Spot Report – 051005–01"; DGSD, PSD Incident Report, 10 May 2005.
- 98 US Department of State Diplomatic Security Service, "DS Report for June 20, 2005"; Blackwater, PSD Incident Report, 20 June 2005, 28 August 2005, 18 March 2006, 2 May 2006, 22 September 2006, 31 January 2007, 4 February 2007, 19 March 2007; Prince, *Civilian Warriors*, 260.
- 99 US Embassy, Baghdad, "Spot Report – 082905–01"; US Department of State Diplomatic Security Service, "DS Report Number 2005–0076"; Blackwater, PSD Incident Report, 29 August 2005.
- 100 US Embassy, Baghdad, "Spot Report – 042205–1"; Blackwater, PSD Incident Report, 21 April 2005.
- 101 Al-Hillah Police, "Police Reports"; Al-Hillah Investigation Court, "Investigation Court's Reports"; Blackwater, PSD Incident Report, 24 October 2005; US Embassy, Baghdad, "Spot Report – 102405–06".
- 102 US Embassy, Baghdad, "Decision Memorandum Issued".
- 103 Majority Staff, "Memorandum", 8; House Committee on Oversight and Government Reform, "Hearing on Blackwater USA", 149; Fainaru, *Big Boy Rules*, 164.
- 104 Majority Staff, "Memorandum", 8.
- 105 Beckman, *Blackwater from the Inside Out*, Loc. 790–792.
- 106 Ibid., Loc. 794.
- 107 Scahill, *Blackwater*, 1st edn, 161–163; Levesque, "Clearwater Security Worker".
- 108 Fainaru, *Big Boy Rules*, 178; Glanz and Rubin, "Errand to Fatal Shot".
- 109 Fainaru, *Big Boy Rules*, 178; Scahill, "Blackwater's Youngest Victim".
- 110 Raghavan, "Tracing the Paths".
- 111 Ibid.
- 112 Fainaru, *Big Boy Rules*, 178; Scahill, *Blackwater*, 2nd edn, 7.
- 113 Taylor, Kohl and Malis, "Factual Proffer", 5; Scahill, *Blackwater*, 2nd edn, 8.
- 114 DGSD, PSD Incident Report, 16 July 2007; US Embassy, Baghdad, "Spot Report – 071607–07"; US Department of State Diplomatic Security Service, "DS Report Number 7/16/2007".
- 115 Unfortunately, the Office of the Inspector General did not collect comparable data for every year of the 2003 to 2009 period. However, since approximately 52 per cent of the violent incidents under study occurred in 2005, analyzing the data for that year should provide a reasonably accurate assessment of each firm's propensity to use violence.
- 116 Prince, *Civilian Warriors*, 216.
- 117 House Committee on Oversight and Government Reform, "Hearing on Blackwater USA", 54.
- 118 Prince, "Statement of Erik D. Prince", 2.
- 119 US Army, "Improved Explosive Device".
- 120 US Army, "Escalation of Force by Blackwater".
- 121 Blackwater, PSD Incident Report, 1 November 2005; US Embassy, Baghdad, "Spot Report – 110105–01"; US Embassy, Baghdad, "Spot Report – 1005–6".
- 122 Blackwater, PSD Incident Report, 22 March 2005.
- 123 Fainaru, *Big Boy Rules*, 137.
- 124 Scahill, *Blackwater*, 2nd edn, 10–11; Fainaru, *Big Boy Rules*, 164–166; Majority Staff, "Memorandum", 13.
- 125 Both firms exhibited similar recruiting patterns, with the most sought-after personnel being veterans of American and other Western special operations units, such as the US Navy SEALs, the US Army Rangers and Special Forces ("Green Berets"), and the British Special Air Service. Both firms also hired veterans of regular US Army and Marine and civilian police units. Isenberg, *Shadow Force*, 37; Fainaru, *Big Boy Rules*, 52; Singer, *Corporate Warriors*, 17;

Engbrecht, *America's Covert Warriors*, 20; Pelton, *Licensed to Kill*, 221; Middle East Regional Office, "Performance Evaluation", 5 and 17; Laguna, *You Have to Live Hard*, Loc. 326–342.
126 In an email sent to other Iraq-based special agents of the Department of State's DSS, Special Agent John Hislop wrote that, all of the private security firms working for the State Department in Iraq, "operate under the same EOF (Escalation of Force) procedures through out theatre". Hislop, "ROI, SR and Statements EOF".
127 Hislop, "ROI, SR and Statements EOF".

References

Al-Hillah Investigation Court. "Investigation Court's Reports based on Accounts from Iraqi Eyewitnesses and Medical Examiners with Knowledge of 24 October 2005, Incident in Al-Hillah". Al-Hillah, Iraq: Al-Hillah Investigation Court, 24 October 2005.

Al-Hillah Police. "Police Reports based on Accounts from Iraqi Eyewitnesses and Medical Examiners with Knowledge of 24 October 2005, Incident in Al-Hillah". Al-Hillah, Iraq: Al-Hillah Police, 24 October 2005.

Amin, Rizgar Muhamad. "Statement". Erbil, Iraq: Kurdistan Judges Union, 18 July 2007.

Beckman, Tim. *Blackwater from the Inside Out*. Kindle edn. New York: HDTI, 2010.

Blackwater. PSD Incident Reports and Sworn Statements. Baghdad: Blackwater, 2005–2009.

Bonfiglio, Brian. "BW SIR Karbala PSD (E-mail) sent to Frederick M. Piry, Paul Nassen, and Mike Rush". Moyock, NC: Blackwater, 13 April 2005.

Burke, Susan L., William T. O'Neil, Elizabeth M. Burke, Rosemary B. Healy and Katherine B. Hawkins. "Second Amended Complaint in Abtan v. Blackwater". Washington, DC: The United States District Court for the District of Columbia, 28 March 2008.

Carafano, James Jay. *Private Sector, Public Wars: Contractors in Combat – Afghanistan, Iraq, and Future Conflicts*. Westport, CT: Praeger Security International, 2008.

Ciralsky, Adam. "Tycoon, Contractor, Soldier, Spy". *Vanity Fair*, January 2010.

Commission on Wartime Contracting in Iraq and Afghanistan. "At What Cost? Contingency Contracting in Iraq and Afghanistan". Washington, DC: Commission on Wartime Contracting in Iraq and Afghanistan, June 2009.

Cotton, Sarah K., Ulrich Petersohn, Molly Dunigan, Q. Burkhart, Megan Zander-Cotugno, Edward O'Connell and Michael Webber. *Hired Guns: Views About Armed Contractors in Operation Iraqi Freedom*. Santa Monica, CA: The Rand Corporation, 2010.

Daskal, Jennifer. "Blackwater in Baghdad". *Salon*, 14 December 2007.

DeYoung, Karen. "Other Killings by Blackwater Staff Detailed". *Washington Post*, 2 October 2007.

DGSD (DynCorp Government Services Division). PSD Incident Reports and Sworn Statements. Falls Church, VA: DynCorp, 2005–2008.

Dunigan, Molly. *Victory for Hire: Private Security Companies' Impact on Military Effectiveness*. Stanford, CA: Stanford Security Studies, 2011.

Dunning, Rebecca. "Heroes or Mercenaries? Blackwater, Private Security Companies, and the US Military". Case study. Durham, NC: The Kenan Institute for Ethics, Duke University, 2010.

Engbrecht, Shawn. *America's Covert Warriors: Inside the World of Private Military Contractors.* Washington, DC: Potomac Books, 2011.

Engel, Richard. "Blackwater's Ugly Americans". *MSNBC World Blog,* 28 September 2007.

Fainaru, Steve. "Guards in Iraq Cite Frequent Shootings; Companies Seldom Report Incidents, US Officials Say". *Washington Post,* 3 October 2007.

Fainaru, Steve. "How Blackwater Sniper Fire Felled 3 Iraqi Guards". *Washington Post,* 8 November 2007.

Fainaru, Steve. "Warnings Unheeded on Guards in Iraq". *Washington Post,* 24 December 2007.

Fainaru, Steve. *Big Boy Rules: America's Mercenaries Fighting in Iraq.* Philadelphia: Da Capo Press, 2008.

Fainaru, Steve, and Saad al-Izzi. "US Security Contractors Open Fire in Baghdad; Blackwater Employees were Involved in Two Shooting Incidents in Past Week". *Washington Post,* 27 May 2007.

Finer, Jonathan. "State Department Contractors Kill 2 Civilians in N. Iraq". *Washington Post,* 9 February 2006.

Glanz, James. "Security Guard Fires from Convoying, Killing Iraqi Driver". *New York Times,* 12 November 2007.

Glanz, James, and Alissa J. Rubin. "From Errand to Fatal Shot to Hail of Fire to 17 Deaths". *New York Times,* 3 October 2007.

Glanz, James, and Sabrina Tavernise. "Blackwater Shooting Scene was Chaotic". *New York Times,* 28 September 2007.

Global Security.org. "Vehicle Borne IEDs (VBIEDs)". Global Security.org, 2011.

Hislop, John T. "ROI, SR and Statements EOF Kirkuk 7/6/07". Kirkuk, Iraq: US Department of State, 7 July 2007.

House Committee on Oversight and Government Reform. "Hearing on Blackwater USA". Washington, DC: House of Representatives, Congress of the United States, 2 October 2007.

Human Rights First. "Private Security Contractors at War: Ending the Culture of Impunity". New York: Human Rights First, 2008.

Iraq Body Count. "Man Shot Dead by Blackwater Security Forces in Mosul". Iraq Body Count, 24 October 2005.

Iraq Body Count. "Ambulance Driver Shot Dead by Blackwater Convoy in Baghdad". Iraq Body Count, 2 May 2006.

Isenberg, David. *Shadow Force: Private Security Contractors in Iraq.* Westport, CT: Praeger Security International, 2009.

Johnston, David, and John M. Broder. "F.B.I. Says Guards Killed 14 Iraqis Without Cause". *New York Times,* 14 November 2007.

Joint Contracting Command – Iraq. "Blue (Blackwater) on White in Baghdad: 1 Civ Killed, 0 cf. Inj/Damage: Redacted Report 7–2". Baghdad: Joint Contracting Command – Iraq, 2 May 2006.

Jordan, Lara Jakes. "FBI Finds Blackwater Trucks Patched". Associated Press, 12 January 2008.

Karadsheh, Jomana, and Alan Duke. "Blackwater Incident Witness: 'It Was Hell'". *CNN.com,* 2 October 2007.

Kirkuk Police. "Police Reports based on Accounts from Iraqi Eyewitnesses and Medical Examiners with Knowledge of February 7, 2006, Incident in Kirkuk". Kirkuk, Iraq: Kirkuk Police, 7 February 2006.

Krugman, Paul. "Hired Gun Fetish". *New York Times*, 28 September 2007.
Laguna, Dan. *You Have to Live Hard to Be Hard: One Man's Life in Special Operations*. Kindle edn. Bloomington, IN: Authorhouse, 2010.
Levesque, William R. "Clearwater Security Worker Killed in Iraq". *St. Petersburg Times*, 8 June 2004.
Majority Staff. "Memorandum – Additional Information about Blackwater USA". Washington, DC: Congress of the United States, 1 October 2007.
Middle East Regional Office. "Performance Evaluation of the DynCorp Contract for Personal Protective Services in Iraq". US Department of State and the Broadcasting Board of Governors Office of Inspector General, June 2009.
Miller, T. Christian. *Blood Money: Wasted Billions, Lost Lives, and Corporate Greed in Iraq*. New York: Little Brown and Company, 2006.
Palmer, Elizabeth. "'I Went to a Meeting and Somebody Died'". *CBS News*, 23 January 2010.
Partlow, Joshua, and Zaid Sabah. "US Security Firm Involved in Shooting of Iraqi Driver". *Washington Post*, 12 November 2007.
Pelton, Robert Young. *Licensed to Kill: Hired Guns in the War on Terror*. New York: Crown Publishers, 2006.
Prince, Erik. "Statement of Erik D. Prince to the House Committee on Oversight and Government Reform". Washington, DC: Congress of the United States, 2 October 2007.
Prince, Erik. *Civilian Warriors: The Inside Story of Blackwater and the Unsung Heroes of the War on Terror*. Kindle edn. New York: Portfolio, 2013.
Raghavan, Sudarsan. "Tracing the Paths of 5 Who Died in a Storm of Gunfire". *Washington Post*, 4 October 2007.
Scahill, Jeremy. *Blackwater: The Rise of the World's Most Powerful Mercenary Army*. 1st edn. New York: Nation Books, 2007.
Scahill, Jeremy. *Blackwater: The Rise of the World's Most Powerful Mercenary Army*. 2nd edn. New York: Nation Books, 2008.
Scahill, Jeremy. "Blackwater's Youngest Victim". *The Nation*, 22 February 2010.
Schwartz, Moshe. "The Department of Defense's Use of Private Security Contractors in Afghanistan and Iraq: Background, Analysis, and Options for Congress". Washington, DC: Congressional Research Service, 13 May 2011.
Sengupta, Kim. "The Real Story of Baghdad's Bloody Sunday". *The Independent*, 21 September 2007.
Simons, Suzanne. *Master of War: Blackwater USA's Erik Prince and the Business of War*. New York: Harper, 2009.
Singer, Peter W. *Corporate Warriors: The Rise of the Privatized Military Industry*. Ithaca, NY: Cornell University Press, 2003.
Stanger, Allison. *One Nation Under Contract: The Outsourcing of American Power and the Future of Foreign Policy*. New Haven, CT: Yale University Press, 2009.
Stein, Jeff. "Wikileaks Files Likely Pose Little Threat to Blackwater". *Washington Post Official Blog*, 22 October 2010. Available at http://blog.washingtonpost.com/spy-talk/2010/10/wikileaks_report_of_talibans_n_1.html?wprss=spy-talk.
Tavernise, Sabrina. "US Contractor Banned by Iraq over Shooting". *New York Times*, 18 September 2007.
Taylor, Jeffrey A., Kenneth C. Kohl, and Jonathan M. Malis. "Factual Proffer in Support of Guilty Plea – United States of America v. Jeremy P. Ridgeway". United States District Court for the District of Columbia, 18 November 2008.

Thurner, Jeffrey S. "Drowning in Blackwater: How Weak Accountability over Private Security Contractors Significantly Undermines Counterinsurgency Efforts". *Army Lawyer* (July 2008): 64–90.

Tiefer, Charles. "No More Nisour Squares: Legal Control of Private Security Contractors in Iraq". *Oregon Law Review* 88, no. 3 (2009): 745–775.

Uesseler, Rolf. *Servants of War: Private Military Corporations and the Profit of Conflict.* Translated by Jefferson Chase. Berkeley, CA: Soft Skull Press, 2008.

US Army. "Improved Explosive Device Attack on Civilian Convoy in the Vicinity of Habbaniyah: 0 Inj/Damage". Habbaniyah, Iraq: Wikileaks, 16 March 2004.

US Army. "Small Arms Attack on DynCorp SET Convoy (6 Veh) in the Vicinity of Balad: 5 NEU Inj". Balad, Iraq: Wikileaks, 12 October 2004.

US Army. "Escalation of Force by Blackwater in Baghdad (Zone 13): 1 Civilian Inj, 0 Coalition Forces Inj/Dama". Baghdad: Wikileaks, 12 December 2005.

US Army. "Escalation of Force Conducted by BWS IVO Kirkuk: 2 Civ Killed, 0 cf. Inj/Damage". Kirkuk, Iraq: Wikileaks, 7 February 2006.

US Army. "Green on Green in Al Karkh: 3 IA Wounded in Action/Sedan Destroyed, 0 Coalition Forces Inj/Damage". Baghdad: Wikileaks, 26 August 2006.

US Department of Justice. "Transcript of Blackwater Press Conference". Washington, DC: US Department of Justice, 8 December 2008.

US Department of State. "Blackwater Personnel Security Detail Involved in Lethal Incident". Washington, DC: US Department of State, 17 September 2007.

US Department of State. "First Meeting of the Joint Commission on PSD Issues". Washington, DC: US Department of State, 10 October 2007.

US Department of State. "PM Malaki on Blackwater, Oil Contracts, UM QASR Port, and Elections". Washington, DC: US Department of State, 8 January 2010.

US Department of State and the Broadcasting Board of Governors Office of the Inspector General. "Status of the Secretary of State's Panel on Personal Protective Services in Iraq Report Recommendations". Washington, DC: US Department of State and the Broadcasting Board of Governors Office of Inspector General, December 2008.

US Department of State Diplomatic Security Service. "24 January 2005 Lethal Force Incident Involving INL PSD". Baghdad: US Department of State, 24 January 2005.

US Department of State Diplomatic Security Service. "DS Report for 20 June 2005 Incident". Baghdad: US Department of State, 20 June 2005.

US Department of State Diplomatic Security Service. "DS Report Number 2005-0028". Baghdad: US Department of State, 10 May 2005.

US Department of State Diplomatic Security Service. "DS Report Number 2005-0076". Baghdad: US Department of State, 30 August 2005.

US Department of State Diplomatic Security Service. "DS Report Number 2005-0084". Baghdad: US Department of State, 11 September 2005.

US Department of State Diplomatic Security Service. "DS Report Number 2005-0093". Baghdad: US Department of State, 20 September 2005.

US Department of State Diplomatic Security Service. "DS Report Number 2005-0118". Baghdad: US Department of State, 18 October 2005.

US Department of State Diplomatic Security Service. "DS Report Number 2006-0019". Baghdad: US Department of State, 7 February 2006.

US Department of State Diplomatic Security Service. "DS Report Number 2006-0095". Baghdad: US Department of State, 12 August 2006.

Military culture and threat casualties 135

US Department of State Diplomatic Security Service. "DS Report Number 2007–00025". Baghdad: US Department of State, 19 February 2007.
US Department of State Diplomatic Security Service. "DS Report Number 7/16/2007 – Kirkuk". Baghdad: US Department of State, 16 September 2007.
US Embassy, Baghdad. "2005BAGHDA01554 – Vehicle Threat Engaged by PSD Team Resulting in the Death of One Local National". Baghdad: US Department of State, 13 April 2005.
US Embassy, Baghdad. "Decision Memorandum Issued by the Embassy Baghdad Claims and Condolence Payment Program Committee". Baghdad: US Department of State, 23 December 2005.
US Embassy, Baghdad. "Preliminary Spot Report". Baghdad: US Department of State, 13 April 2005.
US Embassy, Baghdad. "Spot Report – 1005–3 – Use of Deadly Force Against a Vehicle Resulting in Death". Baghdad: US Department of State, 24 October 2005.
US Embassy, Baghdad. "Spot Report – 1005–6 – Use of Deadly Force During a Motorcade Movement – Possible KIA". Baghdad: US Department of State, 1 November 2005.
US Embassy, Baghdad. "Spot Report – 020706–02 – COM PSD Fires on Aggressive Vehicle". Baghdad: US Department of State, 7 February 2006.
US Embassy, Baghdad. "Spot Report – 020707–01 – SAF Attack on a COM PSD". Baghdad: US Department of State, 7 February 2007.
US Embassy, Baghdad. "Spot Report – 021907–01 – COM TST Team Fires on Three Aggressive Vehicles". Baghdad: US Department of State, 19 February 2007.
US Embassy, Baghdad. "Spot Report – 032505–1 – PSD Team Fires on Vehicle". Baghdad: US Department of State, 25 March 2005.
US Embassy, Baghdad. "Spot Report – 042205–1 – Attack on Chief of Mission Motorcade". Baghdad: US Department of State, 22 April 2005.
US Embassy, Baghdad. "Spot Report – 051005–01 – DynCorp COM PSD Team Fires on Aggressive Vehicle". Baghdad: US Department of State, 10 May 2005.
US Embassy, Baghdad. "Spot Report – 062005–7 – PSD Motorcade Hit with IED and SAF". Baghdad: US Department of State, 20 June 2005.
US Embassy, Baghdad. "Spot Report – 071607–07 – COM PSD Team Fires on Aggressive Vehicle". Baghdad: US Department of State, 16 July 2007.
US Embassy, Baghdad. "Spot Report – 081206–01 – COM PSD Team Fires on an Aggressive Vehicle". Baghdad: US Department of State, 12 August 2006.
US Embassy, Baghdad. "Spot Report – 082905–01 – COM PSD Team Fires on Aggressive Vehicle". Baghdad: US Department of State, 29 August 2005.
US Embassy, Baghdad. "Spot Report – 091105–03 – COM PSD Team Fires on Aggressive Vehicle". Baghdad: US Department of State, 11 September 2005.
US Embassy, Baghdad. "Spot Report – 092005–02 – COM PSD Team Fires on Aggressive Vehicle". Baghdad: US Department of State, 20 September 2005.
US Embassy, Baghdad. "Spot Report – 092406–01 – REO PSD Vehicle Accident ". Baghdad: US Department of State, 24 September 2006.
US Embassy, Baghdad. "Spot Report – 101805–02 – COM PSD Team Fires on Aggressive Vehicle". Baghdad: US Department of State, 18 October 2005.
US Embassy, Baghdad. "Spot Report – 102405–06 – COM PSD Team Fires on Aggressive Vehicle". Baghdad: US Department of State, 24 October 2005.
US Embassy, Baghdad. "Spot Report – 110105–01 – COM PSD Team Fires on Aggressive Vehicle". Baghdad: US Department of State, 1 November 2005.

Welch, Michael. "Fragmented Power and State-Corporate Killings: A Critique of Blackwater in Iraq". *Crime, Law and Social Change* 51, no. 3–4 (2009): 351–364.

Williams, Timothy. "Iraqis Angered as Blackwater Charges are Dropped". *New York Times*, 2 January 2010.

Zittle, Zachariah. "RE: OEF in Erbil – UPDATE". Erbil, Iraq: US Department of State, 17 July 2007.

Zittle, Zachariah. "Re: Claim filed by". Erbil, Iraq: US Department of State, 30 July 2007.

5 The relationship between military culture, tactical behaviour and friendly casualties

Much like the previous chapter, this chapter examines the relationship between the firms' military cultures, the use of violence by their security personnel and the casualties they inflicted during their security operations. However, while Chapter 4 concentrated on the casualties the firms inflicted against civilians, this chapter focuses on the deaths and series injuries they inflicted on the insurgents they encountered in Iraq and also the casualties they suffered during their security operations. It consists of four main parts. It first analyzes the theory's predictions regarding the relationship between military culture, tactical behaviour and the casualties inflicted and suffered by each firm's personnel. Second, it addresses the question of whether Blackwater's behaviour during the Iraq War may have actually undermined the security of its personnel and clients. Third, it discusses a number of possible alternative explanations for these findings. Finally, it concludes with a summary of the findings.

Predictions of the ideational theory of tactical violence

The ideational theory of tactical violence offers specific, testable predictions about how the behavioural norms contained in a PSC's military culture should influence the tactical behaviour exhibited by its security personnel.

Engagement time

The theory predicts that the security personnel of PSCs that place strong emphasis on norms encouraging personal initiative, proactive use of force and an exclusive approach to security should tend to employ violence more quickly after observing a suspected threat than the security personnel of firms that do not place strong emphasis on these norms. For instance, although the security personnel of firms that strongly emphasize these norms should often issue non-violent warnings to suspected threats before firing their weapons, they should escalate to using deadly force more quickly than their counterparts in firms that do not strongly emphasize these norms. Security personnel who behave in this manner in effect reduce the amount of time available for a suspected threat to alter its behaviour and attempt to convince the security personnel that it means them no harm – by, for example, dropping a weapon, halting its approach or altering its course away from the security personnel and their clients – before they engage the suspected threat with deadly force. This, in turn, means that security personnel who behave in this manner are more likely to kill or seriously injure a suspected threat during an incident than are security personnel who behave in a less violent manner.

This prediction was supported. Blackwater's tendency to fire relatively quickly at suspected threats certainly placed civilians at severe risk of harm; however, this behaviour was also highly effectively at neutralizing genuine insurgent threats. The firm's employees inflicted at least 32 of the 33 known insurgent deaths (97 per cent) during incidents where they fired as their first or second behavioural response to a suspected threat. The firm also only lost personnel during four incidents out of a total of 54 (7 per cent) where they fired relatively quickly at insurgents. Rapidly engaging insurgents provided them very little time to inflict harm by, for instance, firing a weapon, detonating an explosive or accelerating a vehicle toward the firm's personnel and clients. As a result, the behaviour exhibited by Blackwater's personnel almost certainly reduced the casualties suffered by themselves and their clients.

In the immediate aftermath of a VBIED attack on 19 September 2005 in Mosul, which killed three of the firm's security personnel, the surviving members of the AT quickly spotted and fired at a group of gunmen who had positioned themselves to carry out a follow-on ambush against the team.[1] The initial attack occurred approximately 15 minutes after a Blackwater AT, made up of a lead vehicle, a limousine, a follow vehicle, a K9 vehicle and a CAV bringing up the rear, departed the US Department of State's Regional Embassy Office (REO) in Mosul en route to Provincial Hall. Four kilometres into the journey, the convoy encountered a silver-grey Opel Omega car driven by an Arab male, just one of the many civilian cars and trucks that had pulled over to the side of the road to let them go by. The Opel pulled back onto the road slightly ahead of the approaching convoy but initially kept to the right and travelled more slowly, at about 55 kilometres per hour, than the convoy, which was travelling at about 80 kilometres per hour. Personnel in the lead vehicle noticed the potential threat right away, and called over the radio to "Watch that car". The Opel swerved toward the convoy's lead vehicle as it drove past, but missed. The lead vehicle then attempted to push the Opel back onto the right shoulder, but the suspicious vehicle maneuverer out of the way before being struck.

The Opel next tried to force itself between the lead vehicle and the convoy's limousine, but failed and drifted three to five metres to the right side of the road. It then tried to squeeze between the limousine and the follow vehicle, an armoured GMC Suburban that carried three Blackwater personnel, Kenneth Webb, Peter J. Tocci and David R. Shephard, as well as DSS Special Agent Stephen Sullivan, the acting regional security officer for Mosul.[2] The follow vehicle's driver sped up to both close the gap and try to push the Opel back toward the right shoulder yet again. This manoeuvre was initially successful; however, the Opel detonated just as the follow vehicle passed it. The force of the explosion, with the power of multiple 122 mm and 155 mm artillery shells, set the follow vehicle on fire and blasted it across six lanes of traffic into a concrete wall running along the edge of the road. Before coming to a stop, the vehicle crushed a car driven by an Iraqi national, who died instantly. Shephard, Sullivan and Tochi were thrown about 25 metres from their vehicle by the blast while Webb remained inside. All four died instantly.

When questioned by a Congressional panel about Blackwater's tactical behaviour in Iraq, Prince used this incident to highlight the costs of responding too slowly to a potential threat. In response to questions from Congressman John Tierney about why the firm's personnel tended to use deadly force before a suspected threat had fired at them, Prince stated that:

> The terrorists have figured out how to make a precision weapon with a car loaded with explosives with a suicidal driver.... [T]his is what happens when our guys are not able to prevent a suicide car bomb. This happened. This blew up three Blackwater personnel and one State Department security officer up in Mosul. It tossed a 9,000 pound armored Suburban 50 feet [15 metres] into the side of a building, followed by a whole bunch of small arms fire from the rooftops, a very serious ambush, killed four Americans that fast.[3]

The security team did, however, rapidly respond to a follow-up attack launched by insurgent gunmen. The lead vehicle and limousine stopped about 100 metres away from the follow vehicle and set up a defensive perimeter. At this point, at least three insurgents who had established an ambush position in a nearby building with assault rifles and a PKM belt-fed machine gun opened fire on the lead vehicle and limousine. The personnel in these vehicles responded very quickly with gunfire from their own assault rifles and machine guns. The firm's incident report states that the lead vehicle's right rear gunner called out "Belt Fed, rooftop", before he "immediately engaged the enemy, killing the primary gunner".[4] Other personnel rapidly blew through entire 200-round belts of machine gun bullets. Blackwater's speedy response soon forced the insurgents to stop firing and drop out of sight, all presumably dead. Once the enemy fire was suppressed, a team member radioed the firm's tactical operations centre to report the attacks and request backup. Meanwhile, the personnel in the K9 and counter assault vehicles were frantically searching for their comrades in the follow vehicle, a risky undertaking due not only to the insurgent gunfire but also the fact that numerous rounds of ammunition in the follow vehicle were cooking off and firing randomly in all directions. After locating the destroyed follow vehicle, they extinguished the fire and set up a defensive perimeter.

Within three minutes of receiving the call for backup, four US Army Stryker vehicles arrived from the south to provide perimeter security for Blackwater's AT. They were joined by one US Army AH-64 Apache and one OH-58D Kiowa Warrior helicopter. At the same time, the limousine's vehicle commander reported receiving fire from a mosque adjacent to the buildings containing the insurgents' main ambush position. A gunner from the lead vehicle quickly engaged and killed the threat. The US Army helicopters then engaged the fleeing insurgents, killing 15. A Blackwater QRF arrived shortly after to bolster perimeter security around the attack site so that the firm, with help from US Army personnel, could recover the bodies of their fallen comrades, the remains of the suicide bomber and the follow vehicle. Ultimately, the Blackwater AT's decision to rapidly resort to deadly force resulted in the deaths of four insurgents and serious injury to an unknown number of other insurgents and prevented the surviving team members from suffering further harm.[5]

Another telling incident took place in mid-September 2003, when a four-man Blackwater team was ambushed by insurgent gunmen while entering a rural village north of Baghdad.[6] In response to the gunfire emanating from multiple structures in the village, one detail member, Ben Thomas, quickly fired at the gunmen using his M4 carbine. Prior to embarking on that mission, Thomas had equipped his rifle with a magazine of experimental armour-piercing, limited-penetration ammunition designed to easily penetrate tough materials, such as steel plates or body armour, but shatter on contact with human flesh, creating, according to a report in the *Army Times*, "untreatable wounds".[7] When combined with his rapid resort to deadly force, this ammunition allowed Thomas to kill one of the gunmen, who was approximately 100 to 110 metres away, almost immediately through a shot that, in Thomas' words, "completely destroyed everything in the lower left section of his stomach ... everything was torn apart".[8] Through this action and gunfire from the other members of the security detail, they quickly drove off the remaining insurgents, after which they inspected the wounds of the gunmen killed by Thomas and proceeded to return to base.[9]

The firm's personnel likewise quickly responded with deadly force when one of its PSDs came under small-arms fire near Amanat City Hall in Baghdad on 23 May 2007.[10] Although this convoy was ambushed by insurgents firing assault rifles and RPGs from the street and a building to their west, its personnel promptly unleashed a "flurry of gunfire" at the insurgents.[11] They were soon reinforced by a nearby TST, which came in firing. A second TST later joined and immediately directed more firepower at the insurgents, who had established new firing positions in buildings to the north, south, and east of the City Hall. The security teams involved did not suffer any serious injuries during the engagement, which lasted for approximately 15 minutes, but, with additional fire support from a US Army unit and some of the firm's Little Bird door gunners, they killed at least five of their attackers and seriously injured 17 others before escorting their clients back to the Green Zone.[12] As these examples illustrate, by rapidly engaging insurgents with deadly force, Blackwater's personnel enhanced the security of themselves and their clients by shortening the window of opportunity available for the insurgents to launch attacks and undermined the security of at least some of the insurgents they encountered by neutralizing them before they could escape to safety.

The theory's prediction on engagement time was also supported by the behaviour of Blackwater's air crews. Although their primary task was to provide reconnaissance for Blackwater's security convoys, the firm's Little Bird crews regularly exposed themselves to danger by providing extra firepower when security convoys or their fellow air crews came under threat.[13] Laguna stated in his account of the firm's air operations in Iraq that air crews frequently launched operations on their own initiative and on numerous occasions chose to risk their lives by providing air support for their ground-based colleagues.[14] In an email written while he was serving as Blackwater's Aviation Program Manager in Iraq, Laguna wrote that he and the firm's other pilots decided for themselves to rapidly provide fire support for their ground-based colleagues and clients and noted that "we always go when someone is in harm's way".[15] Once on station, the door gunners "are expected to seek out hostile threats and engage targets with precision rifle fire".[16] Unlike many US Army or Marine helicopters, the firm's Little Birds lacked armour, or even doors; their crews were, consequently, highly vulnerable to insurgent gunfire and relied largely on the proactive use of firepower from their two door gunners along with intentionally erratic flying to avoid being shot down.[17] Nevertheless, Laguna said that the firm's air crews were highly motivated to brave enemy fire to support their ground-based colleagues because

> in this business every second counts; it literally could mean life or death for one of our Blackwater brothers. As the Quick Reaction Force (QRF) for all teams, the Little Bird crews are never far from their helicopter and are always ready when a call requesting help comes in.[18]

He went on to state that the air crews would "typically ... fly immediately to the ambush site, provide enough firepower to help the convoy disengage, then escort them back into the Green Zone".[19]

When the firm's air crews quickly fired on a vehicle or insurgent on foot, they tended to rapidly neutralize potential threats to their colleagues.

For example, on 24 November 2004, a Blackwater helicopter crew used multiple bursts of machine gun fire to disable a white-and-orange taxi that attempted to flee a mosque being used by insurgents as a sniper position to fire at US military personnel.[20] The Little Bird crew issued one nonviolent warning, in the form of hand signals, to try to convince the vehicle's driver to head back to the mosque before firing two bullets directly in front of the vehicle, followed shortly by four more bullets into the vehicle's engine. The two men in the taxi then exited and walked back to the mosque where they were detained by the firm's ground personnel until coalition forces could take them into custody. By preventing the suspected insurgents from escaping, Blackwater's personnel may have not only forced them to face an investigation by the coalition forces but also neutralized a future threat to their own personnel, clients or other friendly forces. Firing at these suspected threats relatively quickly may, therefore, have prevented significant future harm.

A somewhat similar incident occurred on 20 September 2005, while two Blackwater Little Bird crews were returning from a mission to escort a PSD in Baghdad.[21] Spotting an explosion approximately three kilometres from their intended landing zone, the crews flew over to investigate and noticed a US military convoy with three vehicles, one of which was disabled, stopped about 100 metres from the blast site. Just as Iraqi police arrived to secure the scene so that the military personnel could prepare to tow the disabled vehicle away, one of the air crews spotted a white pickup truck, occupied by a lone male, about 400 metres from the beleaguered convoy and carrying a large box in its bed. The crew successfully used non-violent signals to convince the driver to move further away from the convoy, but he stopped after travelling only a short distance. The crew then fired a single round into the dirt in front of the truck. This motivated the driver to move a second time but, despite having clear, unobstructed road ahead of him, he stopped after travelling a short distance and, to the crew's alarm, attempted to pull a U-turn and head back toward the convoy. In response, one of the door gunners disabled the truck's engine with two well-aimed rounds. The driver then exited the vehicle and fled toward some nearby buildings. At this point, a second US Army convoy arrived to assist, which allowed the Little Birds to return to base. However, shortly after they left, these US military personnel experienced another insurgent attack and reportedly suffered six casualties.[22]

Moreover, during an incident on 28 May 2006, two Blackwater air crews rapidly responded to small-arms fire emanating from two shooters on a bridge in Baghdad.[23] The insurgents were armed with AK-47 assault rifles and managed to hit one of the Little Birds in the tail boom and front windscreen. The latter shot entered one side of the windscreen, passed through an instrument panel and exited out the other side of the windscreen but did not inflict any injuries. A door gunner rapidly killed one of the shooters and forced the other one to disengage, at which point the crews safely returned to base.

Furthermore, after being fired at by three insurgents on 25 February 2007 near a wooded area of Baghdad that provided a great deal of concealment and protection, a door gunner of a Blackwater Bell 412 helicopter immediately responded with two 15 round bursts of machine gun fire to suppress the shooters and allow the aircraft to break contact and return to base.[24] According to a Department of State cable, "the incoming fire ceased almost immediately" after the door gunner engaged the suspected threats.[25] The unarmoured helicopter was hit by eight rounds of assault rifle ammunition during the first few seconds of the attack, which damaged three out of four of its rotor blades and punctured at least one fuel tank. Being able to suppress the hostile fire long enough to break contact was thus vital for preventing further damage to the aircraft and preserving the safety of the crew and passengers. Likewise, when a Bell 412 air crew spotted an insurgent pointing an RPG at them in Baghdad on 14 March 2007, a door gunner immediately fired a burst of between 15 and 20 rounds at the suspected threat, who dropped to the ground and did not fire his weapon.[26] The insurgent was approximately 250 metres away from the helicopter at the time, which was 18 metres off the ground and travelling at 170 kilometres per hour, so he would have had to make the shot of his life to actually hit the aircraft with his unguided, single-shot weapon. Nevertheless, the door gunner's rapid resort to deadly force quickly eliminated the potential threat to the aircraft and allowed its crew to complete their mission without further incident.

This aspect of Blackwater's behaviour also led to 57 of the 58 known serious insurgent injuries (98 per cent) that the firm inflicted during the Iraq War. DynCorp likewise inflicted all four of its serious insurgent injuries during incidents where its personnel fired relatively quickly. While providing security for an event at the Religious University in Al-Hillah on 8 February 2007, two members of one of Blackwater's ATs shot and incapacitated a suspected sniper "within 2 seconds" of spotting his scoped rifle.[27] The shooting occurred shortly before three Department of State personnel were scheduled to leave a meeting at the university and enter their armoured limousine outside, during which time they would have been in the open and within the insurgent's field of fire.

Likewise, one of the firm's security teams responded within seconds to an insurgent ambush in Baghdad on 2 February 2007 by engaging the gunmen with small-arms fire.[28] Two severely injured insurgents were the only casualties suffered by either side during the incident. The value of rapidly employing military force to assist colleagues under threat was also demonstrated on 5 June 2004, when a Blackwater security team made up of seven employees in two GMC Suburbans – only one of which had armour – was chased down and attacked by "four to five vehicles, full of [approximately 20] armed men, all with automatic weapons", and at least one rocket-propelled grenade launcher.[29] The convoy was travelling from the Green Zone to the Baghdad airport along Route Irish when the "well-orchestrated" attack occurred.[30] The gunmen hit the lead, soft-skinned SUV's gas tank with an RPG, which engulfed the vehicle in flames, but faced a rapid counterattack by the personnel in the firm's armoured vehicle, who reportedly "expended all of their ammunition" at the insurgents.[31] The team members in the armoured SUV then placed themselves between the insurgents and their fallen comrades, including Americans Christopher Neidrich and Jarrod "J.C." Little and Poles Kryzysztof "Kaska" Kaskos and Artur "Zuku" Zukoski.[32] However, their vehicle soon lost a tyre and caught fire when two of the insurgent vehicles stopped to their rear and engaged them with copious volumes of small-arms fire.[33] The firm's surviving personnel were eventually forced to break contact and flag down a civilian vehicle to link up with coalition forces. The four contractors in the vehicle that was hit by the RPG did not survive the firefight, but their colleagues' actions prevented the insurgents from stealing their bodies.

Finally, members of multiple Blackwater ground and air teams chose to quickly respond with deadly force to an attack by approximately 30 to 50 insurgents, armed with assault rifles and belt-fed machine guns, near Amanat City Hall in Baghdad on 9 September 2007.[34] The incident began when an AT, escorting a PSD, received small-arms fire from a location approximately 200 metres south of their position. Despite suffering mechanical difficulties, one of the firm's TSTs soon arrived and immediately provided fire support to allow the PSD to escape with their clients while the firm's Little Birds provided reconnaissance and standby air support. The two remaining ground teams continued firing a large quantity of ammunition at insurgents attacking from the roofs and windows of multiple buildings, including the old headquarters of the Iraqi Ministry of Commerce, a Ministry of Justice building, a nearby mosque and at least one other.[35] A Department of State after-action report noted that this attack was more sophisticated than the one attempted against Blackwater on 23 May 2007 at the same location, since it involved a greater number of firing positions.[36] Several of the firm's vehicles suffered minor damage during the engagement and one employee was injured. In exchange, the firm's personnel swiftly killed at least five of the insurgents, all suspected of being members of the Jaysh al-Mahdi militia, and seriously injured at least 10 others before withdrawing under heavy fire to the Green Zone.

Reflecting on Blackwater's generally rapid resort to deadly force, a study of private security operations in Iraq concluded that "The tactical advantage that these teams derive from this approach is not only overwhelming firepower but also a certain deterrent factor", since would-be insurgents may have come to understand that they had a relatively low probability of carrying out a successful attack against a trigger-happy Blackwater security team.[37] Put differently, would-be insurgents may have come to believe that they had a better chance of successfully attacking convoys operated by other firms that were less prone to rapidly using deadly force.[38] Ultimately, Blackwater's tendency to rapidly resort to the use of deadly force could be the single most important factor that allowed the Secretary of State's Panel on Personal Protective Services to conclude that "The Department's security operations in Iraq have been highly effective in ensuring the safety of mission personnel" and may be why numerous other commentators, regardless of their views of Blackwater's behaviour in Iraq, have acknowledged that none of the firm's clients in Iraq were killed or seriously injured while under its protection.[39]

Engagement distance[40]

The ideational theory of tactical violence predicts that the security personnel of PSCs that place strong emphasis on norms encouraging personal initiative, proactive use of force and an exclusive approach to security should tend to employ violence against suspected threats at greater distances than the security personnel of firms that do not place strong emphasis on these norms. Employing the assumption that the suspected threats encountered by various firms travel, on average, at the same speed, security personnel who behave in this manner again reduce the amount of time available for a suspected threat to alter its behaviour and attempt to convince the security personnel that it means them no harm before they engage the suspected threat with deadly force. This, in turn, means that security personnel who behave in this manner are more likely to kill or seriously injure a suspected threat during an incident than are security personnel who behave in a less violent manner.

This prediction was supported, with Blackwater inflicting at least 21 of its 33 known insurgent deaths (64 per cent) during incidents where its personnel fired at suspected threats at distances exceeding the mean engagement distance of DynCorp's personnel. As discussed in Chapter 4, the figures on deaths and seriously injuries in this section may not reflect all of the casualties inflicted by Blackwater's personnel during relatively long-distance engagements because any incident for which the engagement distances were not known was excluded from this analysis. The firm also lost personnel during only three incidents out of a total of 48 (6 per cent) where they are known to have fired at insurgents at distances exceeding the mean engagement distance of DynCorp's personnel. The tendency by Blackwater's personnel to fire at potential threats that were relatively far away not only reduced the amount of time that would-be gunmen or suicide bombers had to attack the firm's convoys but also maintained a safety buffer between the convoys and potential attackers, which lowered the probability that an insurgent could strike a convoy with either bullets or an explosive charge.[41] Beckman, for example, recounted how his team "drilled several cars and trucks in the engine" during their operations in order to prevent these suspected threats from getting close to their comrades and clients.[42] One of the firm's DDMs shot an insurgent sniper in the head at a distance of approximately 480 metres during an incident in Mosul on 1 September 2005.[43] The firm's personnel also killed several hundred insurgents during an incident on 4 April 2004 in Najaf by engaging the gunmen at distances of up to 800 metres.[44]

Blackwater likewise inflicted at least 26 out of 58 known insurgent injuries (45 per cent) during relatively long-distance engagements. One of the firm's TSTs injured three insurgents during a firefight at the Adhamiyah Court House in Baghdad on 18 February 2007, which saw engagements at distances of 60 and 200 metres.[45] The incident began approximately 30 minutes after an AT arrived at the court house to conduct a technical support survey. At that time, the team reported receiving small-arms fire from the north, and a TST responded to provide additional security. Shortly after arriving, one of the TST's members noticed a moped carrying two Iraqi males driving up and down an alleyway about 200 metres north-west of his location. The moped's passenger, who was armed with an assault rifle, fired one bullet at the TST's lead vehicle, but he failed to hit anyone because he was too far away to take accurate shots with his AK-47. A TST member immediately returned fire with his more accurate M4 carbine and struck the shooter in the back. The moped crashed a few seconds later, leading the TST to conclude that the bullet had probably passed through the passenger and severely injured the driver as well. A TST member then noticed two other Iraqi males dashing between bits of cover as they attempted to approach the team's location. One was armed with an AK-47 while the other had a grenade. At a distance of about 60 metres, as the insurgent armed with the grenade prepared to throw his explosive, a TST member shot and severely injured him. The gunman then dragged his partner off the road. The grenade did not explode because the insurgent was shot before he pulled the pin. Finally, engaging at a distance of 250 metres, one of the firm's PSDs shot and seriously injured an insurgent at the Doura Power Plant in Baghdad on 2 September 2007.[46]

Number of bullets fired

The ideational theory of tactical violence predicts that the security personnel of PSCs that place strong emphasis on norms encouraging personal initiative, proactive use of force and an exclusive approach to security should tend to fire a greater number of bullets at suspected threats than the security personnel of firms that do not place strong emphasis on these norms. Since each bullet fired could, of course, hit a suspected threat, security personnel who behave in this manner are more likely to kill or seriously injure a suspected threat during an incident than are security personnel who behave in a less violent manner.

This prediction was supported, since Blackwater's personnel inflicted at least 27 out of 33 known insurgent deaths (82 per cent) during incidents where they fired more than five bullets. The firm also only lost personnel during three incidents out of a total of 42 (7 per cent) where they fired more than five bullets at insurgents and, as discussed later in this chapter, these were incidents where insurgents employed a great deal of violence. One of these took place on 5 June 2004, when one of the firm's two vehicle convoys was attacked by about 20 vehicle-borne insurgents who fired more than 50 bullets and at least one RPG round. The two others were part of the "Blackwater Down" event on 23 January 2007, when the firm took on approximately 1,000 well-armed insurgents in the centre of Baghdad who fired well in excess of 50 bullets at the firm's security teams.

Several incidents indicate that high volumes of fire were very helpful at neutralizing genuine threats.[47] While escorting clients to the US Embassy in Baghdad on 16 February 2005, a Blackwater AT fired far more than 50 bullets toward an approaching car containing two insurgents, killing one of them.[48] The incident occurred as the team was returning to the Embassy after conducting a security check at a venue in the Green Zone in advance of a scheduled diplomatic meeting. As the team's convoy moved with traffic, it was approached from the rear by a gray car occupied by two men dressed entirely in black. The car emerged from a side road and attempted to drive around the traffic separating it from the convoy. After the car was struck in the grille by one round, the car's driver accelerated toward the then-stationary convoy while his passenger opened his door and began firing with a handgun. In response, three members of the security detail opened fire simultaneously with "long sustained bursts" of up to 100 rounds. They struck the driver several times through the windscreen and brought the car to a halt. The passenger then fled on foot into the surrounding neighbourhood as the convoy resumed its journey to the embassy. In addition, the firm's personnel fired far in excess of 50 bullets during the incident on 19 September 2005 to neutralize insurgent gunmen in the immediate aftermath of a VBIED attack on one of the firm's convoys in Mosul.[49]

Moreover, during a series of incidents associated with an event known as "Blackwater Down", the firm's personnel fired thousands of bullets and inflicted an untold number of deaths and serious injuries in the centre of Baghdad on 23 January 2007.[50] In response to a request for support from a Blackwater PSD that was ambushed while transporting a client to the US Embassy from the Iraqi Public Works Annex, two air crews rushed to their Little Birds.[51] The convoy, using the call sign Raven 7, reported coming under "very heavy" fire from small arms, including assault rifles and light machine guns, and heavier weapons, including rocket-propelled grenades and at least one 12.7mm heavy machine gun.[52] Accounts of the incident estimated that the convoy was assaulted by nearly a thousand insurgents firing from the streets, out of buildings and vehicles and from rooftops.[53] Steve "G-Man" Gernet, a Little Bird door gunner, was killed by insurgent fire shortly after his helicopter arrived on station.[54] Gernet's body was still tethered to the aircraft by a safety harness when his team returned to the firm's Baghdad airbase, Landing Zone (LZ) Washington, where it was met by a dozen other air crew members who reportedly "all volunteered" to head back to assist Raven 7 on the next flight.[55] Two additional Blackwater Little Bird crews then took off to join the firefight. The firm's lead pilot and air commander, Dan Laguna, who had previously served as a Special Operations Aviator in the US Army's 160th SOAR, said that the "astounding" volume of enemy fire made this the most intense firefight he had ever participated in.[56]

The firm's air crews were soon joined by three more teams of ground personnel. These included a CAT operating under the call sign Raven 24 and a TST called Raven 26. Both teams were equipped with armoured vehicles, which certainly helped as they fought their way to Raven 7's location to rescue that team's personnel and client and attempted to escape to the Green Zone.[57] Moreover, an LRMT soon deployed to offer further tactical support. During the next few hours, these snipers saved one of the firm's air crews by killing multiple insurgents that were attempting to shoot down a Little Bird.[58] Blackwater's assets were supported by a US Army Stryker brigade that also rushed to assist Raven 7.[59]

During this and other engagements during the Iraq War, the firm's air crews flew at very low altitudes, of 30 metres or even less, because this made it easier for their door gunners to see and hit potential threats.[60] This tactic simultaneously made it easier for insurgents to see and hit the unarmoured helicopters. During the rescue of Raven 7, a Little Bird operating under the call sign Blackwater 3–5 was hit by insurgent fire while flying characteristically close to the ground and crashed a few blocks away from the epicentre of the Raven 7 firefight.[61] Another Little Bird crew, operating under the call sign Blackwater 3–4, braved intense insurgent gunfire to mount an aggressive search for their fallen comrades.[62] They were soon joined by three other Blackwater air crews and Raven 26, which re-entered the Red Zone after dropping off the client rescued from Raven 7 at the US Embassy.[63] During the search, Blackwater 3–4 was hit by dozens of light machine gun bullets and several rounds from a 12.7mm heavy machine gun operating from the back of a truck.[64] The crew's door gunners attempted to suppress numerous insurgents with fire from their own light machine guns, but they had trouble spotting the heavy weapon because the insurgents camouflaged it with a canopy immediately after firing.

With three punctured rotor blades and a great deal of other damage, the crew of Blackwater 3–4 was forced to make an emergency landing near the headquarters of the Iraqi Ministry of Health.[65] They took off again moments later after spotting a mob of several dozen insurgents rushing toward them. Under the protection of another air crew, operating under the call sign Blackwater 3–3, Blackwater 3–4 safely returned to LZ Washington.[66] After only 10 minutes on the ground, during which the firm's mechanics replaced the damaged rotor blades, Blackwater 3–4 lifted off again in their heavily damaged aircraft to resume the search for Blackwater 3–5.[67] As during the earlier return of the Little Bird carrying Gernet's body, every member of the firm's air crews reportedly volunteered to join the search for the missing helicopter.[68]

Most of the crew of Blackwater 3–5 died instantly when their aircraft crashed into the pavement with enough force to snap the tail boom, shatter the glass canopy, and bend the rotor blades.[69] The dead included Casey "Rooster" Casavant, Shane "War Baby" Stanfield, Ron "Cat Daddy" Johnson, and Arthur "Art" Laguna, Blackwater 3–4 pilot Dan Laguna's younger brother.[70] Johnson survived the impact but was shot in the head by an insurgent as he attempted to escape to safety.[71] Blackwater 3–4's crew risked a similar fate when they chose to land next to the crashed Little Bird and, along with Raven 26, helped the US Army Stryker unit maintain a defensive perimeter to keep the insurgents from capturing the bodies of the downed security contractors.[72] Vargas, one of Raven 26's turret gunners, stated that his team engaged in "intense fighting" as they forced their way to the crash site in the face of considerable insurgent fire: "it was their stronghold, and we made it our stronghold upon arrival.... Tears filled my eyes through my goggles, and lead filled the air to cover these brave men on the ground".[73] He also recalled "seeing many AK-47s and just parts of forearms and hands over walls and in windows. Too bad for them (the nearby insurgents) the cement wasn't the strongest, which made them easy to deal with".[74] His team employed "intense gunfire at the insurgents" to help protect Dan Laguna as he identified the bodies of the downed air crew.[75] Despite being told that they could return to LZ Washington, Blackwater 3–3's crew volunteered to provide tactical support above the crash site.[76]

If any of these assets had declined to respond to Raven 7's distress call, then most, if not all, of that team's members and their principal likely would have been surrounded and killed by the veritable horde of insurgents bearing down on them. However, the firm's use of large quantities of ammunition allowed every person travelling in Raven 7 to survive the attack.[77] Summarizing the behaviour of both the private and public troops that took part in events reminiscent of the Battle of Mogadishu in 1993, one of the participants rightly concluded that "Uncommon valor was common on that morning".[78] It is also clear that, by engaging insurgents with a relatively large number of bullets during these incidents, Blackwater's personnel not only enhanced the security of themselves and their clients but also undermined the security of the insurgents they encountered by increasing their chances of hitting and neutralizing the insurgents before they could escape or launch further attacks.

Finally, one of the deadliest incidents that saw Blackwater personnel fire well in excess of 50 bullets occurred on 4 April 2004, when eight of the firm's personnel played a central role in a multi-hour pitched battle against insurgents in Najaf.[79] The incident took place at the CPA's local headquarters, a site that Blackwater was contracted to protect.[80] The firm's personnel were joined on the day of the incident by a US Marine, three US Army military police, three Salvadorian soldiers, and Philip Kosnett, the top US civilian official in Najaf.[81] According to Corporal Lonnie Young, the Marine who took part in the fighting, the battle began when a large crowd of insurgents, who had been protesting near the CPA building, charged toward the main gate of a wall surrounding the building and began firing at the rooftops of the structure, where the soldiers and security contractors were located.[82] The Shiitte insurgent force, made up of members of Muqtada al-Sadr's Mahdi Army, numbered in the hundreds and were armed with AK-47 assault rifles, sniper rifles and rocket-propelled grenades.[83]

Young requested permission to return fire with his M249 Squad Automatic Weapon, a light machine gun, but since there were no Marine officers on the rooftop, the Blackwater personnel took command of the situation and "gave the call to commence firing".[84] Video shot on the roof of the CPA building that day confirmed this account, since it showed the firm's personnel telling the American and Salvadorian soldiers when and where to fire their weapons. The firm's personnel also operated weapons during the siege, including M4 carbines, light machine guns, grenade launchers and at least one sniper rifle, to "engage whatever targets of opportunity presented themselves" amongst the insurgent force.[85]

During the intense battle, the personnel defending the CPA building "were continuously pounded by RPGs and AK-47 gunfire".[86] In response, Blackwater's personnel, along with the American and Salvadorian soldiers, fired "clip after clip ... thousands of rounds and hundreds of 40 mm grenades into the crowd".[87] Rapidly burning through their ammunition, they were forced to pause every 15 minutes to allow their overheated gun barrels to cool.[88] One account of the battle stated that the insurgents attacked four Salvadoran soldiers who were trapped outside the CPA compound. They allegedly stuffed a grenade in the mouth of one of the soldiers and pulled the pin, shot another to death, and beat and captured the other two.[89] Without question, the insurgents wounded three of the American military personnel on the CPA rooftops with gunfire during the battle.[90] Moreover, one of the firm's personnel was struck in the face by an insurgent bullet and was treated by a colleague at the scene.[91]

Due to concessions made to Shiitte leaders, who sought to minimize the presence of foreign troops in Najaf, the US military maintained very few assets in the city.[92] As a result, when the defenders at the CPA compound radioed for support, they were informed that the US military could not respond quickly.[93] Once they learned that military support was not going to arrive any time soon, multiple Blackwater air crews, led by the firm's top pilot in Iraq, Steven "Hacksaw" Chilton, launched their own support operation and braved the insurgents' gunfire during three flights to the

CPA compound to drop off weapons and ammunition and extract Young, who had been wounded, for medical treatment.[94] Prince later recalled that:

> This was a highly unusual development; every bit of paperwork with the State Department stipulated that those Little Birds were in Baghdad for Bremer's protection detail. Nothing in our contracts said anything about military rescue or resupply operations – though, technically, our men reasoned, nothing explicitly forbade it, either. The horrors of Fallujah were fresh in everyone's minds – so much so that when Gallagher put out the word that Americans were in trouble in Najaf, more Blackwater personnel volunteered to go than our four-man helicopters could carry.[95]

These actions not only saved the Marine's life but also likely saved those of the personnel who remained on the rooftops, because they eventually would have run out of useable weapons and ammunition and been defenceless without the supplies.[96] According to Patrick Toohey, a senior Blackwater executive, the firm's men "were down to single digits of ammo" at one point.[97] Moreover, the rescue of the wounded Marine indicates that the firm had the capacity to remove at least some of its personnel from the CPA compound. However, despite this, all of the firm's ground personnel chose to remain at their posts and continue to risk their lives in defence of each other, the state-based military troops and their client's facility, in the face of considerable danger. Chris Taylor, a Blackwater employee, later reflected on his colleagues' choice to remain in the battle: "When there are rounds firing, coming at you from down range, everybody pulls together to do what needs to be done".[98]

Despite being heavily outnumbered, the Blackwater-led force prevented the insurgents from capturing the CPA compound.[99] Although they suffered some casualties, they inflicted far more to the insurgents. Young recalled that, before being extracted from the battle, he saw the bodies of hundreds of dead insurgents on the ground outside the compound.[100] This is consistent with the video footage of the incident, which showed a Blackwater employee describing the one-sided battle as "a fucking turkey shoot".[101] The engagement ended several hours after it began with the arrival of multiple US Army AH-64 Apache attack helicopters and a unit of US Special Forces soldiers that, together, convinced the insurgents to break off their attack.[102] The actions of Blackwater's personnel in Najaf earned considerable praise from senior US military officials. Referring to the firm's personnel as "coalition soldiers", US General Mark Kimmitt told reporters on 5 April 2004:

> I know on a rooftop yesterday in An Najaf, with a small group of American soldiers and coalition soldiers … who had just been through

about three and a half hours of combat, I looked in their eyes, there was no crisis. They knew what they were here for. They'd lost three wounded. We were sitting there among the bullet shells – the bullet casings – and, frankly, the blood of their comrades, and they were absolutely confident.[103]

Rather than ask to be extracted, the firm's personnel stayed to fight off a second, smaller-scale assault on the compound the next day.[104]

DynCorp similarly inflicted all eight of its insurgent deaths during an incident where its personnel fired more than 50 bullets. This occurred on 20 June 2005, in Kirkuk, when one of the firm's security teams was attacked by an IED and at least eight insurgent gunmen.[105] By firing a very large number of bullets at their attackers, the security team neutralized the threat before suffering any deaths.

Firing large numbers of bullets also allowed Blackwater's personnel to inflict at least 50 out of 58 known serious insurgent injuries (86 per cent). After an insurgent fired approximately 12 rounds at a Department of State facility in Mosul during the night of 13 April 2006, the Blackwater personnel on-site fired approximately 30 rounds toward the insurgent.[106] Hearing screams from the direction of the insurgent attack, the security team believed that they had wounded at least one of their attackers. Another of the firm's PSDs fired between 10 and 15 bullets at a gunman stationed on the roof of a building at the Doura power plant in Baghdad on 2 September 2007.[107] Despite taking the security team by surprise with his initial 10-to-15-round volley, the gunman failed to hit the team members or their clients. After receiving fire from a team member, the injured insurgent ended his attack and fell out of sight.

The firm's personnel seriously injured a further 10 insurgents during a firefight near Amanat City Hall on 9 September 2007, an incident in which the firm's personnel fired far more than 50 bullets.[108] Likewise, after suffering an IED attack in the centre of Baghdad on 12 September 2007, one of the firm's TSTs took part in a particularly violent engagement.[109] Immediately after their armoured Puma vehicle was disabled by the explosive, the victims of the initial surprise attack came under insurgent gunfire emanating from surrounding rooftops and windows and also from nearby streets. The rest of the TST's personnel fired well in excess of 50 bullets during this incident as they evacuated their injured comrades to a safer location about 300 metres away from the attack site. Their defensive fire inflicted serious injuries to at least five of their attackers. These incidents demonstrate particularly well that, by engaging insurgents with a relatively large number of bullets, Blackwater's personnel not only enhanced the security of themselves and their clients but also undermined the security of the insurgents they encountered by increasing their chances of hitting and neutralizing the insurgents before they could escape or launch further attacks.

Propensity to abandon the victims of violence

The ideational theory of tactical violence predicts that the security personnel of PSCs that place strong emphasis on norms encouraging personal initiative, proactive use of force and an exclusive approach to security should tend to abandon a greater proportion of the victims they produce through their use of violence, rather than offer them assistance, than the security personnel of firms that do not place strong emphasis on these norms. Since the security personnel of these firms have been strongly encouraged to care only about the security of their own colleagues and clients, they should feel no obligation to assist any insurgents, civilians or other actors that they harm through their use of violence. Moreover, since abandoning wounded victims could allow their injuries to worsen or even allow them to die, security personnel who behave in this manner are more likely to kill or seriously injure a suspected threat during an incident than security personnel who behave in a less violent manner.

This prediction was supported, since Blackwater's personnel abandoned at least 24 of the 33 known insurgents they are known to have killed (73 per cent) and at least 50 of the 58 insurgents they are known to have seriously injured (86 per cent) during their security operations. The firm lost personnel during only two incidents out of the total of 46 (4 per cent) where they abandoned insurgents after using violence against them. DynCorp's personnel likewise abandoned all eight of the insurgents they are known to have killed in Iraq. The tendency of Blackwater's personnel to abandon the insurgents they attacked likely enhanced the security of their colleagues and clients for several reasons. For instance, remaining at the site of a violent incident, let alone offering wounded insurgents medical attention, could have exposed the firm's personnel and clients to reprisal attacks by their victims, other insurgents or enraged civilians. As Prince informed a congressional committee:

> Our job is to get them [the firm's clients] off the X. The X is what we refer to in our business ... [as] the preplanned ambush site where bad guys have planned to kill you. So our job is to get them away from that X, to get them to a safe place. So we can't stay and secure the terrorist crime scene.[110]

The widely publicized actions of the largely civilian mob that assembled following a deadly insurgent attack on four Blackwater personnel in Fallujah in March 2004, including burning, mutilating and hanging the contractors' bodies from a bridge spanning the Euphrates River, vividly illustrated the dangers associated with remaining on-site in the aftermath of a violent incident.[111]

Moreover, insurgents mounted rapid follow-on ambushes on a number of occasions during the 2003 to 2009 period when the firm's ground security teams loitered near the site of recent insurgent attacks.[112] For example, the AT that suffered a devastating VBIED attack in Mosul on 19 September 2005 came under small-arms fire less than a minute after the explosion took place.[113] Similarly, when one of the firm's TSTs responded to an – initially brief – insurgent ambush of an AT on 9 September 2007 in Baghdad, it came under small-arms and RPG fire from multiple directions.[114] In this incident, the insurgents may have sought to lure additional Blackwater personnel into the line of fire. One of the TST's members received shrapnel wounds during this engagement. Likewise, another of the firm's TSTs came under small-arms fire shortly after stopping to assess the damage inflicted on one of its Puma armoured vehicles by an IED in Baghdad on 12 September 2007.[115] DynCorp's security teams also faced follow-on attacks. For example, on 20 June 2005, mere moments after an IED struck one of its PSDs in Kirkuk, the team came under small-arms fire.[116] The team's lead vehicle, a GMC Suburban, was disabled in a blast that also sprayed shrapnel throughout the cabin and broke one of the occupants' legs. The follow-on ambush occurred as this team member was being extracted from his vehicle. On 4 January 2006, while a DynCorp team was stopped to change the tyres of a vehicle damaged by an IED strike, it was hit with a secondary IED.[117] Finally, a DynCorp PSD en route from the Green Zone to the Iraqi Ministry of Electricity on 19 April 2006 faced small-arms fire almost immediately after suffering an IED attack that disabled one of its vehicles and injured its four passengers. The two most seriously wounded were transported to hospital by Blackwater helicopters.[118] Taking examples such as these into account, it is clear that Prince was not being disingenuous when he told a Congressional committee that "there would be a lot more firefight ... there would be a lot more shooting" if his firm's personnel routinely chose to remain at the location of violent incidents.[119] Therefore, although their tendency to abandon the victims of their violence likely contributed to several civilian and insurgent deaths during the Iraq War, it may also have prevented several friendly casualties.

Finally, remaining with a victim could have exposed a firm's personnel to the risk of arrest by coalition or Iraqi security forces, which would have deprived the firm's clients of some or all of their protection detail. The general unwillingness of Blackwater's personnel to be taken into custody by the Iraqi police was clearly demonstrated on 24 May 2007, when, following the shooting of a civilian driver by a Blackwater TST near the headquarters of the Iraqi Ministry of Interior, dozens of Ministry of Interior commandos, supported by four trucks with mounted machine guns, surrounded the team's vehicles, with AK-47s drawn, in an effort to prevent the team from escaping to the Green Zone.[120] This provoked an armed standoff in the Ministry of Interior compound as the commandos and Blackwater personnel aimed their guns at each other, waiting for the first shot to be fired. At such close quarters, even an accidental weapons discharge would have quickly degenerated into a bloodbath. Despite the arrival of American soldiers, who, during three hours of tense negotiations, attempted to defuse the situation, the Blackwater personnel refused to be taken into custody and, instead, proceeded to their compound.

Broad predictions regarding the relationship between military culture, tactical behaviour and security outcomes

The central claims of the ideational theory of tactical violence are that the behavioural norms that make up a PSC's military culture have a strong influence on the degree of violence employed by that firm's personnel and that, in turn, the degree of violence employed by these personnel strongly affects two security outcomes. These include, first, the degree of security enjoyed by the people under the firm's protection, such as the firm's personnel and clients, and, second, the degree of security enjoyed by other actors in the firm's operating environment, such as insurgents, civilians, the personnel of other PSCs and the members of state-based security and military forces. The theory predicts that if the employees of a PSC tend to employ a great deal of violence during their security operations, then they and the clients under their protection should suffer a lower casualty rate than their counterparts in firms that behave in a less violent manner. It also predicts that if the employees of a PSC tend to employ a great deal of violence during their security operations, then they should kill and seriously injure a greater number of suspected threats and innocent bystanders than the security personnel of firms that behave in a less violent manner.

This chapter has largely focused on the first prediction and demonstrated that Blackwater's military culture motivated its personnel to fire upon suspected threats more quickly, at greater distances and with a greater number of bullets and to abandon the people they shot at more readily when compared to DynCorp's personnel, who maintained a military culture that encouraged far less violent behaviour. These actions, in turn, allowed Blackwater's personnel to kill and seriously injure numerous insurgents and achieve a much lower casualty rate among themselves and the clients under their protection than their counterparts in DynCorp.

Some observers may be surprised by this conclusion, given that 20 of Blackwater's security personnel were killed in insurgent attacks during the Iraq War while DynCorp lost only 14 security personnel to enemy fire during the conflict. Indeed, at first glance, serving with Blackwater in Iraq appears noticeably more dangerous. However, Blackwater suffered its 20 deaths during eight out of the 118 total incidents where its personnel were attacked by insurgents, which meant that it suffered deaths in 6.8 per cent of these engagements and lost, on average, 0.17 employees per attack. On the other hand, DynCorp suffered its 14 deaths during 8 out of just 22 total incidents where insurgents attacked its personnel, which means that fully 36 per cent of these engagements proved deadly and that it lost, on average, 0.64 employees per attack – a casualty rate almost four times higher than Blackwater's. In other words, the members of DynCorp's security teams stood a much greater chance of being killed when they were attacked by insurgents than their counterparts in Blackwater did.

Moreover, Blackwater made it through the entire war without losing a client to enemy fire, a record the firm's personnel are fiercely proud of. As Prince put it:

> Critics may have questioned my company's tactics, but to this day no one has ever doubted our results: In some fifty thousand completed personal security detail missions, we never suffered a single loss of life or serious injury to those in our care.[121]

The *Washington Post*'s Steve Fainaru, a long-time critic of the firm's behaviour in Iraq, acknowledged "Blackwater's ruthless efficiency", since it "kept its clients safe, come hell or high water".[122] Even Jeremy Scahill, likely the firm's most ardent critic, noted that "Blackwater had done its job in Iraq: to keep the most hated US occupation officials alive by any means necessary".[123] The US Secretary of State's Panel on Personal Protective Services likewise concluded that "The Department's security operations in Iraq have been highly effective in ensuring the safety of mission personnel".[124] Finally, US Ambassador to Iraq Ryan Crocker informed a reporter that Blackwater's personnel "guard my back.... And I have to say they do it extremely well".[125] This prediction was, however, only partially supported by the empirical evidence in this case because DynCorp's more passive security personnel also managed to avoid losing any clients to enemy fire during the Iraq War.

Did Blackwater's tactical behaviour undermine the security of its personnel and clients?

Skeptical readers could argue that the relatively violent behaviour exhibited by Blackwater's employees in Iraq may have had a counterproductive effect on the security of their colleagues and clients because it may have encouraged insurgent forces to increase the frequency of their attacks against the firm's security teams. If insurgents knew or at least strongly suspected that Blackwater had killed numerous insurgents and civilians, then this may have driven them to seek out and try to harm its employees and principals. At least one major insurgent force, al-Qaeda, may have specifically targeted two of Blackwater's chief principals early in the conflict and encouraged other would-be insurgents to do the same. In May 2004, a website posted an audio file, purportedly recorded by Osama bin Laden, in which he offered a reward of 10 kilograms of gold, worth approximately US$137,000 at the time, to anyone who could penetrate Blackwater's defences and assassinate Bremer or his deputy in the CPA, Richard Jones: "We in the al-Qaeda organization will guarantee, God willing, 10,000 grams of gold to whoever kills the occupier, Bremer, or the American chief commander, or his deputy in Iraq".[126] To anyone who died in an attempt to kill these individuals, bin Laden also promised that "the great prize will be for us and for him when God grants him martyrdom".[127] Other insurgent groups reportedly offered up to US$50,000 in rewards for killing Blackwater employees.[128]

While it is clear that the behaviour of Blackwater's employees drove at least some insurgents to want to harm them or their clients, it is not clear that this desire actually increased the frequency of attacks against the firm's security teams. To be sure, Blackwater's personnel were attacked by insurgents over five times as often as their counterparts in DynCorp during the 2003 to 2009 period (118 versus 22). However, it is probable that Blackwater's personnel suffered a greater number of attacks simply because they conducted a far greater number of security operations and, consequently, spent considerably more time in the "Red Zone", where they were exposed to the threat of IEDs, VBIEDs and insurgent gunmen seeking to engage any target of opportunity that came near them. Moreover, targeting a specific firm's security teams is more challenging than it might first appear. Due to the fact that multiple firms used similar models of armoured vehicles and SUVs, insurgents probably found it difficult to distinguish between the security teams fielded by different firms.[129] Therefore, the insurgents that attacked Blackwater's convoys using firearms, VBIEDs or command-detonated IEDs were probably not able to tell which firm they were targeting. As Frank Gallagher put it in his account of the 6 December 2003 attack on Bremer's convoy, "I'm still not sure who the bad guys thought they were attacking or why no one ever took credit for the attack ... I think we were just a target of opportunity. Wrong place, wrong time".[130] Furthermore, pressure-detonated IEDs, another common insurgent weapon, are designed to detonate when a vehicle – any vehicle – drives over a pressure plate and thus could not possibly distinguish Blackwater's security vehicles from heavy civilian vehicles, vehicles operated by other firms or vehicles operated by Iraqi or coalition security forces.

Finally, even if insurgents were adept at specifically targeting Blackwater's security teams, the fact that this firm was responsible for transporting many of the most hated people in Iraq, such as Bremer, subsequent US ambassadors to Iraq, US secretaries of state, and British Prime Minister Tony Blair, likely provided sufficient motivation to attack its convoys, regardless of how its personnel behaved. The 2004 audio message attributed to bin Laden makes clear that Bremer and his deputy should be the primary targets of would-be insurgents. Regardless, neither this call to action nor the financial and spiritual incentives attached to it, which were offered just a month before Bremer's period of rule in Iraq ended, had an observable effect since Bremer's security team did not suffer any direct attacks during this period.[131] According to Prince and Gallagher, no one on Bremer's detail was even seriously injured during their entire 11-month assignment.[132] Likewise, none of the available evidence suggests that any of the financial and spiritual incentives offered by other insurgent groups influenced the frequency of attacks against the firm's security teams. The threats made against the Bremer detail's members actually suggests that the insurgents' willingness to attack a security detail was not closely linked to that detail's behaviour, since Bremer's ground security teams never fired their weapons at suspected threats, nor did they kill or injured anyone.[133]

Of perhaps greatest importance, if the deaths and serious injuries inflicted by Blackwater's personnel actually encouraged insurgents to attack them, then they should have experienced a significant increase in attacks following the scandalous Nisour Square incident in September 2007. Unlike the vast majority of other incidents where the firm's personnel used deadly force, this incident received extensive coverage from the Iraqi news media, virtually all of which explicitly blamed the firm for killing and seriously injuring over 40 Iraqi civilians. However, neither Blackwater nor DynCorp were attacked by insurgents during the three months following the Nisour Square incident. This compares favourably to the same period in 2005, when insurgents attacked Blackwater's personnel 12 times and DynCorp's twice, and in 2006, when Blackwater's personnel suffered five insurgent attacks.

Alternative explanations for Blackwater's relatively low casualty rate

A number of alternative explanations can be offered to try to account for Blackwater's relatively low casualty rate. Clearly, any notion that Blackwater's personnel faced less potent security threats in Iraq must be set aside from the start. Indeed, the firms' incident reports demonstrate that Blackwater's personnel were attacked over five times as often as their counterparts in DynCorp. Blackwater also tended to face more violent attacks. For instance, the insurgents that attacked Blackwater's personnel employed violence as their initial form of behaviour during 87 per cent of their assaults (see Table 5.1). The insurgents faced by DynCorp, in contrast, employed violence as their initial form of behaviour during 77 per cent of their assaults. These results suggest that Blackwater's personnel tended to receive less time to prepare for an attack than their counterparts in DynCorp did. These incidents, which were often ambushes or other surprise attacks, tended to be quite deadly for both firms, since Blackwater suffered nine deaths during these incidents and DynCorp suffered 10 deaths during them.

Table 5.1 First behaviour exhibited by insurgents

	Approached PSC force on foot or in vehicle	Fired a gun, RPG or mortar	Detonated an IED	Detonated a VBIED
Blackwater	15 12.71%	70 59.32%	32 27.12%	1 0.85%
DynCorp	5 22.73%	8 36.36%	9 40.91%	0 0.00%

Blackwater's personnel were not only shot at far more often than their counterparts in DynCorp, at 77 incidents to 11, but also tended to be on the receiving end of a far greater number of bullets (see Table 5.2). Of the insurgent attacks against Blackwater, 34 (29 per cent of the total) saw the insurgents fire more than five bullets at the firm's security teams, and 21 of these attacks saw the insurgents fire more than 50 rounds. DynCorp, in contrast, is only known to have suffered two attacks with more than five bullets, representing 9 per cent of its total attacks by insurgents. Blackwater suffered 14 of its 20 deaths during incidents where insurgents fired more than five bullets at its personnel. Besides the infamous Fallujah incident on 25 February 2004, where Jerko "Jerry" Zovko, Michael "Iron Mike" Teague, Stephen "Scott" Helvenston and Wesley "Wes" J.K. Batalona were ambushed and killed in multiple hails of gunfire, the firm lost another employee to gunfire on 10 May 2005, when one of its PSDs came under sporadic fire while they were exiting their vehicle at a venue.[134] Their client was not hurt by the barrage of approximately six to 20 bullets but one member of the team, Thomas "Bama" Jaichner, was shot through the hand and throat and bled to death. The firm also lost four employees, Christopher Neidrich, Jarrod "J.C." Little, Kryzysztof "Kaska" Kaskos and Artur "Zuku" Zukoski, on 5 June 2004, when their two-vehicle convoy was attacked with more than 50 bullets and at least one RPG round on Route Irish by approximately 20 vehicle-borne insurgents.[135] DynCorp did not suffer any deaths during the two incidents where its personnel were definitely attacked with more than five bullets, but in one of the attacks that

Table 5.2 Number of bullets fired by insurgents

	Unknown	No bullets	1 bullet	2–5 bullets	6–20 bullets	21–50 bullets	Over 50 bullets
Blackwater	25 21.19%	41 34.75%	7 5.93%	11 9.32%	10 8.47%	3 2.54%	21 17.80%
DynCorp	9 40.91%	11 50.00%	0 0.00%	0 0.00%	1 4.55%	0 0.00%	1 4.55%

saw insurgents fire an unknown number of bullets and RPG rounds at one of its teams, a team member named Christian Kilpatrick died instantly.[136]

A comparison of attacks with the insurgents' other preferred weapons – explosives, including IEDs, VBIEDs, grenades and RPGs – once again indicates that Blackwater's personnel faced a tougher challenge. They were attacked with explosives during 60 incidents, while DynCorp was attacked by these weapons during only 15 incidents (Table 5.3). In addition, DynCorp's security teams were known to have been attacked by multiple explosives during only one incident, whereas Blackwater's personnel were attacked with multiple explosives during at least seven incidents. In addition, Blackwater's personnel were also attacked with very large but ultimately unknown numbers of RPGs during some incidents, such as the 2004 Najaf CPA compound siege and the 2007 "Blackwater Down" incidents.[137]

There is a strong connection between the insurgents' use of explosives and their ability to kill the firms' personnel. Blackwater suffered 19 out of its 20 deaths during incidents where insurgents used explosives, such as the VBIED attack against one of its ATs in Mosul on 19 September 2005 that resulted in the deaths of Kenneth Webb, Peter Tocci and David Shephard.[138] In addition, when the rearmost armoured vehicle in one of the firm's convoys was struck by a roadside IED in Baghdad on 25 February 2005, the blast spun the vehicle around and fatally launched Bruce "Bee" Durr and James "Tracker" Cantrell out onto the pavement.[139] Likewise, an employee named Curtis "Sparky" Hundley was killed on 21 April 2005 when an IED struck his armoured vehicle in Ramadi.[140]

All but one of DynCorp's deaths occurred during incidents where insurgents used explosives. Ignatius Du Preez, Johannes Potgieter and Miguel Tablai died on 14 November 2005, when their convoy was struck by a single IED while en route to the Iraqi Ministry of Justice in Baghdad.[141] A DynCorp employee named Glen Joyce died when insurgents struck The Baghdad Hotel, which he was stationed at, with a 122mm rocket on 15 February 2007.[142] Another of the firm's employees, Jose Mauricio Mena Puerto, was killed in a VBIED attack while travelling on Route Irish on 30 November 2004.[143] Furthermore, a DynCorp team was attacked with an IED and assault rifle fire on 16 August 2004.[144] The insurgents disabled at least one vehicle in the convoy and captured a team member named

Table 5.3 Number of explosive rounds/devices used by insurgents

	Unknown	None	1	2–5	6–9
Blackwater	12 10.17%	58 49.15%	41 34.74%	5 4.24%	2 1.70%
DynCorp	1 4.55%	7 31.82%	13 59.09%	1 4.55%	0 0.00%

Herman Pretorius. It is clear that both firms suffered great losses from these attacks, but it is also clear that Blackwater weathered them better, given that it was attacked far more often and sometimes with a much higher quantity of explosives.

The notion that Blackwater's personnel tended to operate in "safer" areas of Iraq is also a non-starter because DynCorp's primary areas of operations were relatively peaceful cities in northern Iraq, such as Erbil and Kirkuk.[145] Blackwater, in contrast, primarily operated in the most unstable areas of the country, such as Baghdad, Ramadi, Najaf, Karbala and Mosul.[146] Data compiled by the US Department of Defense on the deaths of US military personnel in Iraq bear this out. For instance, no US military personnel were killed in Erbil between 2003 and 2009, and 32 were killed in Kirkuk.[147] In contrast, 962 were killed in Baghdad during the war, along with 265 in Ramadi, 21 in Najaf, 15 in Karbala and 162 in Mosul. Overall, the US military suffered more than 44 times as many deaths in Blackwater's primary operating areas as they did in DynCorp's.[148]

Data compiled by the Iraq Body Count Project on civilian deaths in Iraq tell a similar story.[149] For instance, Erbil experienced 120 insurgent-caused civilian deaths between 2003 and 2009 and just eight insurgent attacks. Kirkuk saw 740 insurgent-caused civilian deaths and 275 insurgent attacks during this period. The figures for some of Blackwater's primary areas of operations were much higher, with Baghdad experiencing 5,011 insurgent-caused civilian deaths and 1,357 attacks, Najaf seeing 255 deaths and 33 attacks, Karbala seeing 169 deaths and 33 attacks, Ramadi seeing 2,039 deaths and 558 attacks, and Mosul seeing 2,234 deaths and 867 attacks. Overall, Blackwater's primary areas of operation experienced over 10 times as many insurgent attacks against civilians (2,848 vs. 283) and suffered over 11 times as many civilian deaths (9,708 vs. 860) as DynCorp's primary areas of operation during this period.[150]

Data contained in the PSCVID lend further support. Of the incidents where insurgents employed violence against Blackwater's personnel, 66 per cent occurred in the vicinity of Baghdad, while 9 per cent occurred in the vicinity in Mosul, 4 per cent in the vicinity of Al Hillah, 3 per cent in the vicinity of Najaf, 2 per cent in the vicinity of Ramadi, 1 per cent in the vicinity of Kirkuk and none in the vicinity of Karbala or Erbil (see Table 5.4). Likewise, the vast majority of insurgent attacks on DynCorp's personnel, 68 per cent, occurred in the vicinity of Baghdad, compared to 5 per cent in the vicinity of Kirkuk and none in the vicinity of Erbil. From this it is clear that Blackwater had by far the most dangerous primary operating areas. Moreover, the firms' casualty figures indicate that not only was Baghdad easily the deadliest city that either firm operated in during the war but also that Blackwater's personnel achieved a much lower casualty rate during its operations in this city. Blackwater suffered 11 deaths (out of 20 total) over the course of 78 insurgent assaults in this city, or 0.14 deaths per attack. DynCorp, in contrast, suffered 12 deaths (out of 14

Table 5.4 Insurgent attacks per city

	Baghdad	Mosul	Al Hillah	Tikrit	Najaf	Ramadi	Kirkuk	Erbil	Other
Blackwater	78 66.10%	11 9.32%	5 4.24%	4 3.39%	4 3.39%	2 1.69%	1 0.85%	0 0.00%	13 11.01%
DynCorp	15 68.18%	2 9.09%	0 0.00%	2 9.09%	0 0.00%	0 0.00%	1 4.55%	0 0.00%	2 9.09%

total) over the course of just 15 insurgent assaults in Baghdad, which means it averaged 0.8 deaths per attack in this city – a casualty rate almost six times higher than Blackwater's.

Finally, other observers may presume that Blackwater's relatively low casualty rate was due to it having access to significantly better equipment than that available to DynCorp's personnel. However, both firms tended to use quite similar vehicles, with a mixture of medium-armoured personnel carriers, such as Mambas and Bearcats, and light-armoured HMMWVs and sport utility vehicles, such as GMC Suburbans, constituting a standard load out for both firms on many missions.[151] Therefore, both firm's employees generally enjoyed the same degree of armoured protection during their missions. Both firms also equipped their personnel with a similar range of assault rifles and light machine guns; as a result, neither firm's ground teams had a clear advantage in offensive capabilities. This is due to the fact that the Department of State determined the type and level of armour on the vehicles that would be used to transport its personnel in Iraq and the weapons that its security contractors would employ.[152] The only area where Blackwater enjoyed a distinct advantage over DynCorp was in its small fleet of Little Bird and Bell 412 helicopters, each of which usually flew with two door gunners armed with 5.56mm carbines or belt-fed machine guns.[153] However, while these assets certainly enhanced Blackwater's ability to inflict casualties upon suspected threats, they were also the most vulnerable assets in the firm's arsenal since they lacked armour and were, thus, easily damaged by insurgent gunfire. In fact, despite making up a small fraction of the firm's total security personnel, the air crews suffered 25 per cent of the firm's total deaths during the war, and the crews of multiple helicopters that were heavily damaged by insurgent gunfire narrowly escaped this fate. For example, Steve "G-Man" Gernet was shot to death on 23 January 2007 while manning a door-mounted machine gun on a Little Bird.[154] During the same day, the firm lost all four crew members of another Little Bird, Arthur "Art" Laguna, Casey "Rooster" Casavant, Shane "War Baby" Stanfield and Ron "Cat Daddy" Johnson, when it was shot down over Baghdad.[155]

Conclusion

The data discussed in this chapter indicate that the most plausible reason for Blackwater's comparatively low casualty rate is the relatively violent culturally-driven behaviour exhibited by its personnel in Iraq (see Table 5.5). Although the firm's willingness to fire at suspected threats relatively quickly resulted in the death or serious injury of dozens of non-insurgents during the war, it also allowed the firm to rapidly eliminate genuine threats to their personnel and clients. Likewise, the firm's willingness to fire at suspected threats that were relatively far away from its convoys also produced unnecessary non-insurgent casualties but, again, helped neutralize plenty of

164 *Military culture and friendly casualties*

Table 5.5 Support for the predictions of the ideational theory of tactical violence

The security personnel of PSCs that place strong emphasis on norms encouraging personal initiative, proactive use of force and an exclusive approach to security should tend to employ violence more quickly after observing a suspected threat than the security personnel of firms that do not place strong emphasis on these norms.	Supported
The security personnel of PSCs that place strong emphasis on norms encouraging personal initiative, proactive use of force and an exclusive approach to security should tend to employ violence against suspected threats at greater distances than the security personnel of firms that do not place strong emphasis on these norms.	Supported
The security personnel of PSCs that place strong emphasis on norms encouraging personal initiative, proactive use of force and an exclusive approach to security should tend to fire a greater number of bullets at suspected threats than the security personnel of firms that do not place strong emphasis on these norms.	Supported
The security personnel of PSCs that place strong emphasis on norms encouraging personal initiative, proactive use of force and an exclusive approach to security should tend to abandon a greater proportion of the victims they produce through their use of violence, rather than offer them assistance, when compared to the security personnel of firms that do not place strong emphasis on these norms.	Supported
The security personnel and clients of PSCs that tend to employ a great deal of violence during their security operations should suffer a lower casualty rate than their counterparts in firms that behave in a less violent manner.	Partially supported
The security personnel of PSCs that tend to employ a great deal of violence during their security operations should kill and seriously injure a greater number of suspected threats and innocent bystanders than their counterparts in firms that behave in a less violent manner.	Supported

genuine threats before they could get close enough to take more accurate, close-range shots, throw grenades, or detonate a VBIED. The firm's willingness to fire relatively large numbers of bullets at suspected threats had deleterious effects on the civilians and other non-insurgents they mistakenly targeted, but it is also closely connected with their ability to kill and seriously injure insurgents. Indeed, the firm's ground teams survived several well-organized assaults by large groups of insurgents by firing hundreds of rounds of rifle and machine gun ammunition at their attackers. Finally, the firm's propensity to abandon nearly all of the people they used violence against helped reduce their exposure to both ad hoc and pre-planned follow-on attacks. DynCorp's comparatively passive behaviour, in contrast, likely prevented numerous unnecessary civilian deaths and serious injuries but also may have exposed the firm's personnel and clients to greater risk of harm. With this said, however, the theory's prediction that the security personnel of PSCs that tend to employ a great deal of violence during their security operations should suffer a lower casualty rate than their counterparts in firms that behave in a less violent manner was only partially supported: although DynCorp's relatively passive security personnel suffered a higher casually rate, they, like Blackwater, did not lose any clients to enemy fire. Chapter 7 discusses the implications of these findings for the use and development of private armed forces.

Notes

1 Blackwater, PSD Incident Report, 19 September 2005; US Department of State Diplomatic Security Service, "DS Report Number 2005–0092"; US Embassy, Baghdad, "Spot Report – 091905–01"; House Committee on Oversight and Government Reform, "Hearing on Blackwater USA", 78–79; Oppel and Tavernise, "Attacks in Iraq".
2 BVA Honor Roll.
3 House Committee on Oversight and Government Reform, "Hearing on Blackwater USA", 78–79.
4 Blackwater, PSD Incident Report, 19 September 2005.
5 Blackwater, PSD Incident Report, 19 September 2005; US Department of State Diplomatic Security Service, "DS Report Number 2005–0092"; US Embassy, Baghdad, "Spot Report – 091905–01"; House Committee on Oversight and Government Reform, "Hearing on Blackwater USA", 78–79; Oppel and Tavernise, "Attacks in Iraq".
6 Scahill, *Blackwater*, 1st edn, 77.
7 Scahill, *Blackwater*, 1st edn, 77; Roos, "1-shot killer".
8 Scahill, *Blackwater*, 1st edn, 78; Roos, "1-shot killer".
9 Roos, "1-shot killer".
10 Fainaru, *Big Boy Rules*, 173; Welch, "Fragmented Power", 354; Blackwater, PSD Incident Report, 23 May 2007.
11 Simons, *Master of War*, 163; Welch, "Fragmented Power", 354; Blackwater, PSD Incident Report, 23 May 2007.
12 Blackwater, PSD Incident Report, 23 May 2007; Cave, Burns and Adeeb, "Roadside Bombings"; Fainaru and al-Izzi, "US Security Contractors"; Simons, *Master of War*, 163. Two of the firm's personnel suffered minor shrapnel wounds during the incident.
13 Laguna, *You Have to Live Hard*, Loc. 332–333 and 3160–3161; Kimberlin, "Blackwater's 'Little Birds'"; Simons, *Master of War*, 154–155; Dunigan, *Victory for Hire*, 145.
14 Laguna, *You Have to Live Hard*, Loc. 388–390.
15 Quoted in Kimberlin, "Blackwater's 'Little Birds'".
16 Laguna, *You Have to Live Hard*, Loc. 394; Staff, "Five Killed".
17 Laguna, *You Have to Live Hard*, Loc. 381; Kimberlin, "Blackwater's 'Little Birds'"; Batty, "Rock Stars of Baghdad".
18 Laguna, *You Have to Live Hard*, Loc. 422–424.
19 Ibid., Loc. 438–439.
20 Majority Staff, "Memorandum", 8–9; Blackwater, PSD Incident Report, 24 November 2004.
21 Blackwater, PSD Incident Report, 20 September 2005; US Embassy, Baghdad, "Spot Report – 092005–03".

22 Blackwater, PSD Incident Report, 20 September 2005.
23 Blackwater, PSD Incident Report, 28 May 2006; US Embassy, Baghdad, "Spot Report – 052806–02".
24 US Embassy, Baghdad, "Spot Report – 022507–01"; Blackwater, PSD Incident Report, 25 February 2007.
25 Howard, "COM Helicopter".
26 Blackwater, PSD Incident Report, 14 March 2007; US Embassy, Baghdad, "Spot Report – 031407–04".
27 US Embassy, Baghdad, "Spot Report – 020807–01"; Blackwater, PSD Incident Report, 8 February 2007.
28 US Embassy, Baghdad, "RS-2007–00011".
29 Neff and Price, "Ambush Kills 4 Workers"; Levesque, "Clearwater Security Worker"; Scahill, *Blackwater*, 1st edn, 163; Agence France-Presse, "Four Hired Guns"; Kirka, "Four Employees"; Deutsche Presse-Agentur, "Four Private Security Workers"; *The Warsaw Voice*, "Have Gun"; Chachere, "Palm Harbor Man"; CIS World Services, "In Memory of Chris Neidrich"; Prince, *Civilian Warriors*, 158; Gallagher and Del Vecchio, *The Bremer Detail*.
30 Levesque, "Clearwater Security Worker"; Prince, *Civilian Warriors*, 158.
31 Chachere, "Palm Harbor Man"; *The Warsaw Voice*, "Have Gun"; Kirka, "Four Employees"; Scahill, *Blackwater*, 1st edn, 163; Agence France-Presse, "Four Hired Guns"; Levesque, "Clearwater Security Worker"; Deutsche Presse-Agentur, "Four Private Security Workers"; Neff and Price, "Ambush Kills 4".
32 BVA Honor Roll.
33 CIS World Services, "In Memory of Chris Neidrich".
34 Burke *et al.*, "Second Amended Complaint", 10–11; Scahill, *Blackwater*, 2nd edn, 12; Partlow and Raghavan, "Iraq Probe"; US Department of State Diplomatic Security Service, "DS Report Number 2007–00096"; Blackwater, PSD Incident Report, 9 September 2007; US Embassy, Baghdad, "Spot Report – 090907–01"; US Department of State Diplomatic Security Service, "City Hall Engagement".
35 US Department of State Diplomatic Security Service, "City Hall Engagement".
36 Ibid.
37 Lonsdale, "Convoy Security", 7–8.
38 Beckman, *Blackwater from the Inside Out*, Loc. 609–613.
39 House Committee on Oversight and Government Reform, "Hearing on Blackwater USA", 18 and 26; Dunning, "Heroes or Mercenaries?", 7; Fainaru, *Big Boy Rules*, 140; Laguna, *You Have to Live Hard*, Loc. 326–342; Beckman, *Blackwater from the Inside Out*, Loc. 422–423; Boswell *et al.*, "Secretary of State's Panel", 5; Scahill, *Blackwater*, 2nd edn, 16; Associated Press, "US Ambassador"; Sands, "Bush Lauds Security Firm"; House Committee on Oversight and Government Reform, "Hearing on Blackwater USA", 56 and 68.
40 Eight Blackwater incidents were intentionally excluded from this analysis of mean engagement distances. These incidents were extreme outliers, for they involved engagement distances of 482, 500, 550, 600, 800 and 1,300 metres, which are considerably longer than the firm's next-longest engagement distance of 350 metres. Including these incidents would have therefore increased the firm's mean engagement distances to a point where they would no longer accurately reflect the firm's general behaviour.
41 House Committee on Oversight and Government Reform, "Hearing on Blackwater USA", 54–55.
42 Beckman, *Blackwater from the Inside Out*, Loc. 368–369 and 662–675.
43 US Embassy, Baghdad, "Spot Report – 090105–01". The Iraqi sniper died instantly.

44 Chatterjee, *Iraq, Inc.*, 129–130; Human Rights First, "Private Security Contractors", 24; Sizemore and Kimberlin, "Blackwater"; Majority Staff, "Memorandum", 8; Miller, *Blood Money*, 165; Gallagher and Del Vecchio, *The Bremer Detail*, Loc. 2246.
45 US Embassy, Baghdad, "Spot Report – 021807–01"; Blackwater, PSD Incident Report, 18 February 2007.
46 Blackwater, PSD Incident Report, 2 September 2007.
47 Fainaru, *Big Boy Rules*, 88; Carafano, *Private Sector, Public Wars*, 107; Simons, *Master of War*, 176 and 262; Dunigan, *Victory for Hire*, 71–72; Scahill, *Blackwater*, 2nd edn, 8.
48 Blackwater, PSD Incident Report, 16 February 2005; US Department of State Diplomatic Security Service, "DS Report Number 2005–0005".
49 Blackwater, PSD Incident Report, 19 September 2005; US Department of State Diplomatic Security Service, "DS Report Number 2005–0092"; US Embassy, Baghdad, "Spot Report – 091905–01"; House Committee on Oversight and Government Reform, "Hearing on Blackwater USA", 78–79; Oppel and Tavernise, "Attacks in Iraq".
50 US Embassy, Baghdad, "Spot Report – 012307–02".
51 Kimberlin, "Blackwater's 'Little Birds'".
52 Laguna, *You Have to Live Hard*, Loc. 432–433 and 498–500; Simons, *Master of War*, 154.
53 Laguna, *You Have to Live Hard*, Loc. 441, 469–470 and 499–500.
54 Ibid., Loc. 442–443; Kimberlin, "Blackwater's 'Little Birds'"; Simons, *Master of War*, 154–155; Associated Press, "US Helicopter Crashes"; Staff, "Five Killed"; BVA Honor Roll.
55 Laguna, *You Have to Live Hard*, Loc. 476–477; Simons, *Master of War*, 155.
56 Laguna, *You Have to Live Hard*, Loc. 350 and 498–499.
57 Ibid., Loc. 585–593.
58 Ibid., Loc. 556–564.
59 Ibid., Loc. 496, 501, 649–654, 662–667 and 696–728; Batty, "Rock Stars of Baghdad".
60 Laguna, *You Have to Live Hard*, Loc. 501–502; Staff, "Five Killed".
61 Laguna, *You Have to Live Hard*, Loc. 504–522; Kimberlin, "Blackwater's 'Little Birds'"; Batty, "Rock Stars of Baghdad"; Associated Press, "US Helicopter Crashes"; Staff, "Five Killed".
62 Laguna, *You Have to Live Hard*, Loc. 531–550; Simons, *Master of War*, 154–155; Staff, "Five Killed".
63 Laguna, *You Have to Live Hard*, 565 and 590–593.
64 Ibid., Loc. 549–556; Simons, *Master of War*, 156–157.
65 Laguna, *You Have to Live Hard*, Loc. 593–596; Simons, *Master of War*, 157.
66 Laguna, *You Have to Live Hard*, Loc. 604–623; Kimberlin, "Blackwater's 'Little Birds'"; Simons, *Master of War*, 155.
67 Laguna, *You Have to Live Hard*, Loc. 622–633; Simons, *Master of War*, 157.
68 Laguna, *You Have to Live Hard*, Loc. 633–640.
69 Ibid., Loc. 650–667; Kimberlin, "Blackwater's 'Little Birds'"; Batty, "Rock Stars of Baghdad"; Simons, *Master of War*, 156–157; Associated Press, "US Helicopter Crashes".
70 BVA Honor Roll.
71 Gallagher and Del Vecchio, *The Bremer Detail*, Loc. 2491.
72 Laguna, *You Have to Live Hard*, Loc. 675–690; Kimberlin, "Blackwater's 'Little Birds'"; Simons, *Master of War*, 157.
73 Quoted in Laguna, *You Have to Live Hard*, Loc. 669–670, 698–701 and 3570–3581.
74 Quoted in Laguna, *You Have to Live Hard*, Loc. 3559–3561.

75 Laguna, *You Have to Live Hard*, Loc. 700–701.
76 Kimberlin, "Blackwater's 'Little Birds'"; Simons, *Master of War*.
77 Staff, "Five Killed".
78 Laguna, *You Have to Live Hard*, Loc. 668–669.
79 Chatterjee, *Iraq, Inc.*, 129–130; Human Rights First, "Private Security Contractors", 24; Sizemore and Kimberlin, "Blackwater"; Majority Staff, "Memorandum", 8; Miller, *Blood Money*, 165; Gallagher and Del Vecchio, *The Bremer Detail*, Loc. 2246.
80 Rosen, *Contract Warriors*, 38–39; Priest, "Private Guards"; Scahill, *Blackwater*, 1st edn, 118; Wiltrout, "If I Had to Die".
81 Barstow, "Security Firm Says"; Rosen, *Contract Warriors*, 38–39; Priest, "Private Guards"; Scahill, *Blackwater*, 1st edn, 122; Human Rights First, "Private Security Contractors", 24; Prince, *Civilian Warriors*, 133–135.
82 Scahill, *Blackwater*, 1st edn, 123–124; *US Fed News*, "True Grit".
83 Rosen, *Contract Warriors*, 38–39; Priest, "Private Guards"; Scahill, *Blackwater*, 1st edn, 118–119; Human Rights First, "Private Security Contractors", 5; Wiltrout, "If I Had to Die"; Miller, *Blood Money*, 165; Prince, *Civilian Warriors*, 142. Estimates of the size of the insurgent force ranged from 300 to 2,000 fighters.
84 Scahill, *Blackwater*, 1st edn, 123; *US Fed News*, "True Grit".
85 Scahill, *Blackwater*, 1st edn, 125–130; Majority Staff, "Memorandum", 8; Human Rights First, "Private Security Contractors", 24.
86 Rosen, *Contract Warriors*, 38–39; Scahill, *Blackwater*, 1st edn, 123–124; Wiltrout, "If I Had to Die"; Priest, "Private Guards".
87 Scahill, *Blackwater*, 1st edn, 124; Priest, "Private Guards"; *US Fed News*, "True Grit".
88 Wiltrout, "If I Had to Die"; Barstow, "Security Firm Says".
89 Shadid, *Night Draws Near*.
90 Rosen, *Contract Warriors*, 38–39; Scahill, *Blackwater*, 1st edn, 125–130.
91 Scahill, *Blackwater*, 1st edn, 125–126.
92 Ibid., 122.
93 Rosen, *Contract Warriors*, 38–39; Chatterjee, *Iraq, Inc.*, 129–130; Miller, *Blood Money*, 165.
94 Chatterjee, *Iraq, Inc.*, 129–130; Priest, "Private Guards"; Rosen, *Contract Warriors*, 38–39; Wiltrout, "If I Had to Die"; Scahill, *Blackwater*, 1st edn, 125–130; Barstow, "Security Firm Says"; Human Rights First, "Private Security Contractors", 16; Majority Staff, "Memorandum", 8; Miller, *Blood Money*, 165; Prince, *Civilian Warriors*, 142–144.
95 Prince, *Civilian Warriors*, 143.
96 Wiltrout, "If I Had to Die"; Sizemore and Kimberlin, "Blackwater".
97 Barstow, "Security Firm Says".
98 Wiltrout, "If I Had to Die".
99 Barstow, "Security Firm Says"; Scahill, *Blackwater*, 1st edn, 125–130.
100 *US Fed News*, "True Grit"; Scahill, *Blackwater*, 1st edn, 125–130; Gallagher and Del Vecchio, *The Bremer Detail*, Loc. 2249.
101 Scahill, *Blackwater*, 1st edn, 125–130; Sizemore and Kimberlin, "Blackwater".
102 Priest, "Private Guards"; Human Rights First, "Private Security Contractors", 24.
103 Quoted in Rosen, *Contract Warriors*, 38–39; Scahill, *Blackwater*, 1st edn, 129–130.
104 Gallagher and Del Vecchio, *The Bremer Detail*, Loc. 2249–2276.
105 US Embassy, Baghdad, "Spot Report – 062005-7"; US Department of State Diplomatic Security Service, "DS Report for June 20, 2005".
106 US Embassy, Baghdad, "Spot Report – 041306–02".

Military culture and friendly casualties 169

107 Blackwater, PSD Incident Report, 2 September 2007; US Department of State Diplomatic Security Service, "DS Report Number RS-2007–00351"; US Embassy, Baghdad, "RS-2007–00351".
108 Scahill, *Blackwater*, 2nd edn, 12; Partlow and Raghavan, "Iraq Probe"; US Embassy, Baghdad, "Spot Report – 090907–01"; Blackwater, PSD Incident Report, 9 September 2007; US Department of State Diplomatic Security Service, "DS Report Number 2007–00096".
109 Blackwater, PSD Incident Report, 12 September 2007; Partlow and Raghavan, "Iraq Probe"; US Embassy, Baghdad, "Spot Report – 091207–01"; Scahill, *Blackwater*, 2nd edn, 12.
110 House Committee on Oversight and Government Reform, "Hearing on Blackwater USA", 61 and 71.
111 Chan, "US Civilians Mutilated"; Schmitt, "Test in a Tinderbox".
112 Blackwater, PSD Incident Report, 31 January 2007; US Embassy, Baghdad, "Spot Report – 013107–01"; Blackwater, PSD Incident Report, 19 September 2005; US Department of State Diplomatic Security Service, "DS Report Number 2005–0092"; US Embassy, Baghdad, "Spot Report – 091905–01".
113 Blackwater, PSD Incident Report, 19 September 2005; US Department of State Diplomatic Security Service, "DS Report Number 2005–0092"; US Embassy, Baghdad, "Spot Report – 091905–01"; House Committee on Oversight and Government Reform, "Hearing on Blackwater USA", 78–79; Oppel and Tavernise, "Attacks in Iraq".
114 Burke *et al.*, "Second Amended Complaint", 10–11; Scahill, *Blackwater*, 2nd edn, 12; Partlow and Raghavan, "Iraq Probe"; US Department of State Diplomatic Security Service, "DS Report Number 2007–00096"; Blackwater, PSD Incident Report,
9 September 2007; US Embassy, Baghdad, "Spot Report – 090907–01".
115 Blackwater, PSD Incident Report, 12 September 2007; Partlow and Raghavan, "Iraq Probe"; US Embassy, Baghdad, "Spot Report – 091207–01"; Scahill, *Blackwater*, 2nd edn, 12.
116 US Embassy, Baghdad, "Spot Report – 062005–7"; US Department of State Diplomatic Security Service, "DS Report for June 20, 2005".
117 US Embassy, Baghdad, "Spot Report – 010406–02"; DGSD, PSD Incident Report, 4 January 2006.
118 US Embassy, Baghdad, "Spot Report – 041906–01"; DGSD, PSD Incident Report, 19 April 2006.
119 House Committee on Oversight and Government Reform, "Hearing on Blackwater USA", 60–61.
120 Blackwater, PSD Incident Report, 24 May 2007; Fainaru, *Big Boy Rules*, 173–175; Scahill, *Blackwater*, 2nd edn, 11–12; Simons, *Master of War*, 163; Prince, *Civilian Warriors*, 214.
121 Prince, *Civilian Warriors*, 312.
122 Fainaru, *Big Boy Rules*, 176.
123 Scahill, *Blackwater*, 2nd edn, 16.
124 Boswell *et al.*, "Secretary of State's Panel", 5.
125 Associated Press, "US Ambassador".
126 CNN Staff, "Purported bin Laden Tape"; Scahill, *Blackwater*, 2nd edn, 137; Prince, *Civilian Warriors*, 81; Gallagher and Del Vecchio, *The Bremer Detail*, Loc. 2600–2603.
127 CNN Staff, "Purported bin Laden Tape".
128 Pelton, "Riding Shotgun"; Prince, *Civilian Warriors*, 81; *Virginian-Pilot* Staff, "In His Own Words"; Gallagher and Del Vecchio, *The Bremer Detail*, Loc. 1650.
129 Prince, *Civilian Warriors*, 159.

130 Gallagher and Del Vecchio, *The Bremer Detail*, Loc. 1309.
131 Security teams affiliated with the Bremer detail were attacked only three times: on 6 December 2003, on 27 January 2004 and in February 2004. Gallagher and Del Vecchio, *The Bremer Detail*, Loc. 1265–1317, 1684, 1718 and 1962.
132 Prince, *Civilian Warriors*, 81; Gallagher and Del Vecchio, *The Bremer Detail*, Loc. 1650.
133 Gallagher and Del Vecchio, *The Bremer Detail*.
134 Blackwater, PSD Incident Report, 10 May 2005; BVA Honor Roll.
135 Neff and Price, "Ambush Kills 4 Workers"; Levesque, "Clearwater Security Worker"; Scahill, *Blackwater*, 1st edn, 163; Agence France-Presse, "Four Hired Guns"; Kirka, "Four Employees"; Deutsche Presse-Agentur, "Four Private Security Workers"; *The Warsaw Voice*, "Have Gun"; Chachere, "Palm Harbor Man"; CIS World Services, "In Memory of Chris Neidrich"; BVA Honor Roll.
136 Associated Press, "News in Brief"; McClintock, "Ranger Christian Kilpatrick"; Fimrite, "Tears Flow".
137 Laguna, *You Have to Live Hard*, Loc. 442–443; Kimberlin, "Blackwater's 'Little Birds'"; Simons, *Master of War*, 154–155; Associated Press, "US Helicopter Crashes"; Staff, "Five Killed"; BVA Honor Roll.
138 Blackwater, PSD Incident Report, 19 September 2005; US Department of State Diplomatic Security Service, "DS Report Number 2005–0092"; US Embassy, Baghdad, "Spot Report – 091905–01"; House Committee on Oversight and Government Reform, "Hearing on Blackwater USA", 78–79; Oppel and Tavernise, "Attacks in Iraq".
139 Blackwater, PSD Incident Report, 12 March 2005.
140 Burns, "Video"; Scahill, *Blackwater*, 2nd edn, 362.
141 Semple and Wong, "US–Iraqi Assault"; Anderson, "US Widens Offensive"; DGSD, "Two Dead"; DGSD, "South African Man Dies".
142 Nelson, "West Union Security Guard"; Associated Press, "Iowa Native Injured"; DGSD, "DynCorp International Security Supervisor Killed".
143 Martinez, "Soldado Hondureno Muere".
144 Phildander and Ekron, "They Want Money"; Brink, "Complaint for Damages"; Cropley, "Big Risks".
145 Majority Staff, "Memorandum", 4; US Department of State and the Broadcasting Board of Governors Office of the Inspector General, "Joint Audit", 7.
146 Uesseler, *Servants of War*, 86; US Department of State and the Broadcasting Board of Governors Office of the Inspector General, "Joint Audit", 7; Dunning, "Heroes or Mercenaries?", 8.
147 US Department of Defense, "US Military Hostile Casualties".
148 Ibid.
149 Iraq Body Count, "Database of Incidents".
150 Ibid.
151 Beckman, *Blackwater from the Inside Out*, Loc. 343, 492–496, 640–642, 887–890 and 981–985; Simons, *Master of War*, 243; Pelton, *Licensed to Kill*, 9; Thurner, "Drowning in Blackwater", 64; Prince, *Civilian Warriors*, 159; Fainaru, *Big Boy Rules*, 52; DGSD, PSD Incident Report, 15 August 2008; Blackwater, PSD Incident Report, 8 May 2008; US Embassy, Baghdad, "Spot Report – 091207–01"; US Embassy, Baghdad, "Spot Report – 050905–01"; Blackwater, PSD Incident Report, 20 June 2005, 24 September 2006; US Department of State and the Broadcasting Board of Governors Office of the Inspector General, "Review of Security Programs", 2, 29 and 33–34; Thurner, "Drowning in Blackwater", 64; Schumacher, *A Bloody Business*, 74; US Embassy, Baghdad, "Spot Report – 091507–01"; DGSD, PSD Incident Report, 1 February 2006; Blackwater, PSD Incident Report, 17 July 2007, 15 June 2008, 15 January 2009.

152 Prince, *Civilian Warriors*, 156.
153 Beckman, *Blackwater from the Inside Out*, Loc. 354–355; Simons, *Master of War*, 72.
154 Laguna, *You Have to Live Hard*, Loc. 442–443; Kimberlin, "Blackwater's 'Little Birds'"; Simons, *Master of War*, 154–155; Associated Press, "US Helicopter Crashes"; Staff, "Five Killed"; BVA Honor Roll.
155 Laguna, *You Have to Live Hard*, Loc. 504–522; Kimberlin, "Blackwater's 'Little Birds'"; Batty, "Rock Stars of Baghdad"; Associated Press, "US Helicopter Crashes"; Staff, "Five Killed"; Gallagher and Del Vecchio, *The Bremer Detail*, Loc. 2491.

References

Agence France-Presse. "Four Hired Guns Killed in Baghdad Ambush Saturday". *Agence France-Presse*, 6 June 2004.
Anderson, John Ward. "US Widens Offensive in Far Western Iraq". *Washington Post*, 15 November 2005.
Associated Press. "News in Brief from California's North Coast". 21 May 2004.
Associated Press. "US Helicopter Crashes in Iraq in the Past 6 Months". 7 February 2007.
Associated Press. "Iowa Native Injured in Iraq during Private Security Duty". 21 February 2007.
Associated Press. "US Ambassador Calls Blackwater Shooting Horrific, but Still Feels High Regard for Guards". 25 October 2007.
Barstow, David. "Security Firm Says Its Workers Were Lured Into Iraqi Ambush". *New York Times*, 9 April 2004.
Batty, Roy. "Rock Stars of Baghdad". *Military.com*, 8 February 2007.
Beckman, Tim. *Blackwater from the Inside Out*. Kindle edn. New York: HDTI, 2010.
Blackwater. PSD Incident Reports and Sworn Statements. Baghdad: Blackwater, 2005–2009.
Boswell, Eric J., George A. Joulwan, J. Stapleton Roy and Patrick F. Kennedy. "Report of the Secretary of State's Panel on Personal Protective Services in Iraq". Washington, DC: US Department of State, October 2007.
Brink, Daniel. "Complaint for Damages and Declaratory and Injunctive Relief". Washington, DC: The United States District Court for the District of Columbia, 26 September 2011.
Burke, Susan L., William T. O'Neil, Elizabeth M. Burke, Rosemary B. Healy and Katherine B. Hawkins. "Second Amended Complaint in Abtan v. Blackwater". Washington, DC: The United States District Court for the District of Columbia, 28 March 2008.
Burns, John F. "Video Appears to Show Insurgents Kill a Downed Pilot". *New York Times* (23 April 2005).
BVA Honor Roll (Blackwater Veterans Association. "Honor Roll – Blackwater Personnel Killed in Action". 6 January 2013. Available at: https://bwvets.com/index.php?forums/honor-roll-blackwater-personnel-killed-in-action.63/).
Carafano, James Jay. *Private Sector, Public Wars: Contractors in Combat – Afghanistan, Iraq, and Future Conflicts*. Westport, CT: Praeger Security International, 2008.
Cave, Damien, John F. Burns and Ali Adeeb. "Roadside Bombings Kill 2 More G.I.'s in Iraq". *New York Times*, 28 May 2007.

Chachere, Vickie. "Palm Harbor Man Among Dead in Ambush on Iraq Convoy". Associated Press, 7 June 2004.

Chan, Sewell. "US Civilians Mutilated in Iraq". *Washington Post*, 1 April 2004.

Chatterjee, Pratap. *Iraq, Inc.: A Profitable Occupation*. New York: Seven Stories Press, 2004.

CIS World Services. "In Memory of Chris Neidrich (Raven 18)". CIS World Services, 2004. Available from www.cisworldservices.org/memorial/RAVEN18.html.

CNN Staff. "Purported bin Laden Tape Offers Gold for Bremer". *CNN.com*, 7 May 2004.

Cropley, Ed. "Big Risks, Big Rewards for Iraq's 'Dogs of War'". *Reuters News*, 20 September 2004.

Deutsche Presse-Agentur. "Four Private Security Workers Killed in Iraq". *Deutsche Presse-Agentur*, 6 June 2004.

DGSD. "Two Dead and Two Seriously Injured in Iraq". Falls Church, VA: DynCorp, 14 November 2005.

DGSD. "South African Man Dies from Injuries Received in Iraq". Falls Church, VA: DynCorp, 19 November 2005.

DGSD (DynCorp Government Services Division). "DynCorp International Security Supervisor Killed in Baghdad". Baghdad: DynCorp, 19 February 2007.

DGSD. PSD Incident Reports and Sworn Statements. Falls Church, VA: DynCorp, 2005–2008.

Dunigan, Molly. *Victory for Hire: Private Security Companies' Impact on Military Effectiveness*. Stanford, CA: Stanford Security Studies, 2011.

Dunning, Rebecca. "Heroes or Mercenaries? Blackwater, Private Security Companies, and the US Military". Case study. Durham, NC: The Kenan Institute for Ethics, Duke University, 2010.

Fainaru, Steve. *Big Boy Rules: America's Mercenaries Fighting in Iraq*. Philadelphia: Da Capo Press, 2008.

Fainaru, Steve, and Saad al-Izzi. "US Security Contractors Open Fire in Baghdad; Blackwater Employees Were Involved in Two Shooting Incidents in Past Week". *Washington Post*, 27 May 2007.

Fimrite, Peter. "Tears Flow in Santa Rosa for Civilian Slain in Iraq". *San Francisco Chronicle*, 5 May 2004.

Gallagher, Frank, and John M. Del Vecchio. *The Bremer Detail: Protecting the Most Threatened Man in the World*. Kindle edn. New York: Open Road Media, 2014.

House Committee on Oversight and Government Reform. "Hearing on Blackwater USA". Washington, DC: House of Representatives, Congress of the United States, 2 October 2007.

Howard, Joseph J. "COM Helicopter Suffers Damage from Ground Fire South of Baghdad". Baghdad: US Department of State, 26 February 2007.

Human Rights First. "Private Security Contractors at War: Ending the Culture of Impunity". New York: Human Rights First, 2008.

Iraq Body Count. "Database of Incidents of Civilian Deaths from Violence in Iraq". Iraq Body Count, 2 February 2012.

Kimberlin, Joanne. "Blackwater's 'Little Birds' of Baghdad Pack Quite a Sting". *Virginian-Pilot*, 1 March 2007.

Kirka, Danica. "Four Employees of US Company Killed in Ambush in Baghdad". Associated Press (6 June 2004).

Laguna, Dan. *You Have to Live Hard to Be Hard: One Man's Life in Special Operations.* Kindle edn. Bloomington, IN: Authorhouse, 2010.
Levesque, William R. "Clearwater Security Worker Killed in Iraq". *St. Petersburg Times*, 8 June 2004.
Lonsdale, Mark V. "Convoy Security in Semi-permissive War Zones (Iraq and Afghanistan)". Washington, DC: Operational Studies, 2007.
Majority Staff. "Memorandum – Additional Information about Blackwater USA". Washington, DC: Congress of the United States, 1 October 2007.
Martinez, Renan. "Soldado Hondureno Muere en Irak Opciones". *La Prensa*, 12 December 2004.
McClintock, Mike. "Ranger Christian Kilpatrick Remembered". *Ranger Register XI-4*, 6–7.
Miller, T. Christian. *Blood Money: Wasted Billions, Lost Lives, and Corporate Greed in Iraq.* New York: Little, Brown and Company, 2006.
Neff, Joseph, and Jay Price. "Ambush Kills 4 Workers in Iraq; Men Worked for N.C. Security Firm". *News and Observer*, 7 June 2004.
Nelson, Josh. "West Union Security Guard Injured in Iraq". *Waterloo Courier*, 20 February 2007.
Oppel, Richard A., and Sabrina Tavernise. "Attacks in Iraq Kill 9 Americans, Including State Dept. Aide". *New York Times*, 21 September 2005.
Partlow, Joshua, and Sudarsan Raghavan. "Iraq Probe of US Security Firm Grows; Blackwater, Accused of Killing 11 on Sunday, Cited in Earlier Deaths". *Washington Post*, 22 September 2007.
Pelton, Robert Young. "Riding Shotgun in Baghdad". *Popular Mechanics* (April 2005).
Pelton, Robert Young. *Licensed to Kill: Hired Guns in the War on Terror.* New York: Crown Publishers, 2006.
Phildander, Rusana, and Ziegfried Ekron. "They Want Money for His Body". *Die Burger*, 7 September 2004.
Priest, Dana. "Private Guards Repel Attack on US Headquarters". *Washington Post*, 6 April 2004.
Prince, Erik. *Civilian Warriors: The Inside Story of Blackwater and the Unsung Heroes of the War on Terror.* Kindle edn. New York: Portfolio, 2013.
Roos, John G. "1-shot Killer; This 5.56 mm Round has All the Stopping Power you Need – but you Can't Use It". *The Army Times*, 1 December 2003.
Rosen, Fred. *Contract Warriors: How Mercenaries Changed History and the War on Terrorism.* New York: Alpha, 2005.
Sands, David R. "Bush Lauds Security Firm; Blackwater Chief Sought Defense". *Washington Times*, 18 October 2007.
Scahill, Jeremy. *Blackwater: The Rise of the World's Most Powerful Mercenary Army.* 1st edn. New York: Nation Books, 2007.
Scahill, Jeremy. *Blackwater: The Rise of the World's Most Powerful Mercenary Army.* 2nd edn. New York: Nation Books, 2008.
Schmitt, Eric. "Test in a Tinderbox". *New York Times*, 28 April 2004.
Schumacher, Gerry. *A Bloody Business: America's War Zone Contractors and the Occupation of Iraq.* Osceola, WI: Zenith Press, 2006.
Semple, Kirk, and Edward Wong. "US–Iraqi Assault Meets Resistance Near Syrian Border". *New York Times*, 15 November 2005.
Shadid, Anthony. *Night Draws Near: Iraq's People in the Shadow of America's War.* New York: Henry Holt, 2005.

Simons, Suzanne. *Master of War: Blackwater USA's Erik Prince and the Business of War*. New York: Harper, 2009.

Sizemore, Bill, and Joanne Kimberlin. "Blackwater: On the Front Lines". *Virginian-Pilot*, 25 July 2006.

Staff. "Five Killed in Attack on 2 Blackwater Helicopters". *Virginian-Pilot*, 24 January 2007.

The Warsaw Voice. "Have Gun ... Will Travel". *Warsaw Voice*, 23 June 2004.

Thurner, Jeffrey S. "Drowning in Blackwater: How Weak Accountability over Private Security Contractors Significantly Undermines Counterinsurgency Efforts". *Army Lawyer* (July 2008): 64–90.

Uesseler, Rolf. *Servants of War: Private Military Corporations and the Profit of Conflict*. Translated by Jefferson Chase. Berkeley, CA: Soft Skull Press, 2008.

US Department of Defense. "US Military Hostile Casualties in Support of Operations Iraqi Freedom and New Dawn". Washington, DC: US Department of Defense, 15 July 2011.

US Department of State and the Broadcasting Board of Governors Office of the Inspector General. "Review of Security Programs at US Embassy Baghdad". Washington, DC: US Department of State and the Broadcasting Board of Governors Office of Inspector General, July 2005.

US Department of State and the Broadcasting Board of Governors Office of the Inspector General. "Joint Audit of Blackwater Contract and Task Orders for Worldwide Personal Protective Services in Iraq". Washington, DC: US Department of State and the Broadcasting Board of Governors Office of Inspector General, June 2009.

US Department of State Diplomatic Security Service. "DS Report Number 2005–0005". Baghdad: US Department of State, 16 February 2005.

US Department of State Diplomatic Security Service. "DS Report for 20 June 2005 Incident". Baghdad: US Department of State, 20 June 2005.

US Department of State Diplomatic Security Service. "DS Report Number 2005–0092". Baghdad: US Department of State, 19 September 2005.

US Department of State Diplomatic Security Service. "DS Report Number RS-2007–00351". Baghdad: US Department of State, 2 September 2007.

US Department of State Diplomatic Security Service. "City Hall Engagement 09 Sep 2007". Baghdad: US Department of State, 9 September 2007.

US Department of State Diplomatic Security Service. "DS Report Number 2007–00096". Baghdad: US Department of State, 9 September 2007.

US Embassy, Baghdad. "RS-2007–00011: 2FEB07 Escalation of Force 28". Baghdad: US Department of State, 2 February 2007.

US Embassy, Baghdad. "RS-2007–00351: 20070902, UODFI, Baghdad". Baghdad: US Department of State, 2 September 2007.

US Embassy, Baghdad. "Spot Report – 010406–02 – International Narcotics and Law Enforcement (INL) Convoy Attacked by IED". Baghdad: US Department of State, 4 January 2006.

US Embassy, Baghdad. "Spot Report – 012307–02 – Complex Attack on COM PSD Resulting in Five KIA". Baghdad: US Department of State, 23 January 2007.

US Embassy, Baghdad. "Spot Report – 013107–01 – Small Arms Fire on RSO Air Asset". Baghdad: US Department of State, 31 January 2007.

US Embassy, Baghdad. "Spot Report – 020807–01 – Threat Engaged by COM PSD Team". Baghdad: US Department of State, 8 February 2007.

US Embassy, Baghdad. "Spot Report – 021807–01 – SAF Attack on a COM PSD". Baghdad: US Department of State, 18 February 2007.
US Embassy, Baghdad. "Spot Report – 022507–01 – RSO Air Asset Attacked by SAF". Baghdad: US Department of State, 25 February 2007.
US Embassy, Baghdad. "Spot Report – 031407–04 – RSO Air Asset Fires at an RPG Assailant". Baghdad: US Department of State, 14 March 2007.
US Embassy, Baghdad. "Spot Report – 041306–02 – FOB Courage Receives Small Arms Fire". Baghdad: US Department of State, 13 April 2006.
US Embassy, Baghdad. "Spot Report – 041906–01 – IED/SAF Attack on Com Convoy". Baghdad: US Department of State, 19 April 2006.
US Embassy, Baghdad. "Spot Report – 050905–01 – Tactical Support Team Fires on Vehicle". Baghdad: US Department of State, 9 May 2005.
US Embassy, Baghdad. "Spot Report – 052806–02 – Blackwater Aircraft Attacked with SAF". Baghdad: US Department of State, 28 May 2006.
US Embassy, Baghdad. "Spot Report – 062005–7 – PSD Motorcade Hit with IED and SAF". Baghdad: US Department of State, 20 June 2005.
US Embassy, Baghdad. "Spot Report – 090105–01 – COM PSD Fires on an Anti-Iraq Forces (AIF) Sniper in Mosul". Baghdad: US Department of State, 31 January 2007.
US Embassy, Baghdad. "Spot Report – 090907–01 – Complex Attack Against COM PSD Teams". Baghdad: US Department of State, 9 September 2007.
US Embassy, Baghdad. "Spot Report – 091207–01 – Complex Attack against COM Team". Baghdad: US Department of State, 12 September 2007.
US Embassy, Baghdad. "Spot Report – 091507–01 – PSD Team EOF on Aggressive Vehicle". Baghdad: US Department of State, 15 September 2007.
US Embassy, Baghdad. "Spot Report – 091905–01 – COM PSD Team Attacked by VBIED Causing Fatal Injuries to Four US Citizens". Baghdad: US Department of State, 19 September 2005.
US Embassy, Baghdad. "Spot Report – 092005–03 – COM Blackwater Air Team Fires on Suspicious Vehicle". Baghdad: US Department of State, 20 September 2005.
US Fed News. "True Grit: Real-Life Account of Combat Readiness". *US Fed News*, 2 September 2004.
Virginian-Pilot Staff. "In His Own Words: 'The Guys Who do This are Not Money-Hungry Pigs'". *Virginian-Pilot*, 28 July 2006.
Welch, Michael. "Fragmented Power and State-Corporate Killings: A Critique of Blackwater in Iraq". *Crime, Law and Social Change* 51, no. 3–4 (2009): 351–364.
Wiltrout, Kate. "If I Had to Die, It Would Be Defending My Country". *Virginian-Pilot*, 18 September 2004.

6 The implications of Blackwater and DynCorp's tactical behaviour in Iraq

The Nisour Square incident on 16 September 2007 proved to be a turning point for not only Blackwater but also the broader private military industry. As this chapter illustrates, while this incident was certainly not the only controversial use of deadly force by either firm in Iraq, it provoked political and legal scandals of unprecedented scale that, in turn, strongly influenced the government of the United States' approach to the use of PSCs and undermined Blackwater's ability to compete in the marketplace for private armed forces. This chapter focuses almost entirely on Blackwater because the relatively passive behaviour exhibited by DynCorp's personnel, and the comparatively low number of civilian casualties they inflicted, allowed that firm to largely escape scrutiny. As a result, unlike Blackwater, DynCorp was rarely directly embroiled in scandals. This chapter consists of four main parts. It first discusses the legal and regulatory implications of Blackwater's behaviour in Iraq. Second, it explores the political implications of the firm's behaviour. Third, it discusses the implications of the firm's behaviour for its own corporate development. Finally, it concludes with a summary of these implications.

Legal and regulatory implications

The behaviour exhibited by both firms' personnel in Iraq sometimes embroiled them in legal trouble. As could be expected, given the disparity in the amount of violence they employed, Blackwater's personnel generated far more and more serious legal scandals, all of which involved incidents where they caused the death or serious injury of non-insurgents.[1] For example, when a Blackwater CAT member shot and seriously injured the driver of an approaching Toyota car in Al Kut on 19 May 2005, the US Department of State issued a US$1,200 payment to compensate the victim for the two bullet wounds he received during the incident and the damage to his car.[2] Likewise, when a Blackwater PSD shot and killed one of the passengers in an approaching Kia car on 13 April 2005, the Department of State paid US$3,000 in condolence money to the victim's family.[3] In addition, after one of the firm's PSDs shot an Iraqi civilian named Munther

Kadhum Abid Ali in Al-Hillah on 24 October 2005, the Department of State issued a US$5,000 condolence payment to his son.[4] On the other hand, DynCorp's personnel were involved in only a single recorded incident in Iraq where the Department of State felt their actions warranted issuing a condolence payment. This occurred in Erbil on 16 July 2007, when one of its security teams shot and seriously injured the driver of an approaching Isuzu SUV.[5] The victim, an Iraqi judge, accepted a US$2,500 payment to compensate him for his injuries and damage to his vehicle.

The Nisour Square incident of 16 September 2007 sparked the most serious legal troubles experienced by either firm during their operations in Iraq. The Iraqi police secured Nisour Square shortly after the shooting stopped and began collecting statements from surviving victims and other eye witnesses. They also collected physical evidence in the form of hundreds of bullet casings from the kinds of US-made firearms favoured by Blackwater's security teams, blood and body parts from the victims, and over a dozen bullet-ridden civilian vehicles.[6] The Iraqi police claimed to have not found any bullet casings from AK-47s, the preferred weapons of Iraqi insurgents and police. However, lawyers for some of the members of Raven 23 that stood trial for their role in the incident stated that AK-47 bullet casings were, in fact, found in the traffic circle and accused the Iraqi police of removing this critical evidence to undercut the defendants' claim that they had been attacked by gunmen dressed in civilian clothes and Iraqi police uniforms.[7]

Prosecuting the accused shooters in Iraqi courts proved impossible. Due to the legal protection afforded by CPA Order 17, which granted immunity under Iraqi law to all foreign contractors, Iraqi courts lacked jurisdiction to prosecute foreign security personnel, regardless of their suspected crimes. Complicating matters for the Iraqi authorities, the accused were also flown back to the United States a few days after the shooting.[8] Some Iraqi politicians demanded that their government attempt to extradite the accused back to Iraq but this effort was quashed under pressure from the Department of State. The unenviable task of trying to hold the suspected shooters to account for a crime that took place half a world away then fell to the American justice system.

Shortly after the shooting stopped, as DSS agents were conducting the first of several legally questionable interviews with members of Raven 23, soldiers from the US Army's First Cavalry Division arrived in Nisour Square to conduct a physical investigation of the crime scene.[9] The Iraqi police controlled access to the traffic circle but the soldiers were permitted to conduct their own inspection of the scene and interview Iraqi witnesses. In their report, the unit's personnel echoed the Iraqi police's claim that no AK-47 bullet casings were found in Nisour Square.[10] They did, however, find a large number of shell casings from US-made M4 carbines, M203 grenade launcher rounds and M240 machine guns, all of which were used by Blackwater's security teams as well as most US Army and Marine combat units.[11] They also reported seeing numerous civilian vehicles that had been riddled with bullets and/or set alight. The report characterized the incident as a "criminal event" and concluded that there was "no enemy activity involved", meaning that all of the shooting victims were civilians.[12]

The DSS's Baghdad Regional Security Officer sent six investigators to Mansour police station on 18 September 2007 to interview 14 Iraqi witnesses about the shootings.[13] These included Iraqi Army and police personnel and also civilians. DSS agents first visited the traffic circle on 20 September, four days after the shooting occurred.[14] There they observed some of the debris left over from the incident but, given the passage of time and the fact that the crime scene was not under American control, they were not able to determine how, if at all, the scene had been altered after the shooting stopped. Normally, the DSS handled every investigation of possible criminal acts involving the Department of State's private security personnel, most of which, as discussed in Chapter 4, involved a handful of civilian deaths or serious injuries. However, after issuing their initial report in October 2007 to Greg Starr, the Director of the Department of State's Bureau of Diplomatic Security, which oversees the DSS, the magnitude of the offenses prompted senior Department of State officials to ask the US Department of Justice's FBI to take over the case.[15]

The FBI agents that arrived in Iraq in October 2007 faced a challenging investigation. Critically, after speaking to DSS agents, who had promised that nothing said during their interviews could be used against the firm's personnel in a court of law, many members of Raven 23 refused to be interviewed by FBI investigators who, quite correctly, would not offer a similar guarantee.[16] Like their DSS counterparts, the FBI's investigators deemed the crime scene to be severely compromised.[17] This made it impossible for them to know what, if any, physical evidence, such as bullet casings and bullet fragments, had been left during the incident, or either removed or planted at some point after the incident. Complicating matters, Blackwater quickly repaired and repainted the armoured vehicles that Raven 23 had used during the incident.[18] This destroyed a critical piece of physical evidence that investigators could have used to evaluate the team members' claim that someone in the traffic circle was shooting at them, since it is highly likely that armed insurgents would have been able to hit at least one of the vehicles during the 15 minute altercation. In fact, Prince claimed that three of the team's vehicles were damaged by hostile gunfire and that one vehicle's radiator was "shot out and disabled".[19] The initial incident report also claimed that this disabled vehicle was towed out of the traffic circle by another vehicle.[20] Anne E. Tyrrell, Blackwater's spokesperson, claimed that the firm conducted the repairs "at the government's direction", but the Department of State did not confirm this assertion.[21]

Despite these challenges, the FBI completed its investigation, which largely reflected the conclusions of the Iraqi police and the First Cavalry Division. On 8 December 2008, the Department of Justice charged six of the firm's employees with multiple counts of voluntary manslaughter, attempt to commit manslaughter and weapons violations for their alleged role in the incident.[22] Five of these personnel – Paul Slough, Evan Liberty, Dustin Heard, Donald Ball and Nicholas Slatten – decided to contest the charges in court. The sixth employee, Jeremy Ridgway, pled guilty to voluntary manslaughter and attempt to commit manslaughter and agreed to testify against his former colleagues.[23]

Although many scholars agree that 17 Iraqi civilians were killed and 24 seriously injured as a result of Raven 23's actions in the traffic circle, the Department of Justice only laid charges in connection to 14 of the deaths and 20 of the seriously injured victims.[24] Nevertheless, if convicted for offenses committed against this fraction of the total pool of victims and sentenced to serve consecutive prison terms, then each of the defendants could have faced up to 10 years in prison for each of the 14 manslaughter counts, seven years in prison for each of the 20 attempted manslaughter counts, and a mandatory minimum sentence of 30 years on the firearms charge, for a total of 310 years behind bars.[25]

To the surprise of many, especially the government of Iraq, the trial planned for February 2010 ended before it began when Judge Ricardo M. Urbina of the Federal District Court in Washington, DC dismissed all charges on 31 December 2009.[26] Basing his 90-page ruling on the content of grand jury sessions and other pre-trial proceedings, Urbina concluded that investigators and prosecutors had mishandled the case to such an extent that their actions warranted dismissing the indictment against all of the defendants.[27] Describing their actions as a "reckless violation of the defendants' constitutional rights", Urbina ruled that, during interviews conducted shortly after the shootings, DSS agents illegally compelled members of Raven 23 to make incriminating statements by threatening to fire them if they declined to cooperate.[28] The agents also wrongly told the team members that their statements could not be used against them in a court of law. As a result, the firm's employees provided investigators with information about their behaviour in Nisour Square that they probably would have withheld in the absence of the investigators' threats and misleading statements.

Of critical importance, some of the team members told investigators that they had fired their weapons during the incident. This served as the most damning evidence against them because, even though prosecutors presented evidence that US and Iraqi investigators found numerous bullet fragments and casings that matched the kinds of firearms carried by the team, they could not establish unassailable links between specific weapons and specific victims. Therefore, in the absence of the defendants' statements about firing their weapons during the incident, prosecutors might not have been able to prove beyond a reasonable doubt that these particular members of Raven 23 were responsible for the deaths and injuries that occurred in Nisour Square.

Since investigators and prosecutors relied heavily on the defendants' statements to build their case, Urbina concluded that the case was tainted and not fit for trial. Moreover, he also ruled that "The explanations offered by the prosecutors and investigators in an attempt to justify their actions and persuade the court that they did not use the defendants' compelling testimony were all too often contradictory, unbelievable and lacking in credibility".[29] Furthermore, he criticized prosecutors for withholding "substantial evidence" from the grand jury that decided to indict the team members and for presenting "distorted versions" of witnesses' testimony, such as telling the grand jury that the defendants had incriminated themselves in their statements to the DSS investigators.[30]

The fact that this ruling hinged largely on the investigators' and prosecutors' alleged misconduct, rather than on the defendants' guilt or innocence, proved confusing to the government of Iraq. In the wake of the ruling, US Embassy officials reported that "a consistent theme in our engagements with Iraqi contacts and in Iraqi media reporting on the dismissal of the case against Blackwater employees has been a failure to grasp the legal nuances behind Judge Urbina's decision".[31] The Department of Justice pledged to appeal the ruling.[32]

After taking several months to rebuild their case against the accused, Department of Justice prosecutors made good on their pledge and, in April 2011, the United States Court of Appeals for the District of Columbia reopened the criminal case against members of Raven 23.[33] The three-judge appeals panel found that Urbina's ruling depended on "an erroneous view of the law" and called on the lower court to review the case and determine, for each individual defendant, "what evidence – if any – the government presented against him that was tainted" and to then determine whether this justified dismissing the charges.[34] Prosecutors opted to dismiss the charges against Donald Ball, one of the defendants during the earlier legal proceedings, in September 2013, but recharged the other four defendants during the following month and sought a new trial.[35] Slatten was initially charged with 14 counts of voluntary manslaughter and 16 counts of attempt to commit manslaughter, but he was later recharged with a single count of first degree murder; Slough was charged with 13 counts of voluntary manslaughter and 18 counts of attempt to commit manslaughter; Liberty and Heard were charged with 13 counts of voluntary manslaughter and 16 counts of attempt to commit manslaughter; and all four defendants were charged with one count of using and discharging a firearm during and in relation to a crime of violence.[36] The 10-week trial took place in July and August 2014.

Prosecutors presented 71 witnesses at the trial, while the defence called only four.[37] In addition to a number of Iraqi eyewitnesses, some members of Raven 23 testified against their former colleagues during the trial. Matthew Murphy, one of the team's turret gunners, testified that he saw his teammates "firing wildly" at civilians, including children.[38] In response to several questions from a prosecutor about the degree of threat the team may have faced in Nisour Square, such as "Did he appear to be a threat to you?", "Did you see any threats to the Raven 23 convoy?", "Did you see any men with AK-47s around that area?", "Did you see any (of the victims) armed at all?", Murphy answered that he had not.[39] He also testified that he saw "people completely unarmed, people doing nothing wrong, get shot", and described the shootings as "the most horrible, botched thing I've ever seen in my life".[40] Adam Frost, another team member, testified that he "saw people huddled down in their cars, trying to shield their children with their bodies" from the team's gunfire.[41] Still another team member, Mark Mealy, stated that one of his colleagues shot an unarmed Iraqi man who was holding his hands up.[42] However, Murphy also testified that, although he did not recall seeing anyone armed with an AK-47, he heard AK-47 gunfire during the incident.[43] Frost likewise testified that he was certain that someone was shooting at his convoy.[44] A number of witnesses also provided testimony suggesting that Ridgeway, the only team member to plead guilty, deserved a great deal of the blame for what happened in the traffic circle.[45]

Whether the defendants had actually fired the bullets that inflicted so many deaths and serious injuries in Nisour Square was not at issue during the trial. Rather, the trial hinged on the questions of whether the defendants believed they were under threat and whether they used a reasonable amount of force in response to that suspected threat. Summarizing the defendants' perspective, William Coffield, one of the defence lawyers, argued that "There's a lot of tragedy here. But it's not the fault of these four".[46] Defence lawyers pointed to the fact that a VBIED had exploded in the vicinity of Nisour Square shortly before the incident took place and used this to argue that the defendants were reasonable in their belief that at least the first vehicle they fired at, a Kia car containing Ahmed and Mahasin al-Rubaie, could have been another VBIED.[47] Brian Heberlig, another defence lawyer, conveyed this argument when he stated that "Perhaps their perception was erroneous.... It does appear that this was not a [VBIED]. It does appear that this was a medical student and his mother, but our clients did not know that".[48] The defence also argued that AK-47 bullet casings had actually been found at the scene after the shootings and that this corroborated the claim that Raven 23 had been shot at.[49] Finally, the defence also argued that because the Iraqi police, a force known to be highly hostile to PSCs, had controlled the crime scene, it was impossible for US investigators to know whether physical evidence was removed or planted in order to incriminate the firm's employees.[50]

The lead prosecutor, Assistant US Attorney Anthony Asuncion, countered that "There was not a single dead insurgent on the scene" and that "none of these people were armed".[51] He disagreed with defence lawyers' claims that the team's first target, the Kia car, was moving toward them when they fired at it, suggesting instead that the vehicle was initially stationary and started rolling toward the convoy only after the team killed its driver.[52] In addition, he argued that if any damage was done to the team's vehicles, which itself was under dispute because the vehicles were repaired and repainted before investigators could examine them, this was most likely caused by shrapnel from the grenades the team fired during the incident.[53] Moreover, he argued that finding AK-47 bullet casing at the scene did not constitute proof that insurgents had fired at the convoy that day because finding AK-47 bullets casings on the streets of Baghdad is "as common as finding cigarette butts in the streets of a US city or finding sea shells at the beach".[54] During his closing arguments, Asuncion stated that the accused "took something that did not belong to them: the lives of 14 human beings ... they were turned into bloody, bullet-riddles corpses at the hands of these men".[55] He went on to speculate that, for the Iraqi civilians at the scene, "it must have seemed like the apocalypse was here".[56] He singled out Slatten as the incident's instigator, and claimed that the team's DDM fired the lethal first bullet at the Kia's driver.[57] In Asuncion's words, Slatten "lit the match that ignited the firestorm".[58] Prosecutors also argued that Slatten and Slough had fired at civilians during earlier security operations in Iraq.[59]

On 22 October 2014, after seven weeks of deliberations, the jury convicted all four of the defendants on all but three charges. Slough was convicted on 13 counts of voluntary manslaughter and 17 counts of attempted manslaughter. Heard was convicted on six counts of voluntary manslaughter and 11 counts of attempted manslaughter. Liberty was convicted on eight counts of voluntary manslaughter and 12 counts of attempted manslaughter. Slatten was found guilty of first-degree murder for the premeditated killing of Ahmed al-Rubaie, the first civilian to die during the incident.[60] All of the defendants were also convicted on the charge of using a firearm while committing a felony. The jury did not acquit the defendants of any of the charges, but they were unable to reach a verdict on three voluntary manslaughter charges levied against Heard.[61]

The verdict pleased the government of Iraq. Mohamad al-Quraishy, Deputy Chief of Mission at the Iraqi Embassy to the United States, heard the jury's verdict in person. Referring to his government, he stated that "They will welcome this decision".[62] At the same time, the defendants' attorneys appeared stunned by the verdict and promised to appeal. Heard's attorney, David Schertler, stated that "The verdict is wrong; it's incomprehensible. We're devastated. We're going to fight it every step of the way. We still think we're going to win".[63] For his part, Liberty's attorney, William Coffield, said that "There are a lot of appellate issues here".[64] Each voluntary manslaughter conviction carries a penalty of up to 15 years in prison and each attempted manslaughter conviction carries a penalty of up to seven years in prison. Slatten faces a maximum penalty of life in prison for the murder conviction. Slough, Heard, and Liberty also face a mandatory minimum of 30 years in prison due to the firearms conviction.

Blackwater's legal troubles were not confined to criminal proceedings. Shortly after the Nisour Square shootings took place, Iraqi politicians and civilians began calling on the firm to pay compensation to the victims and their families.[65] Department of State officials agreed to these demands and placed pressure on the firm's executives to comply.[66] Due to Blackwater's frequent use of deadly force against civilians, the department had already established a Claims and Condolence Program to distribute "blood money" to victims or their families in exchange for a pledge to refrain from suing either the department or the firm involved.[67] The department did, however, announce that it would streamline the approval process for the victims of the Nisour Square shootings and their families.[68] By 27 December 2007, the US Embassy to Iraq had paid a total of US$40,000 to the families of four people killed during the Nisour Square incident, US$65,000 to 13 people who had been seriously injured during the incident, and US$27,500 to 11 people who suffered damage to their vehicles during the incident.[69] Thus condolence payments for deaths associated with the incident were valued at approximately US$10,000, serious injuries warranted US$5,000 and vehicle damage deserved US$2,500 – fully a quarter of the value placed on a human life. The Department of State issued several additional condolence payments at later dates.

Less than a month after the shootings, on 11 October 2007, several survivors of the Nisour Square shootings and families of two of the dead filed a lawsuit against Blackwater in US federal court. The suit alleged that "Blackwater created and fostered a culture of lawlessness amongst its employees, encouraging them to act in the company's financial interests at the expense of innocent human life".[70] It also alleged that Raven 23's behaviour in Nisour Square amounted to "war crimes".[71] Moreover, it alleged that "Blackwater benefits financially from its willingness to kill innocent bystanders" because the firm's willingness to employ deadly force indiscriminately helped it ensure the safety of its clients.[72] Besides compensatory damages for the deaths, injuries and associated financial losses suffered by the plaintiffs, the plaintiffs also sought "punitive damages in an amount sufficient to strip Defendants of all of the revenue and profits earned from their pattern of constant misconduct and callous disregard for human life".[73] Blackwater settled with seven of the plaintiffs in January 2010.[74] Although the terms of the settlement prevented Prince from discussing how much money his firm paid out, he repeated the Associated press's claim that his firm paid US$100,000 to each of the families of the deceased and US$30,000 to each of the seriously injured victims.[75] The firm settled another lawsuit in 2012 by paying similar amounts.[76]

On 18 January 2008, representatives from Blackwater briefed officials at the US Embassy to Iraq about the firm's plans to provide condolence payments to all of the shooting victims, including those that were attempting to sue the firm at the time.[77] They claimed to have allocated "a generous pot" of money for these payments and had hired Iraqi lawyers with expertise in condolence payments to contact the victims and their families.[78] They also pledged to provide at least twice as much money to each victim and family as the Department of State had and substantially larger amounts in cases where the death or serious injury of a victim posed an especially significant economic hardship for a family, such as if the victim was a family's primary breadwinner.[79] This suggests that the firm intended to pay considerably more in response to the death or serious injury of adult men, who tend to be the chief source of income for Iraqi families, than for women and children.

According to an account provided by US Embassy officials, the firm intended to use its promise to make condolence payments as leverage in its ongoing negotiations with the Iraqi Ministry of Interior to obtain a new license to provide security services in Iraq. The embassy officials informed the firm's representatives that it was morally correct for Blackwater to make condolence payments but that this would not influence the Department of State's future decisions on whether to retain the firm's services in Iraq. These officials also indicated that they viewed the firm's decision to link condolence payments with their attempts to obtain an operating license to be akin to bribing the Ministry of Interior, and stated that the embassy would not be a party to these negotiations.[80] The firm's representatives claimed that their attempts to obtain a new operating license would be "straightforward and transparent".[81] However, the Department of Justice later investigated allegations that Blackwater paid up to one million dollars in bribes to Iraqi officials to either issue an operating license or ignore the fact that the firm was operating without one.[82]

Blackwater's use of violence in Iraq also prompted the government of the United States to develop more robust regulations for monitoring and controlling the behaviour of its private security personnel in overseas conflict zones. In October 2007, US Secretary of State Condoleezza Rice established the Panel on Personal Protective Services in Iraq to produce a "serious, probing, and comprehensive" report on the department's management of these actors and how this could be improved.[83] After conducting two weeks of investigations in Iraq, the panel issued a report on 23 October 2007 containing recommendations for improving how the department managed its use of private security personnel, many of which were taken up.[84] For instance, the Department of State adopted a long-standing practice of many police forces in the United States by placing GPS locator beacons and cameras inside the vehicles used by its private security personnel.[85] In one of its more expensive regulatory changes, due to the need to hire additional staff, the department also required DSS agents to accompany every private security team during their operation in Iraq.[86] The department also revised its mission firearms policy to further discourage its private security personnel from unnecessarily resorting to deadly force.[87] In addition, the department barred its private security personnel from consuming alcohol when deployed overseas.[88] Finally, it also required these personnel to undertake country-specific cultural awareness training prior to their deployments.[89]

Although Blackwater's primary client in Iraq was the Department of State, the Nisour Square incident prompted US Secretary of Defense Robert M. Gates to send a team of investigators to Iraq to gather information about his department's relationship with PSCs in that country.[90] Gates acted quickly on the team's findings. Just 10 days after the incident, the Department of Defense issued a memorandum outlining ways to improve its management and oversight of security firms.[91] Of particular importance, the memorandum instructed the commanders of every US military unit in Iraq to ensure that they apply the use of force provisions in the Uniform Code of Military Justice (UCMJ) to private security personnel working for the department and that they apprehend, disarm and detain any contractors suspected of violating the UCMJ.[92] It also instructed them that, if an employee of a PSC is suspected of committing a criminal act, then US military officers must work with the Department of Justice to hold the employee to account under the Military Extraterritorial Jurisdiction Act (MEJA).

As they developed their separate responses to the Nisour Square incident, the Departments of State and Defense also signed a memorandum of agreement (MOA) on 5 December 2007 that established procedures for coordinating their respective uses of PSCs in overseas conflict zones.[93] The MOA includes jointly agreed standards for sharing information on the location and intended routes of security convoys and more stringent provisions on the use of force by PSCs, their authority to carry firearms, their authority to travel within overseas conflict zones, their responsibility to report serious incidents and their legal accountability in the event that they are suspected of committing a crime.[94] The central objective of this MOA is to ensure that PSCs working for either department are required to behave and be treated in the same manner. Department of Defense officials were particularly keen to ensure that the employees of every PSC hired by either department received instruction in the laws of war and developed a thorough understanding of how to behave to avoid violating these laws.[95] With respect to rules of engagement, the Department of Defense sought to ensure that every employee of a PSC hired by either department understood that they did not operate under the US military's rules of engagement, which allowed for proactive uses of deadly force against suspected threats, but were, instead, only allowed to fire their weapons in self-defence or to "prevent life threatening offenses against civilians".[96] For its part, the Department of State's clarified rules on the use of force stated that private security personnel must take care to fire only well-aimed shots with "due regard for the safety of innocent bystanders" in order to minimize civilian casualties.[97] The MOA called for these provisions to be included in every contract signed between the departments and private security firms.

The new regulations also required firms working for either department to provide the US military with information on the routes their security teams intended to use during their operations, except when emergencies and other circumstances do not allow for this, and to cancel or reschedule operations in the event that the US military deems them too dangerous.[98] This provision was intended to reduce the probability that private security teams would become involved in friendly fire incidents with US military personnel or other firms or be attacked by insurgents. It was also intended to allow the US military to rapidly respond to violent incidents involving private security personnel and, depending on the circumstances, rescue the security personnel or negotiate peaceful resolutions to disputes arising between them and Iraqi authorities.

The Nisour Square incident also prompted the government of Iraq to demand further legal and regulatory authority over the dozens of foreign PSCs operating on its soil. In November 2008, the governments of the United States and Iraq signed a Status of Forces Agreement (SOFA) to establish a new framework under which foreign armed forces, including the US military and most PSCs, could operate within Iraq.[99] This document granted the government of Iraq criminal and civil jurisdiction over American private security personnel that worked for the Department of Defense in their country and therefore partially overturned the blanket immunity afforded by CPA Order 17. Iraq did not, however, gain jurisdiction over private security personnel, such as the employees of Blackwater, DynCorp and Triple Canopy, that worked for the Department of State. Moreover, the 2008 SOFA was not a legally binding document, since it could be unilaterally cancelled by either government at any time. Therefore, the agreement granted little, if any, tangible legal and regulatory authority to the government of Iraq.

These regulatory changes may have contributed to a significant decrease in the frequency of incidents where either firm opted to use violence. According to data contained in the PSCVID, Blackwater's personnel used violence in 348 incidents between 2003 and September 2007, but only resorted to violence in five incidents from October 2007 to 2009. DynCorp likewise resorted to violence in just three incidents from October 2007 to 2009, down markedly from 57 incidents between 2003 and September 2007. Both the US Embassy to Iraq and the Commission on Wartime Contracting in Iraq and Afghanistan found a similar decrease in deadly force incidents during this period.[100] Moreover, Blackwater's personnel did not kill anyone in Iraq after September 2007 and seriously injured only two people between October 2007 and December 2009. DynCorp's personnel killed just one person after the Nisour Square incident and did not seriously injure anyone after that event. The political and legal scandals generated by the Nisour Square incident likely affected the firms' behaviour, since this motivated the Department of State to impose new regulations and to greatly enhance oversight of its private security personnel in Iraq.

With this said, however, it is also plausible that the firms' behaviour changed in response to the significant decrease in insurgent violence that began in 2007 as the surge in US military personnel and other counterinsurgency efforts started having an effect.[101] Deaths of US military personnel from hostile acts decreased by almost 80 per cent from 1,765 in the 27 months preceding the Nisour Square incident (July 2005 to September 2007) to 365 in the 27 months after the incident (October 2007 to December 2009). According to figures provided by the Iraq Body Count Project, insurgent-caused civilian deaths also declined from 7,401 to 4,022 and the number of insurgent attacks against civilians fell from 2,336 to 1,435 between these two periods. Finally, insurgent attacks against Blackwater's personnel declined from 94 to four between these periods, while those against DynCorp declined from seven to none. Taking this into account, it makes sense that both firms curtailed their use of violence during the post-Nisour Square period.

Finally, Blackwater's behaviour in Iraq also prompted American lawmakers to try to pass legislation designed to enhance their government's ability to control American private security personnel working in overseas conflict zones and hold them to account for their behaviour. The Panel on Personal Protective Services in Iraq's October 2007 report concluded that there was no basis in US law to prosecute private security personnel working for a department, other than the Department of Defense, for their actions in overseas conflict zones.[102] Just a month after the report's release, Congress explored the possibility of banning the use of private security personnel altogether in American military operations. The Stop Outsourcing Security Act, introduced in November 2007, sought to phase out the use of PSCs "wherever Congress has authorized the use of force, including Iraq and Afghanistan" by 1 January 2009.[103] The press release that accompanied the bill's introduction clearly reflected the public image that Blackwater's employees had acquired in Iraq, for it described these actors as "reckless", "cowboy contractors" that are "unaccountable to the military" and claimed that they "put our troops in harm's way" and were responsible for "the unnecessary deaths of many innocent Iraqi civilians".[104] An updated version of the Stop Outsourcing Security Act was introduced into the US Senate in February 2010. Like the earlier bill, it sought to ban the use of PSCs for the protection of US diplomatic personnel and facilities.[105] It also sought to ban the use of these firms in a range of other roles, such as gathering intelligence, administering prisons, maintaining weapons and providing security advice and planning, that the bill's authors thought should be handled exclusively by the US military. One-third of the bill was made up of examples of negative acts committed by private security personnel, many of which involved Blackwater's employees, to justify the bill's attempt to curtail the use of these actors. As of November 2014, neither version of the Stop Outsourcing Security Act had been passed by Congress.

The belief that the Department of State's private security personnel were operating without sufficient legal constraints motivated Senator Patrick Lehy and Congressman David Price to introduce bills to create a Civilian Extraterritorial Jurisdiction Act in 2010. Unlike the MEJA, which regulates the behaviour of US military personnel and private security contractors working for the Department of Defense, this legislation would have granted the Department of Justice the authority to prosecute private security personnel "employed by or accompanying any department or agency of the United States *other than* the Department of Defense" for a wide range of crimes, such as murder, assault, theft and fraud, committed outside the United States.[106] However, like the Stop Outsourcing Security Act, this legislation was not passed.

Perhaps the most successful attempts to legislate enhanced oversight and control over the behaviour of American PSCs, given that they have actually been passed into law, are provisions contained in annual National Defense Authorization Acts since 2008 that are designed to enhance the United States' capacity to monitor and regulate the activities of these actors. For instance, the 2008 and 2011 National Defense Authorization Acts included provisions requiring the Secretaries of Defense and State to improve their management and regulation of PSCs in overseas conflict zones.[107] These provisions specifically called upon these officials and their staff to monitor, report and account for every incident where an employee of a PSC fires a weapon or injures or kills someone. The 2009 National Defense Authorization Act stated that PSCs should not perform "inherently governmental functions", such as providing security for people or facilities in overseas conflict zones; however, this provision has so far been ignored by both departments.

Since 2008, the government of the United States has also supported the development of international agreements, sets of standards and codes of conduct designed to regulate the use and behaviour of PSCs. The 2008 Montreux Document highlights several existing international legal obligations of states, PSCs and their personnel and recommends good practices to follow when states decide to hire firms.[108] The 2010 International Code of Conduct for Private Security Service Providers puts forward a set of standards to help PSCs comply with international humanitarian and human rights laws.[109] As of November 2014, 708 PSCs were signatories to the code, including a number of prominent American firms such as DynCorp, Triple Canopy and one of Blackwater's later iterations, Academi. Finally, the ANSI/ASIS PSC series of standards, which were completed in 2013, built on both the code and the Montreux Document by articulating an administrative mechanism that may be used by PSCs and their clients to help them adhere to the provisions contained in these earlier initiatives.[110] It remains to be seen whether these initiatives will significantly influence how the government of the United States uses and regulates the behaviour of American PSCs. Its direct involvement in their development could be viewed as a sign of strong support for their provisions. However, none of these initiatives imposes binding legal constraints on either the United States or American PSCs. The tangible effects, if any, of these initiatives will likely be determined by whether the government of the United States and American PSCs conclude that their interests will be best served by adhering to their provisions.

Political implications

In his memoirs, Prince acknowledged the political drawbacks of his employees' violent behaviour in Iraq:

> Our job was to create for ... [the Department of State] a "high-visibility deterrent" to attackers and keep State's personnel safe no matter what. It didn't matter if it was probably the worst approach for the department actually achieving its diplomatic objectives in Iraq.[111]

He rightly argued that, at least until the Nisour Square incident, the Department of State seemed quite satisfied with Blackwater's operations in Iraq since, despite the civilian deaths and serious injuries regularly caused by its personnel, the department repeatedly selected the firm to serve as its primary security provider.[112] Nisour Square was certainly not Blackwater's first controversial use of deadly force in Iraq. For example, the *Washington Post* reported that "a furious phone call" between Iraqi Vice President Abdel Abdul Mahdi and US Ambassador Zalmay Khalilzad took place on 25 December 2006, during which the vice president demanded an immediate meeting and the arrest of an American employee of Blackwater who had shot one of his bodyguards on the previous evening.[113] Khalilzad refused the vice president's demand, a decision that strained US–Iraqi relations for a time.[114] Moreover, after an incident in Kirkuk on 7 February 2006, when one of the firm's security teams shot and killed a 65-year-old taxi driver who failed to rapidly get out of the team's way on a two-lane road, also killing his passenger and a nearby pedestrian, hundreds of protesters gathered outside the US consulate in Kirkuk to vent their outrage.[115] Some in the crowd reportedly wanted to burn down the facility and were only dissuaded by local politicians. Rizgar Ali, an influential Kurdish politician, claimed that this shooting incident rendered all Americans "hated and ostracized" in the Kirkuk region.[116] Among those left embittered was the taxi driver's son, Khursheed Muhammad, who told a reported that "Now, every time I hear that someone targeted Americans and killed them, I feel happy".[117] Another dicey episode occurred on 24 May 2007, when dozens of Ministry of Interior commandos decided to chase down and surround one of the firm's security teams on a Baghdad street shortly after witnessing it shooting at a civilian driver.[118] The commandoes sought to arrest the team at gunpoint but the private security personnel, also with guns drawn, refused. It took the intervention of a US Army unit to break up the tense three-hour standoff that ensued. None of these incidents shook the Department of State's staunch commitment to retaining the firm as its primary security force in Iraq.

The diplomatic firestorm sparked by the Nisour Square incident was, however, unprecedented in scale and forever changed Blackwater's relationship with its primary client in Iraq.[119] Iraqi government officials immediately took the position that the shootings were unprovoked and unnecessary and therefore constituted the wanton murder of innocent civilians.[120] Within days of the shootings, Iraqi Prime Minister Nouri al-Maliki declared that his government "will not allow Iraqis to be killed in cold blood" and acknowledged that "There is a sense of tension and anger among all Iraqis, including the government, over this crime".[121] Just a week after the shootings, during a diplomatic visit to the United States, he told reporters that the firm's actions were "a serious challenge to the sovereignty of Iraq" that "cannot be accepted" by his government.[122] In contrast, Sean McCormack, a Department of State spokesman, described the incident as "a firefight" – that is, an event during which at least two armed combatants were shooting at each other – during a press briefing on 18 September.[123] Claims by Blackwater officials that their personnel had "acted lawfully and appropriately in response to a hostile attack" and that "Blackwater professionals heroically defended American lives in a war zone" not only failed to convince the Iraqi government of its innocence but were considered so inflammatory in Iraq that the Department of State asked the firm to stop talking to the press.[124]

The heightened degree of anger generated by this incident motivated the Department of State to impose a four-day hold on Blackwater's movements in Iraq and to curtail the operations of two of its other mobile security providers, DynCorp and Triple Canopy.[125] Since most of the Department of State's personnel lived and worked in Baghdad, they were effectively on "lock down" and could not leave the relative safety of the Green Zone during this period.[126]

Furious officials at the Iraqi Ministry of Interior, which, by 2007, had taken to issuing licenses permitting certain PSCs to operate in their country, threatened to immediately revoke Blackwater's license and expel all of its employees.[127] Since the firm was serving as the Department of State's primary protection force at the time, with far more personnel than DynCorp and Triple Canopy combined, this would have crippled the department's ability to protect some of its most important facilities in Iraq, including the US Embassy in Baghdad, and would also have prevented its diplomats from travelling outside the Green Zone.[128] As an internal Department of State document put it:

> Chief of Mission personnel in Iraq rely heavily on Blackwater PSDs and assets for travel in the Red Zone. Any action curtailing Blackwater's

operations in Iraq would severely limit COM personnel movement, impacting the Embassy's ability to support [the work of the government of Iraq].[129]

On 19 September US Embassy officials met with the Iraqi Minister of Interior, Jawad al-Bulani, to express their regret over the loss of life but also to encourage him to refrain from issuing inflammatory statements and threatening to revoke the firm's license.[130] Al-Bulani agreed but stressed that no one in Iraq is above the law, that such an incident must never happen again, and that the Iraqi people must feel respected and be able to move around their own country freely and safely.[131] The Ministry of Interior did, however, eventually revoke Blackwater's operating license in January 2009.[132]

Condoleezza Rice telephoned Maliki shortly after the incident to express her regrets.[133] However, she also held a press conference on 21 September during which she declared that "we need protection for our diplomats" in Iraq.[134] Striking a somewhat more conciliatory tone, the US Embassy to Iraq's *chargé d'affaires* and regional security officer met with Mowaffak al-Rubaie, the Iraqi national security advisor, on 17 September to explain that their government was taking the incident very seriously and to express regret for the loss of life.[135] Nevertheless, the *chargé d'affaires* also attempted to rationalize the shootings by pointing out that the team involved had responded to an explosion in the vicinity of their principal's meeting place and that US diplomatic facilities and security personnel had been attacked multiple times during the 10 days preceding the incident.[136] This provoked a hostile response from al-Rubaie, who brought up the high death toll in Nisour Square and claimed that the Western PSCs had been involved in at least three other deadly shooting incidents during the preceding month.

On 18 September the Department of State agreed to jointly investigate the incident and other "issues of security and safety related to USG-affiliated personal security detail operations" with the government of Iraq.[137] A classified internal Department of State document revealed that the department sought to maintain strict control over the commission to ensure that it "does not commit us to a specific course of action" regarding its private security operations in Iraq.[138] US Embassy officials met with the Iraqi co-chair of the commission, Minister of Defence Abdul Qadr, on 20 September to express regret for the loss of life and to convey how seriously the government of the United States took the commission's work. In contrast to some of his cabinet colleagues, Qadr refrained from issuing new recriminations and, instead, stated that the incident should be viewed as the actions of a few individuals rather than as a central feature of the bilateral relationship between their governments.[139]

A second diplomatic firestorm erupted on 1 January 2010, when Iraqi officials learned that Judge Urbina had dismissed the charges against five of the Blackwater personnel accused of killing and injuring Iraqi civilians in Nisour Square. Two Iraqi members of parliament, Omar Khalaf Jabouri and Omar Jaikal al-Jabouri, likely voiced the most extreme reaction from any Iraqi government official when they argued that their government should retaliate against Urbina's decision by releasing every Iraqi sentenced to death for killing Americans in Iraq.[140] Other members of parliament claimed that they would call for a national referendum on whether to continue to permit US military forces to operate on Iraqi soil.[141] In addition, multiple Iraqi politicians demanded that their government extradite and prosecute the accused, but this effort was quashed under pressure from the Department of State.[142]

During a meeting with US Senator John McCain on 5 January 2010, Maliki called on the government of the United States to appeal Urbina's ruling and claimed that the Iraqi people wanted the United States to make public expressions of sympathy for the victims of the Nisour Square incident and their families.[143] He softened his tone during a meeting with the US Ambassador to Iraq on 8 January by acknowledging the US government's concerted efforts to prosecute Blackwater's personnel and the possibility that the Department of Justice could attempt to appeal the ruling.[144] However, he also stated that members of his government "were shocked" by the judge's decision. Among the outraged was Sadiq Rakabi, one of Maliki's senior advisors, who argued on 10 January 2010 that the ruling "complicated" efforts by Americans to gain compensation for infractions committed under the Hussein regime, and stated that "No one will go to Washington now and negotiate an agreement on these claims".[145] He also informed US Embassy officials that the government of Iraq would behave obstinately on this issue in order to demonstrate its displeasure with the ruling.[146]

Finally, multiple officials in the government of Iraq declared that they sought to deport everyone that had ever worked for Blackwater from their country, including dozens of employees of Triple Canopy and DynCorp.[147] The Ministry of Interior sent a letter to Triple Canopy on 5 January 2010, requesting

> an officially signed and sealed letter issued by the authorized director and attorney of your company stating that no Blackwater employees have been employed, or added to the list of personnel in your company ... otherwise Triple Canopy shall pledge to bear the legal responsibility before the Iraqi judiciary.[148]

DynCorp received a similar letter. Both firms were operating on expired licenses at the time, placing the Ministry of Interior in a position to exercise considerable leverage over them. The Ministry did not follow through with its threat.

Blackwater's violent behaviour also infuriated the Iraqi people and likely undermined support for the United States' occupation forces.

Drawing comparisons with the scandalous slaughter of hundreds of Vietnamese civilians by US soldiers on 16 March 1968, a trio of US-based commentators dramatically argued that "the fallout from the September 16 shooting by Blackwater guards in Baghdad was as publicly damaging to US efforts in Iraq as was the My Lai massacre in Vietnam".[149] Reflecting on a more recent scandal involving American security forces in a foreign conflict zone, a US military officer told a reporter shortly after the shootings that "This is a nightmare.... This is going to hurt us badly. It may be worse than Abu Ghraib, and it comes at a time when we're trying to have an impact for the long term".[150] Hatred of Blackwater peaked in the aftermath of the Nisour Square incident as news media in Iraq and other Arab countries provided intensive coverage of the incident. A classified Department of State cable rightly concluded that "most of the coverage tended to focus on differing accounts of the incident and body counts" but also included inflammatory statements from officials working for the Iraqi Ministry of Interior, who threatened to revoke Blackwater's operating license, and from the radical Shia cleric Muqtada al-Sadr, who blamed the Iraqi government for its failure to control Western firms and called for the expulsion of all Western PSCs from the country.[151] The US Embassy to Iraq also lamented that the editorial content in this coverage was extremely negative, with commentators criticizing the government of Iraq for its lack of control over Western PSCs and claiming that the government of the United States used these firms to undertake "dirty" operations that violated normal US military procedures.[152]

Commenting on how ordinary Iraqis viewed Blackwater, retired US Marine Colonel Thomas X. Hammes argued that

> The problem is [that] in protecting the principal, they had to be very aggressive, and each time they went out they had to offend locals, forcing them to the side of the road, being overpowering and intimidating, at times running vehicles off the road, making enemies each time they went out.[153]

He went on to argue that the Iraqi populace also

> holds the [Iraqi] government responsible for everything that the contractors do or fail to do. Since insurgency is essentially a competition for legitimacy between the government and insurgents, this factor elevates the issue of quality and tactical control to the strategic level.[154]

Reflecting on the harm caused by the firm's use of violence to harass suspected threats, a senior official with the Department of Defense similarly argued that Blackwater's personnel

> were very difficult to work with, (and) overly aggressive. Part of counterinsurgency is kicking down doors and getting people, but part of it

is winning the people ... how do you do that when they see Suburbans, with the guys with big muscles and machine guns hanging out the side, driving through checkpoints?[155]

Mosche Schwartz, an analyst with the Congressional Research Service, likewise noted that ordinary Iraqis considered Blackwater's personnel to be official representatives of the United States and that their behaviour, consequently, "undermined the US mission in ... Iraq".[156] He also argued that, since ordinary Iraqis believed that Blackwater's personnel operated without any oversight or control by the government of Iraq, the deaths and serious injuries they inflicted during their operations threatened that government's legitimacy in the eyes of its citizens.[157]

Extensive negative media coverage of Blackwater's behaviour in Iraq also caused political fallout inside the United States.[158] For example, several articles in the *New York Times* and the *Washington Post* suggested that the deaths of the four Blackwater employees in Fallujah in March 2004, a city that Blackwater was not authorized to enter at the time, forced the US Marines to launch a major offensive in that city that otherwise would not have happened.[159] One article contained a quote from Brigadier General Mark Kimmitt, a spokesperson for American military forces in Iraq, who stated that "the reason we went into Falluja included the killing of the four contractors".[160] In addition, several articles correctly reported that the behaviour of PSCs in Iraq, particularly attacks on civilians and Iraqi security personnel, had strained diplomatic relations between the US and Iraqi governments.[161] For example, one article contained a quote from an American official in Iraq, who noted that "I would say that Iraqi officials are no different than other Iraqi citizens: They can't stand the western security companies.... Blackwater is particularly egregious, but I guess they've been told to use those procedures by the US Embassy".[162] Another contained a quote from Mathew Degn, a one-time senior American advisor to the Iraqi Ministry of Interior, who recalled that "The Iraqis despised them [private security companies], because they were untouchable".[163] Beyond this, several articles suggested that Blackwater's violent behaviour resulted in direct harm to Iraqi civilians.[164] For example, one *Washington Post* article included quotes from General Karl R. Horst, deputy commander of the US Army's 3rd Infantry Division, who argued that "These guys run loose in this country and do stupid stuff.... They shoot people, and someone else has to deal with the aftermath. It happens all over the place".[165] In addition, a *New York Times* article printed statements from an Iraqi policeman who argued that Blackwater's personnel were "butchering" ordinary Iraqi citizens without cause.[166]

American media coverage also argued that Blackwater's actions undermined US efforts to win over the hearts and minds of the Iraqi populace.[167] For example, one article in the *New York Times* suggested that the actions of PSCs "stoked outrage among Iraqis", another stated that "Blackwater's behavior is ... proving counterproductive to American efforts to gain support for its military efforts in Iraq" and still others contained references to crowds of Iraqi civilians cheering the deaths of the firm's employees.[168] Likewise, a highly critical article in the *Washington Post* contained a statement from an official in the Iraqi Ministry of Interior, who argued that the behaviour of Blackwater's employees is an important "reason for all the hatred that is directed at Americans, because people don't know them as Blackwater, they know them only as Americans. They are planting hatred because of these irresponsible acts" against Iraqi civilians.[169]

Moreover, numerous articles suggested that Blackwater's employees were rarely punished for their violent behaviour.[170] One article stated, for example, that "the laws governing contractors on the battlefield are vague and rarely enforced".[171] Another suggested that "it is exceedingly unlikely that ... [Blackwater's employees] will be called to account" for their actions in Iraq.[172] Yet another included quotes stating that the employees of Blackwater are "repeat offenders, and yet they continue to prosper in Iraq" because the Department of State turned a blind eye to their violent behaviour.[173] Amid this criticism, the head of the Department of State's Bureau of Diplomatic Security, Richard Griffin, resigned in October 2007.[174]

The extensive negative media coverage of Blackwater's behaviour in Iraq motivated multiple Congressional committees, including the Senate Armed Services Committee, the Senate Homeland Security and Governmental Affairs Committee, the House Committee on Oversight and Government Reform, the House Committee on Armed Services and the House Judiciary Committee, to hold hearings on these matters.[175] An October 2007 report endorsed by the Democratic majority members of the House Committee on Oversight and Government Reform concluded that "Blackwater's use of force in Iraq is frequent and extensive, resulting in significant casualties and property damage".[176] The report and subsequent hearing also criticized the DSS's apparent enabling attitude toward Blackwater's violent behaviour. For example, it noted that

> Even in cases involving the death of Iraqis, it appears that the Department of State's primary response was to ask Blackwater to make monetary payments to "put the matter behind us", rather than to insist upon accountability or to investigate Blackwater personnel for potential criminal liability.[177]

It also drew attention to an email written by a DSS agent in the wake of a violent 2006 incident involving Blackwater's personnel that indicated that the agency viewed the firm's operations through rose-coloured glasses:

> This was an unfortunate event but we feel that it doesn't reflect on the ... overall Blackwater performance. They do an exceptional job under

very challenging circumstances. We would like to help them resolve this so we can continue with our protective mission.[178]

Blackwater's personnel had fired their weapons during more than 200 incidents in Iraq before this email was written.

The 2 October 2007 hearing conducted by this committee saw its members voice numerous criticisms of the firm's behaviour in Iraq. For example, after quoting General David Petraeus' widely-respected counter-insurgency manual, which states that "Counterinsurgents that use excessive force to limit short-term risk alienating the local populace. They deprive themselves of support or tolerance of the people. This situation is what insurgents want. It increases the threat they pose", Congressman John Tierney told Prince that, in his opinion, "It does appear from some of the evidence here that Blackwater and other companies, sometimes at least, conduct their missions in ways that lead exactly in the opposite direction that General Petraeus wants to go".[179] He highlighted incidents where the firm's employees shot at civilian vehicles and ran them off the road as examples of particularly problematic behaviour:

> So when we look at Blackwater's own records that show that you regularly move traffic off the roads and you shoot up cars ... we see, I think, why the tactics you use in carrying out your contract might [militate] against what we're trying to do in the insurgency.[180]

To these and similar lines of inquiry, Prince responded that he "disagreed with" the assertion that his employees had harmed innocent civilians in Iraq and claimed that the civilian deaths associated with his firm were most likely the unintended result of "ricochets" and "traffic accidents".[181] Subsequent questions posed by the committee members indicated that were not convinced by these explanations. Taken together, it is clear that many members of the House and Senate eventually came to hold a highly negative view of Blackwater's actions.

The extensive negative media coverage of Blackwater's behaviour in Iraq also likely influenced the attitudes of officials working in the US government's executive branch.[182] Senior policymakers in the first and second Obama administrations, including the president, Secretaries of State Hillary Clinton and John Kerry, and Secretary of Defense Robert M. Gates, publicly criticized the use of PSCs in Iraq in the wake of the Nisour Square shootings.[183] Speaking less than a month after the incident, then-Senator Obama reflected the tone of prominent media coverage of Blackwater when he argued that "private security contractors ... go out and they're spraying bullets and hitting civilians and that makes it more dangerous for our troops".[184] While serving in the US Senate, Clinton co-sponsored the 2007 version of the Stop Outsourcing Security Act, which called on "the Secretary of State ... [to] ensure that all personnel at any United States diplomatic or consular mission in Iraq are provided security services only by federal government personnel".[185] While voicing her support for the bill, Clinton described firms such as Blackwater as "reckless" and stated that "The time to show these contractors the door is long past due".[186] In February 2011, Gates told a Senate committee that he wanted the Department of State to stop using PSCs in overseas conflict zones.[187] Clinton's successor as Secretary of State, John Kerry, offered similar sentiments before a Senate Committee on 20 December 2012.[188] During the hearing, he voiced support for fielding an "expeditionary diplomatic corps" that would routinely travel "outside the wire" – that is, outside of secure American embassies and other Department of State compounds – to interact with normal citizens in countries all over the world, even in highly unstable countries experiencing terrorism and insurgency.[189] However, probable in reflection of the political fallout generated by Blackwater's behaviour in Iraq, he expressed concern about the likelihood that local citizens would view US diplomats protected by convoys of armed and armoured vehicles with fear and suspicion:

> As you pass through a village with masses of guns and big armoured personnel carriers and Humvees, the look of confusion and alienation from average Iraqis or Afghans, who just don't understand why we're rumbling through their streets that way, is unmistakable.[190]

This statement may be interpreted as a direct rebuke of the "high-visibility deterrent" approach favoured by Blackwater in Iraq.

Corporate implications

As Prince argued in his memoirs, Blackwater's security operations for the Department of State in Iraq proved "lucrative, tumultuous, successful, and ultimately devastating" for the company.[191] In October 2007, he acknowledged that the scandals generated by the Nisour Square incident were "a source of huge controversy and hassle for us" and told reporters that his firm might voluntarily cease operating in Iraq because "We see the security market diminishing".[192] He also spoke of expanding his company into one capable of providing "more of a full-spectrum" of services, including conducting the kinds of highly dangerous and violent counterterrorism and counternarcotics operations that are traditionally handled by elite military and law enforcement units.[193]

Despite these assertions, Prince sought to maintain the firm's valuable security contracts in Iraq for as long as possible. The Iraqi Ministry of Interior effectively sealed Blackwater's fate as a top-tier PSC when it announced, in January 2009, that it would not grant the firm a new license to provide security services in Iraq.[194] Although pressure from the Department of State delayed this decision for more than a year, it had no choice but to comply once the decision was made.[195] Coincidently, all three of the Department's Iraq-based contracts with Blackwater were scheduled to expire in 2009, which made it easier to sever these ties.[196] Prince made an eleventh-hour attempt to preserve these contracts by proposing to establish a corporate alliance with an Iraqi security firm, but the department refused to even consider this.[197] Instead, two of the department's other major PSCs, DynCorp and Triple Canopy, along with a few other firms, took over Blackwater's responsibilities and hired dozens of its former employees.[198] As Blackwater's operating revenue sharply declined, Triple Canopy emerged as the department's new lead private security force in Iraq, providing the bulk of the security teams, including those for the US Ambassador and visiting American politicians, and DynCorp took over the prestigious aerial security and transport role.[199] The fact that the two firms had a large number of former Blackwater personnel on their payrolls angered the Ministry of Interior, but it continued to renew their operating licenses.[200]

Blackwater's operations in Iraq ended on 23 December 2009, with the final flight of its subsidiary, Presidential Airways.[201] The loss of the Iraq contracts left Prince embittered with his former chief client: "I was strung up so the politicians could feign indignation and pretend my men hadn't done exactly what they had paid us handsomely to do".[202] Nevertheless, the firm continued to work for the department on a smaller scale.[203] It also continued to work for the less image-conscious CIA long after the Nisour Square incident.[204] For example, it signed a US$120 million contract in June 2010 to protect US consulates in Afghanistan and signed a US$100 million contract during the same month to guard CIA facilities there.[205] On the other hand, by getting itself banned from providing security services in Iraq, the firm lost out on a highly lucrative opportunity to take part in the Department of State's efforts to field a greatly expanded force of up to 5,500 private security personnel to protect its staff and facilities in the country.[206] If the firm had maintained its position as the department's lead security provider, then it likely would have fielded approximately 3,850 members (70 per cent) of this force and reaped billions of dollars in revenue from this contract.[207]

In an attempt to repair its reputation after the Nisour Square incident, the firm deemphasized its American roots by changing its name from Blackwater USA to Blackwater Worldwide in October 2007.[208] It also introduced a new, less threatening, logo that, rather than featuring a bear paw in the crosshairs of a sniper scope, set the bear paw in between a pair of crescent-shaped brackets.[209] The firm underwent a much more significant rebranding in February 2009 by changing its name to Xe Services and rolling out an entirely new logo.[210] Prince put Xe Services up for sale in June 2010, and it was purchased by USTC Holdings in December of that year.[211] In a conscious effort to reshape the firm's image and military culture, Prince's replacement as CEO, Ted Wright, instituted a new code of conduct that all employees were required to follow, fired more than 80 per cent of the instructors who had indoctrinated employees into the old, belligerent military culture, and changed the firm's name to the intentionally "boring" Academi.[212] In June 2014, Academi merged with its former rival, Triple Canopy, to form a new company called Constellis Holdings that, due to its size, could become a dominant player in the private security industry.[213] Despite these efforts to outrun Blackwater's controversial past, every new iteration of the firm will likely operate under a cloud of suspicion because few scholarly and media accounts of its activities, regardless of its current name, fail to either mention that it was founded as Blackwater USA and/or draw attention to the numerous violent acts committed by its employees in Iraq. As of November 2014, DynCorp continues to provide largely non-controversial security services for the Department of State and other clients around the world.

Conclusion

Blackwater's comparatively belligerent behaviour in Iraq, especially the 15 minutes of carnage its personnel unleashed in Nisour Square, profoundly influenced the firm's own corporate development and also sparked significant political and legal scandals. Indeed, while the firm's personnel proved quite adept at protecting themselves and their clients from harm, their behaviour drove a wedge between the governments of Iraq and the United States, motivated the firm to pay out large sums of money to some of its victims and their families, led to the conviction of multiple employees in an American court, motivated the government of the United States to develop numerous new regulations to improve its ability to monitor and control the behaviour of PSCs, and undermined the firm's ability to compete in the contemporary market for private armed forces. The next chapter provides a summary of the findings of this book and discusses multiple implications for the future use and development of private armed forces.

Notes

1 The Iraqi Media Network attempted to sue Blackwater in an Iraqi court to provide compensation for the three security guards killed by the firm's DDMs on 7 February 2007. However, citing the firm's blanket legal immunity under Coalition Provisional Authority Order 17, an Iraqi judge rejected the case. Fainaru, *Big Boy Rules*, 170 and 173; Fainaru, "Blackwater Sniper Fire"; Scahill, *Blackwater*, 1st edn, 11; US Embassy, Baghdad, "Spot Report – 020707–01"; Simons, *Master of War*, 163; Prince, *Civilian Warriors*, 214.
2 Blackwater, PSD Incident Report, 19 May 2005; US Embassy, Baghdad, "Receipt for Compensation".
3 US Embassy, Baghdad, "Preliminary Spot Report"; US Embassy, Baghdad, "2005BAGHDA01554"; Bonfiglio, "BW SIR Karbala PSD".
4 Al-Hillah Police, "Police Reports"; Al-Hillah Investigation Court, "Investigation Court's Reports"; Blackwater, PSD Incident Report, 24 October 2005; US

Embassy, Baghdad, "Spot Report – 102405–06"; US Embassy, Baghdad, "Decision Memorandum Issued".
5 DGSD, PSD Incident Report, 16 July 2007; US Embassy, Baghdad, "Spot Report – 071607–07"; US Department of State Diplomatic Security Service, "DS Report Number 7/16/2007"; Zittle, "RE: OEF in Erbil"; Amin, "Statement"; Zittle, "Re: Claim filed".
6 US Embassy, Baghdad, "First Meeting".
7 Roberts, "Blackwater Trial".
8 Dunning, "Heroes or Mercenaries?", 9–10.
9 Fainaru, *Big Boy Rules*, 180–181.
10 Fainaru, *Big Boy Rules*, 180–181.
11 Raghavan and White, "Blackwater Guards Fired".
12 Ibid.
13 US Embassy, Baghdad, "Prime Minister Agrees".
14 US Department of State, "Embassy Continues Outreach".
15 Simons, *Master of War*, 186.
16 DeYoung, "Immunity Jeopardizes Iraq Probe".
17 Johnston and Broder, "F.B.I. Says".
18 Fainaru, *Big Boy Rules*, 181; Jordan, "FBI Finds".
19 Jordan, "FBI Finds".
20 Scahill, *Blackwater*, 2nd edn, 32; US Embassy, Baghdad, "Spot Report – 091607–07".
21 Jordan, "FBI Finds"; Scahill, *Blackwater*, 2nd edn, 32.
22 Dunning, "Heroes or Mercenaries?", 9–10; US Department of Justice, "Transcript".
23 US Department of Justice, "Transcript".
24 Ibid.
25 Ibid.
26 Dunning, "Heroes or Mercenaries?", 10.
27 Urbina, "Memorandum Opinion", 59.
28 Ibid., 89.
29 Ibid., 3.
30 Ibid., 23.
31 US Embassy, Baghdad, "Public Outrage".
32 Dunning, "Heroes or Mercenaries?", 10.
33 Risen, "Ex-Blackwater Guards".
34 Ibid.
35 Frommer and Tucker, "Ex-Blackwater Contractors".
36 Ibid.
37 Hsu, St Martin and Alexander, "Four Blackwater Guards".
38 Apuzzo, "Witnesses Testify".
39 Ibid.
40 Ibid.
41 Ibid.
42 Ibid.
43 Ibid.; Roberts, "Trial of Four".
44 Apuzzo, "Witnesses Testify".
45 Ibid.
46 Usborne, "Blackwater Mercenaries Face Justice".
47 Karadsheh and Duke, "Blackwater Incident Witness"; Fainaru, *Big Boy Rules*, 177; Cotton *et al.*, *Hired Guns*, 25–26; Simons, *Master of War*, 176 and 261; Welch, "Fragmented Power", 355; Thurner, "Drowning in Blackwater", 64–65; US Department of Justice, "Transcript", 2–3; Scahill, *Blackwater*, 2nd edn, 5 and 32–33; US Department of State, "Blackwater Personnel";

Usborne, "Blackwater Mercenaries Face Justice"; Roberts, "Blackwater Trial".
48 Roberts, "Blackwater Trial".
49 Ibid.
50 Ibid.
51 Usborne, "Blackwater Mercenaries Face Justice".
52 Roberts, "Trial of Four".
53 Ibid.
54 Roberts, "Blackwater Trial".
55 Ibid.
56 Ibid.
57 Hsu, St Martin and Alexander, "Four Blackwater Guards"; Yost, Hananel and Tucker, "Blackwater Guards Found Guilty".
58 Hsu, St Martin and Alexander, "Four Blackwater Guards".
59 Hsu, St Martin and Alexander, "Four Blackwater Guards"; Roberts, "US Jury Convicts".
60 Viswanatha and Edwards, "US Jury Convicts".
61 Yost, Hananel and Tucker, "Blackwater Guards Found Guilty".
62 Viswanatha and Edwards, "US Jury Convicts".
63 Hsu, St Martin and Alexander, "Four Blackwater Guards"; Yost, Hananel and Tucker, "Blackwater Guards Found Guilty".
64 Hsu, St Martin and Alexander, "Four Blackwater Guards".
65 REO Hillah, "Najaf Governor Marja'iyya"; US Embassy, Baghdad, "Update on Joint Commission"; US Embassy, Baghdad, "PM Advisor Cites Impact"; Simons, *Master of War*, 181; Prince, *Civilian Warriors*, 192.
66 US Embassy, Baghdad, "Embassy Continues Outreach".
67 US Embassy, Baghdad, "Update on Joint Commission"; US Department of State, "Claims and Condolence Payment Program".
68 US Embassy, Baghdad, "Update on Joint Commission".
69 US Embassy, Baghdad, "Implementation of Recommendations".
70 Burke *et al.*, "Second Amended Complaint", 3.
71 Ibid., 16.
72 Ibid., 12.
73 Ibid., 19.
74 Prince, *Civilian Warriors*, 303–304.
75 Ibid., 303–304.
76 Ibid., 304.
77 US Embassy, Baghdad, "Implementation of Recommendations".
78 Ibid.
79 Ibid.
80 Ibid.
81 Ibid.
82 Risen, "Ex-Blackwater Guards"; Devereaux, "Blackwater Guards Lose Bid".
83 Thurner, "Drowning in Blackwater", 83–84; Simons, *Master of War*, 181–182; Human Rights First, "Private Security Contractors", 19.
84 Commission on Wartime Contracting in Iraq and Afghanistan, "At What Cost?", 66–67.
85 Ackerman, "US Blocks Oversight"; Commission on Wartime Contracting in Iraq and Afghanistan, "At What Cost?", 66–67; Thurner, "Drowning in Blackwater", 83–84; US Department of State, "Secretary of State's Panel", 9; Human Rights First, "Private Security Contractors", 19.
86 Commission on Wartime Contracting in Iraq and Afghanistan, "At What Cost?", 66–67; Thurner, "Drowning in Blackwater", 83–84; US Department of State, "Secretary of State's Panel", 9.

87 Ackerman, "US Blocks Oversight"; Kennedy, "Statement by Patrick F. Kennedy", 5.
88 Kennedy, "Statement by Patrick F. Kennedy", 5.
89 Ibid., 5.
90 Thurner, "Drowning in Blackwater", 81–82; England, "Memorandum"; Behn, "Pentagon Hints".
91 Human Rights First, "Private Security Contractors", 18.
92 Thurner, "Drowning in Blackwater", 81–82; England, "Memorandum"; Dunning, "Heroes or Mercenaries?", 11; Human Rights First, "Private Security Contractors", 18.
93 US Department of Defense and US Department of State, "Memorandum"; Office of the Special Inspector General for Iraq Reconstruction, "Monitoring Responsibilities", 1; Human Rights First, "Private Security Contractors", 18 and 20.
94 Commission on Wartime Contracting in Iraq and Afghanistan, "At What Cost?", 66–67; Thurner, "Drowning in Blackwater", 82–83; US Department of State, "Secretary of State's Panel", 9; US Department of Defense and US Department of State, "Memorandum of Agreement".
95 Thurner, "Drowning in Blackwater", 82–83.
96 Ibid., 82–83.
97 Thurner, "Drowning in Blackwater", 83–84; US Department of Defense and US Department of State, "Memorandum of Agreement".
98 Thurner, "Drowning in Blackwater", 84; US Department of Defense and US Department of State, "Memorandum of Agreement".
99 Dunning, "Heroes or Mercenaries?", 11–12; Governments of the United States and Iraq, "Agreement".
100 Commission on Wartime Contracting in Iraq and Afghanistan, "At What Cost?", 66–67; US Department of State and the Broadcasting Board of Governors Office of the Inspector General, "Status of the Panel", 12; US Embassy, Baghdad, "NSA Rubaie".
101 Commission on Wartime Contracting in Iraq and Afghanistan, "At What Cost?", 66–67; REO Basra, "Foreign Security Firms"; Office of the Special Inspector General for Iraq Reconstruction, "SIGIR 11–019", 5; Carafano, *Private Sector, Public Wars*, 107.
102 Boswell *et al.*, "Secretary of State's Panel", 5.
103 Schakowsky, "Senate and House Members", 461; Scahill, *Blackwater*, 2nd edn; Scahill, "Bush's Shadow Army".
104 Schakowsky, "Senate and House Members"
105 Senate of the United States, "Stop Outsourcing Security Act".
106 Doyle, "Civilian Extraterritorial Jurisdiction Act", 5.
107 Schwartz, "Department of Defense's Use".
108 International Committee of the Red Cross, "The Montreux Document".
109 Swiss Federal Department of Foreign Affairs, "International Code of Conduct".
110 ASIS International, "ANSI/ASIS PSC1–2012".
111 Prince, *Civilian Warriors*, 157.
112 Prince, *Civilian Warriors*, 169 and 216.
113 DeYoung, "State Department Struggles".
114 Ibid.
115 Fainaru, *Big Boy Rules*, 139–140; US Army, "Escalation of Force".
116 Ibid., 139–140.
117 Ibid., 139–140.
118 Blackwater, PSD Incident Report, 24 May 2007; Fainaru, *Big Boy Rules*, 173–175; Scahill, *Blackwater*, 2nd edn, 11–12; Simons, *Master of War*, 163; Prince, *Civilian Warriors*, 214.
119 Simons, *Master of War*, 181.

Implications of tactical behaviour 203

120 Human Rights First, "Private Security Contractors", 5.
121 DeYoung, "Other Killings".
122 Rubin and Kramer, "Iraqi Premier".
123 Simons, *Master of War*, 181–182.
124 CNN Staff, "Blackwater: Employees 'Acted Lawfully' "; US Embassy, Baghdad, "Prime Minister Agrees".
125 US Embassy, Baghdad, "Prime Minister Agrees"; US Department of State, "Embassy Continues Outreach"; Scahill, *Blackwater*, 2nd edn, 13–14.
126 Thurner, "Drowning in Blackwater", 80–81; Kramer, "Blackwater Resumes Guarding".
127 Simons, *Master of War*, 181; Office of the Secretary of State, "Blackwater Personal Security Detail"; US Embassy, Baghdad, "Prime Minister Agrees"; Thurner, "Drowning in Blackwater", 80–81; Office of the Secretary of State, "Blackwater Personal Security Detail".
128 Kramer, "Blackwater Resumes Guarding"; Scahill, *Blackwater*, 2nd edn, 13–14; Simons, *Master of War*, 181.
129 Office of the Secretary of State, "Blackwater Personal Security Detail".
130 Office of the Secretary of State, "Blackwater Personal Security Detail".
131 US Department of State, "Embassy Continues Outreach".
132 Avant *et al.*, "The Mercenary Debate: Three Views", 40.
133 Thurner, "Drowning in Blackwater", 83–84.
134 Rice, "Transcript".
135 Office of the Secretary of State, "Blackwater Personal Security Detail".
136 Ibid.
137 Thurner, "Drowning in Blackwater", 83–84; Kramer, "Blackwater Resumes Guarding"; Scahill, *Blackwater*, 2nd edn, 14; US Embassy, Baghdad, "Prime Minister Agrees".
138 Office of the Secretary of State, "Blackwater Personal Security Detail".
139 US Embassy, Baghdad, "Initial Discussion with Iraqi MOD".
140 US Embassy, Baghdad, "Public Outrage".
141 US Embassy, Baghdad, "Public Outrage"; US Embassy, Baghdad, "Fallout Over Blackwater Continues".
142 US Embassy, Baghdad, "Public Outrage".
143 US Embassy, Baghdad, "GOI Leaders Request"; US Embassy, Baghdad, "CODEL McCain Meetings".
144 US Embassy, Baghdad, "PM Maliki on Blackwater".
145 US Embassy, Baghdad, "PM Advisor Cites Impact".
146 Ibid.
147 US Embassy, Baghdad, "Public Outrage"; US Embassy, Baghdad, "Fallout Over Blackwater Continues".
148 Quoted in US Embassy, Baghdad, "Fallout Over Blackwater Continues".
149 Carstens, Cohen and Küpçü, "Changing the Culture".
150 Raghavan and Ricks, "Private Security".
151 US Embassy, Baghdad, "Prime Minister Agrees".
152 US Embassy, Baghdad, "Update on Joint Commission".
153 Quoted in Luban, "Blackwater Pays Price".
154 Hammes, "Private Contractors", 29.
155 Simons, *Master of War*, 161.
156 Schwartz, "Department of Defense's Use", 16.
157 Ibid., 16.
158 Prince, *Civilian Warriors*, 314–315.
159 Gettleman, "Mix of Pride and Shame"; Gettleman, "4 from U.S. Killed"; Knickmeyer, "Insurgents Down Civilian Helicopter"; Chan and Vick, "U.S. Vows"; Fainaru, *Big Boy Rules*; Risen, "Iraq Contractor".

160 Schmitt, "Test in a Tinderbox".
161 Barstow, "Security Companies"; Broder and Risen, "Armed Guards in Iraq"; Finer, "Security Contractors in Iraq"; Glanz and Tavernise, "Security Firm Faces Criminal Charges"; Thompson, "5 Guards Face U.S. Charges".
162 Partlow and Pincus, "Iraq Bans Security Contractor".
163 Fainaru, "Where Military Rules Don't Apply".
164 Dao, "Private Guards Take Big Risks"; Kramer and Glanz, "U.S. Guards Kill 2"; Partlow and Pincus, "Iraq Bans Security Contractor"; Raghavan and DeYoung, "5 Witnesses Insist"; DeYoung, "Other Killings".
165 Finer, "Security Contractors in Iraq".
166 Kramer and Glanz, "U.S. Guards Kill 2".
167 Finer, "Security Contractors in Iraq".
168 Broder and Risen, "Blackwater Tops All Firms"; Dao, "Private Guards Take Big Risks"; Gettleman, "4 from U.S. Killed"; Glanz, "Security Guard Kills Iraqi Driver"; Schmitt, "Test in a Tinderbox".
169 Fainaru, "Where Military Rules Don't Apply".
170 Broder and Risen, "Armed Guards in Iraq"; Risen, "Limbo for U.S. Women"; Witte, "New Law Could Subject Civilians"; Risen, "Iraq Contractor".
171 Broder and Risen, "Armed Guards in Iraq".
172 Rubin and Von Zielbauer, "Judgment Gap".
173 Broder and Risen, "Blackwater Tops All Firms".
174 Schwartz, "State Department Official Resigns".
175 Majority Staff, "Memorandum"; House Committee on Oversight and Government Reform, "Hearing on Blackwater USA"; House Committee on Oversight and Government Reform, "Private Military Contractors"; Senate Committee on Armed Services, "Contracting in a Counterinsurgency"; Subcommittee on National Security, Emerging Threats, and International Relations, "Private Security Firms"; Senate Committee on Homeland Security and Governmental Affairs, "An Uneasy Relationship".
176 Majority Staff, "Memorandum", 6.
177 Ibid., 9.
178 Ibid., 11.
179 House Committee on Oversight and Government Reform, "Hearing on Blackwater USA", 77.
180 Ibid., 77.
181 Ibid., 71.
182 Robinson, "Policy-Media Interaction Model".
183 Brodsky, "Clinton Supports Bill"; Goodman, "Amy Goodman Questions Obama".
184 Davenport, "Obama Criticizes".
185 Brodsky, "Clinton Supports Bill".
186 Ibid.
187 Pincus, "Gates Pleads for Funding".
188 Ackerman, "Blackwater Wins the Battle"; McGreal, "Kerry Defends Diplomacy".
189 Ackerman, "Blackwater Wins the Battle"; McGreal, "Kerry Defends Diplomacy".
190 McGreal, "Kerry Defends Diplomacy".
191 Prince, *Civilian Warriors*, 155–156.
192 Kimberlin, "At Blackwater"; Cole, "Blackwater Vies for Jobs".
193 Cole, "Blackwater Vies for Jobs".
194 Simons, *Master of War*, 263; Avant *et al.*, "The Mercenary Debate", 40; US Embassy, Santiago, "Chile Media Report".
195 Thurner, "Drowning in Blackwater", 80–81; US Embassy, Baghdad, "NSA Rubaie"; US Embassy, Baghdad, "RSO Aviation Support".
196 US Embassy, Baghdad, "RSO Aviation Support".

197 Simons, *Master of War*, 263–264.
198 Scahill, *Blackwater*, 2nd edn, 462; Fainaru, *Big Boy Rules*, 137; House Committee on Oversight and Government Reform, "Hearing on Blackwater USA", 24 and 98; Uesseler, *Servants of War*, 87.
199 Ciralsky, "Tycoon"; US Embassy, Baghdad, "GOI Leaders"; Prince, *Civilian Warriors*, 316–317.
200 US Embassy, Baghdad, "GOI Leaders"; US Embassy, Baghdad, "Public Outrage"; US Embassy, Baghdad, "Fallout Over Blackwater Continues".
201 US Embassy, Baghdad, "Public Outrage".
202 Prince, *Civilian Warriors*, 6.
203 Ackerman, "Blackwater 3.0"; Ackerman, "Blackwater Wins the Battle"; Ackerman, "What Would it Take"; Dunning, "Heroes or Mercenaries?", 10.
204 Ackerman, "What Would it Take".
205 Ibid.
206 Ackerman, "US Blocks Oversight"; Dunning, "Heroes or Mercenaries?", 10.
207 Uesseler, *Servants of War*, 86; Dunning, "Heroes or Mercenaries?", 8; House Committee on Oversight and Government Reform, "Hearing on Blackwater USA", 133 and 141; Elsea and Serafino, "Private Security Contractors", 7; Ackerman, "US Blocks Oversight".
208 Von Zielbauer, "Blackwater Softens Logo".
209 Scahill, *Blackwater*, 2nd edn, 41; Scahill, "Blackwater's Business".
210 Avant *et al.*, "The Mercenary Debate", 40; Elay, "WikiLeaks Reveals"; Boone, "Afghanistan lets Blackwater Stay".
211 Risen, "Founder".
212 Prince, *Civilian Warriors*, 317–318.
213 Gibbons-Neff, "Blackwater Back Under Scrutiny"; Risen, "Before Shooting in Iraq".

References

Ackerman, Spencer. "What Would it Take to Get Xe Fired". *The Economist*, 24 June 2010.
Ackerman, Spencer. "US Blocks Oversight of its Mercenary Army in Iraq". *Wired.com*, 22 July 2011.
Ackerman, Spencer. "Blackwater 3.0: Rebranded 'Academi' Wants Back in Iraq". *Wired.com*, 12 December 2011.
Ackerman, Spencer. "Blackwater Wins the Battle of Benghazi". *Wired.com*, 20 December 2012.
Al-Hillah Investigation Court. "Investigation Court's Reports based on Accounts from Iraqi Eyewitnesses and Medical Examiners with Knowledge of 24 October 2005, Incident in Al-Hillah". Al-Hillah, Iraq: Al-Hillah Investigation Court, 24 October 2005.
Al-Hillah Police. "Police Reports based on Accounts from Iraqi Eyewitnesses and Medical Examiners with Knowledge of 24 October 2005, Incident in Al-Hillah". Al-Hillah, Iraq: Al-Hillah Police, 24 October 2005.
Amin, Rizgar Muhamad. "Statement". Erbil, Iraq: Kurdistan Judges Union, 18 July 2007.
Apuzzo, Matt. "Witnesses Testify Against Ex-Blackwater Colleagues in Case of 2007 Iraq Killings". *New York Times*, 15 July 2014.
ASIS International. "ANSI/ASIS PSC1-2012: Management System for Quality of Private Security Company Operations – Requirements with Guidelines". Alexandria, VA: ASIS International, 2012.

Avant, Deborah, Max Boot, Jorg Friedrichs and Cornelius Friesendorf. "The Mercenary Debate: Three Views". *The American Interest* (May/June 2009): 32–48.

Barstow, David. "Security Companies: Shadow Soldiers in Iraq". *New York Times*, 19 April 2004, A1.

Behn, Sharon. "Pentagon Hints Contractors Can be Tried in Military Courts". *Washington Times*, 27 September 2007.

Blackwater. PSD Incident Reports and Sworn Statements. Baghdad: Blackwater, 2005–2009.

Bonfiglio, Brian. "BW SIR Karbala PSD (E-mail) sent to Frederick M. Piry, Paul Nassen, and Mike Rush". Moyock, NC: Blackwater, 13 April 2005.

Boone, Jon. "Afghanistan lets Blackwater Stay Despite Shakeup of Security Contractors". *Guardian*, 7 March 2011.

Boswell, Eric J., George A. Joulwan, J. Stapleton Roy and Patrick F. Kennedy. "Report of the Secretary of State's Panel on Personal Protective Services in Iraq". Washington, DC: US Department of State, October 2007.

Broder, John M., and James Risen. "Armed Guards in Iraq Occupy a Legal Limbo". *New York Times*, 20 September 2007, A1.

Broder, John M., and James Risen. "Blackwater Tops All Firms in Iraq in Shooting Rate". *New York Times*, 27 September 2007, A1.

Brodsky, Robert. "Clinton Supports Bill to Ban Use of State Department Private Security Contractors". *Government Executive.com*, 3 March 2008.

Burke, Susan L., William T. O'Neil, Elizabeth M. Burke, Rosemary B. Healy and Katherine B. Hawkins. "Second Amended Complaint in Abtan v. Blackwater". Washington, DC: The United States District Court for the District of Columbia, 28 March 2008.

Carafano, James Jay. *Private Sector, Public Wars: Contractors in Combat – Afghanistan, Iraq, and Future Conflicts*. Westport, CT: Praeger Security International, 2008.

Carstens, Roger D., Michael A. Cohen and Maria Figueroa Küpçü. "Changing the Culture of Pentagon Contracting". Washington, DC: New America Foundation, 2008.

Chan, Sewell, and Karl Vick. "U.S. Vows to Find Civilians' Killers". *Washington Post*, 2 April 2004, A01.

Ciralsky, Adam. "Tycoon, Contractor, Soldier, Spy". *Vanity Fair*, January 2010.

CNN Staff. "Blackwater: Employees 'Acted Lawfully'". *CNN.com*, 19 September 2007.

Cole, August. "Blackwater Vies for Jobs Beyond Security". *Wall Street Journal*, 15 October 2007.

Commission on Wartime Contracting in Iraq and Afghanistan. "At What Cost? Contingency Contracting in Iraq and Afghanistan". Washington, DC: Commission on Wartime Contracting in Iraq and Afghanistan, June 2009.

Cotton, Sarah K., Ulrich Petersohn, Molly Dunigan, Q. Burkhart, Megan Zander-Cotugno, Edward O'Connell and Michael Webber. *Hired Guns: Views About Armed Contractors in Operation Iraqi Freedom*. Santa Monica, CA: The Rand Corporation, 2010.

Dao, James. "Private Guards Take Big Risks, For Right Price". *New York Times*, 2 April 2004, A1.

Davenport, Jim. "Obama Criticizes Private Iraq Guards". Associated Press, 7 October 2007.

Devereaux, Ryan. "Blackwater Guards Lose Bid to Appeal Charges in Iraqi Civilian Shooting Case". *Guardian*, 5 June 2012.

DeYoung, Karen. "Other Killings by Blackwater Staff Detailed". *Washington Post*, 2 October 2007.
DeYoung, Karen. "State Department Struggles to Oversee Private Army". *Washington Post*, 21 October 2007, A01.
DeYoung, Karen. "Immunity Jeopardizes Iraq Probe". *Washington Post*, 30 October 2007.
DGSD (DynCorp Government Services Division). PSD Incident Reports and Sworn Statements. Falls Church, VA: DynCorp, 2005–2008.
Doyle, Charles. "Civilian Extraterritorial Jurisdiction Act: Federal Contractor Criminal Liability Overseas". Washington, DC: Congressional Research Service, United States Congress, 15 February 2012.
Dunning, Rebecca. "Heroes or Mercenaries? Blackwater, Private Security Companies, and the US Military". Durham, NC: The Kenan Institute for Ethics, Duke University, 2010.
Elay, Tom. "WikiLeaks Reveals Private Security Contractors Killed Iraqis with Impunity". *World Socialist Website*, 27 October 2010.
Elsea, Jennifer K., and Nina M. Serafino. "Private Security Contractors in Iraq: Background, Legal Status, and Other Issues". Washington, DC: Congressional Research Service, 21 June 2007.
England, Gordon. "Memorandum: Management of DoD Contractors and Contractor Personnel Accompanying US Armed Forces in Contingency Operations Outside the United States". Washington, DC: US Department of Defense, 25 September 2007.
Fainaru, Steve. "How Blackwater Sniper Fire Felled 3 Iraqi Guards". *Washington Post*, 8 November 2007.
Fainaru, Steve. "Where Military Rules Don't Apply". *Washington Post*, 20 September 2007.
Fainaru, Steve. *Big Boy Rules: America's Mercenaries Fighting in Iraq*. Philadelphia: Da Capo Press, 2008.
Finer, Jonathan. "Security Contractors in Iraq Under Scrutiny After Shootings". *Washington Post*, 10 September 2005, A01.
Frommer, Frederic, and Eric Tucker. "Ex-Blackwater Contractors Face Fresh Charges in Iraq Attack". Associated Press, 17 October 2013.
Gettleman, Jeffrey. "4 from U.S. Killed in Ambush in Iraq; Mob Drags Bodies". *New York Times*, 1 April 2004, A1.
Gettleman, Jeffrey. "Mix of Pride and Shame Follows Killings and Mutilations by Iraqis". *New York Times*, 2 April 2004, A1.
Gibbons-Neff, Thomas. "Blackwater Back Under Scrutiny". *Washington Post*, 30 June 2014.
Glanz, James, and Sabrina Tavernise. "Security Firm Faces Criminal Charges in Iraq". *New York Times*, 23 September 2007, A1.
Glanz, James. "Security Guard Kills Iraqi Driver". *New York Times*, 12 November 2007, A1.
Goodman, Amy. "Amy Goodman Questions Sen. Obama on Heeding Iraqis' Call for Full US Withdrawal". *Democracy Now.org*, 28 March 2008.
Governments of the United States and Iraq. "Agreement Between the United States of America and the Republic of Iraq on the Withdrawal of United States Forces from Iraq and the Organization of their Activities during their Temporary Presence in Iraq". Washington, DC and Baghdad: Governments of the United States and Iraq, November 2008.

Hammes, Thomas X. "Private Contractors in Conflict Zones: The Good, the Bad, and the Strategic Impact". *Joint Forces Quarterly*, no. 60 (2011): 26–37.

House Committee on Oversight and Government Reform. "Private Military Contractors in Iraq: An Examination of Blackwater's Actions in Fallujah". Washington, DC: House of Representatives, Congress of the United States, September 2007.

House Committee on Oversight and Government Reform. "Hearing on Blackwater USA". Washington, DC: House of Representatives, Congress of the United States, 2 October 2007.

Hsu, Spencer S., Victoria St Martin and Keith L. Alexander. "Four Blackwater Guards Found Guilty in 2007 Iraq Shootings of 31 Unarmed Civilians". *Washington Post*, 22 October 2014.

Human Rights First. "Private Security Contractors at War: Ending the Culture of Impunity". New York: Human Rights First, 2008.

International Committee of the Red Cross. "The Montreux Document: On Pertinent International Legal Obligations and Good Practices for States Related to Operations of Private Military and Security Companies during Armed Conflict". Geneva: International Committee of the Red Cross, 2008.

Johnston, David, and John M. Broder. "F.B.I. Says Guards Killed 14 Iraqis Without Cause". *New York Times*, 14 November 2007.

Jordan, Lara Jakes. "FBI Finds Blackwater Trucks Patched". Associated Press, 12 January 2008.

Karadsheh, Jomana, and Alan Duke. "Blackwater Incident Witness: 'It Was Hell' ". *CNN.com*, 2 October 2007.

Kennedy, Patrick F. "Statement by Patrick F. Kennedy before the Commission on Wartime Contracting". Washington, DC: The Commission on Wartime Contracting, 6 June 2011.

Kimberlin, Joanne. "At Blackwater, Time Is Now Told in 'Before' and 'After' ". *Virginian-Pilot*, 28 October 2007.

Knickmeyer, Ellen. "Insurgents Down Civilian Helicopter Near Iraqi Capital". *Washington Post*, 22 April 2005, A01.

Kramer, Andrew E. "Blackwater Resumes Guarding US Envoys in Iraq". *New York Times*, 22 September 2007.

Kramer, Andrew E., and James Glanz. "U.S. Guards Kill 2 Iraqi Women in New Shooting". *New York Times*, 10 October 2007, A1.

Luban, Daniel. "Blackwater Pays Price for Iraqi Firefight". *Asia Times* (19 September 2007).

Majority Staff. "Memorandum – Additional Information about Blackwater USA". Washington, DC: Congress of the United States, 1 October 2007.

McGreal, Chris. "Kerry Defends Diplomacy Over Military at Senate hearing on Benghazi Report". *The Guardian*, 20 December 2012.

Office of the Secretary of State. "Blackwater Personal Security Detail Involved in Lethal Incident". Washington, DC: US Department of State, 17 September 2007.

Office of the Special Inspector General for Iraq Reconstruction. "Monitoring Responsibilities for Serious Incidents involving Private Security Contractors once US Military Forces Leave Iraq have Not been Determined (SIGIR 11–019)". Washington, DC: Special Inspector General for Iraq Reconstruction, 29 July 2011.

Partlow, Joshua, and Walter Pincus. "Iraq Bans Security Contractor". *Washington Post*, 18 September 2007, A01.

Pincus, Walter. "Gates Pleads for Funding to Keep Iraq Work Going". *Washington Post*, 18 February 2011.
Prince, Erik. *Civilian Warriors: The Inside Story of Blackwater and the Unsung Heroes of the War on Terror*. Kindle edn. New York: Portfolio, 2013.
Raghavan, Sudarsan, and Karen DeYoung. "5 Witnesses Insist Iraqis Didn't Fire on Guards". *Washington Post*, 29 September 2007, A01.
Raghavan, Sudarsan, and Ricks. "Private Security puts Diplomats, Military at Odds". *Washington Post*, 26 September 2007.
Raghavan, Sudarsan, and Josh White. "Blackwater Guards Fired at Fleeing Cars, Soldiers Say". *Washington Post*, 12 October 2007.
REO Basra. "Foreign Security Firms Adapt to Changing Conditions". Basra, Iraq: US Department of State, 23 January 2010.
REO Hillah. "Najaf Governor Marja'iyya Contributing to Peace". Al Hillah, Iraq: US Department of State, 27 September 2007.
Rice, Condoleezza. "Transcript of US Department of State Press Conference". Washington, DC: US Department of State, 21 September 2007.
Risen, James. "Limbo for U.S. Women Reporting Iraq Assaults". *New York Times*, 13 February 2008, A1.
Risen, James. "Iraq Contractor in Shooting Case Makes Comeback". *New York Times*, 10 May 2008.
Risen, James. "Founder Puts Blackwater Security Firm Up for Sale". *New York Times*, 8 June 2010.
Risen, James. "Ex-Blackwater Guards Face Renewed Charges". *New York Times*, 23 April 2011.
Risen, James. "Before Shooting in Iraq, a Warning on Blackwater". *New York Times*, 29 June 2014.
Roberts, Dan. "Blackwater Trial Reaches Emotional and Legal Climax as Prosecution Rests". *Guardian*, 27 August 2014.
Roberts, Dan. "Trial of Four Blackwater Security Guards Hinges on Belief, Not Reality, of a Threat". *Guardian*, 6 September 2014.
Roberts, Dan. "US Jury Convicts Blackwater Guards in 2007 Killing of Iraqi Civilians". *Guardian*, 22 October 2014.
Robinson, Piers. "The Policy–Media Interaction Model: Measuring Media Power during Humanitarian Crises". *Journal of Peace Research* 37, no. 5 (2000): 613–633.
Robinson, Piers. "The CNN Effect Revisited". *Critical Studies in Media Communication* 22, no. 4 (October 2005): 344–349.
Rubin, Alissa J., and Andrew E. Kramer. "Iraqi Premier says Blackwater Shootings Challenge his Nation's Sovereignty". *New York Times*, 24 September 2007.
Rubin, Alissa J., and Paul von Zielbauer. "The Judgment Gap in a Case Like the Blackwater Shootings, There are Many Laws but More Obstacles". *New York Times*, 11 October 2007, A1.
Scahill, Jeremy. *Blackwater: The Rise of the World's Most Powerful Mercenary Army*. 1st edn. New York: Nation Books, 2007.
Scahill, Jeremy. "Bush's Shadow Army". *The Nation*, 2 April 2007.
Scahill, Jeremy. "Blackwater's Business". *The Nation*, 24 December 2007.
Scahill, Jeremy. *Blackwater: The Rise of the World's Most Powerful Mercenary Army*. 2nd edn. New York: Nation Books, 2008.
Schakowsky, Jan. "Senate and House Members Introduce Bill to Phase-Out Private Security Contractors". Press release, 7 November 2007.

Schmitt, Eric. "Test in a Tinderbox". *New York Times*, 28 April 2004, A1.

Schwartz, Moshe. "The Department of Defense's Use of Private Security Contractors in Afghanistan and Iraq: Background, Analysis, and Options for Congress". Washington, DC: Congressional Research Service, 21 February 2011.

Schwartz, Moshe. "The Department of Defense's Use of Private Security Contractors in Afghanistan and Iraq: Background, Analysis, and Options for Congress". Washington, DC: Congressional Research Service, 13 May 2011.

Schwartz, Rhonda. "State Department Official Resigns in Wake of Blackwater Criticism". *ABC News.com*, 24 October 2007.

Senate Committee on Armed Services. "Contracting in a Counterinsurgency: An Examination of the Blackwater–Paravant Contract and the Need for Oversight". Washington, DC: Senate of the United States, Congress of the United States, 24 February 2010.

Senate Committee on Homeland Security and Governmental Affairs. "An Uneasy Relationship: US Reliance on Private Security Firms in Overseas Operations". Washington, DC: Senate of the United States, Congress of the United States, 27 February 2008.

Senate of the United States. "Stop Outsourcing Security Act". Washington, DC: Senate of the United States, 23 February 2010.

Simons, Suzanne. *Master of War: Blackwater USA's Erik Prince and the Business of War*. New York: Harper, 2009.

Subcommittee on National Security, Emerging Threats, and International Relations. "Private Security Firms: Standards, Cooperation and Coordination on the Battlefield". Washington, DC: House of Representatives, Congress of the United States, 13 June 2006.

Swiss Federal Department of Foreign Affairs. "International Code of Conduct for Private Security Service Providers". Bern: Swiss Federal Department of Foreign Affairs, 2010.

Thompson, Ginger. "5 Guards Face U.S. Charges in Iraq Deaths". *New York Times*, 6 December 2008, A1.

Thurner, Jeffrey S. "Drowning in Blackwater: How Weak Accountability over Private Security Contractors Significantly Undermines Counterinsurgency Efforts". *Army Lawyer* (July 2008): 64–90.

Uesseler, Rolf. *Servants of War: Private Military Corporations and the Profit of Conflict*. Translated by Jefferson Chase. Berkeley, CA: Soft Skull Press, 2008.

Urbina, Ricardo M. "Memorandum Opinion: United States of America v. Paul A Slough *et al.*". Washington, DC: United States Court for the District of Columbia, 31 December 2009.

US Army. "Escalation of Force Conducted by BWS in the Vicinity of Kirkuk: 2 Civilian Killed, 0 Coalition Forces Inj/Damage". Kirkuk, Iraq: Wikileaks, 2 February 2006.

Usborne, David. "Blackwater Mercenaries Face Justice for Bloodbath in Baghdad that Caused 14 Civilian Deaths". *Independent*, 31 August 2014.

US Department of Defense and US Department of State. "Memorandum of Agreement Between the Department of Defense and the Department of State on USG Private Security Contractors". Washington, DC: US Department of Defense and US Department of State, 5 December 2007.

US Department of Justice. "Transcript of Blackwater Press Conference". Washington, DC: US Department of Justice, 8 December 2008.

Implications of tactical behaviour 211

US Department of State. "United States Department of State Claims and Condolence Payment Program". Washington, DC: US Department of State, 2005.

US Department of State. "Blackwater Personnel Security Detail Involved in Lethal Incident". Washington, DC: US Department of State, 17 September 2007.

US Department of State. "Embassy Continues Outreach on Personal Security Detail Incident". Washington, DC: US Department of State, 19 September 2007.

US Department of State. "Report of The Secretary of State's Panel on Personal Protective Services in Iraq". Washington, DC: US Department of State, 3 October 2007.

US Department of State and the Broadcasting Board of Governors Office of the Inspector General. "Status of the Secretary of State's Panel on Personal Protective Services in Iraq Report Recommendations". Washington, DC: US Department of State and the Broadcasting Board of Governors Office of Inspector General, December 2008.

US Department of State Diplomatic Security Service. "DS Report Number 7/16/2007 – Kirkuk". Baghdad: US Department of State, 16 September 2007.

US Embassy, Baghdad. "2005BAGHDA01554 – Vehicle Threat Engaged by PSD Team Resulting in the Death of One Local National". Baghdad: US Department of State, 13 April 2005.

US Embassy, Baghdad. "CODEL McCain Meetings with Prime Minister Maliki and Deputy Prime Minister Issawi". Baghdad: US Department of State, 14 January 2010.

US Embassy, Baghdad. "Decision Memorandum Issued by the Embassy Baghdad Claims and Condolence Payment Program Committee". Baghdad: US Department of State, 23 December 2005.

US Embassy, Baghdad. "Embassy Continues Outreach on Personal Security". Baghdad: US Department of State, 19 September 2007.

US Embassy, Baghdad. "Fallout Over Blackwater Continues, Albeit Diminished". Baghdad: US Department of State, 11 January 2010.

US Embassy, Baghdad. "First Meeting of the Joint Commission on PSD Issues". Baghdad: US Department of State, 7 October 2007.

US Embassy, Baghdad. "GOI Leaders Request USG Appeal of Blackwater Decision". Baghdad: US Department of State, 5 January 2010.

US Embassy, Baghdad. "Implementation of Recommendations on Personal Protective Services: Status Report Update #3". Baghdad: US Department of State, 7 February 2008.

US Embassy, Baghdad. "Initial Discussion with Iraqi MOD, Co-Chair of Joint Commission on Personal Security Detail Issues". Baghdad: US Department of State, 20 September 2007.

US Embassy, Baghdad. "NSA Rubaie on Current Security Issues and Blackwater Contract Renewal". Baghdad: US Department of State, 8 April 2008.

US Embassy, Baghdad. "PM Advisor Cites Impact of Blackwater Decision on AMCIT Civil Claims". Baghdad: US Department of State, 11 January 2010.

US Embassy, Baghdad. "PM Maliki on Blackwater, Oil Contractors, Um Qasr Port, and Elections". Baghdad: US Department of State, 8 January 2010.

US Embassy, Baghdad. "Preliminary Spot Report". Baghdad: US Department of State, 13 April 2005.

US Embassy, Baghdad. "Prime Minister Agrees to Joint Commission on Personal Security Detail Operations in Iraq". Baghdad: US Department of State, 18 September 2007.

US Embassy, Baghdad. "Public Outrage over Blackwater Decision Generating Heavy Fallout". Baghdad: US Department of State, 4 January 2010.
US Embassy, Baghdad. "Receipt for Compensation". Baghdad: US Department of State, 12 June 2005.
US Embassy, Baghdad. "RSO Aviation Support for Iraq". Baghdad: US Department of State, 21 March 2009.
US Embassy, Baghdad. "Spot Report – 020707–01 – SAF Attack on a COM PSD". Baghdad: US Department of State, 7 February 2007.
US Embassy, Baghdad. "Spot Report – 071607–07 – COM PSD Team Fires on Aggressive Vehicle". Baghdad: US Department of State, 16 July 2007.
US Embassy, Baghdad. "Spot Report – 091607–07 – SAF Attack on COM Team". Baghdad: US Department of State, 16 September 2007.
US Embassy, Baghdad. "Spot Report – 102405–06 – COM PSD Team Fires on Aggressive Vehicle". Baghdad: US Department of State, 24 October 2005.
US Embassy, Baghdad. "Update on Joint Commission on PSD Issues and Status of Investigation". Baghdad: US Department of State, 28 September 2007.
US Embassy, Santiago. "Chile Media Report – January 30, 2009". Santiago: US Department of State, 30 January 2009.
Viswanatha, Aruna, and Julia Edwards. "US Jury Convicts Ex-Blackwater Guards in 2007 Baghdad Killings". Reuters, 22 October 2014.
Von Zielbauer, Paul. "Blackwater Softens its Logo from Macho to Corporate". *New York Times*, 22 October 2007.
Welch, Michael. "Fragmented Power and State-Corporate Killings: A Critique of Blackwater in Iraq". *Crime, Law and Social Change* 51, no. 3–4 (2009): 351–364.
Witte, Griff. "New Law Could Subject Civilians to Military Trial". *Washington Post*, 15 January 2007, A01.
Yost, Pete, Sam Hananel and Eric Tucker. "Blackwater Guards Found Guilty in Iraq Shootings". Associated Press, 22 October 2014.
Zittle, Zachariah. "RE: OEF in Erbil – UPDATE". Erbil, Iraq: US Department of State, 17 July 2007.
Zittle, Zachariah. "Re: Claim filed by". Erbil, Iraq: US Department of State, 30 July 2007.

7 Conclusion

The findings of this book reveal that the employees of PSCs that place strong emphasis on norms encouraging personal initiative, proactive use of force and an exclusive approach to security tend to use a great deal of violence during their security operations. When compared to DynCorp's personnel, who did not strongly emphasize any of these norms, Blackwater's security teams, whose tactical behaviour was guided by these norms, tended to employ violence against suspected threats more quickly, at greater distances and with a greater number of bullets; they were also considerably more likely to abandon the insurgents they attacked. The gross disparity in the behaviour exhibited by the firms' personnel, in turn, contributed to a significant disparity in the number of deaths and serious injuries they inflicted during their security operations in Iraq, with Blackwater's personnel killing at least 71 people and seriously injuring at least 122 more, and DynCorp's personnel killing 11 people and seriously injuring five. At the same time, while neither firm lost any clients to enemy fire, Blackwater's relatively belligerent personnel in Iraq enjoyed a considerably lower casualty rate than their more passive counterparts in DynCorp. This concluding chapter offers a summary of how well the ideational theory of tactical violence's predictions were supported by the empirical evidence on the firms' security operations in Iraq (see Table 7.1, a reproduction of Table 4.6). It then builds on the book's findings by highlighting their implications for the use and development of private armed forces.

The ideational theory of tactical violence

The central claims of the ideational theory of tactical violence, the primary theoretical contribution of this book, are that the behavioural norms that make up a PSC's military culture have a strong influence on the degree of violence employed by that firm's personnel and that, in turn, the degree of violence employed by these personnel strongly affects two security outcomes. These are, first, the degree of security enjoyed by the people under the firm's protection, such as the firm's personnel and clients, and,

214 *Conclusion*

Table 7.1 Support for the predictions of the ideational theory of tactical violence

The security personnel of PSCs that place strong emphasis on norms encouraging personal initiative, proactive use of force and an exclusive approach to security should tend to employ violence more quickly after observing a suspected threat than the security personnel of firms that do not place strong emphasis on these norms.	Supported
The security personnel of PSCs that place strong emphasis on norms encouraging personal initiative, proactive use of force and an exclusive approach to security should tend to employ violence against suspected threats at greater distances than the security personnel of firms that do not place strong emphasis on these norms.	Supported
The security personnel of PSCs that place strong emphasis on norms encouraging personal initiative, proactive use of force and an exclusive approach to security should tend to fire a greater number of bullets at suspected threats than the security personnel of firms that do not place strong emphasis on these norms.	Supported
The security personnel of PSCs that place strong emphasis on norms encouraging personal initiative, proactive use of force and an exclusive approach to security should tend to abandon a greater proportion of the victims they produce through their use of violence, rather than offer them assistance, when compared to the security personnel of firms that do not place strong emphasis on these norms.	Supported
The security personnel and clients of PSCs that tend to employ a great deal of violence during their security operations should suffer a lower casualty rate than their counterparts in firms that behave in a less violent manner.	Partially supported
The security personnel of PSCs that tend to employ a great deal of violence during their security operations should kill and seriously injure a greater number of suspected threats and innocent bystanders than their counterparts in firms that behave in a less violent manner.	Supported

second, the degree of security enjoyed by other actors in the firm's operating environment, such as insurgents, civilians, the personnel of other PSCs and the members of national security and military forces.

The theory reasons that if a PSC's military culture is made up of norms that actively encourage its personnel to employ violence quite freely against suspected threats, then its personnel should, indeed, tend to do so during their security operations. It further reasons that if a firm's personnel tend to employ a great deal of violence during their security operations, then they should also tend to enhance the security of themselves and the people under their protection and undermine the security of other actors in their operating environment. This is because when a PSC uses violence in this manner by, for instance, firing off great numbers of bullets at suspected threats, this increases the chance that it will harm not only legitimate threats, such as insurgents, but also civilians and other non-threatening actors in a conflict zone. Therefore, the theory posits that the very same behavioural norms that can help make a PSC's personnel very good at protecting themselves and their clients can also help make them a menace to the society they operate in.

The ideational theory of tactical violence offers specific, testable predictions about how the behavioural norms contained in a PSC's military culture should influence the tactical behaviour exhibited by its security personnel. Specifically, this book examined the relationship between norms encouraging security personnel to exercise personal initiative, proactive use of force and an exclusive approach to security and the speed and distance at which these personnel tended to engage suspected threats, the number of bullets they tended to fire and the rate at which they tended to abandon the people they fired at. This book also examined the relationship between the particular patterns of tactical behaviour exhibited by different PSCs and the casualties they inflicted and suffered during the Iraq War.

Engagement time

The ideational theory of tactical violence predicts that the security personnel of PSCs that place strong emphasis on norms encouraging personal initiative, proactive use of force and an exclusive approach to security should tend to employ violence more quickly after observing a suspected threat than the security personnel of firms that do not place strong emphasis on these norms. For instance, although the security personnel of firms that strongly emphasize these norms should often issue non-violent warnings to suspected threats before firing their weapons, they should escalate to using deadly force more quickly than their counterparts in firms that do not strongly emphasize these norms. Security personnel who behave in this manner, in effect, reduce the amount of time available for a suspected threat to alter its behaviour and attempt to convince the security personnel that it means them no harm by, for example, dropping a weapon, halting its approach or altering its course away from the security personnel and their clients, before they engage the suspected threat with deadly force. This, in turn, means that security personnel who behave in this manner are more likely to kill or seriously injure a suspected threat during an incident than are security personnel who behave in a less violent manner. This prediction was supported by the behaviour exhibited by both Blackwater and DynCorp's personnel. Blackwater's personnel were much more likely than their counterparts in DynCorp to employ deadly force against suspected threats relatively quickly during an engagement. Therefore, unlike DynCorp's personnel, Blackwater's security teams frequently provided very little time for the suspected threats they faced to alter their behaviour and attempt to convince the team that they meant no harm. At least 63 out of the 71 known deaths and at least 102 of the 122 known serious injuries inflicted by Blackwater's personnel occurred during these incidents. A fairly typical incident occurred on Route Irish on 14 May 2005, when, after issuing a brief non-violent warning, a Blackwater security team shot up an approaching civilian vehicle.[1] Their actions caused the death of a father, who was driving the vehicle, and severe injuries to his wife and daughter. Similarly, after one of its security teams was attacked with an IED near Tikrit on 16 August 2006, one of the team members shot and killed a civilian in a passing vehicle without warning.[2] In contrast, although DynCorp's personnel fired their weapons in several dozen incidents during the war, such as when they shot three machine gun rounds at an approaching civilian Chevrolet in Baghdad on 12 November 2007, they virtually always issued multiple non-violent warnings before employing deadly force.[3]

Engagement distance[4]

The ideational theory of tactical violence also predicts that the security personnel of PSCs that place strong emphasis on norms encouraging personal initiative, proactive use of force and an exclusive approach to security should tend to employ violence against suspected threats at greater distances than the security personnel of firms that do not place strong emphasis on these norms. On the assumption that the suspected threats encountered by various firms travel, on average, at the same speed, security personnel who behave in this manner again reduce the amount of time available for a suspected threat to alter its behaviour and attempt to convince the security personnel that it means them no harm before they engage the suspected threat with deadly force. This, in turn, means that security personnel who behave in this manner are more likely to kill or seriously injure a suspected threat during an incident than are security personnel who behave in a less violent manner. This prediction was also supported by the behaviour exhibited by both firms' personnel in that regardless of whether Blackwater's personnel fired their weapons immediately after observing a suspected threat or at a later stage of an incident, they tended to engage suspected threats at far greater average distances than their counterparts in DynCorp. Blackwater's actions effectively robbed suspected threats of crucial time to alter their behaviour and demonstrate that they posed no danger to a security team or its clients. At least 39 out of the 71 known deaths and at least 53 of the 122 known serious injuries inflicted by Blackwater's personnel occurred during incidents where its security teams fired at suspected threats at distances exceeding the mean engagement distance of DynCorp's personnel. For example, one of Blackwater's DDMs shot an insurgent sniper in the head at a distance of approximately 480 metres during an incident in Mosul on

1 September 2005.[5] In addition, another Blackwater security team engaged in a firefight with insurgent gunmen near Baghdad on 18 March 2007 at a distance of 600 metres.[6] Even though DynCorp's personnel killed some civilians during their security operations, such as the driver of an approaching Hyundai SUV on 10 November 2007 at a distance of 50 metres, they tended to allow more time for suspected threats to get closer to a security team and its clients and to demonstrate their true intentions before firing at them.[7]

Number of bullets fired

The ideational theory of tactical violence also predicts that the security personnel of PSCs that place strong emphasis on norms encouraging personal initiative, proactive use of force and an exclusive approach to security should tend to fire a greater number of bullets at suspected threats than the security personnel of firms that do not place strong emphasis on these norms. Since each bullet fired could, of course, hit a suspected threat, security personnel who behave in this manner are more likely to kill or seriously injure a suspected threat during an incident than are security personnel who behave in a less violent manner. This prediction was likewise supported since Blackwater's personnel were much more prone to firing multiple bullets toward a suspected threat than their counterparts in DynCorp. At least 58 out of the 71 known deaths and at least 93 of the 122 known serious injuries inflicted by Blackwater's personnel occurred during incidents where its security teams fired more than five bullets at a suspected threat. Among those killed was the driver of a blue car that approached a Blackwater security team on 20 September 2005 in Baghdad.[8] When the vehicle was about 65 metres away from the rearmost vehicle in the convoy, the vehicle's well gunner fired approximately 30 rounds into its bonnet and windscreen, the left rear gunner fired approximately 14 rounds into its front grille and windscreen, the tactical commander fired approximately five rounds into its front grille and windscreen and the right rear gunner fired approximately 10 rounds into its front grille and windscreen. In contrast, even when facing unambiguous threats, such as the multiple insurgent gunmen who shot and injured a member of a DynCorp security convoy near Samarra on 29 September 2004, that firm's personnel routinely chose to fire very few, if any, bullets to defend themselves and their clients.[9]

Propensity to abandon the victims of violence

Moreover, the ideational theory of tactical violence also predicts that the security personnel of PSCs that place strong emphasis on norms encouraging personal initiative, proactive use of force and an exclusive approach to security should tend to abandon a greater proportion of the victims they produce through their use of violence, rather than offer them assistance, than the security personnel of firms that do not place strong emphasis on these norms. Since the security personnel of these firms have been strongly encouraged to care only about the security of their own colleagues and clients, they should feel no obligation to assist any insurgents, civilians or other actors they harm through their use of violence. Moreover, since abandoning wounded victims could allow their injuries to worsen or even allow them to die, security personnel who behave in this manner are more likely to kill or seriously injure a suspected threat during an incident than security personnel who behave in a less violent manner. As with the theory's other specific predictions, this one was supported by the behaviour exhibited by both firms' personnel, since Blackwater's security teams proved much more likely to abandon the people they used violence against than DynCorp's were. It is challenging to establish precisely how many of the victims of Blackwater's violence would have survived if they had received prompt medical attention; however, the accounts of the firm's incidents indicate that its security personnel abandoned multiple wounded victims who, having not received prompt medical treatment, later died of their injuries.

Broad predictions regarding the relationship between military culture, tactical behaviour and security outcomes

Furthermore, the ideational theory of tactical violence predicts that if the employees of a PSC tend to employ a great deal of violence during their security operations, then they and the clients under their protection should suffer a lower casualty rate than their counterparts in firms that behave in a less violent manner. Finally, it also predicts that if the employees of a PSC tend to employ a great deal of violence during their security operations, then they should kill and seriously injure a greater number of suspected threats and innocent bystanders than the security personnel of firms that behave in a less violent manner. This chapter has already demonstrated that the second prediction was well-supported by empirical evidence on the firms' security operations during the Iraq War. The first prediction received partial support because although neither firm lost any clients to enemy fire, Blackwater's belligerent personnel achieved a casualty rate almost four times lower than their more passive counterparts in DynCorp. Blackwater achieved this despite suffering a far higher number of insurgent attacks and facing insurgents that tended to attack more quickly, fire more bullets and employ explosives more often and in greater quantities. In addition, Blackwater achieved this despite having far more dangerous primary operating areas that suffered considerably more insurgent attacks against US military personnel, Iraqi civilians and private security teams. Finally, Blackwater achieved this despite not having access to significantly better equipment than that fielded by DynCorp's security teams. Taking all of these findings into account, it is clear that, in more ways than one, Blackwater lived up to the pledge it once posted on its corporate website to "exceed ... customers' stated needs and expectations".[10]

When compared to some of the other major PSCs that took part in the Iraq War, Blackwater stands out as a relatively violent and destructive firm that was also relatively successful at protecting its personnel and clients from harm. Hart, a British firm with a well-earned reputation for passivity, having used violence in just eight known incidents during the Iraq War, is known to have killed only a single person during the war and is not known to have injured anyone. This is, of course, far fewer than the 71 known deaths and 122 known serious injuries that Blackwater's personnel inflicted during their security operations. On the other hand, Hart's security personnel suffered at least 33 deaths during 10 out of the 49 total incidents where its personnel were attacked by insurgents, which means that it suffered deaths in 20 per cent of its engagements against insurgents and lost, on average, 0.67 employees per attack. In other words, the proportion of deadly incidents and the casualty rate experienced by this relatively passive firm were far higher than those suffered by Blackwater (6.8 per cent and 0.17 deaths per attack). In addition, while Blackwater was able to keep all of its clients safe, multiple Hart clients were killed and seriously injured during the war. ArmorGroup, another relatively passive British firm, is known to have used violence during only 20 incidents and to have killed 10 people and seriously injured eight people during the war. It was attacked by insurgents more often than Blackwater, at 138 times to 118, but suffered only slightly more deaths (21) and enjoyed a lower casualty rate (0.15 deaths per attack). On the other hand, a greater proportion of the attacks against its personnel (9 per cent) proved deadly. Some of its clients were also wounded during the war.

Finally, Control Risks, yet another British firm, was never known to have used violence during its security operations and, consequently, did not kill or injure anyone in Iraq. Its personnel were, however, attacked by insurgents 24 times, and the firm lost four employees and one client over the course of three deadly incidents. The firm matched Blackwater's casualty rate (0.17 deaths per attack), but experienced a higher proportion of deadly incidents, at 13 per cent. Overall, these firms demonstrate that it is possible to achieve a fairly low personnel casualty rate without routinely resorting to deadly force. However, the fact that insurgents were able to harm clients under the protection of all of these firms indicates that adopting relatively passive behaviour is a high risk approach to protective security operations. Likewise, the fact that all of these firms suffered numerous insurgent attacks during the war, despite their passive behaviour and the relatively small number of casualties they inflicted during their security operations, suggests that insurgents were not motivated to reward their attempts to avoid inflicting harm on others.

Implications for the use and development of private armed forces

Private armed forces have existed throughout human history and they show no signs of disappearing. It is therefore important to consider how potential clients in the market for private security services can make informed decisions about which firms to hire; how security firms can be used safely to carry out more ambitious security operations, such as peace-keeping and counterinsurgency missions, that Western governments no longer want their ground forces to participate in; and how the owners and managers of security firms can shape their military culture to enhance their suitability for certain roles.

Implications for the use of private security companies in private security operations

This book has demonstrated that it is clearly risky to employ firms that maintain a military culture like Blackwater's because their personnel are likely to inflict more deaths and serious injuries than the personnel of firms, like DynCorp, that maintain a less bellicose culture. As a result, governments and other potential clients that choose to employ violence-prone firms, like Blackwater, could face significant criticism from the news media, human rights organizations, other governments, and the citizens, police and soldiers who live and work in the firm's operating environment. Despite being just one of dozens of PSCs that participated in the Iraq War, Blackwater's unparalleled record of violence received far more negative news coverage than the actions of DynCorp or any other firm. In addition, Blackwater's actions in Iraq have been the subject of numerous government investigations, criminal and civil legal proceedings, and protests staged by Iraqi citizens.[11] Moreover, its behaviour eventually motivated the government of Iraq to bar it from operating in that country.[12] Furthermore, the US Department of State's decision to continue and defend its use of Blackwater's security personnel, even after some of their most egregious acts became public knowledge, tarnished the reputation of the government of the United States at home and abroad.[13] Clients who choose to employ a firm with a military culture akin to Blackwater's risk facing a similar backlash.

At least until the scandalous Nisour Square incident, the Department of State seemed willing to give Blackwater's personnel free rein to behave as they saw fit. As Prince put it, "The people who wrote the rule book ... certainly didn't seem to have a problem with our approach".[14] The US Department of Defense, which organized Blackwater's contract for protecting Bremer during 2003 and 2004, likewise gave the firm considerable leeway: "The Pentagon basically said, 'Do whatever you have to. Just keep him alive.'"[15] Other potential clients of private security services should take a more active role in overseeing the work of the firms they hire by not merely demanding that the firms submit detailed, standardized daily reports of their security operations – including information on their behaviour, the behaviour of the suspected threats they encountered and any casualties they inflicted or suffered – but also reviewing and acting on the content of these reports on at least a monthly basis. Clients should also demand the right to have a representative accompany the firm's security teams in order to monitor their behaviour.

The findings of this book also indicate a need for potential clients in the market for private armed forces to evaluate the military culture of the firms vying for their business when deciding which firm to hire, rather than relying exclusively on easily quantifiable factors, such as the size of a firm's personnel roster or its fleet of armoured vehicles, or the projected financial costs of its services. Potential clients should examine accounts of a firm's development and activities in conflict zones and discuss a firm's military culture with its executives, middle managers, trainers and front-line security personnel. Specifically, potential clients should pose questions regarding how the firm's security personnel are encouraged to behave. Moreover, potential clients should demand access to the firm's incident reports to gain insight into how its personnel actually behaved during their previous security operations. Through this process, a potential client ought to be able to determine the nature of the firm's military culture, which should allow them to develop reasonable expectations about how the firm's personnel will behave in a conflict zone. Taking this into account, potential clients that intend to prioritize their own security above all other considerations, including the safety of other actors in their operating environment, should consider hiring a firm that shares Blackwater's bellicose military culture. On the other hand, potential clients that are willing to accept a higher risk of friendly casualties in order to reduce the risk of inflicting unnecessary civilian casualties, and the scandals that could accompany these acts, should consider hiring a more passive, DynCorp-like firm.

The deadly 11 September 2012 attacks on US facilities in Benghazi, Libya, vividly illustrated the potential downsides to a client of employing a relatively passive firm to conduct security operations in an unstable conflict zone. In contrast to the multiple teams of approximately 20 heavily armed and armoured personnel that Blackwater fielded in various cities in Iraq, the primary defensive forces assigned to protect the Department of State's Benghazi compound in the midst of a civil war included five unarmed employees of the British PSC Blue Mountain, three armed members of the unreliable Libyan 17th February Brigade militia, and five DSS agents.[16] Unlike many other US diplomatic posts, the Benghazi compound lacked US Marine guards.[17]

The main insurgent attack on the compound began at 9:40 p.m. local time, when at least 60 gunmen swept through the front gate.[18] Meeting no resistance from the on-site security forces, they entered buildings at will and quickly set fire to the 17th February Brigade's barracks before proceeding to set the main building, containing US Ambassador J. Christopher Stevens and US Foreign Service Information Management Officer Sean Smith, aflame. Soon after the attack began, one of the on-site DSS agents contacted a CIA facility, located two kilometres away, for assistance. However, the six CIA security personnel who responded to this distress signal failed to even leave their facility for approximately 20–25 minutes.[19] Recall from Chapter 1 that Blackwater's quick reaction forces could deploy within five minutes of receiving a call for help.[20] While waiting for the CIA personnel to arrive, a single DSS agent attempted to get Stevens and Smith to safety inside the compound's blazing main building. Amidst the toxic diesel-fueled smoke, he lost track of the principals, who ultimately succumbed to smoke inhalation.[21] None of the DSS agents fired a shot during the attack. Well over 30 minutes after the attack began, the CIA security personnel and some members of the 17th February Brigade, who had previously offered no resistance, started to fight back against the insurgents. Both principals were dead by this point and the compound had suffered extensive fire damage. The DSS agents and CIA personnel eventually fled the compound and returned to the CIA's nearby facility. Two CIA contractors were killed later that night during a follow-on attack against that facility.[22]

Blackwater's personnel faced a somewhat similar situation on 4 April 2004, when a much larger force, made up of hundreds of Iraqi insurgents, attacked a CPA compound in Najaf.[23] During that incident, a handful of Blackwater employees immediately opted to mount a vigorous defence of the compound by firing thousands of assault rifle, machine gun and sniper rounds at their attackers. Over the course of hours of fierce fighting, they killed hundreds of insurgents in exchange for a single serious injury to one of their comrades and just three injuries among the American military personnel under their command, and they succeeded in holding the compound.[24] Similarly, the firm responded within a few minutes of receiving a distress call from a convoy under siege from over a thousand insurgents in the centre of Baghdad on 23 January 2007.[25] It quickly deployed multiple additional ground security teams and air crews to rescue the convoy and its principal, killing hundreds of insurgents in the process. It is, of course, impossible to know for certain whether a Blackwater team could have successfully defended the Benghazi compound and kept the principals alive, but the firm's track record in Iraq suggests that they likely would have put up a much more determined defence than the one offered by the compound's relatively passive on-site security forces.

Implications for the use of private armed forces in peacekeeping and counterinsurgency operations

This book's findings also have implications for the prospect of contracting out peacekeeping and counterinsurgency operations to private armed forces. These initiatives have largely been driven by widespread unwillingness on the part of Western governments to risk their own soldiers' lives on these missions.[26] As of October 2014, no Western countries are among the top 20 contributors of personnel to UN peacekeeping missions.[27] Likewise, despite acknowledging that insurgencies, such as the Islamic State of Iraq and Syria (ISIS), constitute a serious security and humanitarian threat, US President Barack Obama has pledged that he "will not commit … our armed forces to fighting another ground war" in a foreign land to try to defeat them.[28]

The notion that all or part of a UN peacekeeping operation could be contracted out to private actors has already received cautious support. For example, the United Kingdom's Foreign Affairs Committee stated in 2002 that it "sees no difficulty of principle in private companies offering support to humanitarian or peacekeeping missions directly to the UN or to other international bodies that mandate or co-ordinate such missions".[29] Similarly, Shaista Shameen, the former UN Special Rapporteur on Mercenaries, argued that private actors "could help compensate the deficiencies of the UN when the latter is confronted with widespread violations of human rights and genocide".[30] A private armed force called Executive Outcomes, which successfully defeated insurgencies on behalf of the governments of Angola and Sierra Leone during the 1990s, actually proposed to field armed intervention forces in Rwanda in 1994 and the Democratic Republic of the Congo in 1996, though neither offer was ultimately accepted by UN officials.[31] Blackwater's Prince felt so strongly about the notion that private armed forces could undertake peacekeeping operations that he established an affiliated firm called Greystone that, in his words, could rapidly deploy a "privately trained, seventeen-hundred-man peacekeeping package with its own air force, helicopters, cargo ships, aerial surveillance, medical supply chain, and combat group" in conflict zones to which Western governments do not want to send their state-based armed forces.[32]

Likewise, in 2014 prominent media personalities, along with Prince, urged the government of the United States to field private armed forces to fight against ISIS in areas of Iraq and Syria where the US-led aerial bombing campaign cannot easily find and attack its members.[33] Prince surmised that "The American people are clearly fatigued" of ground warfare and argued that "If the (Obama) Administration cannot rally the political nerve or funding to send adequate active duty ground forces to answer the call, let the private sector finish the job".[34] Providing more specifics, he argued that, "If the old Blackwater team were still together, I have high confidence that a multi-brigade-size unit of veteran American contractors or a multi-national force could be rapidly assembled and deployed to be that necessary ground combat team".[35]

The private sector is already heavily involved in some aspects of peacekeeping and counterinsurgency. For instance, several firms, such as MPRI,

Northrop Grumman, PAE and DynCorp, have trained cohorts of state-based peacekeeping forces.[36] Private companies have also provided intelligence collection and analysis services in support of peacekeeping operations. Private security personnel have served as weapons inspectors and border monitors during peacekeeping operations organized by the UN and the Organization for Security and Cooperation in Europe (OSCE).[37] Moreover, the UN has hired private pilots to fly helicopters in combat environments, where they could be expected to utilize deadly force, at least occasionally, in self-defence.[38] Furthermore, a substantial portion of demining operations in UN peacekeeping missions are currently performed by private firms.[39] Private companies have also constructed military bases and provided transportation and other logistical services in several UN missions.[40] Finally, this book has illustrated the important roles that PSCs are already playing, such as defending people, places and things, in the midst of a raging insurgency.

With this said, however, Western governments and the UN have good reasons to be skeptical about contracting out entire peacekeeping and counterinsurgency operations to private armed forces. Even if one sets aside the question of whether the member states of the UN should absolve themselves of their responsibility to protect vulnerable civilians and to fight back against murderous insurgencies, this scheme remains problematic.[41] In contrast to the nature of private security operations during the Iraq War, where most firms operated in areas of the country that were under at least some degree of control by coalition or Iraqi government security forces, the private armed forces hired to conduct peacekeeping and counterinsurgency operations might operate in completely lawless territories where no legitimate authority exists to check any of their behavioural excesses.

As discussed in Chapter 6, the employees of US-based firms are not likely to be held accountable for committing murders, sexual assaults or other grievous behaviour if they are hired by the Department of State or the US Agency for International Development because it is not clear that US laws apply to private security personnel contracted by these institutions. Perhaps because he understood this, Prince proposed that Greystone should seek contracts with the Department of State.[42] Likewise, it is unclear whether the employees of a firm contracted directly by the UN would be subject to any laws save for international war crimes statutes. This makes a firm's military culture especially important since it will greatly influence how its personnel will behave in environments where they can effectively do whatever they want with little fear of reprisal.

Complicating matters, few private security workers will be successfully prosecuted for egregious behaviour in the absence of testimony and evidence provided by well-respected, neutral third parties. Taking this into account, if a state or international organization chooses to hire a private armed force to undertake a peacekeeping or counterinsurgency operation, then it must also deploy a separate but integrated force of observers to monitor and document the behaviour exhibited by their personnel and the suspected threats they face during their missions. The observer force would have to be able to keep up with the PSC and avoid endangering its personnel and should, therefore, be made up of either active-duty soldiers from the armed forces of UN member states or qualified veterans employed by a separate, unaffiliated firm.

Policymakers wishing to pursue this scheme must carefully consider which type(s) of firms to hire to undertake peacekeeping and counterinsurgency operations. A Blackwater-like firm that tends to employ violence relatively quickly and at great distances, fire relatively large numbers of bullets and abandon the vast majority of the people they attack would probably be well-suited for a fairly limited range of roles in UN peacekeeping missions. These could include assaulting local belligerents to degrade their military capabilities or in response to violations of cease-fire agreements, attacks against peacekeepers and civilian safe areas, attempts to stockpile weapons, and other behaviour that runs contrary to the goal of establishing and maintaining peace and stability.[43] This particularly dangerous role is the very one that governments are most reluctant to undertake with their own state-based armed forces. Ideally, a private armed force would carry out this role in rural areas, far away from civilian population centres, where they would be free to behave in a manner that would allow them to inflict plentiful casualties to hostile armed forces and minimize losses among their own personnel. A more passive, DynCorp-like firm, on the other hand, that tends to employ violence more slowly, allow suspected threats more time and distance to demonstrate their true intentions, fire smaller numbers of bullets and abandon a smaller proportion of the people they attack would probably be better suited to undertake such roles as guarding civilian safe areas and patrolling through civilian population centres, where the risk of insurgent attacks is relatively low and the probability of encountering large numbers of non-combatants on a regular basis is particularly high.

Moreover, the very areas of Iraq and Syria where air power is least effective – civilian towns and cities – are also areas where a firm in the vein of Blackwater is poorly suited to serve as the international community's "pointy end of the spear" in a fight against insurgents that can easily blend in with civilians.[44] Indeed, if war planners choose to avoid bombing population centres in order to reduce the risk of inflicting civilian casualties, then deploying a private ground force that is likely to inflict large numbers of civilian casualties would probably prove counterproductive. A more passive firm would be better suited to conduct operations in these areas.

Furthermore, regardless of their degree of passivity or belligerence, PSCs are by no means a panacea. These actors are best suited to undertaking roles in peacekeeping and counterinsurgency operations that traditionally require armed soldiers. Other personnel, whether provided by governments, corporations or non-governmental organizations, would be needed to perform the humanitarian relief, diplomatic and peacebuilding functions that are essential to resolving inter- and intrastate conflicts and reconstituting post-conflict societies.

Implications for the development of private security companies

Finally, the owners and managers of PSCs must determine the nature of the military culture they wish to indoctrinate their employees into since, as this book has shown, this can have a powerful effect on the behaviour exhibited by a firm's employees. The value of fostering a military culture that will encourage the kind of highly violent behaviour that should help a firm achieve an exemplary record of personnel and client protection cannot be overstated, since potential clients will likely want to avoid hiring a firm that failed to protect every single one of its principals, even in high-threat environments such as post-invasion Iraq. As Prince put it when describing the importance of protecting Bremer during his 11 month term as proconsul of Iraq:

> Keeping the ambassador safe would prove we could keep anyone safe, anywhere. Screwing it up, on the other hand, could cripple Blackwater. We couldn't pitch security services to prospective clients by saying, "Everything with Bremer went well – you know, until he got killed."[45]

Frank Gallagher, the head of Bremer's Blackwater security detail in Iraq, expressed similar sentiments:

> Succeed in keeping Ambassador Bremer alive, and your company will have accomplished something no private company has ever achieved before. However, if Bremer gets killed, your company will serve as a poster child for those who believe a private company cannot possibly provide the level of protection required to safeguard government officials. Oh, and by the way, your company will, in all likelihood, never receive another government contract.[46]

At the same time, however, Blackwater and DynCorp's experiences in Iraq suggest that a firm interested in its long-term survival cannot place personnel and client protection above all other considerations. DynCorp's relatively passive approach resulted in a higher friendly casualty rate but it continues to work for the Department of State in Iraq and still operates under the name it used when the Iraq War started. Conversely, Blackwater lost its chief client and has been rebranded and sold multiple times in efforts to escape the reputation it earned through killing and injuring numerous civilians in Iraq.

Taking this into account, if a firm wishes to specialize in highly violent operations against genuine threats, far away from civilian areas, then they

Conclusion 227

would be well-served by fostering a military culture that strongly encourages personal initiative, proactive use of force and an exclusive approach to security. Such a firm is likely to be especially adept at neutralizing threats to their personnel and clients, even in highly dangerous environments, and, through this, minimizing friendly casualties. Blackwater's actions during the Iraq War demonstrated that a firm that encourages its personnel to use a great deal of violence against suspected threats can effectively protect widely hated symbols of foreign occupation from regular insurgent attacks. In contrast, the owners and managers of firms seeking to conduct security operations in areas where they are likely to encounter large numbers of civilians should avoid fostering a military culture that strongly emphasizes these norms; they should rather encourage more passive behaviour and thus reduce the chance that their employees will inflict a large number of civilian casualties.

Notes

1 US Army, "Escalation of Force".
2 US Army, "Possible Loac".
3 US Army, "(Friendly Action) Escalation of Force Rpt Civ Psd".
4 Eight Blackwater incidents were intentionally excluded from this analysis of mean engagement distances. These incidents were extreme outliers, for they involved engagement distances of 482, 500, 550, 600, 800 and 1,300 metres, which are considerably longer than the firm's next-longest engagement distance of 350 metres. Including these incidents would have therefore increased the firm's mean engagement distances to a point where they would no longer accurately reflect the firm's general behaviour.
5 US Embassy, Baghdad, "Spot Report – 090105–01". The Iraqi sniper died instantly.
6 US Army, "Attack (Small Arms, Rocket)".
7 US Army, "(Friendly Action) Escalation of Force Report 5–1/6 IA".
8 Blackwater, PSD Incident Report, 20 September 2005; US Embassy, Baghdad, "Spot Report – 092005–02".
9 US Army, "Small Arms Attack".
10 Quoted in Isenberg, *Shadow Force*, 26.
11 Risen and Williams, "Iraq Tries to Oust Blackwater"; Williams, "Iraqis Angered"; Risen, "Ex-Blackwater Guards"; House Committee on Oversight and Government Reform, "Hearing on Blackwater USA"; House Committee on Oversight and Government Reform, "Private Military Contractors"; Landler, "Contractor to Continue"; Thompson and Risen, "5 Guards Face US Charges".
12 Risen and Williams, "Iraq Tries to Oust Blackwater"; Williams, "Iraqis Angered"; Risen, "Ex-Blackwater Guards"; House Committee on Oversight and Government Reform, "Hearing on Blackwater USA"; House Committee on Oversight and Government Reform, "Private Military Contractors"; Landler, "Contractor to Continue"; Thompson and Risen, "5 Guards Face US Charges".
13 Landler, "Clinton Tries to Reassure"; US Department of State, "Embassy Continues Outreach"; Risen, "End of Immunity"; Rubin, "Talks with US".
14 Prince, *Civilian Warriors*, 216.
15 Ibid., 78.
16 Ackerman, "Blackwater Wins"; Prince, *Civilian Warriors*, 325–326; Senate Select Committee on Intelligence, "Review of Terrorist Attacks", 6.

228 *Conclusion*

17 Prince, *Civilian Warriors*, 325.
18 Senate Select Committee on Intelligence, "Review of Terrorist Attacks", 3; Clapper, "Joint Statement", 3.
19 Senate Select Committee on Intelligence, "Review of Terrorist Attacks", 4.
20 Laguna, *You Have to Live Hard*, Loc. 3541–3543.
21 Senate Select Committee on Intelligence, "Review of Terrorist Attacks", 5–6; Lamb, "Statement for the Record", 6.
22 Senate Select Committee on Intelligence, "Review of Terrorist Attacks", 8.
23 Chatterjee, *Iraq, Inc.*, 129–130; Human Rights First, "Private Security Contractors", 24; Sizemore and Kimberlin, "Blackwater: Front Lines"; Majority Staff, "Memorandum", 8; Miller, *Blood Money*, 165.
24 Barstow, "Security Firm Says"; Scahill, *Blackwater*, 125–130.
25 US Embassy, Baghdad, "Spot Report – 012307-02"; Kimberlin, "Blackwater's 'Little Birds'"; Laguna, *You Have to Live Hard*, Loc. 350, 432–433, 442–443, 476,477, 496–522, 531–556, 564–565, 585–595, 604–667, 675–690, 696–728, 3559–3561 and 3570–3581; Simons, *Master of War*, 154–157; Associated Press, "US Helicopter Crashes"; Staff, "Five Killed in Attack"; BVA Honor Roll; Batty, "Rock Stars of Baghdad".
26 Spearin, "UN Peacekeeping", 197 and 201; Cilliers, "Role for Private Military Companies", 147; Pattison, "Outsourcing the Responsibility", 2.
27 Department of Peacekeeping Operations, "Ranking".
28 Kaplan, "Obama Says it Again".
29 Foreign Affairs Committee, "Private Military Companies", 4.
30 Cited in Ghebali, "United Nations", 218.
31 Bures, "Private Military Companies", 539; Spearin, "UN Peacekeeping", 203; Pattison, "Outsourcing the Responsibility", 6.
32 Prince, *Civilian Warriors*, 94.
33 Thompson, "Ex-Blackwater Chief"; Richter, "O'Reilly: US Should Hire"; Rosen, "Will Private Contractors".
34 Thompson, "Ex-Blackwater Chief".
35 Rosen, "Will Private Contractors".
36 Ostensen, "Business of Peace", 39; Bures, "Private Military Companies", 538.
37 Bures, "Private Military Companies".
38 Venter, *Gunship Ace*.
39 Ostensen, "Business of Peace", 42; Bures, "Private Military Companies", 558; O'Brien, "What Future", 55.
40 Pattison, "Outsourcing the Responsibility", 9; Bures, "Private Military Companies", 538.
41 Baker and Pattison have addressed at some length the issue of a state "paying someone to do what it is morally required to do itself". Baker and Pattison, "Principled Case", 1–18.
42 Prince, *Civilian Warriors*, 94.
43 Pattison, "Outsourcing the Responsibility", 7; Singer, *Corporate Warriors*, 187.
44 Rosen, "Will Private Contractors".
45 Prince, *Civilian Warriors*, 78.
46 Gallagher and Del Vecchio, *The Bremer Detail*, Loc. 153.

References

Ackerman, Spencer. "Blackwater Wins the Battle of Benghazi". *Wired.com*, 20 December 2012.
Associated Press. "US Helicopter Crashes in Iraq in the Past 6 Months". 7 February 2007.

Baker, Deane-Peter, and James Pattison. "The Principled Case for Employing Private Military and Security Companies in Interventions for Human Rights Purposes". *Journal of Applied Philosophy* 29, no. 1 (2012): 1–18.

Barstow, David. "Security Firm says its Workers were Lured into Iraqi Ambush". *New York Times*, 9 April 2004.

Batty, Roy. "Rock Stars of Baghdad". *Military.com*, 8 February 2007.

Blackwater. PSD Incident Reports and Sworn Statements. Baghdad: Blackwater, 2005–2009.

Bures, Oldrich. "Private Military Companies: A Second Best Peacekeeping Option?" *International Peacekeeping* 12, no. 4 (2005): 533–546.

BVA Honor Roll (Blackwater Veterans Association. "Honor Roll – Blackwater Personnel Killed in Action". 6 January 2013. Available at https://bwvets.com/index.php?forums/honor-roll-blackwater-personnel-killed-in-action.63/).

Chatterjee, Pratap. *Iraq, Inc.: A Profitable Occupation*. New York: Seven Stories Press, 2004.

Cilliers, Jackie. "A Role for Private Military Companies in Peacekeeping". *Conflict, Security and Development* 2, no. 3 (2002): 145–151.

Clapper, James R. "Joint Statement for the Record before the Senate Select Committee on Intelligence". Washington, DC: Senate of the United States, Congress of the United States, 15 November 2012.

Department of Peacekeeping Operations. "Ranking of Military and Police Contributions to UN Operations". New York: Department of Peacekeeping Operations, United Nations, 31 October 2014.

Foreign Affairs Committee. "Private Military Companies: Response of the Secretary of State for Foreign and Commonwealth Affairs". London: Foreign Affairs Committee, 2002.

Gallagher, Frank, and John M. Del Vecchio. *The Bremer Detail: Protecting the Most Threatened Man in the World*. Kindle edn. New York: Open Road Media, 2014.

Ghebali, Victor-Yves. "The United Nations and the Dilemma of Outsourcing Peacekeeping Operations". In *Private Actors and Security Governance*, edited by A. Bryden and M. Caparini. Berlin: LIT Verlag, 2006, 213–230.

House Committee on Oversight and Government Reform. "Private Military Contractors in Iraq: An Examination of Blackwater's Actions in Fallujah". Washington, DC: House of Representatives, Congress of the United States, September 2007.

House Committee on Oversight and Government Reform. "Hearing on Blackwater USA". Washington, DC: House of Representatives, Congress of the United States, 2 October 2007.

Human Rights First. "Private Security Contractors at War: Ending the Culture of Impunity". New York: Human Rights First, 2008.

Isenberg, David. *Shadow Force: Private Security Contractors in Iraq*. Westport, CT: Praeger Security International, 2009.

Kaplan, Rebecca. "Obama Says it Again: No Ground Troops in Iraq". *CBS News*, 17 September 2014.

Kimberlin, Joanne. "Blackwater's 'Little Birds' of Baghdad Pack Quite a Sting". *Virginian-Pilot*, 1 March 2007.

Laguna, Dan. *You Have to Live Hard to Be Hard: One Man's Life in Special Operations*. Kindle edn. Bloomington, IN: Authorhouse, 2010.

Lamb, Charlene. "Statement for the Record for the House Committee on Oversight and Government Reform Hearing on the Security Failures of Benghazi".

Washington, DC: House of Representatives, Congress of the United States, 10 October 2012.

Landler, Mark. "Clinton Tries to Reassure a State Dept. in Transition". *New York Times*, 5 February 2009.

Landler, Mark. "Contractor to Continue Work in Iraq Temporarily". *New York Times*, 3 September 2009.

Majority Staff. "Memorandum – Additional Information about Blackwater USA". Washington, DC: Congress of the United States, 1 October 2007.

Miller, T. Christian. *Blood Money: Wasted Billions, Lost Lives, and Corporate Greed in Iraq*. New York: Little Brown and Company, 2006.

O'Brien, Kevin A. "What Future, Privatized Military and Security Activities?" *RUSI Journal* 152, no. 2 (2007): 54–61.

Ostensen, Ase Gilje. "In the Business of Peace: The Political Influence of Private Military and Security Companies on UN Peacekeeping". *International Peacekeeping* 20, no. 1 (2013): 33–47.

Pattison, James. "Outsourcing the Responsibility to Protect: Humanitarian Intervention and Private Military and Security Companies". *International Theory* 2, no. 1 (March 2010): 1–31.

Prince, Erik. *Civilian Warriors: The Inside Story of Blackwater and the Unsung Heroes of the War on Terror*. Kindle edn. New York: Portfolio, 2013.

Richter, Greg. "O'Reilly: US should Hire Mercenary Army to Fight ISIS". *Newsmax*, 22 September 2014.

Risen, James. "End of Immunity Worries US Contractors in Iraq". *New York Times*, 1 December 2008.

Risen, James. "Ex-Blackwater Guards Face Renewed Charges". *New York Times*, 23 April 2011.

Risen, James, and Timothy Williams. "As Iraq Tries to Oust Blackwater, US Lines Up Other Security Options". *New York Times*, 30 January 2009.

Rosen, Armin. "Will Private Contractors like Blackwater Join the Fight Against ISIS?" *Business Insider*, 13 October 2014.

Rubin, Alissa J. "Talks with US on Security Pact are at an Impasse, the Iraqi Prime Minister Says". *New York Times*, 14 June 2008.

Scahill, Jeremy. *Blackwater: The Rise of the World's Most Powerful Mercenary Army*. 1st edn. New York: Nation Books, 2007.

Senate Select Committee on Intelligence. "Review of the Terrorist Attacks on US Facilities in Benghazi, Libya, September 11–12, 2012". Washington, DC: Senate of the United States, Congress of the United States, 15 January 2014.

Simons, Suzanne. *Master of War: Blackwater USA's Erik Prince and the Business of War*. New York: Harper, 2009.

Singer, Peter W. *Corporate Warriors: The Rise of the Privatized Military Industry*. Kindle edn. Ithaca, NY: Cornell University Press, 2007.

Sizemore, Bill, and Joanne Kimberlin. "Blackwater: On the Front Lines". *Virginian-Pilot*, 25 July 2006.

Spearin, Christopher. "UN Peacekeeping and the International Private Military and Security Industry". *International Peacekeeping* 18, no. 2 (2011): 196–209.

Staff. "Five Killed in Attack on 2 Blackwater Helicopters". *Virginian-Pilot*, 24 January 2007.

Thompson, Ginger, and James Risen. "5 Guards Face US Charges in Iraq Deaths". *New York Times*, 6 December 2008.

Thompson, Mark. "Ex-Blackwater Chief Urges Hired Guns to Take on ISIS". *Time*, 10 October 2014.
US Army. "Attack (Small Arms, Rocket) on Blackwater Convoy in the Vicinity of (Route Tampa): 0 Inj/Dam". Baghdad: Wikileaks, 18 March 2007.
US Army. "Small Arms Attack on Civilian Convoy (DynCorp) in the Vicinity of Samarra: 1 NEU Inj". Samarra, Iraq: Wikileaks, 29 September 2004.
US Army. "Escalation of Force by Blackwater Psd in Baghdad (Zone 37N): 1 Civilian Killed in Action, 2 Civilians Wounded". Baghdad: Wikileaks, 14 May 2005.
US Army. "Possible Loac by Coalition Forces Contractor in the Vicinity Of Forward Operating Base Speicher: 1 Civilian Killed, 0 Coalition Forces Inj/Damage". Tikrit, Iraq: Wikileaks, 16 August 2006.
US Army. "(Friendly Action) Escalation of Force Report 5–1/6 IA: 1 Civilian Killed in Action". Baghdad: Wikileaks, 10 November 2007.
US Army. "(Friendly Action) Escalation of Force Rpt Civ Psd: 0 Inj/Dam". Baghdad: Wikileaks, 12 November 2007.
US Department of State. "Embassy Continues Outreach on Personal Security Detail Incident". Washington, DC: US Department of State, 19 September 2007.
US Embassy, Baghdad. "Spot Report – 012307–02 – Complex Attack on COM PSD Resulting in Five KIA". Baghdad: US Department of State, 23 January 2007.
US Embassy, Baghdad. "Spot Report – 090105–01 – COM PSD Fires on an Anti-Iraq Forces (AIF) Sniper in Mosul". Baghdad: US Department of State, 31 January 2007.
US Embassy, Baghdad. "Spot Report – 092005–02 – COM PSD Team Fires on Aggressive Vehicle". Baghdad: US Department of State, 20 September 2005.
Venter, Al. *Gunship Ace: The Wars of Neall Ellis, Helicopter Pilot and Mercenary*. London: Casemate, 2011.
Williams, Timothy. "Iraqis Angered as Blackwater Charges are Dropped". *New York Times*, 2 January 2010.

Index

1st Special Forces Operational Detachment-Delta 83
5 Commando 24
32 Battalion 24

Abu Ghraib 193
Academi *see* Blackwater
advance team 40–1, 138, 140, 144, 146–7, 154
Afghanistan 4, 6, 13, 25–8, 82, 102, 186–7, 198
Africa 29
AGM-114 Hellfire missile 45
AH-6 Little Bird 45, 151
AH-64 Apache 140, 151
Ahmed, Sebhan 114
air teams 31, 41–2, 104, 144
AK-47 assault rifle 29–31, 40, 45, 101, 108, 142, 146, 149–50, 154–77, 181–2
AK-74 assault rifle 29
Al Hillah 34, 37, 161–2
Al Kut 176
al-Bulani, Jawad 191
al-Jabouri, Omar Jaikal 192
al-Maliki, Azhar Abdullah 108
al-Maliki, Nouri 190
al-Qaeda 156–7
al-Quraishy, Mohamad 182
al-Rubaie, Ahmed 101, 181–2
al-Rubaie, Mahasin 101, 181
al-Rubaie, Mowaffak 191
al-Sadr, Muqtada 29, 150, 193
Ali, Munther Kadhum Abid 116, 177
Ali, Rizgar 189
Angola 20–1, 24, 33, 223
ANSI/ASIS PSC standards 188
ArmorGroup 219
armoured personnel carrier 36–7, 44–5, 163, 197

Asia 29
Asuncion, Anthony 181–2
AT *see* advance team
Avant, Deborah 7, 22–4
Azerbaijan 27

Baghdad 1, 28–34, 36, 38–42, 96, 100–1, 103–4, 108, 113, 120, 122–4, 140, 142–4, 146–8, 151–2, 154, 160–3, 178, 182, 189–90, 193, 199, 216–17, 222
Baghdad International Airport 30, 32, 143
Ball, Donald 102, 115, 179–80
Baqubah 109
Basra 28
Batalona, Wesley "Wes" J.K. 30, 159
Bauman, Robert 8
Bearcat 44, 163
Beckman, Tim 13, 38–40, 85, 87, 98, 110, 115, 117, 145
behavioural norm 4–5, 7–8, 14, 65, 82–4, 90, 97–8, 105, 109, 113, 118, 125, 137–8, 145–6, 153, 155, 164, 213–18: definition of 66
Bell 412, 45, 143, 163
Berry, Brian 84
bin Laden, Osama 96, 156–7
Blackwater 1–4, 6–7, 12–65, 67, 71, 75, 82–96, 98, 163, 178, 180, 183–213, 215–23, 225: basic mission types undertaken by 29–35; casualties inflicted by 2, 118, 213, 218–19; casualties suffered by *3*, 155–6, 213, 218–19; civil trials of 183; condolence payments by 183–4; corporate implications of 197–9; criminal trials of 177, 179–82; engagement distance of 106–9, 145–6, 216–17; engagement time of 97–105, 137–45, 215–16;

Index 233

equipment used by 43–5; FBI investigation into 102, 178–9; force structure of 35–43; implications for the use and development of private armed forces of 220–7; legal and regulatory implications of 176–89; military culture of 82–92; number of bullets fired by 109–13, 146–52, 217; origins of 26–7; political implications of 189–97; propensity to abandon victims of its violence 113–18, 153–5, 217–18; threats faced by 29–35
Blackwater Veterans Association 13
Blair, Tony 27, 157
Boot, Max 90
Bosnia 20, 28
Bremer, Paul 3, 13, 27, 30–1, 34–6, 40, 151, 157–8, 220, 226
Broadcasting Board of Governors Office of the Inspector General 119
Bush, George W. 3, 7
BVA *see* Blackwater Veterans Association

California Eastern Airways 27
Callan's Mercenaries 24
Camp Ridgeway 30
Camp Taji 30
Cantrell, James E. "Tracker" 32, 160
Carafano, James Jay 7
Carmola, Kateri 82–3
Casavant, Casey "Rooster" 149, 163
Cassidy, Robert 70
CAT *see* counter assault team
CAV *see* counter assault vehicle
Central Intelligence Agency 24, 26–7, 88, 198, 222
Cerberus Capital Management 27
Chilton, Steven "Hacksaw" 150
Chisholm, Amanda 66
CIA *see* Central Intelligence Agency
Clark, Al 84, 87, 89
Clinton, Hillary 196–7
Coalition Provisional Authority 3, 12, 26–9, 31, 33, 85, 89, 150–1, 157, 160, 177, 186, 199, 222
Coalition Provisional Authority Order 17, 117, 186
Coffield, William 181–2
Columbia 29
command vehicle 37
Computer Sciences Corporation 27
Congressional Research Service 194
Constellis Holdings *see* Blackwater
constructivism 7, 65–7

Control Risks Group 26, 219
Couch, Dick 83, 86–8, 90
Cougar 44
counter assault team 37, 148–9, 163, 176
counter assault vehicle 34, 37, 138–9
counterinsurgency 4, 26, 220, 222–5
CPA *see* Coalition Provisional Authority
Croatia 20
Crocker, Ryan 3, 42, 156

DDM *see* designated defensive marksman
Degn, Mathew 194
Dehart, Jim 84
Democratic Republic of the Congo 24, 33, 223
designated defensive marksman 31, 40, 108, 182
DGSD *see* DynCorp Government Services Division
Diplomatic Security Service 10, 45, 96, 105, 124, 139, 177–80, 184, 195, 221–2
dog piling 111
DSS *see* Diplomatic Security Service
Du Preez, Ignatius 160
Dunigan, Molly 8, 33
Durr, Bruce T. "Bee" 32, 160
Dynalectron Corporation 27
DynCorp 1–4, 6, 10, 12–15, 19–65, 71, 75, 82–96, 98–9, 103–10, 112–14, 116, 118–25, 143, 145, 152, 154, 176–7, 186–8, 190, 192, 198–9, 213, 215–18, 220–1, 224–6: basic mission types undertaken by 29–35; casualties inflicted by 2, 118, 213, 218–19; casualties suffered by 3, 155–6, 213, 218–19; condolence payments by 177; corporate implications of 198–9; engagement distance of 106–9, 145, 216–17; engagement time of 99, 103–5, 143, 215–16; equipment used by 43–5; force structure of 35–43; implications for the use and development of private armed forces of 220–7; legal and regulatory implications of 177, 186–8; military culture of 82–92; number of bullets fired by 109–10, 112–13, 152, 217; origins of 27–8; political implications of 190, 192; propensity to abandon victims of its violence 113–14, 116, 118, 154, 218; threats faced by 29–35
DynCorp Government Services Division 85

Index

EFP *see* explosively-formed penetrator
Engbrecht, Shawn 7, 86, 103
EOF *see* escalation of force
Erbil 28, 34, 38, 105, 120, 124, 161–2, 177
escalation of force 98, 124
Euphrates River 30, 153
exclusive approach to security 4, 71–4, 83, 89–91, 97–8, 105, 109, 113, 125, 137, 145–6, 153, 164, 213–15
Executive Outcomes 20–2, 25, 223
explosively-formed penetrator 44, 111–12

Fainaru, Steve 7, 90, 121, 156, 199
Falls Church, Virginia 27
Fallujah 29–30, 40, 151, 159, 194
Farrell, Theo 66
FBI *see* Federal Bureau of Investigation
Federal Bureau of Investigation 35, 102, 178
Finnemore, Martha 66
First Cavalry Division 177
Fitzsimmons, Scott 8–9
FOB Courage 115
follow vehicle 138–40
Ford Excursion 44
Freedom of Information Act 10
Frost, Adam 181

G3 assault rifle 43
Gallagher, Frank 13, 30, 34, 39, 41, 43, 45, 85, 151, 157–8, 226
Gates, Robert M. 185, 196
GAU-19 Gatling gun 45
Gawker Media 10
Geraghty, Tony 33
Gernet, Steve "G-Man" 147, 149, 163
Glen Joyce 160
Glock 19 pistol 43
GMC Suburban 30, 39, 44, 115, 139, 143, 154, 163
GMC Yukon 44
Goldstein, Judith 68
Green Zone 29, 31, 37–8, 41, 100–1, 104, 111, 141, 143–4, 147–8, 154, 190
Greystone 223
Griffin, Richard 195
Group 4 Securicor 23
Gulf of Aden 27

Habbaniyah 120
Hadi, Nabras Mohammed 108
Hafeez, Ali 117
Haiti 28

Halliburton 20–3, 25
Hammes, Thomas X. 90, 193
Hanner, Darren 102
Hart 15, 23–6, 83, 87, 90, 219
hate truck *see* counter assault vehicle
Heard, Dustin 102, 179–82
Heberlig, Brian 181
Hedahl, Marcus 34
Helvenston, Stephen "Scott" 30, 159
Higate, Paul 66–7
high mobility multipurpose wheeled vehicle 30, 36–8, 117
Hislop, John 124
HMMWV *see* high mobility multipurpose wheeled vehicle
Horst, Karl R. 194
House Committee on Armed Services 195
House Committee on Oversight and Government Reform 34, 102
House Judiciary Committee 195
Human Rights First 87, 102
Hundley, Curtis K. "Sparky" 32, 160
Hussein, Saddam 28, 192

ICDC *see* Iraqi Civil Defence Corps
ideational theory of tactical violence 4–6, 10, 15, 65–81, 97, 105, 109, 113, 118, 124–5, 137, 145–6, 153, 155, 164, 213–18: alternative explanations for results of 6, 118–24, 158–63; assessing predictions of 10–11, 75; broad predictions of 5, 74–5, 118, 155–6, 218–20; core logic of 68–70; dependent variable of 71; independent variables of 71; intervening variable of 71; relationship between norms, tactical behaviour and security outcomes in 70–2; specific predictions of 5, 72–4, 97–118, 137–55, 215–18; theoretical foundations of 65–8
IED *see* improvised explosive device
improvised explosive device 10, 30, 32, 39, 41–2, 44–5, 69, 87, 112, 115, 152, 154, 159–60, 216
inclusive approach to security 91
International Code of Conduct for Private Security Service Providers 188
Iraq 1–6, 8–65, 69, 75, 82–90, 97, 102–3, 110–11, 118–21, 123, 137, 139, 141, 143–5, 148, 150, 153–8, 161, 163, 180, 182–7, 189–213, 215, 218
Iraq Body Count Project 161, 187

Iraq Survey Group 27
Iraq War 1–6, 8–11, 14–15, 19, 22, 26–7, 36, 38, 45, 65, 69, 75, 82, 103, 118, 120, 124–5, 137, 143, 148, 154–6, 215, 218–20, 224, 226
Iraqi Army 104, 115, 178
Iraqi Civil Defence Corps 30
Iraqi Embassy to the United States 182
Iraqi Media Network 108, 199
Iraqi Ministry of Commerce 144
Iraqi Ministry of Electricity 154
Iraqi Ministry of Finance 111
Iraqi Ministry of Health 112, 148
Iraqi Ministry of Interior 100, 154, 184, 189–90, 192–5, 198
Iraqi Ministry of Justice 32, 108, 144, 160
Iraqi Ministry of Oil 117
Iraqi National Guard 109, 112
Irbil *see* Erbil
Isenberg, David 7
ISIS *see* Islamic State of Iraq and Syria
Islamic State of Iraq and Syria 223
Izdihar 100

Jabouri, Omar Khalaf 192
Jackson, Gary 83–4
Jaichner, Thomas W. "Bama" 31, 159
Jaysh al-Mahdi militia 144
Jepperson, Ronald 67
Joachim, Jutta 66
Johnson, Ron "Cat Daddy" 149, 163
Jones, Richard 157
JW GROM 36

K9 unit 40–1, 138–9
Karbala 28, 32, 111, 161, 199
Kaskos, Kryzysztof "Kaska" 144, 159
Katzenstein, Peter 66–7
KBR 20, 22, 25
Keohane, Robert 68
Kerry, John 196–7
Khalil, Ali 104, 117
Khalilzad, Zalmay 189
Khudair, Mohamad Khalil 104
Kilpatrick, Christian 160
Kimberlin, Joanne 41
Kimmitt, Mark 151, 194
Kinsey, Christopher 23–4
Kirkuk 28, 33, 111–12, 116, 124, 152, 154, 161–2, 189
Koevoet 25
Kosnett, Philip 150
Kyle, Chris 84, 88

Laguna, Arthur 149, 163
Laguna, Dan 13, 41–2, 89, 98, 141, 148–9, 163
landing zone 142, 148–9
Lanese, Herb 84–5
Latin America 66
LAU-68D/A rocket launcher 45
lead vehicle 30, 32, 36, 115, 138–40, 146, 154
Lebanon 70
Lehy, Patrick 188
Levy 70
Liberty, Evan 102, 179–80, 182
limousine 30, 37, 43–4, 103–4, 108, 115, 120, 138–40, 143
Lindsay, John 86
Little, Jarrod "J.C." 144, 159
logic of appropriateness 65–6
logic of consequences 65
long-range marksmen team 31, 39, 148
LRMT *see* long-range marksmen team
Lynn, John 70
LZ *see* landing zone

M134 Minigun 45
M203 grenade launcher 43, 101, 177
M240 machine gun 43, 101, 104, 177
M249 machine gun 43, 45, 150
M4 carbine 42–5, 117, 140, 146, 150, 177
M67 grenade 44
Mahdi Army 29, 150
Mahdi Sahib 117
Mahdi, Abdel Abdul 189
Mamba 31, 44, 104, 110–11, 113, 163
Mandel, Robert 21, 23
March, James 65
McCain, John 192
McCormack, Sean 190
McHenry, Patrick 3
MD-530 Little Bird 31, 41–2, 45, 101, 112, 141–2, 144, 147–9, 151, 163
Mealy, Mark 181
MEJA *see* Military Extraterritorial Jurisdiction Act
memorandum of agreement 185
Methodology 10
military culture 4–5, 8–9, 13–15, 42, 65–71, 74, 161, 163, 199, 213–14, 218, 220–1, 224, 226: definition of 66
Military Extraterritorial Jurisdiction Act 25, 185, 188
Military Professional Resources Incorporated 19, 22–3, 223

MOA *see* memorandum of agreement
Mogadishu, Battle of 149
Montreux Document 188
Mosul 33, 114, 138–9, 146–7, 152, 154, 160–2, 216
Moyock, North Carolina 13, 26, 83
MP5 submachine gun 43
Muhammad, Khursheed 189
Murphy, Matthew 180–1
My Lai massacre 193

Najaf 12, 28, 31, 146, 150–1, 160–2, 222
National Defense Authorization Act 25, 188
NATO *see* North Atlantic Treaty Organization
Neidrich, Christopher 117, 144, 159
Nisour Square 1, 29, 35, 100–3, 111, 113, 115, 117, 158, 176–7, 179, 181, 183, 185–7, 189–3, 196–9, 220
North Atlantic Treaty Organization 20, 42
Northrop Grumman 224

Obama, Barack 196, 223
OH-58D Kiowa Warrior 140
Olsen, Johan 65
Organization for Security and Cooperation in Europe 224
OSCE *see* Organization for Security and Cooperation in Europe

PAE 224
Pajero, Mitsubishi 29
Pakistan 27
peacekeeping 4, 222–5
Pelton, Robert Young 7, 44, 83, 87, 90, 96, 110
Pelzman, Kerry 100–1
Percy, Sarah 7, 33
Persian Gulf 70
personal initiative 71–5, 83–6, 97–8, 125, 137, 164, 213–15, 217
Petersohn, Ulrich 8
Petraeus, David 196
Pharrer, Chuck 84, 88, 90–1
Pierson, Paul 68
Pietrzyk, Edward 41–2
PKM machine gun 29, 37, 43, 139
PLSC *see* private logistical support company
PMC *see* private military company
Potgieter, Johannes 32, 160
Presidential Airways 198

Pretorius, Herman 161
Price, David 188
Prince, Erik 7, 13, 26, 29, 34–5, 38, 84–5, 87, 89, 96, 101–2, 114, 116, 119, 139, 151, 153–4, 156, 158, 178, 183, 189, 196–9, 220, 223–4, 226
principal 27, 36–8, 40, 43, 89–91, 149, 156, 191, 193, 222, 226
private logistical support company 20–1, 25: definition of 20
private military company 20, 22, 25: definition of 20
private security company 1–2, 4–11, 14, 19–28, 33, 41, 65–75, 82–3, 87, 89–90, 97–8, 103, 105, 109, 113, 118, 125, 137, 145–6, 153, 155, 159, 164, 176, 181, 185–91, 193–9, 213–21, 224–6: definition of 19
Private Security Company Violent Incident Dataset 10–11, 13, 115, 120, 123–4, 161, 186
private training and consulting company 19: definition of 19
proactive use of force 4–5, 71–5, 84, 86–7, 97, 105, 109, 113, 125, 137, 145–6, 153, 164, 214–17
protective security detail 31–2, 34–41, 44, 100, 103–5, 108–9, 111–12, 114–17, 120, 124, 140, 142, 144, 146–7, 152, 154, 159, 176, 190, 199
PSC *see* private security company
PSCVID *see* Private Security Company Violent Incident Dataset
PSD *see* protective security detail
PTCC *see* private training and consulting company
Puerto, José Mauricio Mena 32, 160
Puma 44, 152, 154

Qadar, Abdul Wahab Adbul 117, 191
Qadr, Abdul 191
QRF *see* quick reaction force
quick reaction force 38–9, 41, 44, 104, 117, 140–1, 222

Rakabi, Sadiq 192
Ramadi 28, 160–2
Ramallah 32
Rasor, Dina 8
rear vehicle 32, 37
Red Zone 38–9, 41, 148, 157, 190
Regional Embassy Office 138
Reisman, Michael 70
REO *see* Regional Embassy Office

Index

Reston, Virginia 28
Rice, Condoleezza 184, 191
Ridgeway, Jeremy 30, 102, 117, 181
rocket-propelled grenade 29, 31, 34, 44, 69–144, 147, 150, 154, 159–60
Ross, Michael 8
Route Irish 143, 160, 216
RPD machine gun 29
RPG *see* rocket-propelled grenade
RPK machine gun 29

Sadr City 29
Sahib, Mahdi 117
Sarhan, Jasem Abed 112
SAS *see* Special Air Service
Saxon 44
Scahill, Jeremy 3, 7, 96, 121, 156, 199
Schertler, David 182
Schneiker, Andrea 66
Schumacher, Gary 84
Schwartz, Mosche 194
Sea Air and Land 13, 26, 83–4, 86–7, 90–6
SEAL *see* Sea, Air and Land
Secretary of State's Panel of Personal Protective Services 145, 156, 184, 187
security outcomes 68, 70–1, 74, 118, 155, 218
Senate Armed Services Committee 195
Senate Homeland Security and Governmental Affairs Committee 195
Shameen, Shaista 223
Shays, Chris 3
Shephard, David R. 139
Shiite 29
Sierawski, Jim 84–5
Sierra Leone 21, 33, 223
Simbas 24
Simons, Suzanne 7, 85, 96, 199
Singer, Peter 6, 21–4, 96
Skylink 13
Slatten, Nicholas 102, 179–80, 182
Slough, Paul A. 102, 179–80, 182
SOAR *see* Special Operations Aviation Regiment
SOFA *see* Status of Forces Agreement
Somalia 27
South Africa 24, 32, 36, 44
Special Air Service 36, 82–3, 90
Special Forces 35, 82–4, 88, 151
Special Maritime and Territorial Jurisdiction Act 25
Special Operations Aviation Regiment 35, 148
Special Weapons and Tactics 26, 35

sports utility vehicle 30, 32, 34, 37–9, 44–5, 105, 144, 157, 177, 217
SR-25 sniper rifle 43
Stanfield, Shane "War Baby" 149, 163
Starr, Ann Exline 89
Starr, Greg 178
Status of Forces Agreement 186
Stop Outsourcing Security Act 187, 196
Sulaymaniyah 116
Sullivan, Stephen 139
Sunni 29
SUV *see* sports utility vehicle
SWAT *see* Special Weapons and Tactics
Syria 223, 225

Tablai, Miguel 32, 160
tactical behaviour 5, 8–9, 34, 66–8, 70–2, 74–5, 87, 97, 118, 122–3, 137, 155–6, 176–213, 215, 218
tactical support team 38–9, 41, 44, 100, 104, 111, 113–15, 117, 120, 140, 144, 146, 148, 152, 154
Tallil 28
Taylor, Chris 34, 151
Teague, Michael "Iron Mike" 30, 159
Terriff, Terry 67–8
Thomas, Ben 140
Tierney, John 87, 139, 196
Tigris River 40
Tikrit 31, 162, 216
Tocci, Peter J. 139, 160
Toohey, Patrick 151
Toyota Land Cruiser 44, 109
Triple Canopy 15, 25–6, 28, 35, 83, 186, 188, 190, 192, 198–9
TST *see* tactical support team
typologies of firms in the private military industry 20–4
Tyrrell, Anne E. 108, 178

UCMJ *see* Uniform Code of Military Justice
UH-60 Blackhawk 41–2
UK Foreign Affairs Committee 223
UN *see* United Nations
Uniform Code of Military Justice 185
United Kingdom 15, 20, 27, 36, 44, 67, 82–3, 87, 90, 157, 219, 221, 223
United Nations 27, 223–5
United States 3, 7, 9, 14, 20, 25–6, 28–9, 35–6, 42–4, 67, 70, 82, 84, 88–9, 96, 100, 103, 119, 124, 150, 155, 157, 176–8, 180, 182, 184, 186–96, 198–9, 220, 222–3

Urbina, Ricardo M. 179–80, 191–2
US Agency for International Development 100, 120, 224
US Air Force 35
US Arms Export Control Act 25
US Army 26, 31, 35, 40, 42, 82–3, 88, 112, 140–2, 148–51, 177, 194
US Commission on Wartime Contracting in Iraq and Afghanistan 102, 186
US Department of Defense 27, 161, 185–8, 193, 220
US Department of Justice 102, 178–80, 185, 188, 192
US Department of State 1, 3, 10–12, 14, 22–4, 27–9, 34–5, 37, 44–5, 84–6, 88, 96, 98, 102, 105, 111, 114, 116, 119, 121, 124, 143–4, 152, 163, 178, 183–6, 188–93, 195, 197–8, 220, 224, 226
US Embassy to Iraq 19, 29, 33, 36, 41–2, 100, 147–8, 180, 183–4, 186, 190–1, 194, 199
US House of Representatives 10–11, 84, 88, 91, 119, 124, 195–6
US House of Representatives Subcommittee on National Security Emerging Threats and International Relations 84–5
US Marine Corps 26, 31, 35, 150, 194, 221
US Navy 13, 26, 35, 82–3
US Senate 10, 124, 187, 195–7
US War Crimes Act 25

USAID *see* US Agency for International Development
USTC Holdings *see* Blackwater

Van Fleet, James 70
Vargas, Tommy 39, 89, 149
VBIED *see* vehicle-based improvised explosive device
vehicle-based improvised explosive device 10, 32–3, 38, 40, 45, 69, 87, 100, 102, 104, 112–15, 120, 138, 147, 154, 157, 159–60, 164, 181
Verkui, Paul 34
Viera, Ken 84

Wasdin, Howard E. 90, 96
Washington, DC 26, 192
Webb, Kenneth 139, 160
Wendt, Alexander 67
Wikileaks 10
Worldwide Personnel Protective Services 28–9, 96
WPPS *see* Worldwide Personnel Protective Services
Wright, Ted 198

Xe *see* Blackwater

Yemen 33
Young, Lonnie 150

Zovko, Jerko "Jerry" 30, 159
Zukoski, Artur 144, 159